D1029701

Reflection Revisited

PERSPECTIVES IN CONTINENTAL PHILOSOPHY

John D. Caputo, series editor

REFLECTION REVISITED

Jürgen Habermas's Discursive Theory of Truth

by

JAMES SWINDAL

Fordham University Press
New York
1999

Copyright © 1999 Fordham University Press
All rights reserved.
LC 99–22493
ISBN 0-8232-1806-6 (*hardcover*)
ISBN 0-8232-1807-4 (*paperback*)
ISSN 1089-3938
Perspectives in Continental Philosophy, No. 5

Library of Congress Cataloging-in-Publication Data

Swindal, James.
    Reflection revisited : Jürgen Habermas's discursive theory of
truth / by James Swindal.
        p.   cm. — (Perspectives in continental philosophy, ISSN
1089-3938 ; no. 5)
    Includes bibliographical references and index.
    ISBN 0-8232-1806-6 (hardcover). — ISBN 0-8232-1807-4 (pbk.)
    1. Habermas, Jürgen—Contributions in concept of truth.   2. Truth.
I. Title.   II. Series.
B3258.H324S95   1999
121'.092—DC21   99-22493
                                                                         CIP

Printed in the United States of America

To
Mary

CONTENTS

ABBREVIATIONS

The following is a list of abbreviations of the works of Habermas most frequently cited in this study.

BFN   *Between Facts and Norms.* Trans. William Rehg. Cambridge, Mass.: The MIT Press, 1996.

CES   *Communication and the Evolution of Society.* Trans. Thomas McCarthy. Boston: Beacon, 1979.

KHI   *Knowledge and Human Interests.* Trans. J. Shapiro. Boston: Beacon, 1971.

JA   *Justification and Application.* Trans. C. Cronin. Cambridge, Mass.: The MIT Press, 1993.

LC   *Legitimation Crisis.* Trans. Thomas McCarthy. Boston: Beacon, 1975.

MCCA   *Moral Consciousness and Communicative Action.* Trans. C. Lenhard and S. Weber Nicholsen. Cambridge, Mass.: The MIT Press, 1990.

OPC   *On the Pragmatics of Communication.* Trans. and ed. M. Cooke. Cambridge, Mass.: The MIT Press, 1998.

PDM   *The Philosophical Discourse of Modernity: Twelve Lectures.* Trans. F. Lawrence. Cambridge, Mass.: The MIT Press, 1987.

PT   *Postmetaphysical Thinking: Philosophical Essays.* Trans. W. M. Hohengarten. Cambridge, Mass.: The MIT Press, 1992.

TCA   *The Theory of Communicative Action.* 2 vols. Trans. Thomas McCarthy. Boston: Beacon, 1984, 1987.

TK   *Texte und Kontexte.* Frankfurt am Main: Suhrkamp, 1990.

WT   *"Wahrheitstheorien": Vorstudien und Ergänzungen zur Theorie des kommunikativen Handelns.* 2nd ed. Frankfurt am Main: Suhrkamp, 1986. Pp. 127–183.

WUP   *"What Is Universal Pragmatics?" Communication and Evolution of Society.* Trans. Thomas McCarthy. Boston: Beacon, 1979. Pp. 1–68.

ACKNOWLEDGMENTS

The inspiration for this work really began eighteen years ago, in an undergraduate course I took on Existentialism. That course left me with the conviction that the purpose of philosophy is not to be curious, but to wonder. Those who have fostered and encouraged this wonder are part of the long list of those deserving my thanks and gratitude for their contributions to this project.

First, I am grateful for The Oregon Province of the Society of Jesus which sustained me for several years of graduate study in philosophy. During this time I was introduced to hermeneutics and critical theory by Jim Loiacono, O.M.I., Hal Sanks, S.J., and Don Gelpi, S.J.

Parts of this particular work benefited from the critical comments of Andy Wallace, Josef Früchtl, Lutz Wingert, Joachim Renn, Axel Honneth, Jodi Dean, Joel Anderson, and Felmon Davis. I am especially indebted to Paul McNellis, S.J., whose journalistically honed editing skills helped tighten up a few slack phrases. Oliva Blanchette made a tremendous contribution by, among other things, helping to show me a novel way to interpret Hegel. Jürgen Habermas's own comments on the introduction and final chapter of this work enabled me to not only better understand but also gain an even deeper appreciation for his project.

I am also indebted to the Graduate School of Arts and Sciences at Boston College for providing me a dissertation grant for research at the University of Frankfurt, and to John Carroll University for its support, both financial and otherwise, for the completion of the project. The philosophy department, and Robert Sweeney in particular, have provided help in untold ways. I must also thank the editors of *Philosophy and Social Criticism* for their permission for me to use material from my article, "The Problem of Problematization," in volume 20 of the journal.

I also am thankful for the help of John Caputo for his support of this project and to Mary Beatrice Schulte for her fine editing. Finally, my greatest thanks goes to David Rasmussen, who provided not only the initial stimulus for this study, but also much of the careful criticism and encouragement by which it was accomplished.

July 31, 1998   JAMES SWINDAL

Reflection Revisited

Introduction: Reflection and Validity

Richard Rorty has proposed a paradigm shift for the discipline of philosophy. He characterizes the former paradigm as one in which all philosophical arguments made a final appeal to a subject's immediate "mirror-like" grasp of objects in the world. In his new paradigm, a philosophical viewpoint justifies itself simply by its ability to equip actors with the tools to "get along with one another" in society. He claims that, although Heidegger, Wittgenstein, and Dewey prepared the way for this new social paradigm,

> neither Heidegger nor Wittgenstein lets us see the historical phenomenon of mirror-imagery, the story of the domination of the mind of the West by ocular metaphors, within a social perspective. Both men are concerned with the rarely favored individual rather than with society. . . . Dewey, on the other hand, though he had neither Wittgenstein's dialectical acuity nor Heidegger's historical learning, wrote his polemics against traditional mirror-imagery out of a vision of a new kind of society.[1]

Rorty places Jürgen Habermas's work squarely within this new paradigm of social philosophy that began with Hegel and continued in Heidegger's deconstructive account of the destiny of the West. Rorty even claims that Habermas, by inquiring into the philosophical vocabulary that best serves individual and social autonomy, is the contemporary philosopher who most closely resembles Dewey.[2]

Habermas would agree with, and perhaps be a bit flattered by, Rorty's likening of him to Dewey. Indeed, both he and Dewey de-

---

[1] *Philosophy and the Mirror of Nature* (Princeton, N.J.: Princeton University Press, 1979), p. 13.

[2] *Philosophical Papers*, 2 vols. (New York: Cambridge University Press, 1991), 2.24, 183. Rorty proposes to achieve this autonomy through an ironic stance toward the world. See also his *Contingency, Irony, and Solidarity* (Cambridge: Cambridge University Press, 1989), pp. 97ff.

velop a social theory that is solidly optimistic about the ability of critical reflection to improve conditions of life in a modern techno-logical society. But on what grounds is Habermas so optimistic about the capacity for a social theory to improve the conditions of life in the modern world, beset as it is by so much injustice and oppression? Just how comprehensive is the social theory he claims to derive from this new socio-philosophical paradigm?

Even a cursory look at Habermas's works reveals that the accom-plishments he anticipates for his emancipatory social theory will af-fect almost every aspect of human life. He hales from a tradition of critical theory that maintains that human emancipation is inextrica-bly linked to socio-economic conditions of society. Max Horkheimer, for instance, urged critical theorists to foster human emancipation by expanding the limits of their analysis beyond their hitherto neu-tral categories of traditional thinking to the explication of exchange relations from which present forces and counterforces of society can be deduced.[3] Habermas believes that once such emancipatory condi-tions are incorporated into individual and collective will-formation processes, individuals will become, though not necessarily happier, more autonomous.[4] He calls the critical reflection that explicates these conditions the "subversive power" that can solve conflicts in society and have an intimate, yet fractured, relationship to the total-ity of the lifeworld (PT 38–39). He argues that "the unity of the world c[an] no longer be secured objectively through the hypostasiz-ing unifying principles (God, being, or nature); henceforth, it c[an] be asserted only reflexively through the unity of reason (or through a rational organization of the world, the actualization of reason)" (CES 105). Thus, critical reflection fixes the procedures for the de-termination of truth required for the delineation of rational solutions to social conflicts and discord. This form of reflection no longer pos-its the subjective conditions of objective and decontextualized knowledge, but performs the function of recovering the praxis of

---

[3] See his "Traditional and Critical Theory," in *Critical Theory: Selected Essays*, trans. M. O'Connell (New York: Herder and Herder, 1972), pp. 226–232.

[4] *The Past as Future* (Lincoln: University of Nebraska Press, 1994), pp. 106–107. He also claims that emancipatory processes never resulted from "extraordinary ex-periences."

thinking that unifies both subjective and objective poles of truth into a social discursive procedure of truth determination.[5]

Critical theorists have aimed to rehabilitate reflection as a necessary component of truth and knowledge determination.[6] Horkheimer argued that reflection must determine that thought is limited, but that "no areas are set aside to which thought is not to be applied."[7] Habermas himself has applied a reflective analysis to a myriad of social issues, such as German unification, student protests, environmental issues, and, more recently, the Gulf War, racism, and the problem of political asylum in Germany. In the *Historikerstreit* debate, for example, Habermas accused certain German historians of promoting a "non-reflective" German national identity uncritical of its National Socialist past.[8] But Habermas's version of critical reflection is unique among critical theorists. It is based on the assumption that *reason itself* demands that individuals employ reflection in order to limit the egoism of their own interests so as to gain a broader social perspective. By its very nature, reason is reflective and argumentative.

Hans Wagner calls reflection the "unifying principle of all philosophy."[9] But many philosophers—Rorty and Habermas included—are aware that previous philosophies of reflection have generally been either incoherent or inconsistent. Theories of reflection have run into problems of circularity, infinite regression, and solipsism. Con-

---

[5] Robert Holub, *Jürgen Habermas: Critic in the Public Sphere* (New York: Routledge, 1991), p. 9.

[6] See Raymond Geuss, *The Idea of a Critical Theory: Habermas and the Frankfurt School* (Cambridge: Cambridge University Press, 1981), p. 2; and Theodor Adorno, *Negative Dialectics*, trans. E. B. Ashton (New York: Seabury, 1973), especially pp. 4–5 where Adorno refers to philosophy's "critical self-reflection." See also Adorno and Horkheimer, *Dialectic of Enlightenment*, trans. J. Cumming (New York: Herder and Herder, 1972), pp. 188–192; they note that, though neutral, the problems with projection commence when it is done without reflection: "When the subject is no longer able to return to the object what he has received from it, he becomes poorer rather than richer. He loses the reflection in both directions: since he no longer reflects the object, he ceases to reflect upon himself, and loses the ability to differentiate" (p. 189).

[7] Horkheimer, "Materialism and Metaphysics," in *Critical Theory: Selected Essays*, trans. M. O'Connell (New York: Herder and Herder, 1972), p. 39.

[8] For a good description of Habermas's role in the *Historikerstreit* debate, see Holub, *Critic in the Public Sphere*, pp. 185–187.

[9] See his *Philosophie und Reflexion* (Würzburg: Ernst Reinhardt, 1959), p. i.

fronted with the circular paradoxes of reflective self-reference, Bertrand Russell rejected self-reference altogether in favor of hierarchies of reference.[10] Wittgenstein in the *Tractatus* also argued forcefully against the possibility of reflexive description and reference.[11] He flatly rejected the Augustinian hope that reflection could capture such notions as time in a self-presence to a mind.[12] Rorty claims that Kant's transcendental synthesis, Hegel's self-diremption of the concept, Heidegger's *Sorgen*, and now Derrida's *différance* are all forms of reflection that allegedly overcome the isolation of the individual subject but in fact are mere "gimmicks" that in the final analysis resort to the mirror of a solitary consciousness. Rorty concludes that each of these approaches justifies itself, not by a logical argumentation procedure, but by a "leap" to some kind of transcendent ground: "This insusceptibility to argument is what makes 'the philosophy of reflection'—the tradition of transcendental inquiry within which Gasché wishes to embed Derrida—the bête noire of philosophers who take public discussability as the essence of rationality."[13] Rorty locates Habermas among those who maintain that rationality ought to conform to a standard of public discussability. But Rorty also claims that any theory of emancipation ought to appeal, not to a transcendental or reflexive ground, but only to a "positive" argumentational determination of the conditions of social praxis itself. By implication, Rorty thus insists that one ought to renounce all appeal to reflection and ultimate grounds.

Is Rorty's pessimism about the ability of reflection to set proper limits on social theory, or in fact any theory, well founded? Or does Habermas succeed in developing a unique form of reflection that avoids the pitfalls of earlier theories of reflection? Dieter Henrich shares Rorty's suspicions about the value of Habermas's discursive version of reflection, although for quite different reasons. He argues

---

[10] For a good discussion of Russell's paradoxes of self-reference, see Julian Roberts, *The Logic of Reflection: German Philosophy in the Twentieth Century* (New Haven, Conn.: Yale University Press, 1992), pp. 88–90.

[11] Herbert Schnädelbach, *Reflexion und Diskurs: Fragen einer Logik der Philosophie* (Frankfurt am Main: Suhrkamp, 1977), p. 207. Roberts also argues that Wittgenstein maintained a "lingering Fichtean belief in irreflexivity" (*Logic of Reflection*, p. 130).

[12] See Roger McClure, "St. Augustine and the Paradox of Reflection," *Philosophy*, 69 (1994), 322–323.

[13] *Philosophical Papers*, 2.123. For Gasché's description of reflection, see *The Tain*

that reflection is not a logical structure, but a *spontaneous act* of all conscious and intelligent life. He characterizes reflection as a "break" that determines the consciousness of the difference between the various ways of understanding formed in the course of conscious life. Thus, "whoever reflects understands that he is not home in the world and cannot grow up in it without a rupture."[14] Reflection effectively allows a subject to "distance" itself from the aporias that both the art of understanding and the act of self-description tend to engender. Henrich then concludes that, by relying on the immediacy and reliability of reflection in a lifeworld context alone, Habermas denies modernity its very achievement of having bestowed the "stabilizing" power of self-reflection on individual subjects.

Neither Rorty's suspicions about the use of reflection for theory construction nor Henrich's critique of Habermas's neglect of subjective reflection have garnered universal acceptance. Julian Roberts argues not only that Habermas employs reflection in his social theory, but that it is his "central method."[15] He claims that Habermas, borrowing from Lorenzer's dialogic model of rationality, develops a logic of discourse that successfully overthrows positivism's outright rejection of reflection. He even claims that only a reflective methodology such as Habermas's can provide the contextualization needed for an emancipative social science.

Taking up Roberts's proposal, in this study I shall explore how Habermas uses philosophical reflection in the determination of validity claims that can be utilized for social theory. I shall show how he radically reformulates traditional theories of reflection into a *linguistic-pragmatic* view of reflection by which speaker, in the process of communication, transcends his own viewpoint and takes on the viewpoints of those he addresses. The critical reflection he develops operates only in and through language use understood as embedded in a socio-theoretically explicated lifeworld.

Habermas develops this discursive view of reflection primarily

---

of the Mirror: Derrida and the Philosophy of Reflection (Cambridge, Mass.: Harvard University Press, 1986), chaps. 1–3.

[14] "Was ist Metaphysik—was Moderne? Zwölf Thesen gegen Jürgen Habermas," in *Konzepte: Essays zur Philosophie in der Zeit* (Frankfurt am Main: Suhrkamp, 1987), pp. 19ff. In Chapter 3 I shall examine how Habermas responds to Henrich's criticisms.

[15] See *Logic of Reflection*, pp. 220, 229.

from his critical reading of the history of philosophy. He argues that philosophical thought has gone through three successive stages: the ontology of being, the reflection of consciousness, and finally linguistic, or *postmetaphysical*, thinking (PT 28–29).[16] He then claims that the philosophy of reflection, which was developed at the consciousness stage, can be radically transformed by the critical demands of the postmetaphysical stage. Frege inaugurated the postmetaphysical stage by claiming that the primary elements of meaning are not the conceptual representations of an object, but the "thoughts" (*Gedanken*) about states of affairs expressed by propositions (BFN 10). On Habermas's view, this new understanding of meaning requires a justification that is neither dialectical nor intuitive, but intersubjective and discursive. In later writings Habermas claims that such discursive justification is verified on the basis of the *inherent reflexivity of ordinary language*. He thus situates the reflexive act, not in the agreement between consciousness and object, as previous theories, but in a speaker's aim of communicating a specific content to a hearer. Thus, even at the postmetaphysical stage, reflection plays a crucial role in truth determination.

Habermas's version of postmetaphysical thinking attributes truth determination, not to an isolated consciousness reflecting on its own thought processes, but to an interactive subject raising and redeeming validity claims in discursive argumentation. Postmetaphysical truth claims account for both their origin and their application by means of their "reflective cognitive structure."[17] Rejecting Rorty's belief that some non-argumentational processes of world-disclosure—or, as he calls it, metaphor—aid in the "acquisition of truth," Habermas unequivocally maintains that discursive argumentation

---

[16] Karl-Otto Apel claims that the subject is no longer the "guarantor" of knowledge; rather "we are—because no one can follow a rule alone or only once (Wittgenstein)—destined apriori to intersubjective communication and understanding." This apriori of an actual communicative community is practically identical with human society. See his *Transformation der Philosophie*, 2 vols. (Frankfurt am Main: Suhrkamp, 1973), 1.59–60. Michiel Korthals describes how this development culminates in a speaker's ability to reject non-reflective forms of communication and "commit himself to norms that other, potential justifying agents ought to respect." See his "On the Justification of Societal Development Claims," *Philosophy and Social Criticism*, 18, No. 1 (1992), 13.

[17] *Theorie und Praxis*, 2nd ed. (Frankfurt am Main: Suhrkamp, 1971), p. 19.

must replace *all* other forms of truth determination.[18] Truth is determined neither by an assent to a judgment nor by a privileged representation within a tradition or set of texts, but only by argumentatively reached agreement about a claim. Thus, Habermas grants a "privileged" status only to the idealizations that guide *every* act that aims to attain agreement among disputants.[19]

Rorty's and Henrich's critiques of postmetaphysical philosophies of reflection, though unable to undermine Habermas's commitment to a theory of reflection, nevertheless do raise problems that any theory of reflection must resolve. Can Habermas convincingly show that the intersubjective argumentation he endorses is the *only* means of providing individuals and groups with an emancipative, or edifying, stance toward reality?[20] Can Habermas justify the claim that discursive postmetaphysical reflection has *priority* over all metaphysical forms of reflection?[21] Are the "idealizations" that Habermas requires for argumentation completely immune from Rorty's critique of privileged representations? Is his version of critical reflection applicable to actual conflict situations in everyday life? I shall take up each of these problems in the course of this study.

Before evaluating the effectiveness of Habermas's account of a postmetaphysical critical reflection, I need to analyze briefly the con-

---

[18] Rorty, "Philosophy as Science, Metaphor, Politics," in *Philosophical Papers*, 2.12–14. Rorty argues that world-disclosers like Plato, Heidegger, and Derrida *are* philosophers. But he dislikes the way Gasché blurs the distinction between problem-solvers and world-disclosers. Rorty attributes a similar activity of reflection to their very dissimilar projects.

[19] Geuss, *Idea of a Critical Theory*, p. 66. For a description of the ideal speech situation from which these idealizations are derived, see Karl-Otto Apel, "The Transcendental Conception of Language-Communication and the Idea of a First Philosophy," in *The History of Linguistic Thought and Contemporary Linguistics*, ed. H. Parret (New York: de Gruyter, 1976), pp. 32–61.

[20] Empirical evidence abounds that would seem to refute Habermas's claim that deliberate and reflective consensus formation actually guarantees good political and economic decisions. For instance, Jeffrey Sachs strongly urges governments in the former Soviet bloc to move *rapidly* to a free market system, because the new rules of a free market "have to be established quickly or there will be widespread uncertainty." He points out that countries like Argentina "that have spent all their time arguing about the rules of the game" have done poorly. See "Father of Radical Reform," *Time*, July 22, 1991, pp. 54–55.

[21] For a good treatment of the problem of the priority of communicative over other forms of rationality, see David Rasmussen, *Reading Habermas* (Cambridge, Mass.: Basil Blackwell, 1990), pp. 18–19.

cept of reflection itself. Then I can situate Habermas's use of reflection within a broader framework.

AN ANALYSIS OF THE CONCEPT OF REFLECTION

An analysis of the concept of reflection includes an analysis of the ordinary usage of the term, a philosophical definition of the term and a description of its function, an account of the domains in which it operates and of its types, and, finally, an analysis of its temporal and spatial contextualization.

A semantic analysis of the ordinary language usage term "reflection" reveals that both its nominal and its verbal forms are equivocal. The noun "reflection" can refer either to the *content* to which an act of reflection refers or to the *act* of reflecting itself. Only the specific *context* in which the utterance is used can determine which of the two possible senses a speaker is intending.

What is even more problematic is that the verb "to reflect" has two very different ordinary language meanings:

(1) to reproduce or duplicate a thing or event in an image or concept ("I was reflecting on how nice it was yesterday," or "that reflects the same attitude we've seen before," etc.);

(2) to *distance* oneself from an object in order to imagine it differently ("I will take a moment to reflect before I ever do that again").

These two distinct uses have often been conflated by philosophers, causing much confusion.[22] (1) is the passive form of reflection, criticized by Rorty, that copies, or "mirrors," an object. Roger McClure uses this form when he claims that reflective acts "reproduce earlier phases of the same consciousness as reflects."[23] The temporal status of the object reflected upon is inconsequential: it can be present, past (remembered), or future (anticipated). Most theoretical forms

---

[22] See Roberts, *Logic of Reflection*, pp. 5–6. Roberts's definition of reflection excludes such ordinary uses as "to think hard about something" and such common notions as being introspectively aware of one's empirical self or as referring to oneself logically. Instead he adopts a Kantian definition of reflection as a transcendental act. I shall take up his version of reflection more extensively in Chapter 3.

[23] McClure, "St. Augustine and the Paradox of Reflection," 320.

of reflection adopt this sense of the term. (2) is the active and practical form of reflection in which an agent reflects by "stepping back" in order to imagine a certain past or present state of affairs in a different way. Gadamer calls (1) the act of "being reflected" that results in the substitution of one reality for another, and (2) the "speculative" act that overcomes the dogmatism of everyday experience.[24] I shall call (1) the *analytic* form of reflection, and (2) the *synthetic* form. Habermas employs the synthetic form of reflection when he links reflection with the process by which we determine truth and truth-analogous claims.[25]

More precisely, I will propose the following philosophical definition of synthetic reflection: synthetic reflection is the act by which a subject determines an object (entity or event), not on the basis of the object's properties, but on the basis of the subject's relation to the object relative to a *limit* between them.[26] If the subject makes the synthetic reflective act *itself* an object, it determines an identity relation. Otherwise, a subject's synthetic reflective act is a *second-order* reflection that has two possible intentions: it can determine the limit between itself and the object to which it is referred; or it can determine the limit between its own thinking and itself as a subject. Philosophers have tended to privilege one of the two referents. Aquinas chose the former objective option, claiming that by a reflective act an agent knows a singular object, not directly in the way we abstract intelligible species from our phantasms, but only indirectly by turning from the species back to the phantasm.[27] Rejecting this kind of objective realism, Descartes situated the referent, not in the object, but in the *subject who knows the object*. Most modern philosophers adopt a Cartesian subjective referent for reflective acts.

Hans Wagner has developed a comprehensive analysis of different

---

[24] Gadamer, *Truth and Method*, trans. G. Barden and J. Cumming (New York: Seabury, 1975), p. 423. Gadamer claims that Hegel was aware of the distinction between both forms by acknowledging a distinction between the "in itself" and the "for me."

[25] In this study, any unspecified use of the term reflection will refer to synthetic reflection.

[26] For a further discussion of the link between reflection and relationality, see Hans Wagner, *Kritische Theorie: Systematische und historische Abhandlungen*, ed. K. Bärthlein and W. Flach (Würzburg: Königshausen and Neumann, 1980), p. 57.

[27] Aquinas, *Summa Theologiae*, I, q. 86, a. 1.

models of subjective synthetic reflection. He defines reflection as a consciousness's return from its intended object to *itself as limited* relative to the object. But he modifies the subjective approach in two ways. First, he stipulates that reflection includes *an interest in determining the object's validity.*[28] In this way reflection provides an *objective* grounding for the content of the object in question. Second, he expands the domain of the objects of reflexive consciousness to include not only perceptions and cognitions, but also acts of feeling, planning, knowing, and acting. Habermas will adopt, in modified form, both these approaches. Although hampered by its lack of specific reference to language use, Wagner's theory of reflection nonetheless provides a coherent analysis of the characteristics of all synthetic reflective acts.

Wagner also distinguishes between the sense and the referent of a synthetic reflective act. Its sense correlates with its formal act (*noesis*); its referent, with the content of its terms (*noema*).[29] He then distinguishes between the two levels not only on the basis of their intended objects, but also on the basis of their relation to validity determination as such. *Noematic reflection* does not determine validity; it simply expresses its noematic object as a product of the subject's constitutive act. *Noetic reflection,* on the other hand, by reflecting on both the object and the act, determines the universality of the subject's constitutive act as limited by the object.[30] Nathan Rotenstreich, for example, takes account of such a noetic element by noting that "reflection differs from expression because reflection refers also to itself and is thus inherently bound to present not only

[28] *Philosophie und Reflexion,* pp. 36, 320, 398. Wagner claims that Horkheimer and Adorno understood the reflexive return (*Rückgriff*) in a dialectical and negative sense. See his *Kritische Theorie,* p. 470. Wagner then divides reflection into critical reflection, by which consciousness determines itself, and speculative reflection, by which concepts of finitude and infinitude are interrelated. I will be concerned with critical reflection. Wagner to a large extent anticipates Habermas's own concern that reflection be aware of its own interest in proving validity. See *Philosophie und Reflexion,* pp. 398ff.

[29] Aquinas had also made this distinction, claiming that reflection is directed both to the reproduced image or concept of an object *and* to the act of reflecting itself. See his *De veritate,* I, 9.

[30] See Wagner, *Kritische Theorie,* p. 61. Wagner uses the term *Aktleben,* presumably to give the concept more of an existential feel. One need not understand the subject of a reflexive act as constitutive of the act in a constructivist or decisionistic manner.

contents to which it refers, but also self-understanding implied in self-reference, and the standing topic of the validity of that which is asserted. Expression does not call for validation."[31] Noetic reflection can be applied to all of a subject's acts, whether cognitive, linguistic, or productive. The verificational ground of a noetic synthetic reflection grounds all truth-conditional theories of truth.

Wagner then describes how validity determination functions as a four-step sequence involving both noematic and noetic forms of reflection. Noematic reflection refers to the structure of its object, while noetic reflection synthesizes the difference between the object of the reflection and the act of reflecting itself.[32] Noetic reflection is a formal act that negates the previous limit determinations and as such provides grounds for verification of the intended object. Wittgenstein describes what amounts to noematic reflection in his description of introspection found in his *Lectures on Philosophical Psychology* (1946–1947):

> You observe your own mental happenings. How? By introspection. But if you observe, i.e., if you go about to observe your own mental happenings you alter them and create new ones: and the whole point of observing is that you should not do this—observing is supposed to be just the thing that avoids this. Then the science of mental phenomena has this puzzle: I can't observe the mental phenomena of others and I can't observe my own, in the proper sense of "observe." So where are we?[33]

But according to this account, Wittgenstein's introspection fails to go to the fourth noetic step, which unifies the bifurcation of thought and object of thought. In other words, it does not grasp the *act* that grasps the limit of thinking about thinking *as* a limit and in so doing overcomes, or negates, the difference between a thought and an introspective thought about the thought. This dissolving of the difference, or the "puzzle" as Wittgenstein calls it, provides synthetic reflection with the grounds for determining the validity of the thought.

---

[31] See his "Can Expression Replace Reflection?" *Review of Metaphysics*, 43 (March 1990), 614.

[32] Here I have modified Wagner's schema to make it simpler and clearer.

[33] See *Wittgenstein's Lectures on Philosophical Psychology: 1946–1947*, ed. A. C. Jackson, P. T. Geach, K. J. Shah, as quoted in Ray Monk, *Ludwig Wittgenstein: The Duty of Genius* (New York: The Free Press, 1990), p. 500.

In Wagner's scheme, all partial or intermediate levels of validity are excluded by the principle of "validity difference": that a claim or proposition is either valid or invalid.[34] Although Husserl posited a form of noetic verification based on absolute evidence, Wagner argues that he did not adopt the principle of validity difference. Habermas clearly adopts a validity difference principle in his contention that a validity claim demands either a yes or a no answer. As we will see, Habermas dispenses with the cognitive analysis of the noetic or noematic properties of reflection, concerning himself rather with an *intersubjective* referent for reflection. The act of reflection he terms *argumentation,* and the referents of the reflection are intersubjectively determined claims to validity in a *discourse.*

Having explicated the formal levels of reflection in validity determination, Wagner then specifies how validity can be *applied* as either a theoretical (factual) or an axiomatic (evaluative) measure.[35] Theoretical verification determines genus and species as structures of claims that have intrinsic content; axiomatic verification determines genus and species for claims that lack intrinsic content but acquire content indirectly from the noematic objects to which they refer. Both ethical ways of thinking (*Gesinnungen*) and instrumental actions are axiomatic claims that require this indirect form of verification. The determination of axiomatic validity—that with which Habermas is most interested—thus requires analysis of:

(1) the object or claim,
(2) the action toward the object,
(3) a judgment about the action, and
(4) a judgment about the validity of the judgment.[36]

(4) is the specifically reflexive element of this procedure.[37] Habermas employs several axiomatic forms of reflection: empirical, aesthetic, expressive, pragmatic, ethical-existential, moral, and political. In this

---

[34] *Philosophie und Reflexion,* p. 322.

[35] Ibid., pp. 76, 78; Wagner, *Kritische Theorie,* p. 59.

[36] *Theoretical* validity involves only three steps: the action, a judgment about the action, and a judgment about the judgment of the action.

[37] Wagner, *Philosophie und Reflexion,* pp. 243, 251. Wagner claims that ethical reflection seeks for the determination of the will, not a utilitarian calculation, but a Kantian unconditioned. He thus falls into the Kantian dilemma of trying to determine *conditions,* such as that of pure intention, for an *unconditioned* free act. Roberts avoid this by focusing on the action as conditioned by another mind.

study I shall focus primarily on the ethical-existential and moral forms.

In addition to distinguishing themselves from their theoretic counterparts, axiomatic forms of reflection, Wagner stipulates, must also include an analysis of their own temporal and spatial contexts. With regard to spatial considerations, he argues for a kind of naturalism in which all forms of axiomatic reflection employ bodily expressions that are to be recognized by another in the "space of nature." As for temporal factors, he argues that since noetic reflection refers back to an original act that is no longer "present," it implicitly raises the critical contextualizing problem of the reflective act's "now phase."[38] Husserl analyzed the problem of time-consciousness, but had to weave a complicated web of categories—*Urimpression*, retention, protention, repetition, and expectation—to explicate it. Although Wagner bypasses this plethora of categories, he does argue that the subject achieves a temporal synchronicity of a past and a present state of affairs only through a form of retention.

Roberts also claims that truth determination requires an act of reflection that determines both the spatial and the temporal contextualization of the "bounded situation" in which a truth claim is raised.[39] On his account, the reflective recovery of context both transcends and augments mere predicational description. Roberts links this to what he terms the "principle of partiality": "No truths absolutely transcend their context: even 'necessary' truths relate to some particular set of worlds."[40] Roberts is aware of the subjectivism and psychologism that lurk in such a recovery of context. He avoids these dangers by linking reflection directly to dialogue or discourse with other minds.

Critical theorists, who attribute their inspiration to Marx's critique of capitalism, also adopted his interest in grounding a theoretical reflection *that locates itself historically in time and thus accounts for the possibility of its own standpoint.*[41] Such a critical reflection emerges not from dialogue with other minds, as Roberts holds, but from actual material conditions of society. But, as a critical theorist,

---

[38] Ibid., p. 341.

[39] *Logic of Reflection*, p. 43.

[40] Ibid., p. 103.

[41] See Moishe Postone, *Time, Labor, and Social Domination* (Cambridge: Cambridge University Press, 1993), p. 16.

Habermas has moved in a direction that places less emphasis on critique aware of its own historical conditioning. He hinges his theory of truth on the *ahistorical* social conditions of consensual inquiry into normative claims. But I will examine how his undetermination of the contextual factors involved in his own theory has hampered its emancipatory potential.

Having defined the framework by which we can analyze Habermas's theory of reflection, I need to specify how he actually employs reflection in his emancipatory theory.

REFLECTION AND THE DETERMINATION OF THE VALIDITY OF TRUTH AND TRUTH-ANALOGOUS CLAIMS

Habermas develops a formal-pragmatic theory of truth. He claims that a propositionally formulated and intersubjectively expressed claim is true if, and only if, all possible problematizations of its validity by both speakers and hearers are resolvable through rationally guided discursive argumentation. Claims that regard ethical norms and aesthetic beliefs are truth-*analogous*: normative claims are determined according to their rightness, and aesthetic and expressive beliefs are determined according to their truthfulness.

Habermas's form of synthetic reflection in his theory of truth thus exhibits three distinctive characteristics:

(1) Habermas limits the attribution of axiomatic reflection to semantically well-formed and intersubjectively meaningful *claims*. He thus excludes all non-propositional forms of meaning from the validity spheres of truth, truthfulness, and rightness. However, he also claims that *all* propositionally formulated claims, whether theoretic or axiomatic, are in principle redeemable by discursive argumentation. The speaker of any claim must yield to the grounds, or "third term," of the rational consensus of all affected by a possible truth or truth-analogous claim. Habermas thus excludes from this validity theory all non-intersubjective forms of verification, such as appeals to authority (Augustine), experience (Locke), transcendental categories (Kant), or intuition (Husserl). As we shall see, Habermas understands reflection to be integral, not to the truth *content* of a claim, but to its *mode* of assertion.

(2) Habermas understands reflection in the history of philosophy

to have evolved from a subject-centered to a discourse-centered act. His discursive theory of reflection replaces consciousness-centered terms such as "subject," "belief," and "intended object" with "speaker," "claim," and "interest." I will analyze his justification of this linguistically centered view of reflection in Chapter 1.

(3) Although Habermas's formal-pragmatic theory of validity does require that we account for

(a)   the comprehensibility of two or more terms related in a propositional claim,

(b)   the way the identity, or unity, of the terms is expressed by the copula of the proposition claim, and

(c)   the verification of (b) through discursive argumentation, he does not adequately account for

(d)   the temporal contextualization of the content of the claim required at level (c).

In Chapter 5, I shall argue that temporal contextualization relies on an act of reflection that can determine both the conditions of assertability of claims in everyday interactions *and* the background conditions by which the conditions themselves are determined for particular contexts. Moreover, this demand for contextualization must include an analysis of the selection of the various forms of linguistic media used in a specific argumentative discourse (symbols, gestures, speech act), the determination of the domain of what can or cannot be brought into a discourse (the determination of a claim *as* truth-claiming), and the motives that compel an actor to engage in a particular discursive reflection in the first place.

OVERVIEW OF THE ARGUMENT

To carry out this analysis and critique of Habermas's theory of reflection, in Chapter 1 I present an historical view of various theories of reflection to which Habermas refers. My purpose is to show how the notion of reflection slowly evolved from a consciousness-centered to a linguistically centered act. Starting with Kant, reflection went through several discernible stages of modification in Fichte, Schelling, and Hegel. Moreover, by sketching the various modifications made throughout the course of the development of reflection,

I can show how certain elements of Habermas's speech-act theoretic version of reflection were anticipated by these earlier theorists, particularly Hegel and Husserl, and how, on Habermas's account, these theories of reflection deviated from a speech-theoretic basis to form what he calls philosophies of consciousness.

Chapter 2 examines Habermas's early development of the idea of a self-reflective emancipatory science. As a critical theorist, Habermas was interested in finding a structure by which unjust and oppressive social practices could be critiqued. Rejecting what he perceived to be Horkheimer's and Adorno's pessimism about the ability of rationality to secure true progress, Habermas reconsidered the possibility of a scientific use of reflection as a tool for both social and individual emancipation. However, he quickly realized deficiencies in his methodological analysis, particularly its failure to distinguish differences in the determinations of scientific, moral, and expressive claims to validity. Nonetheless, he never abandoned his conviction that a methodological determination of normative validity is not only possible but desirable.

Chapter 3 describes how Habermas uses insights from speech act theory and interactive sociology as a way to determine the similarities and differences among the claims to truth, truthfulness, and rightness. Though his motivation to analyze speech act theory arose out of the analysis of social interaction and a need to provide a methodological basis for social science, it also supplies the tools by which social interaction is modified and better ordered. Moreover, I will examine some of the presuppositions required for this analysis, particularly its *phenomenological* analysis of background conditions required for intersubjectivity. My focus will be on the form of reflection that can ground an exclusively discursive view of meaning and truth. I will also examine why speech act theory thus lies at the core of Habermas's theory of emancipation, since it acknowledges the reflective act embodied in ordinary language that provides speakers with the guarantee of unforced cooperation needed for the determination of both truth and truth-analogous claims.

Chapter 4 analyzes how Habermas applies this discursive theory of reflection specifically to two sets of claims in which context determination is of particular importance: moral claims and expressive claims (particularly those relevant to the determination of ego-identity). These two loci of discourse in particular reveal how Habermas uses a synthetic act of reflection to explicate the intersubjectivity needed for actual discourses. I will examine how emancipative intersubjectivity must be reconstructed not only as an unproblematized sharing of perspectives in the lifeworld, but also as an achievement that requires a cognitively guided restructuring of the contexts in which the distorted communication that undermines rightness and truthfulness takes place.

Finally, in Chapter 5 I suggest how Habermas's version of discursive reflection can be made more sensitive to context, particularly to the temporal conditions under which actors are *motivated* to engage in critical and emancipative reflection in the first place. On the basis of Habermas's own methodological presuppositions regarding what he terms communicative speech acts, I reconstruct second-order discourses by which actors in a discursive setting determine the precise nature of the *content* of the claims they discuss relative to the limits imposed on their own interests by the interests of others. I propose a formal pragmatics of the discourse regarding the temporal modalities of validity determination itself.

In closely scrutinizing Habermas's analysis and use of reflection, my overall aim is to increase the suasive power of his unique and compelling theory of truth. I hope to show how he elucidates the peculiar human ability to negate distortions of truth and social order by reflective acts whose power can be utilized not only to repair the damage of oppression and deception, but also to design a just and free society.

1

Habermas's Critique of the Use of Reflection in Theories of Consciousness

Rodolphe Gasché contends that most current usage of the terms "reflection" and "self-reflection" stems from the Hegelian critique of Kant's philosophy of reflection.[1] Habermas's own analysis of reflection and validity does in fact rely heavily on Hegel's critique of the philosophy of reflection, but to suit his own intersubjective and emancipative interests, he also criticizes and modifies key elements of the philosophy of reflection that both precedes and follows Hegel.

Hegel claimed to have achieved a coherent logic of the reflective interplay beyond subject-and-object analysis by raising noetic reflection itself to the rank of the *Begriff* (concept). Hegel's *Begriff* includes both a noematic reflection on the opposed moments of a relation, the subject and object, and a noetic reflection on the totality of the *medium* of the noematic reflection itself.[2] The medium for this noetic reflection is the subject's own *otherness*, the representation of its alienated self: "In the reflection of the mirror-subject as an annulment of the mirroring subject's former alienation, the reflection of other becomes a reflection of self. The mirror's self-reflection is the embracing whole that allows it to release itself into the other, which explains why it faces an object in the first place and why it returns reflexively to itself."[3] Gasché claims that an understanding of Hegel's speculative understanding of reflection is essential for the analysis of all subsequent theories of subjectivity, consciousness, and self-consciousness.

---

[1] Roberts, on the other hand, focuses on Kant's rather than Hegel's analysis of reflection. His study is based upon how reflection functions in "post-Kantian rationality." See *Logic of Reflection*, p. 9.

[2] Gasché, *Tain of the Mirror*, p. 62.

[3] Ibid., p. 21.

Habermas understands reflection to be a necessary feature of any philosophy of consciousness. On his account, a philosophy of consciousness is any theory that privileges representational thinking: the determination of meaning and truth on the basis of formalized, systematized, and perceptually grounded concepts. Beginning with Kant, the function of reflection was to determine how the mind conceives of itself as a subject related to itself and to others. Although each successive philosophy of consciousness tried to address the deficiencies of previous theories, Habermas identifies in each an insurmountable defect. On his account, reflective processes serve a truly emancipative function when they analyze, not mentalistic concepts, but the discursive use of language that coordinates action. Humboldt, Frege, and Mead set the tools in place for a coherent reflective reconstruction of these discursive structures.

Using Hegel's theory as its primary focus, this chapter will present an analysis of consciousness-based theories of reflection that Habermas criticizes in the process of developing his own theory of discursive reflection. The theories to which he refers are found in the works of Kant, Fichte, Schelling, Hegel, Husserl, and Heidegger. My purpose will be threefold: to present Habermas's analysis of these theories, to make a coherent account of the various stages, or levels, of reflection these theories posit (by integrating schemes developed by Gasché, Schnädelbach, and Roberts), and to evaluate Habermas's estimation of the theories of consciousness in each of these theories of reflection. This will prepare the grounds for an analysis of the development of Habermas's own theory of reflection in the next chapter.

THE PRE-KANTIAN ORIGINS OF THE PROBLEM OF REFLECTION

The concept of reflection is as old as philosophy itself. In both Greek and Latin philosophy the term 'reflection' was an optic metaphor that described a kind of mirroring property of an object.[4] Karl-Otto Apel describes how early Greek philosophers employed a first reflection (*intentio recta*) to distinguish between immediate sense experi-

---

[4] Schnädelbach, *Reflexion und Diskurs*, p. 14.

ence and the subject of the experience. This level of reflection that attends to immediate sense experience is:

(R1) *empirical (sensible) reflection,* which "bends in" on the subject and determines its limits relative to objects. It specifically determines that the subject is both distinct from and related to objects. It is the source of all psychological knowledge.[5]

Since the *expression* of this first reflection was problematic, philosophers had to employ a second reflection (*intentio obliqua*), by which one reflected, in a truly philosophical sense, on perception itself.[6] This second level of reflection was:

(R2) *logical (intellectual) reflection,* which turns thought away from its relation to objects themselves (including itself as an empirical reality) to an examination of relations among concepts of objects.

Logical reflection was the "epistemologization" of the concept of *energeia,* the reflexive structure by which a substance actualizes itself.[7] The Greeks attributed reflexive properties to some realities and excluded them from others.

Plato employed logical reflection in turning from ontological questions about the nature and origin of things to questions about the correctness of names, the function of speech, and the meanings and definitions of words. All reflection on the function of language occurs in this second form of reflection. In the *Charmides* Socrates denied that *sophrosyne*—the soul's knowledge regarding good and evil—can refer reflexively both to itself and to an object. But in other Platonic dialogues we hear that the soul is formally reflexive because it has the capacity of self-movement. Yet Plato denied that the self-relationality of the soul's power of movement can also be attributed

---

[5] The typology of stages of reflection I am presenting is derived from Schnädelbach's typology in *Reflexion und Diskurs.* He grounds his typology on the reflexive return to the subject and on the way that this return is justified and structured (pp. 64ff.). One weakness of Schnädelbach's neo-Kantian study, however, is its failure to include Hegel's critique of the philosophy of reflection.

[6] See Apel, "Transcendental Conception of Language-Communication and the Idea of a First Philosophy," pp. 32–61.

[7] See John McCumber's review of *The Tain of the Mirror,* in *Philosophical Review,* 100, No. 2 (April 1991), 302. He notes that Fichte was the first to point out the relation between reflection and *energeia.*

to its power of knowing.[8] Although Plato maintained that knowledge is not reflexive, Rorty argues that he anticipated subsequent levels of reflection by forging an initial link between the perception of particular objects and the knowledge of the universal.[9]

Aristotle distinguished between the sense and the reference of a reflective act. This enabled him to turn from the determination of whether an activity is reflexive to the determination of a first principle whose self-reflexivity would allow it to ground other activities. He found such a noetic grounding principle in the "thinking of thinking" (noesis noeseos). He claimed that knowledge grounded in the self-relationality of this reflective noûs is free of false assumptions and heterogenous causes. Aristotle even placed the essence of God in this noûs.[10] Both the Stoics and the neo-Platonists also adopted noûs as their grounding principle; in medieval Scholasticism the principle of esse served a similar function.[11] Borrowing from Plato's notion of anamnesis, Augustine formulated a form of self-reflection: reditus in se ipsum.[12]

The seventeenth century witnessed a significant development in the idea of reflection. Descartes's methodological doubt redirected Augustine's self-reflection toward practical ends. Descartes claimed that the "I think" is the decisive methodological foundation not only for epistemology, but also for enlightened and autonomous action.[13] Habermas, in fact, locates the origin of all reflexive philosophies of consciousness precisely in this Cartesian reflexive self-consciousness.[14] Applying this reflectively derived autonomy to the religious

---

[8] Gasché, Tain of the Mirror, p. 66.

[9] See Philosophy and the Mirror of Nature, pp. 156–157.

[10] Metaphysics 1072b. For a discussion of Aristotle on reflection, see Werner Marx, Das Selbstbewußtsein in Hegels Phänomenologie des Geistes (Frankfurt am Main: Klostermann, 1986), p. 37.

[11] See Robert Badillo, The Emancipative Theory of Jürgen Habermas (Washington D.C.: The Council for Research in Values and Philosophy, 1991), p. 132. Badillo even correlates Aquinas's explication of relative transcendentals with Habermas's project: the transcendental property of goodness correlates with Habermas's emancipation; and the transcendental of truth, with the notion of being as communicative (pp. 136ff.). But he admits that a completely developed sense of communicative reality is wanting in Aquinas's metaphysics.

[12] See Schnädelbach, Reflexion und Diskurs, p. 18.

[13] Ernst Tugendhat, Self-Consciousness and Self-Determination, trans. Paul Stern (Cambridge, Mass.: The MIT Press, 1986), p. 1.

[14] For Habermas's claims regarding the Cartesian influence on the subsequent philosophy of reflection, see PT 158, 178; and his "Erkenntnis und Interesse," in

domain, La Rochefoucauld extolled the virtue of a "reflective conviction before one's own damnation" that would purify one's intentions
and enable one to attain to a "better I."[15] Fénelon opposed this Jan-
senistic view of reflection, arguing that it was a reflection unaware of
its own interest. Robert Spaemann claims that Fénelon's critique
of reflective self-certainty's exclusion of interest began the modern
problematic of reflection. Fichte's later development of practical reflection, from which Habermas himself borrows, further developed
this initial link between reflection and practical interests.

Locke, Leibniz, and Hume each tried to work out the epistemological relationship between empirical and logical reflection. Locke held
that the subject, by logically reflecting on mental phenomena, could
determine their *validity*.[16] But he based this reflection on an *intentio
recta*, an "inner psychological perception," that Kant claimed merely
sensualized appearances and reduced logical reflection to empirical
reflection.[17] Leibniz, however, did just the opposite: he formulated
an introspective "intellectual actualization" that attends to the innate ideas in the mind and thus reduces empirical reflection to logical reflection. He argued that we come to notions such as the self or
substance by means of reflexive acts distinct from principles of reason such as non-contradiction and sufficient reason.[18] Hume, on the
other hand, did not reduce one form of reflection to the other. He
attributed to logical reflection the power to assert that the distinctions that follow from empirical reflection are real entities: "it cannot
be doubted that the mind is endowed with several powers and facul-
ties, that these powers are distinct from each other, that what is
really distinct to the immediate perception may be distinguished by
reflection."[19] But Hume denied reflection the ability to determine

---

Technologie und Wissenschaft als Ideologie (Frankfurt am Main: Suhrkamp, 1968),
p. 159. Schnädelbach agrees that all reflective concepts emerge from Descartes's
paradigm. Tugendhat also places Husserl in this same Cartesian paradigm. See Ernst
Tugendhat, *Vorlesungen zur Einführung in die sprachanalytische Philosophie* (Frankfurt am Main: Suhrkamp, 1976).

[15] Robert Spaemann, "Unschuld und Reflexion," in *Fénelon: Reflexion und Spontaneität* (Stuttgart: Klett-Cotta, 1990), p. 119. Hegel in *Der Geist des Christentums
und sein Schicksal* also speaks of the value of a "reflexive life."

[16] See Schnädelbach, *Reflexion und Diskurs*, p. 106.

[17] See Rorty, *Philosophy and the Mirror of Nature*, p. 148.

[18] See Roberts, *Logic of Reflection*, pp. 7ff.

[19] *An Inquiry Concerning Human Understanding*, ed. C. Handel (New York: Macmillan, 1955), p. 22.

the validity of causal inference. The intrinsic limitations of the division between empirical and logical reflection had yet to be overcome.

KANT'S SYNTHESIS OF EMPIRICAL AND LOGICAL REFLECTION

The German critical tradition in philosophy to which Habermas is heir begins with Kant. At several points in both his theoretical and his practical work, Habermas recognizes Kant as the founder of a critique of a reason able to inform social critique and action. For Kant, reason takes on a dual role: not only does it reveal its own architectonic, but it also assumes the role of supreme judge, even in relation to culture. Thus, his theory of reflection provides the first systematic treatment of the idea of reflection for Habermas's critique of theories of consciousness.

Habermas claims that Kant's transcendental method developed a form of absolute self-consciousness. Its reflexive structure is that of a "self-relating, knowing subject, which bends back upon itself as object, in order to grasp itself as in a mirror image" (PDM 18). He notes that Kant connects the concept of knowledge with the synthetic accomplishments of the productive imagination and understanding, and borrows from the construction of simple geometric forms and number series to show the operation of producing unities within a previously unordered multiplicity. The synthesis results, not from some overarching intuition, but from the following of apriori categories of thought.

Habermas argues that the transcendent unity of the Kantian "I think" does not produce, but only *accompanies* every synthesis (PT 124). It grounds the identity of the self. But Habermas points out that the "I think" is ambiguous relative to the status of the actual individual. Since the categories of the understanding subsume particulars under universals, the ego's inner nature remains a transcendent ideal that cannot be empirically individuated. So, how does this transcendental self understand the objects of its knowledge? Habermas argues that Kant had to employ a regulatory cosmological idea of the world which represents everything that stands over and against the subject. But this regulative idea has only heuristic value for knowledge. Since it is dependent on the synthetic accomplishments of the subject, it "downgrades" the cosmos into the nomonological range of the natural sciences. For Habermas this entails that the Kantian world of appearance is no longer a "whole organized according to ends"(PT 125).

Habermas's critique of Kant thus focuses on the problem of the inherent limits imposed by a transcendental method. Habermas does acknowledge that the *First Critique* expanded Hume's limited view of the access the self has to an intelligible world. Although the "Transcendental Analytic" employs a Humean version of empirical and logical reflection, the "Amphiboly of Reflection" sets forth a level of reflection that critically determines the very *subjective conditions* by which we distinguish empirical and logical concepts in the first place. This critical form of reflection, in Kant's words, "does not concern itself with objects themselves with a view to deriving concepts from them directly, but is that state of mind in which we first set ourselves to discover the subjective conditions under which [alone] we are able to arrive at concepts."[20] This form of reflection (*Überlegung*) is neither a simple awareness of an empirical self nor a Lockean perception of the operations of a mind. Rather, it determines the relation of given representations to the two different sources of knowledge: the "noumenal" for the concepts of the understanding, and the "phenomenal" for sensible intuition. Within the latter, reflection reveals the spatial and temporal media of sensibility that limit conceptual thought. Concepts of the understanding are systematic and holistic; sensibility is unpredictable and filled with possibility. By this distinction, Kant achieved a third level of reflection:

(R3) *transcendental reflection,* which inquires into the logical apriori constitutive principles of the limits of the subject's ability to conceptualize an empirical object.

From this perspective, logical concepts of the understanding contain "the unity of reflection upon appearances insofar as these appearances should necessarily belong to a possible empirical consciousness."[21] Transcendental reflection grounds both empirical and logical

---

[20] *Critique of Pure Reason,* trans. Norman Kemp Smith (New York: St. Martin's, 1956), B316. Rorty claims that Kant's argument that a non-conscious synthesis of a manifold of intuition is a condition of the possibility of conscious experience "should be viewed as a *reductio ad absurdum* of the very idea of such conditions." See Rorty's "Two Meanings of Logocentrism," in *Philosophical Papers,* 2 vols. (New York: Cambridge University Press, 1991), 2.112.

[21] *Critique of Pure Reason,* B367.

reflection in the noetic and unconditional unity of reflection's own cognitional *activity*. Kant thus set the stage for further analysis of the way this activity relates to transcendental regulative ideas.

Kant's transcendental turn set reflection firmly on a critical ground. Schnädelbach claims that Kantian reflection subsumes a threefold typology:

(*a*) a phenomenological reflection that determines the "inner object" or noema of the *intentio recta*,

(*b*) a validity-theoretic reflection that determines the noetic conditions of validity of its own possibility, and

(*c*) a meaning-explicative reflection that determines that a given representation *belongs to the subject*: the knowledge is "my" knowledge.[22]

(*a*) is a consequence of the synthetic unity of apperception, and (*b*) is a consequence of the amphiboly of reflection. Although (*c*) is absent from the *First Critique*, as we have seen, in his *Logic* Kant does speak of the self-confirmation of "my knowledge."[23] Kant established that a subject cognizes not only a difference with regard to the object (the unknowable thing-in-itself), but also an identity with regard to the *subjective conditions* by which it conceptualizes the object.

Habermas argues that the same limitations as apply to this transcendental reflection's access to the intelligible world apply to its access to itself. He further suggests that neither Fichte nor Schelling overcame these limitations. Kant's denial of intellectual intuition left him without a proper form of mediation between the sphere of physics and the sphere of ethics. His system cannot explain how the subject can either use knowledge of the physical world to determine moral action or even know that his moral actions as posited in the world of sense really belong to it.

Kant claimed to achieve a teleological bridge between the transcendental and the intelligible by a third idea of reason in his *Critique of Judgment*. This idea of reason is an *intellectus archetypus*, a higher form of cognition in which the opposition of universal and

---

[22] *Reflexion und Diskurs*, p. 112.

[23] See his "Logik," in *Schriften zur Metaphysik und Logik* II (Frankfurt am Main: Suhrkamp, 1977), §7. Schnädelbach rightly criticizes Tugendhat's claim that Kant's talk about "my" representations follows merely a "semantic rule of a Cartesian language game" and a transcendental semiotics. See *Reflexion und Diskurs*, p. 113.

particular, at least in nature and history, no longer exists.[24] Fichte
and Schelling later appeal to similar intuitive forms of synthesis. For
Kant, aesthetic judgments of taste do have an immediate empirical
basis: in the pains and pleasure of a perceiving subject. After all, the
pleasure confirmed by a judgment of taste derives, not from an object external to the subject, but from the subject's reflection on the
pleasure of the harmony that the object excites in its cognitive capacities.[25] This is the basis for what Hegel later called Kant's subjective "subject-object," which Hegel used to launch his own view of
reflection. But Habermas argues that these philosophers use forms
of intellectual intuition to view nature only *as if* (Kant's own phrase)
they are capable of constituting teleological principles, such as the
kingdom of ends. He refuses to consider levels of cognition in Kant
other than those presented in the *First Critique*'s transcendental aesthetic and transcendental analytic. This precludes Habermas from
granting any constitutive content to Kant's aesthetic and teleological
judgments.

Though Kant left underdetermined the nature of both the empirical grounds of reflective judgment and the universal communicabil-
ity of an aesthetic judgment, Fichte saw in Kant's analysis the
possibility of a unique way to reunite the intelligible and sensible
realms. Kant had allowed only sensible, not intellectual, intuition
into the determination of objects of experience. But starting from
the third paralogism's claim that the self requires the other for its
own reflexive return to itself, Fichte uses the *productive imagination*
as a tool to establish a practical access both to the self and to the
other. He grants intellectual intuition a role in this unitive determination without rejecting Kant's principle of the primacy of practical
reason.[26]

---

[24] Kant, *Critique of Judgement*, trans. J. Meredith (Oxford: The Clarendon Press,
1973), §76. See also Gasché, *Tain of the Mirror*, p. 27.

[25] *Critique of Judgement*, §39.

[26] See *Johann Gottlieb Fichtes sämmtliche Werke*, ed. I. H. Fichte (Berlin: Veit,
1845–1846), 4:86, 1:466; Kant, *Critique of Practical Reason*, trans. L. Beck (New
York: Bobbs-Merrill, 1956), book 1, chap. 3. Although Fichte never uses the term
"intellectual intuition" explicitly, several scholars have argued that the term is implied in his understanding of action and is made more explicit in the Second Introduction to the *Wissenschaftslehre*.

FICHTE'S REFLEXIVE APPROPRIATION OF THE I

Habermas argues that, by beginning with the act of self-consciousness as the original transcendental experience, Fichte's system stood Kant's denial of an empirical element in the unity of apperception on its head (KHI 37). Like most scholars, Habermas agrees that the architectonic of Fichte's system is found in his *Wissenschaftslehre* (*Science of Knowledge*) of 1794 (PT 162).[27] Here Fichte defined individuality, not as the productive cultivation of one's own essential powers, but only as the renunciation of the possibility of realizing one's own freedom (PT 160). Habermas claims that Fichte's I "can only take possession of itself and 'posit' itself by positing, as it were unconsciously, a not-I and trying gradually to retrieve this thing posited by the I" (PDM 262). But Habermas acknowledges that this act of mediated self-positing can be understood under three different aspects: as a process of self-knowledge, as a process of growing reflective awareness, and as a process of self-formation. Thus, Fichte's I has a double relation: it is in the world "always already" as something that has become itself contingently, and it is endowed by this reflection with the ability to make the world's "in itself" transparent and to elevate it into consciousness "for itself" (PDM 263).

Habermas maintains that this architectonic, though granting the other a necessary role in the constitution of the self, ultimately renders the self too one-sidedly subjective and constructivistic.[28] The

---

[27] Although Fichte published other editions of the *Science of Knowledge* that corrected many of the errors of the first, Hegel is believed to have read only the first edition. Dieter Henrich mentions how difficult Fichte scholarship is since only about half of his written work has so far been "deciphered." See Henrich's "Fichte's Original Insight," in *Contemporary German Philosophy* I, trans. D. Lachterman (University Park: Pennsylvania State University Press, 1982), p. 17. Of the differences in the 1794, 1797, and 1801 versions of the *Science of Knowledge*, the most salient for Henrich are the focus on the "as" of representation in the 1797 version, and the centrality of the analogy of the "eye" for self-consciousness which sees both intuition and concept, separated in Kant, in a simultaneous moment and a reciprocal relation in the 1801 version (pp. 31–34). For a good treatment of recent Fichte scholarship, see Daniel Breazeale, "Editor's Introduction," in *Foundations of Transcendental Philosophy: Wissenschaftslehre nova methodo (1796/99)*, trans. and ed. Daniel Breazeale (Ithaca, N.Y.: Cornell University Press, 1992), pp. 1–49.

[28] Habermas makes these initial claims in his doctoral dissertation on Schelling, *Das Absolute und die Geschichte: Von der Zwiespältigkeit in Schellings Denken* (Dissertation, Universität Bonn, 1954), pp. 123, 141.

Fichtean I that aims at self-knowledge becomes trapped in a circle: "by referring itself to itself, the subject makes itself into an object and thus fails to attain itself as spontaneously generative subjectivity" (PT 207). Entrapped in the subject/object paradigm, the I gains an individuality that is not particular, but only generalized. The I experiences itself as capable of spontaneous activity only *because* it confronts the not-I. Though this grounds our understanding of ourselves as numerical individuals—we are only one of many rational beings—the "balance" among individuals is nullified by the fact that the I unavoidably makes itself into an object in consciously assuring itself. This objectivization obscures the antecedent source of all accomplishments of consciousness.

Habermas concludes that Fichte's objectivization of the self-relation also undermines any possibility of a coherent account of intersubjectivity. Since each subject becomes aware of itself by making itself into an object *after* its originary self-positing, it is alien to itself (PT 159). Since this is the case, it is also alien to the "alien freedoms" of others (PT 160). Moreover, Habermas concludes that no attempt by a philosophy of the subject to properly determine the structures of intersubjectivity has been successful: not Fichte's analysis, not Husserl's fifth Cartesian Meditation, not Sartre's construction of Being-for-another. Such theories operate with the dynamics of a mutual objectification that lacks the communicative distinction between first- and second-person address. Fichte views language, not as a medium in which a speaker confronts the force of linguistically formulated claims, but only as a "glassy medium without properties" (PT 161). Though he made a significant advance by linking reflection and action in the act of self-positing, Fichte remained entangled in the decisionistic error that has beleaguered philosophers from Kierkegaard to Tugendhat: the claim that a person is ultimately constituted by his own individuality (PT 170).[29] Fichte's I is a "practically executed and reflexively recapitulated" act that requires only a minimal dependence on the other (PT 159).[30]

Fichte's system represents for Habermas the very epitome of a theory of consciousness. But Habermas's devastating critique misses some points at which Fichte evaded Kant's de-temporalized tran-

---

[29] Habermas criticizes all theories in which "*das Eigenste die Person ist.*"

[30] Habermas uses the term *nachvollziehbaren* for this recapitulation.

scendental understanding of reflection and in so doing prepared the ground for Hegel's more comprehensive and coherent view of inter-subjectivity. Moreover, a close reading of the *Wissenschaftslehre* from the viewpoint of its theory of reflection yields a theory of inter-subjectivity richer and more complex than Habermas's critique suggests.

In the *Wissenschaftslehre*, Fichte criticized the dogmatism of Kant's arbitrary positing of the necessity of both the thing-in-itself and the categories.[31] According to Fichte, Kant "by no means proved the categories he set up to be conditions of self-consciousness, but merely said that they were so: that still less did he derive space and time as conditions thereof, or that which is separable from them in the original consciousness and fills them both."[32] Fichte deduced the categories from the very *act* of self-consciousness that Kant had introduced in the transcendental unity of apperception. In so doing, he expanded the range of philosophical reflection into the realm of the practical. By claiming that by means of reflection the self can determine both its object and *itself as conditioned by the object*, Fichte gave content to the emptiness of Kant's transcendental reflection and its failure to formulate a coherent account of intersubjectivity. He locates the terms of transcendental reflection, not in the relation between the subject and an unknown thing-in-itself, but in a dialectical struggle between the I and the not-I.

Although Kant constructed his science of knowing from reflections on the forms of deductive and inductive inference, Fichte constructed his "evidential science" simply from reflection on the cognitive conditions for understanding tautological axioms.[33] Fichte

---

[31] Charles Taylor, *Hegel* (Cambridge: Cambridge University Press, 1975), p. 37.

[32] See Jere Paul Surber, "Introduction," in *The Difference Between the Fichtean and Schellingian Systems of Philosophy* (Resada, Calif.: Ridgeview Publishing, 1978), p. xliii. See also Johann Gottlieb Fichte, "Grundlage der gesamten Wissenschafts-lehre (1794)," in *Ausgewählte Werke*, ed. F. Medicus (Darmstadt: Wissenschaftliche Buchgesellschaft, 1962). My page references will refer to the first edition of volume I of the work. I will also refer to John Lach's translation of the *Science of Knowledge* (New York: Cambridge University Press, 1970).

[33] All Fichte's subsequent works can be seen as commentaries on the *Wissen-schaftslehre*. See George Seidel, *Fichte's Wissenschaftslehre of 1794: A Commentary on Part One* (West Lafayette, Ind.: Purdue University Press, 1992). (The English translations I will use of the first volume of the *Sämmtliche Werke* are taken from this text.) See also Robert Williams, *Recognition: Fichte and Hegel on the Other* (Albany: State University of New York Press, 1992), pp. 53ff. Fichte never published

set forth the forms of three logical tautologies—the laws of identity, excluded middle, and contradiction—as the fundamental axioms from which knowledge can be derived and justified.[34] His science thus begins with the purely intelligible productive deed of the knowing I and proceeds to deduce the entire realm of empirical experience.

The key advance that Fichte gained over Kant was the ability to include the negative *within* a system. The negative is revealed in the thinking needed to understand the second axiom: not-A is not equal to A. This transition from positing to counterpositing—a "category of negation"—is possible only through the mediation of the identity of the I. This makes the I's identity neither transcendental nor regulative, but actual. But its actuality is limited, since its actuality is *temporally prior* to its recognition by the subject.[35] Nevertheless, time for Fichte is no longer an apriori form of representation, as it was for Kant, but a form of experience that reflection can determine only retroactively. Both Schelling and Hegel will approach self-reflection from this same de-Kantianized temporal perspective.

Fichte made another important advance over Kant by determining that the mediation between the posited I and the counterposited not-I is not a synthetic unity of apperception, but a divisible *reality*. The I and the not-I are related to each other within a dynamic of limitation and interdetermination within this divisible medium. By grasping this divisibility and limitation determined by the productive imagination, a second reflection is able to separate out two aspects of a unitary judgment: the act of counterpositing and the act of combination. Thus, Fichte provided a second-order analysis of both antithesis and synthesis: in an antithesis, reflection dwells solely on the element of counterpositing and thereby raises it to clear and distinct consciousness; in a synthesis, reflection ignores the act of

---

any of the many subsequent versions of the *Wissenschaftslehre*. For more on the development of the *Wissenschaftslehre*, see Breazeale, *Foundations of Transcendental Philosophy*, pp. 13–16.

[34] For a treatment of Fichte's impact on Hegel, see Richard Kroner's introduction to Hegel's *Early Theological Writings*, trans. T. M. Knox (Philadelphia: University of Pennsylvania Press, 1981), p. 31.

[35] The second axiom entails that one can negate a single term. Tugendhat argues that, since Aristotle, it has been generally agreed that negation applies only to propositions, not to single terms (*Categories* 3b24). But both Fichte and Hegel adopt this non-propositional form of negation.

counterpositing and brings to consciousness only the ground of connection between the terms.[36]

Fichte then examined the synthetic union between these two modes of interdetermination. Here the modality of time is again required, now in order to distinguish the different degrees of the ego's activity or passivity from the *simultaneous* viewpoint of an actual external observer.[37] The I's progressive action in this process of interdetermination is an infinite "striving." This boundless striving is the condition of the possibility of any object for the I: "no striving, no object."[38] Borrowing from the physical science of his day, Fichte used the metaphors of centripetal and centrifugal forces to describe the nature of this striving. The I acts centripetally as a finite self-reflection and centrifugally as an infinite *life force*. This self-determining "harmonizing" of drive and action forms a more comprehensive grounding for a theory of action than Kant's harmonization of nature and freedom in the judgment of taste described in the *Third Critique*.

Fichte thus developed a fourth stage of reflection distinct from Kant's transcendental reflection:

(R4) *critical practical reflection*, which is a form of thinking able to specify its own theoretical and practical limits relative to an infinite not-I, thereby determining itself as an infinitely striving I.

In subsequent revisions of the *Wissenschaftslehre*, Fichte specifies that the two conditions that limit the power of reflection are the temporal succession of the I's activity and the discursive thinking of its determination of activity.[39] Though reflection is by nature *regressive*, there is one unified act that regressive analysis constitutes as a progressive analysis: the act of *will*.[40] Logically, an act of limiting is

---

[36] Fichte, *Ausgewählte Werke*, 1.113–114.

[37] *Science of Knowledge*, p. 140. Kant had taken account of this need for the extension of successive time in the transcendental aesthetic of the *First Critique*.

[38] *Science of Knowledge*, p. 231.

[39] See *Foundations of Transcendental Philosophy*, §15:167, pp. 332–333.

[40] In the "Second Introduction," Fichte takes up more directly the relationship between the speculative and the practical that the realm of life comprises. The philosophical consciousness reflects on and interprets the natural consciousness. See Williams, *Recognition*, p. 39. At this point it is still a regressive analysis, since philosophical reflection can follow its subject, but prescribe no law for it. See Fichte,

impossible unless "I am acquainted with something that is assumed to lie beyond the limits."[41] The will represents that which posits beyond limits. Thus, it has a double aspect: it contains both the positive factor of the "beyond" and the negative factor of limitation. Since this double aspect provides the foundation for a reflection upon the determinate state of the I, it follows that willing and limitation are synthetically united within this act of reflection. Since willing is a condition for knowing, theory and practice are inextricably intertwined.[42]

Fichte realized, however, that reflection is unable to grasp the will in its totality, since the will is limited in time, "and feeling [*Gefühl*] is the immediate expression of this limitation."[43] The origin of the act of reflection that determines the feeling remains shrouded in mystery. We cannot account for the starting point of our empirical life. So, despite his inclusion of feeling and willing in reflection, Fichte realized that he still lacked a transcendental system of the "intelligible world," which was the Kantian term for the intersubjective realm of free moral agents. Yet he was becoming alarmed by Schelling's assertions regarding the relationship between transcendental philosophy and an apriori philosophy of nature, as well as by his claims about the objective character of intellectual intuition.[44]

Recent work by Robert Williams and Alan Singer suggests that Fichte develops a much more coherent account of intersubjective recognition than is acknowledged by the "traditional" critique of German idealism that Habermas adopts. Singer argues that the I's self-positing is a "non-transcendental" posit. Moreover, the I asserts that it is *not* a ground, since "the ground falls outside the grounds."[45] However, Singer does admit that Fichte is nevertheless responsible for perpetuating the transcendental thesis regarding the relation to

---

Ausgewählte Werke, 1:223. The philosopher regards both the I and the not-I as joined in consciousness and then reflects upon this reflection (*Ausgewählte Werke*, 1.161–162). According to Seidel, this task of philosophy is taken upon by Hegel in the *Phenomenology* when "we" the philosophers observe what is going on behind the back of consciousness. See his *Commentary*, p. 107.

[41] *Wissenschaftslehre 1796/99*, §14.161–162, pp. 322–323.

[42] Breazeale, "Editor's Introduction," p. 12.

[43] *Wissenschaftslehre 1796/99*, §14,165, pp. 328–330.

[44] See Breazeale, "Editor's Introduction," pp. 27–30.

[45] See Williams, *Recognition*, pp. 53ff.; Alan Singer, "The Adequacy of the Aesthetic," *Philosophy and Social Criticism*, 20, Nos. 1–2 (1994), 65–66.

the other by maintaining, even in his later writings, the positing of the other as a situation-specific call or summons (*Aufforderung*). The abstract formalism of the interplay between the I and the not-I within a divisible reality remains problematic in Fichte's writings. But despite this failure to determine a coherent theory of the inter-determination between the I and the not-I, Fichte provided the first coherent formulation of the way a reflective act can determine itself relative to an objective other that it both constitutes and is consti-tuted by. Schelling, then, began his analysis of the interplay between the I and the not-I by criticizing Fichte's assumption that the not-I (nature) is merely a postulate of human practical activity.

SCHELLING'S "OBJECTIVIZATION" OF THE EGO

Although Habermas wrote his dissertation on Schelling, he makes scant mention of Schelling's systematic thought in his subsequent works. In his dissertation, he acknowledges that Schelling steered a middle course between a dogmatic Kantian philosophy in which the subject is considered a thing among other things and a critical Fich-tean philosophy in which the subject alone constitutes objects. Schelling transformed Fichte's categories of I and not-I into spirit and nature, and then determined their interrelation through an "ob-jective variation."[46] Schelling was, however, dubious about discursive forms of reflection, arguing at one point that nature speaks to us more the *less* we reflect on it. Nevertheless, Habermas suggests that Schelling derived a new form of reflection that mitigates both the overly subjective and the dialectical aspects of Fichte's critical prac-tical reflection.[47]

Schelling argued that the being of the ego posits itself through an intellectual intuition that precedes all thought and representation.[48] This intuition grounds the deduction of the determination of an

---

[46] For a description of this objective variation, see Habermas, *Das Absolute und die Geschichte*, p. 123; Surber, "Introduction," p. 54.

[47] *Das Absolute und die Geschichte*, p. 141.

[48] See Schelling, *Vom Ich als Prinzip der Philosophie oder über das Unbedingte im menschlichen Wissen* (1795) as quoted in Walter Schulz's "Introduction" to his translation of *System des transzendentalen Idealismus* (Hamburg: Felix Meiner, 1957), pp. xii–xiii.

absolute ego that, as Kant argued, can be comprehended only as immediate. Like Fichte, Schelling posited the terms mediated by intellectual intuition within practical action.[49] But for Schelling the human spirit now faces a different duality: the diremption of nature and spirit. In his *First Outline of a System of Philosophy of Nature* Schelling argued that the highest efficient cause in nature presupposes an "absolute duplicity" forged by a universal dynamic exteriorization. This exteriorization is overcome by the aesthetic harmonization of an intellectual intuition between the self and nature that results in a subject who is fully self-reflexive.[50] When this is achieved, the self finds itself completely free with respect to the very objects, both natural and subjective, by which it is determined. But for Habermas this means that reason can no longer take possession of itself in its own medium of self-reflection; it can only rediscover itself in the medium of art (PDM 90). Like Hegel, Habermas claims such an aesthetic synthesis is insufficient as a ground for rationality.

Habermas argues that Schelling developed a materialist version of metaphysics according to which all contradictions "come together in the venerable concept of matter" by means of intellectual intuition (PT 123). Thus, Schelling set himself against Platonic metaphysics, in which the material is a shading or weakening of the intelligible. He showed how world history is *constructed* through reason and history: reason is the source of world-constituting ideas, and history is the medium through which the mind carries out its synthesis. But Habermas argues that Schelling failed to overcome the Fichtean "gap" between the self's spontaneous synthesis of its activity and its knowledge of such synthesis. On Habermas's account, this gap continued until Hegel made reflection itself absolute (see PT 124–129).

---

[49] Habermas, *Das Absolute und die Geschichte*, p. 126.

[50] Ibid., p. 151. See also Schelling, *Sämmtliche Werke* (Stuttgart: Publisher, 1858), 3:217–18. Schelling completes his philosophy of nature with a speculative aesthetics, whose details I have omitted here. He argues that the complete resolution of the theory/praxis problem is found, not in the observation of nature, but in a work of art. The entire system of transcendental idealism oscillates between two grounds: one determined by the intellectual intuition of the ego; the other, through an aesthetic intuition of the object. See *System*, pp. 299ff. Alan White argues that since the absolute identity remains prior to the self-reflective act, Schelling's philosopher cannot properly know the absolute identity. Thus, his *System* fails to solve this conflict of grounds. See White's *Schelling: An Introduction to the System of Freedom* (New Haven, Conn.: Yale University Press, 1983), p. 71.

Though Schelling's analysis of the self remained dualistic, his analysis of the absolute provided the basis for the eventual solution of the dualism at a higher level. Schelling contended that intellectual intuition provides no determinant knowledge of the absolute: the absolute still stands above every oppositional axiom in an unmediated appearance. Moreover, the intuition does not forge an abstract link between the phenomenal and the noumenal selves; it only embeds them in the activity of life itself.[51] Habermas deduces that Schelling's chief task was to work out the details of the relation of opposition between the self and the absolute within this new medium of life. By appealing to a "divine *sophia*," Schelling overcame the subjectivism of Fichte's critical practical reflection.[52]

From the viewpoint of a philosophy of reflection, Schelling made several advances beyond Fichte. Although he continued to employ the distinction both Kant and Fichte made between theoretical and practical forms of reflection, Schelling clearly sided with Fichte's claim that practical reason provides the ego's fullest satisfaction. But he criticized both the subjective one-sidedness of Fichte's practical formulation of the real and its consequent mechanistic view of nature. He argued that the self is both a reflexive and an active self-conscious spirit. The self interacts with nature, not in a realm in which the concepts of purpose and life are merely thought, but in a living reality that shares in the dynamisms of consciousness itself. Nature is, thus, not Fichte's posited not-I, but rather the more dynamic concept of the "soul's coming to itself."[53]

Schelling did determine a more intersubjective role for reflection than Fichte did. First, he stipulated that nature has the conscious aim of realizing life in a full subjectivity, even though it is the unconscious product of subjectivity.[54] But this subjectivity manifests itself,

---

[51] Habermas points out that Schelling was strongly influenced by Oetinger's *schwäbische* form of *Lebensphilosophie* in which life was viewed as a form of self-reproduction. See *Das Absolute und die Geschichte*, pp. 126–129.

[52] Ibid., p. 137.

[53] *System*, p. xx. In *The First Outline of a System of Philosophy of Nature* (1799) Schelling had posited the primal reflective act of spirit as the "absolute synthesis" and pinnacle of both a transcendental philosophy and a philosophy of nature. See White, *Introduction to the System of Freedom*, pp. 54–55. White notes that the final form of the *System*'s complicated argumentational structure was so precarious that Schelling abandoned it within a year's time.

[54] See Taylor, *Hegel*, p. 41.

not in a Fichtean I, but in two worlds: the unconscious world of nature, and the conscious world of human action. Thus, for Schelling the content of the ego's thought is a not transcendental positing of the conditions of itself as an individual vis-à-vis the other, but as *becoming other* in history.[55] Although the ego can be represented in consciousness as neither a thing nor a fact, Schelling argued that it is an infinitely enduring "non-objective" (*Nichtobjektive*). However, the ego also "returns to itself" in the historically situated immediacy of the unity of the act of self-consciousness. Reflection yields the identity proposition "I think" from representations, but forms the "higher" proposition "I am" from this return of self-consciousness from the other to itself.[56] As we have seen, Hegel adopts a similar synthetic "self-othering" solution to the problem of the relation between self and other.

How does our awareness of this self-othering come about? Discarding Kant's and Fichte's analytic and deductive explanations of how self-consciousness comes to be reflexively aware of itself, Schelling adopted a scheme that investigates the *actual genesis* of the synthesis in time. He claimed that three transitional epochs have occurred in the history of self-consciousness:

(1) from original sense experience to productive intuition;
(2) from productive intuition to reflection; and
(3) from reflection to an absolute act of the will.

(1) situates the ego's unintentional self-limitation in the act of self-consciousness. At this initial level of sense experience, the ego does not reflect upon its own limits and extension. Productive intuition provides the transition from the ego's ability to perceive objects passively to its ability to be an agent that effects change in the world. (2) emerges when reflection conceptually abstracts the ego's actions from what they produce. Although in every act the ego brings about a determinant product, the I intends not the product, but *to make itself appear in the product*.[57] In a similar way, Aristotle had distinguished between *poiesis* (action that aims at any extrinsic end) and *praxis* (action whose end is the actor itself).[58] Thus, the theoretical

---

[55] *System*, p. 33.
[56] Ibid., p. 35.
[57] Ibid., p. 122.
[58] *Nicomachean Ethics*, 1140b.

and the practical are reciprocally related in the ego's subjective formulation of practical action.[59] Finally, (3) indicates that the ego has
attained a "synthesizing thread" for its actions. The series of actions
from which the ego is derived was first posited analytically by a logical reflection that determined each category as a simple formal concept. But now the ego separates itself from the objects of both its
ideal and its real activity by means of a higher reflexive act. Now
the mechanism of the Kantian categories rests upon an opposition
between the object and *either* the theoretical cognitive powers of the
intelligible and sensible *or* the practical cognitive capacities of the
imagination and the understanding.[60] But for Schelling the terms of
reflection are:

(*a*) a relation, when it is directed toward an object, or
(*b*) a quantity or a quality, when directed toward itself, or
(*c*) possibility or causality, when directed toward both itself and
the object.[61]

But synthetic reflection unites these various "categories," not in a
Kantian transcendental ego or in a Fichtean striving, but in a dynamic *intelligence* aware of its limitation as an historical and temporal object relative to nature and spirit.

From this genetic analysis of reflection—several features of which
Hegel will also adopt—Schelling thus attained to another level of
reflection:

(R5) *noetic practical reflection*, which takes account of the limits of theoretical and practical thinking and "decenters" the activity of reflection from an idealized ego vis-à-vis an other to a
synthesizing intelligence in time.

But now the Habermasian question arises: Is Schelling's form of intersubjectivity completely liberated from a Fichtean objectivization
of the self?

---

[59] Walter Cerf claims that Schelling's use of reflection here was later adopted by
Hegel in the *Essays*. Cerf goes on to compare the difference between philosophies
of reflection and speculation in Hegel's and Schelling's day and our contemporary
difference between analytic philosophy (logical positivism) and synthetic philosophy (existentialism). See Cerf's "Speculative Philosophy and Intellectual Intuition:
An Introduction to Hegel's *Essays*," in *Faith and Knowledge*, trans. W. Cerf and H.
Harris (Albany: State University of New York Press, 1977), p. xvii.

[60] *Critique of Judgement*, §35.

[61] *System*, p. 194.

Like Fichte, Schelling claimed that the self determines itself, not by isolated thinking, but by interaction with actual other selves in history. Although explaining consciousness by the timeless "self-determination" of an act of intelligence, Schelling also stipulated that this self-determination has an intersubjective referent.[62] The fulfillment of two conditions is required for the subjective will's realization of ends. First, like Fichte, Schelling argued that an intelligence determines its will autonomously by "reflecting itself" in the mirror of another intelligence that *limits its choices*.[63] But, unlike Fichte, Schelling stressed that the intelligences constitute a *common* "world" that conditions every member.[64] Schelling even maintained that the intersubjective union of intelligences grounds a kind of consensus theory of truth since knowledge depends on others whose "agreement with my representations is truth."[65]

Despite his decisive move in the direction of an intersubjective and discursive community, Schelling provided no procedure by which to guarantee that agents will cooperate to preserve the existence of each member in the community. The world of intelligences, although determined only through each ego, remains independent from them. Thus, he resorted to the positing of a transcendental kind of pre-established harmony among members. This harmony closely approximates Leibniz's pre-established harmony between the objective situation and the conditions needed for self-knowledge.[66]

Schelling's embedding of reflective processes in an historical and temporal development concretized the transcendentality of Kant's and Fichte's versions of reflection. Hegel adopted this same strategy, having become embroiled in the controversy surrounding Fichte's and Schelling's philosophies of reflection immediately upon his arrival at Jena in 1801. According to Habermas, at this juncture the young Hegel inaugurated postmetaphysical thinking. Yet Habermas also acknowledges that Hegel could not have done so without Schelling's elaboration of both the *construction* of the unity of the world

---

[62] Ibid., p. 200.

[63] Ibid., p. 210. The text reads: "Sie kann erfolgen, sobald dem Ich der Begriff des Wollens entsteht, oder sobald es sich selbst reflektiert, sich im Spiegel einer andern Intelligenz erblickt."

[64] See White, *Introduction to the System of Freedom*, pp. 45ff.

[65] *System*, p. 224.

[66] See White, *Introduction to the System of Freedom*, p. 67.

by an intelligence employing reason and the synthesizing power of history (PT 124).

HEGEL'S DEVELOPMENT OF SPECULATIVE REFLECTION

Habermas's Interpretation of Hegel's Development of Reflection

Habermas points out several ways in which the early Hegel modified Schelling's theory. First, Hegel rejected Schelling's claim that spirit posits an ontological difference between principles and concrete nature. Second, Hegel accused Schelling of turning the hitherto ideal opposites of nature and spirit into real opposites that intellectual intuition then dissolves. He replaced Schelling's forms of intuition with a mediation of opposites that preserves real opposites in self-developing processes.[67] Third, although initially accepting the aesthetic intuition Schelling placed at the apex of the systems of consciousness and nature, Hegel later characterized it as a "simplicity" that depicts actuality in a non-actual manner.[68] Instead he maintained that such a synthesizing intuition has to be grasped *in discursive thought*.[69] In his later works he determined logical forms for this thinking.

In "Hegel's Concept of Modernity," Habermas reconstructs the means by which the early Hegel "burst the philosophy of subjectivity from within" (PDM 23). Hegel derived his new power of unification, not from the understanding (*Verstand*), as philosophies of reflection did, but from reason (*Vernunft*). Reason actually demonstrates the very unity it forms from the categories of the understanding.

---

[67] See Surber, "Introduction," p. xxiii. In the "Preface" to the *Phenomenology*, Hegel criticized Schelling's system of identity and its view of the absolute. But the famous "night when all cows are black" characterization probably would *not* have bothered Schelling, because he himself often referred to the absolute as a kind of night (see White, *Introduction to the System of Freedom*, p. 105). But many scholars think that the *Phenomenology*'s critique of Schelling's system of identity nevertheless vexed Schelling; he published only one work after 1806.

[68] Hegel, *Phänomenologie des Geistes* (Frankfurt am Main: Suhrkamp, 1970), p. 19 / *Phenomenology of Spirit*, trans. A. V. Miller (Oxford: Oxford University Press, 1977), p. 7. I will cite all references from both texts.

[69] Taylor argues that although Schelling did not understand the concrete content of the concept, he did understand that its development was logical and demonstrable. See *Hegel*, p. 532.

Habermas traces the development of such a reconciling reason back to Hegel's analysis of the criminal in the "Spirit of Christianity and Its Fate." Hegel argued that a criminal's injuring of a victim causes not only the criminal's self-estrangement, but also the means by which both criminal and victim *recognize* the true basis of their existence. But this recognition cannot be derived by categories of the understanding, since they explain the interaction of autonomous wills only by violence. He thus explained the mutual recognition of criminal and victim, not as the rupture of a subject/object continuum, as Fichte did, but as a disturbance of an intersubjective equilibrium. Habermas acknowledges that at this juncture the early Hegel was on the verge of developing a communication-theoretic retrieval and a reflective concept of reason. But Hegel failed to complete the task, because he was burdened by his residual ties to the exemplary past of the Greeks. Only his later study of political economy convinced him that the ancient ideal of the state could not be restored in a modern world.

In his early lectures on the philosophy of spirit, Hegel modified the dialectical nature of Schelling's formative processes of spirit.[70] Habermas describes how for Hegel the self-formation of spirit emerges in three media:

(1) interaction,
(2) language (symbolization), and
(3) work.

Each of the three moments is a reflexive form of mediation. (1) grounds the ethical relationship between the individual and the community. In his earlier theological writings Hegel had interpreted the ethical relationship on the basis of a mutual love through which each member of the relationship knows itself in an other. Love was the basis of the reconciliation of conflict engendered by the dialectical struggle for recognition. The reconciliation was offered even to the criminal who destroys the ethical totality, as we have seen.[71] (2)

---

[70] These lectures took place in Jena between 1803 and 1806. For a good description of them, see Richard Bernstein, "The Relationship of Habermas's Views to Hegel," in *Hegel's Social and Political Thought* (Atlantic Heights, N.J.: Humanities Press, 1980), pp. 235–239.

[71] Habermas, "Arbeit und Interaktion," *Technik und Wissenschaft als Ideologie* (Frankfurt am Main: Suhrkamp, 1968), p. 16. By the time of the Jena writings, however, Hegel had moved from the problem of criminals to the problem of subjects

is a double form of mediation. Symbol production is consciousness's power both to *subjectivize the other* by representing the other in a symbol and to *objectivize itself* by distancing itself from itself through its production of the symbol.[72] In this way spirit becomes a medium between inner and outer. In (3), labor mediates between the reign of immediate desire and the satisfaction of drives. The laboring subject reflexively suspends the very needs its labor aims to satisfy. Thus, spirit overcomes the immediacy of contingent needs through the mediation of labor. By this threefold description of spirit, Habermas credits Hegel with a crucial insight into the link between developmental processes and levels of reflection.[73] But Habermas argues that a proper science of reflection, which Hegel never fully developed, must formulate a dialectical interrelationship *among* all three levels.

Habermas argues that in the *Phenomenology of Spirit* Hegel explicated the multiple forms of the genesis of the self-reference of spirit. Spirit works its way up out of its substantiality to self-consciousness, "which bears within itself the unity as well as the difference of the finite and the infinite" (PT 129). An absolute form of spirit no longer *precedes* the world process, as it had for Schelling and Fichte; it exists only in the consuming activity of reflection *itself*. Absolute spirit is the mediating process of a self-reference that produces itself unconditionally. The unity of the one and the diversity of the all no longer

---

who attach their entire being to the individuality of a possession acquired from an other. This instantiates the dialectical struggle for life and death we see in the *Phenomenology*.

[72] Ibid., p. 24.

[73] Habermas claims that the level of idealism steadily increased in Hegel's writings. The object facing the speaking and laboring subject became increasingly an opponent (*Gegenspieler*) and not properly an object (*Gegenstand*). See ibid., p. 38. Oliva Blanchette argues, in fact, that Hegel's term *Gegenspiel* can be translated as "plaything," which further captures the idealism of the term. See Blanchette, "Language, the Primordial Labor of History," *Cultural Hermeneutics*, 1 (1974), 367. But Blanchette rejects Habermas's explanation of why Hegel later modified his views. Habermas can see Hegel's absolute only according to a pattern of solitary self-reflection based upon the distinction of spirit and nature, not as the dialogue between "subjects properly speaking" which is "recognition in the true sense" (p. 367). Thus, Habermas himself takes the early Hegel's development of intersubjectivity for granted. But for Blanchette it was only after 1802 that Hegel began to see the necessary link between *inter*subjectivity and *self*-consciousness. He thus abandoned the threefold scheme he used earlier because it presupposed a fully constituted self-consciousness capable of reflecting on itself apart from another and prior to any act of mutual recognition.

stand over and against each other as *relata*; the relation itself, set in motion historically, establishes the unity of its *relata*.

On Habermas's reading, Hegel's description of the self-mediation of spirit is a grammar for understanding the progress of history. Habermas claims that each particular is granted the form of a concrete universal by a specific kind of synthesis that "congeals" the shapes of spirit. Sense certainty, our natural and contingent consciousness of everyday life, is the first shape. Habermas describes how Hegel's sense certainty undergoes a reversal, since "the recollecting power of reflection itself originates in this stratum of experience, whose dogmatic character it unmasks. In reflection consciousness cannot make anything transparent except the context of its own genesis" (KHI 8). Habermas argues that this first reversal starts a process of immanent critique that eventually exposes all the unacknowledged presuppositions of Kant's epistemology. In its early stages, spirit works its way up from sensing to perceiving, then to knowledge of things, to knowledge of the suprasensible world, and finally to self-consciousness. Habermas notes that spirit thus mediates between the needs of the human species and the opposition of its environment by developing formative processes brought about, not by causal forces, but by a determinate negation (KHI 18).

Habermas argues that by appealing to a determinant negation Hegel cured the Kantian view of its "false consciousness" and brought it to "consciousness of itself as reflection" (KHI 10). Hegel thus overcame three of Kant's dualisms: the dualism of sensible and moral, the dualism of constitutive and regulative uses of ideas of reason, and the dualism of form and content (see KHI, chap. 1; PT 130). Moreover, he replaced the violent unification of the understanding with an "unforced identity" (PDM 33).[74] The critique of knowledge that Hegel inaugurated dissolved the normative conceptions of both science and the ego by appealing to a phenomenological experience that

> moves in the medium of a consciousness that reflexively distinguishes between itself, for which an object is given, and the being-in-itself of the object. The transition from the naïve intuition of the object-in-

---

[74] See Hegel's "Differenz des Fichteschen und Schellingschen Systems der Philosophie," in *Jenaer kritische Schriften* I (Hamburg: Felix Meiner, 1979) (hereafter cited as *Differenzschrift*), p. 36.

itself to the reflexive knowledge that this being-in-itself exists for it enables consciousness to have a specific experience of itself via its object [KMI 16].

Since the detached phenomenal observer, the "we," is also drawn into the praxis of reflection, Hegel also nullified the distinction between theoretical and practical reason.

Habermas maintains that although the Hegel of the Jena period was on the verge of discovering a truly discursive role for reflection, his later formulations reverted "to the understanding in fixing the activity of reason in opposition" (PDM 24). Habermas pins this failure on Hegel's refusal to give up the privileging of the "one" of the universal, represented by the absolute, over the "many" of individuality and particularity. On Habermas's reading, the universal of reason takes on two distinct forms in Hegel's view of the modern state: one is as an ethical absolute that includes society within itself as one of its moments, and the other is as a "positive universal" that can check a society's tendencies to self-destruction (PDM 39). Habermas notes that in *The Philosophy of Right* Hegel designated the monarch as the self-knowing subject that could serve as the point of reconciliation between these two universals. The monarch knows himself both as universal, as standing over against the world as the totality of possible objects, and also as individual, as appearing in the historical world as a particular entity. But Habermas claims that such a scheme is in fact monological, since the absolute power of the monarch functions as a universal that still dominates over the individual, limiting his freedom. Thus, Hegel's subsequent formulation of the development of the modern state failed to integrate the individual and the universal in the way that his earlier phenomenological analysis of spirit had promised.

Habermas thus charges Hegel with a failure to develop a higher-level intersubjectivity of uncoerced will formation among members of a community existing under cooperative constraints. Such a universal can be determined only by an uncoerced consensus that would allow individuals a court of appeal. It demands, not a monarchical subjectivization of spirit, but a democratic integration of each individual spirit within the universal. Habermas claims that this conception of uncoerced individuation emerged only later with Mead's "internalization of the agencies that monitor behavior" (PT 152).

Habermas thus finds two substantive inconsistencies in Hegel's analysis. First, since in the *Phenomenology* the last moment of absolute knowing is implicit throughout all the moments of self-formation, the movement of spirit simply *presupposes* what its development is supposed to *justify* (KHI 10). Second, since the *Phenomenology* is supposed to produce a standpoint of absolute knowledge that coincides with authentic scientific knowledge, its explication of the *construction* of knowledge cannot claim the status of scientific knowledge. Thus, Kant's problem of "knowing before knowledge" remains unsolved (KHI 21–22). Moreover, Hegel's later appeal to a logic of pure essences fails to be a proper science, since it reduces phenomenological investigation simply to the level of a metaphysical philosophy of mind and nature. For the later Hegel the *Phenomenology* became simply a ladder we must throw away after climbing it to the standpoint of the *Logic*.[75] Habermas concludes that the advance heralded by Hegel's early analyses of interaction, language, labor, and recognition was undermined by his later explication of absolute knowledge. Hegel considered the absolute as the final stage of all forms of reflection, and thus the *goal* of the progression of forms of consciousness.

One can, *pace* Habermas, conceptualize Hegel's absolute in an alternative way. The alternative interpretation I will endorse—derived from the previous philosophies of reflection to which Hegel is responding—holds that Hegel's absolute reflection is not one *type* of reflection that sublates lesser types, but a *quality*, or formal description, of any actual self-reflection that *recognizes itself as so limited*. In this version, absolute reflection is merely the act of a reason that "decenters" the particular things and events from which it emerges and into which it returns. This interpretation, which I shall explicate below, yields several advantages over Habermas's. First, it supports an evaluation of the overall emancipatory power of Hegel's project that is more optimistic than Habermas's. Second, it provides a more prominent role for the reflection involved in Hegel's description of intersubjective recognition, thus giving more cogency to Habermas's own attempts to build on Hegel's early theory of recognition. Third,

---

[75] Marx, for his part, rejects the idea of nature as that which the mind remembers reflexively while returning to itself from it; he rejects spirit as the absolute ground of nature. See KHI 25ff. I shall discuss this further in the next chapter.

it makes Hegel's presentation of stages of reflection in the *Phenomenology* consistent with his later analysis of determining reflection in the *Logic*. Fourth, it better elucidates the crucial role that individual will formation plays in the ethical life of Hegel's community. This is particularly evident in the processes of reflection Hegel describes in the use of practical reasoning in the *Phenomenology*.

To support the plausibility of this variant reading, Hegel's explication of two key reflective processes, recognition in the *Phenomenology* and determining reflection in the *Logic*, is crucial.

Hegel's Development of Recognition into a Form of Intersubjective Reflection

Hegel had begun his analysis of recognition in his early critiques of the philosophy of reflection.[76] In the *Differenzschrift* Hegel claimed that reason posits a form of recognition that can express the *identity in difference* between the identity and the difference determined by the understanding.[77] By resolving this antinomy, reason brings the "formal essence of reflection" under itself.

Hegel maintained that the understanding's categories of identity and difference cannot fully account for the limits a self experiences vis-à-vis an other. Hegel argued that Fichte's use of the productive imagination to mediate between the I's ideal positings and its opposition relative to the not-I still resulted in a stubborn opposition.[78] Though his concept of striving raised the power of reflection above its immediate object in nature, Fichte's practical demand that the self produce itself as a subject–object had remained just that: a mere demand. The highest synthesis was achieved if the I canceled the not-I. Thus, both the theoretical and the practical capacities of

---

[76] See the analysis of the criminal in *System of Ethical Life (1802/1803) and First Philosophy of Spirit*, trans. H. S. Harris and T. M. Knox (Albany: State University of New York Press, 1977).

[77] See Surber, "Introduction," p. 48.

[78] *Differenzschrift*, p. 47. Robert Pippin states that, according to Hegel, Fichte was the first to see that Kant's idealist revolution meant that there can be no anchor for thought's self-legislation in a beyond, an immediacy, or a pure form. But Fichte drew the wrong conclusion by asserting that a "transcendental positing" is responsible for the I's relation to the not-I. For Hegel there is no such original activity. See Pippin's "Hegel, Modernity, and Habermas," in *The Monist*, 74, No. 3 (July 1991), 341.

Fichte's self remained under the "check" of the not-I. But Hegel showed that reason posits a self-identity that sublates empirical consciousness with respect not only to what it *is not*, but also to what it *is*. The ego confronts the other not only as another intelligence, but also as another subject with empirical needs and demands of its own.[79] Both ego and other must be assured that their own needs are *recognized*.

Hegel stipulated that this recognitional identity occurs when reflection realizes it must presuppose *itself* as a self-reflective agency engaged in everyday life interactions. This results in a sixth form of reflection:

> (R6) *speculative* (or *absolute*) *reflection*, by which reason unifies the distinctions of identity and difference—originally meant to define the limits between self and other (or the alien self)—into a self-formative historical process. All reflection becomes decentering self-reflection.[80]

Werner Marx claims that through this conscious recognition of mediation as such "the individual consciousness breaks out of its self-fixation and abandons its demand for certainty to the power of this mediation between it and the immutable."[81] Speculative reflection

---

[79] See *Differenzschrift*, pp. 65–73. Hegel describes how the relationship between nature and reason emerges in Fichte's two "systems of communities of men" in the *Sittenlehre*. The first is a "community of rational beings" built upon reflection. Individual freedom must be "given up" so that the freedom of all rational beings in the community is secured. Freedom here is rather Hobbesian: it is the characteristic of rationality that sublates all the limitations of the individuals relative to the community. Life is given over to submission and reflection and, thus, is under the control of the understanding. This "state of distress" is determined to be the natural law and is absolutely necessary. Philosophical reflection is unable to think an organic relation between the very opposites it sets forth, so it has a compulsion of making endless "policing" determinations (p. 68). The second community is the "system of moral community of men." Anticipating Hegel's own development in the *Phenomenology*, Fichte holds that in the "reign of morals" the only duties that are lawful are those so recognized by the reason of individuals. Duties collide, but men have the power to choose arbitrarily among them (p. 73). Hegel sees a contradiction: if the moral law demands only self-independence as its determination through the *Begriff*, then nature can come into its own only through a limitation of human freedom.

[80] Gasché, *Tain of the Mirror*, p. 51. Gasché also argues that the Platonic rejection of the "self-relationality of reflexivity" anticipates Hegel's speculative reflection (p. 64).

[81] *Das Selbstbewußtsein in Hegels Phänomenologie des Geistes*, p. 131.

thus acknowledges the apriori wholeness of what the philosophy of reflection up to this point had divided. Hegel thus transforms Schelling's principle of self-othering into an absolute process of the self-relating of reason itself.

Armed with this speculative reflection, the pre-*Phenomenology* Hegel began to transform the instrumentality of a Hobbesian egoistic struggle for self-assertion into an intersubjective struggle for social recognition that takes place in three concrete realms: in the family, in the struggle for abstract rights, and in the struggle for ethical solidarity.[82] In the *Phenomenology*, each formative process, though viewed in the context of an overall developmental telos, makes its own unconditioned "contribution" to spirit that is retained in the medium of *life*. Hegel insisted that reflection returns us from the diversity of life to the genus of life as a whole, a reflexive unity whose moments are sublated in itself as a being-for-another.[83] The specific differences of the genus of life are understood to be the actual differences of many self-consciousnesses.[84] Thus, in later reflections consciousness must determine "the experience of what spirit is—this absolute substance which is the unity of the different independent self-consciousnesses which, in their opposition, enjoy perfect freedom and independence: 'I' that is 'We,' and 'We' that is 'I.' "[85] Recognition reveals the struggle these spiritual unities have with their own difference.[86] Though self-consciousness is able to be represented as "in and for itself," it strives for a self-reflective universality that concretizes the fact that it always is limited by its need for recognition by the "negation" of another self-consciousness.

The reflective mechanisms of recognition begin with the limitation that self-consciousness experiences when confronting the other.

---

[82] See Axel Honneth, "Moralische Entwicklung und sozialer Kampf," *Zwischenbetrachtungen im Prozeß der Aufklärung*, ed. Alex Honneth et al. (Frankfurt am Main: Klostermann, 1989), pp. 571–573. But Honneth, like Habermas, argues that Hegel later omitted these practical dimensions of the struggle for recognition in the *Phenomenology*, focusing only on the formation of self-consciousness. He thus abandoned familial recognition, shortened the analysis of recognition through abstract right, and developed the opposition of labor only in relations between the master and the bondsman.

[83] See Marx, *Das Selbstbewußtsein in Hegels Phänomenologie des Geistes*, p. 143.

[84] Habermas points out that Hegel will later describe religion, art, and science as "self-reflexive histories of mankind." See KHI 19.

[85] *Phenomenology*, p. 110/*Phänomenologie*, p. 145.

[86] Marx, *Das Selbstbewußtsein in Hegels Phänomenologie des Geistes*, p. 63.

Though it sees its identical self in the other, *it still must sublate its own other-being*. But it discovers that the instrumental action (*Tun*) by which this is accomplished is *also* the action of the other, because there is nothing in the other that is not in consciousness. Therefore the struggle for recognition generates an intersubjective reciprocity.[87] Each becomes for the other the means by which self-mediation occurs.[88] By this move Hegel understood that consciousness moves beyond Kant's moment of abstract universality among all self-consciousnesses.

But self-consciousness soon realizes that there is still a difference in its "duplication" of itself. This inequality is exhibited by a middle term split up into extremes both as recognized (*Anerkanntes*) and as recognizing (*Anerkennendes*).[89] To negate this difference, both the self and its alien self must achieve the pure abstraction of being negatively for themselves, not through thinking, but through the concrete and relationally understood act of *service*. In servitude self-consciousness must show that it is not attached by fear to the existence of anything. Thus, the individual can acquire freedom in his servitude by his "ability to abstract from his very existence," even to the point of giving up his life.[90]

This *struggle* for recognition instantiates the interplay between the dependent consciousness (the bondsman) and the independent consciousness (the lord). Although the bondsman's service forms mere things, the lord enjoys them and forms his nature on the basis of them. Then a reversal occurs: although the bondsman fears death, he overcomes his attachment to the natural existence of life by means of work. In fashioning the thing, the bondsman reflexively overcomes alienation and fear but acquires a uniqueness or identity as negative in the order of things.[91] Thus, self-recognition requires

---

[87] This need to fight for recognition Kojève attributes to Hegel's experience of the approach of Napoleon's armies to Jena during the writing of the *Phenomenology*. See Alexandre Kojève, *Introduction to the Reading of Hegel: Lectures on the Phenomenology of Spirit*, trans. J. Nichols, ed. A. Bloom (Ithaca, N.Y.: Cornell University Press, 1969), p. 41.

[88] Quentin Lauer, *A Reading of Hegel's Phenomenology of Spirit* (New York: Fordham University Press, 1976), p. 104.

[89] *Phenomenology*, pp. 112–113/*Phänomenologie*, p. 147.

[90] See Tugendhat, *Self-Consciousness and Self-Determination*, p. 308.

[91] *Phenomenology*, p. 118/*Phänomenologie*, p. 154. Hegel is the first philosopher to have stated explicitly that work contributes significantly to the development of self-consciousness. Kojève claims that the repression of the bondsman's instincts by an

neither the Fichtean not-I nor Schelling's objective nature, but the process of a bondsman's inner nature struggling with outer nature.

The bondsman's emancipation is, however, short-lived. The *Phenomenology* chronicles the fate that befalls the bondsman once his negation of servitude gains him individuality and freedom: he forfeits them. Kojève argues that the bondsman imagines a series of "ideologies"—stoicism, skepticism, unhappy consciousness—by which he seeks in vain to recover the ideal of freedom.[92] Self-consciousness had demonstrated its independence from the other self-consciousnesses only at the cost of negating or destroying some of its *desires*. But the "freed" bondsmen can still achieve a self-reflexive universality if he proceeds, not by a negative extermination of desire and an extreme independence from others, but by a self-determination of right desires and a rational dependence on others.[93]

Reason is the "experience" that begins with the certainty of sense-consciousness and emerges step-by-step to "penetrate its own essence in the certainty that there and only there will it come to terms with reality."[94] In all four manifestations of reason—reason, spirit, religion, and absolute knowing—"we" observe the various forms that this proper "dependence" relation to the other takes. At this level, reflection can attain to *truth*: "not until reason comes on the scene as a *reflection* from this opposite certainty does its affirmation about itself present itself not merely as a certainty and an assertion, but as truth; and not merely alongside other truths but as the sole truth."[95] Reason itself has a reflexive form; it is the self's process of justifying the activities that the understanding proposes.

Each stage of reason represents a more concrete form of mediation between the various sets of differences that the categories of understanding posit. Irritability, for example, is determined by the differ-

---

idea gives rise in the slave to understanding, abstract thought, science, technique, and the arts. See his *Introduction to the Reading of Hegel*, p. 49. Cassirer will also speak of the link between the act of formation and meaning. See his *Philosophie der symbolischen Formen* I, 2nd ed. (Oxford: Bruno Cassirer, 1954).

[92] See his *Introduction to the Reading of Hegel*, p. 53.

[93] See Tugendhat, *Self-Consciousness and Self-Determination*, p. 302.

[94] Lauer, *Reading of Hegel's Phenomenology of Spirit*, p. 127.

[95] *Phenomenology*, p. 141/*Phänomenologie*, p. 181. Categories had been determined with regard to essence but undetermined with regard to existence. Hegel now asserts that a category means the essentiality or simple unity of the existent as a thinking reality, the ego. We now seek a "filling" for what was previously an empty "mine" (*Phenomenology*, p. 145/*Phänomenologie*, p. 185).

ences generated by the inner perspective of the organism confronting its environment. As self-consciousness's awareness of its own pain, it is a form of mediation that expresses a lifelike reflection into self. The "outer" observable perspective of reason involves the use of language. The inner aspect of the organism takes on thè content of being (*Sein*) when its outer environment is externalized in language. The bodily actions of speech and work externalize the subject's inner aspect, exposing it to the other's interpretation.[96] Language at this stage is a naturalistic use of signs that forms a "self-agreement of thought" by which the immediate unity of an individual self-consciousness becomes "universal" for the other.[97]

This externalizing of the inner in an observable and recognizable deed, however, raises the possibility of misunderstanding and misconstrual by others. "The individual is therefore not dumb as regards his external action, because he is thereby at once reflected into himself, and gives expression to this reflectedness into self. This theoretical action, or the individual's speech with himself about the external action, is also perceptible to others, for this speech is itself an expression (*Äußerung*)."[98] In a pragmatic twist, consciousness realizes that *die Sache selbst* is not the content of the utterance, but the being of the observable deed that expresses the utterance. Through the simplicity of the being of the deed, the individual becomes a universal essence for an other and ceases to be merely something meant or intended (*Gemeintes*).[99] Thus, recognition by the other has become essential for the self's own identity. This forges a link between individual self-identity and moral action that spirit will never abandon. The struggle for recognition thus requires not only the individuality of the recognition of personal sovereignty, but also the universality by which the essence of the subject can be recognized behind its deeds by the other.

---

[96] *Phenomenology*, p. 187/*Phänomenologie*, p. 235. We can assume that Hegel is referring to the most primitive kind of language here, the use of gestures or signs, not to higher speech functions such as proposition formation and argumentation. Language contains a seemingly insurmountable difference between—although Hegel does not use these terms—sign and signified. The reflected being in the subject is the sign, which is indifferent with regard to the expressed content.

[97] Werner Marx, *Absolute Reflexion und Sprache* (Frankfurt am Main: Klostermann, 1967), p. 26.

[98] *Phenomenology*, p. 190/*Phänomenologie*, pp. 238–239.

[99] *Phenomenology*, p. 194/*Phänomenologie*, p. 243.

Since its action and existence constitute universally recognizable ethical practices, individual consciousness becomes an existential unity (*seiende Eins*).[100] As Montesquieu had argued, this actualization of self-conscious reason has its fullest reality in the language, culture, and laws which constitute the "ethical life of a nation."[101] Yet, even at this point, self-consciousness has not achieved self-reflective universality. For when the individual realizes that his very being depends upon the community, he loses his initial trust in the totality and places himself in opposition to the community's laws and customs.[102] To ensure his own happiness, the individual needs to secure some form of autonomy *apart* from the community's norms.

This new struggle for autonomy appeals to the demands of practical reason itself. Kant had claimed that the inner voice of practical reason demands a self-sacrifice that challenges the self-serving "way of the world."[103] But spirit realizes that such sacrifice actually undermines the actor's autonomy. Spirit must actualize itself, not by conforming to ends antithetical to it, but by striving toward ends whose categories are its *own* objects. Each individual actor discovers his own specific character—its *Tinktur des Geistes*—which determines the capabilities, talents, and character by which he relates to the other. Through education (*Bildung*) the human spirit emerges from its immersion in nature to realize in itself a form of activity that is in no way derived from without.[104] Although an individual is limited by this nature, he is no longer limited by a Fichtean negative relation

---

[100] Hegel, *The Philosophy of Right*, trans. T. M. Knox (Oxford: Oxford University Press, 1967), §261. In *The Philosophy of Right* Hegel develops the notion of a civil society in which "the particular person is essentially so related to other particular persons that each establishes himself and finds satisfaction by means of the others, and at the same time purely and simply by means of the form of universality" (§182). A system of complete interdependence is formed in which the livelihood, happiness, and legal status of each is interwoven with that of all.

[101] *Phenomenology*, p. 265/*Phänomenologie*, p. 325. In *The Philosophy of Right* Hegel specifically cites Montesquieu's claim that each state possesses a specific character or spirit.

[102] This ethical consciousness goes through two stages: lust and necessity. On the one hand, this leads both to a slavery to natural necessity and to an abandonment of laws and customs. On the other, it also leads to the law of the heart, a utopian reformism that leads only to conflicts and a state of war.

[103] *Critique of Judgement*, §88.

[104] Lauer, *Reading of Hegel's Phenomenology of Spirit*, p. 214.

to an other. Through action (*Handeln*)—as opposed to instrumental action (*Tun*)—the agent makes its "in itself" also "for itself."[105]

The self-fulfilling actor, however, finds himself in a circle. Though he must form an idea of an act before he can act, the very formation of the idea of the act is verified only at the moment the act commences. The actor achieves a way out of this dilemma through the medium of his own *interest*, the "already given answer to the question: whether and what should be done."[106] But the *Phenomenology* explicates neither the genesis nor the nature of this interest. Is this interest inherently intersubjective? Or is it radically individual? Is it able to be made normative in Habermas's sense? This formation of practical action is like Kantian duty, since it avoids reference either to the end, means, or circumstances of the act, or even to the contingent and perishable work it accomplishes. Thus, the agent becomes the sole source of its interest and the work that follows from it. This unity of work and reflection is the true work and "the thing itself" (*die Sache selbst*).

Spirit finds, however, that the demand for universal self-reflection is still not satisfied by determining the *die Sache selbst* as its own particular affair. The particular moral laws that an actor posits must be brought before the tribunal of an even higher reason. But this reason discovers that these laws can be neither justified nor even fully explained. They become mere Kantian types of commandments which have no actuality. The critical reason needed for a proper determination of ethical action is still found only in the ethical whole. But now the mediation of individual ends and social needs comes only through the institutions and laws of a *State*.[107] Spirit finds an internal connection between individual autonomy and the universality of the community. This need not be viewed, as Habermas does, as an imposition of the universal. Rather, the State is a system by which the diverse interests found among its citizens are unified at the level of right. This seems to achieve the very balance of universal-

---

[105] *Phenomenology*, pp. 239–240/*Phänomenologie*, pp. 296–297.

[106] *Phenomenology*, p. 240/*Phänomenologie*, p. 297.

[107] *Phenomenology*, p. 255/*Phänomenologie*, p. 314. In the "Preface" Hegel echoes Schelling's conviction that it is humanity's nature to find agreement (*Übereinkunft*) in an "achieved community of minds" (*Phenomenology*, p. 43/*Phänomenologie*, p. 65). Hegel continues this analysis in *The Philosophy of Right*.

ity, particularity, and individuality that Habermas contends that Humboldt—not Hegel—was the first to posit.[108]

It is at this stage of the development of spirit, situated well before the end of the *Phenomenology*, that the relation between the individual and the universal unfolds. Hegel will further explicate this stage in *The Philosophy of Right*, indicating that the State alone secures the reconciliation of individual and communal interests. As we have seen, Habermas interprets this to mean that the later Hegel abandoned the individual autonomy described in his earliest works and in the later sections of the *Phenomenology*. But it is equally plausible that Hegel excluded examination of individual autonomy in *The Philosophy of Right* on the grounds that a political treatise necessarily functions, not on the level of the *Begriff*, but on the level of representation of the interplay of interests. If I am correct, right is only one, though a necessary, stage in reason's development. An analysis of right need not—and indeed *cannot*—provide an exhaustive account of the way reason commands us to act ethically with regard to others. Moreover, as we will see, Hegel's *Science of Logic* includes an analysis of the *Phenomenology*'s non-representational determinations of self-reflective universality omitted in *The Philosophy of Right*.

The impetus for the development of non-representational forms of mediation between the individual and the community in the *Phenomenology* begins when the facile harmonization of individual ends constituted by the State's decisions fails to produce a persistent and effective role for reason. Though the mediation between the self's autonomy and duty's requirement is represented, it is still neither actual nor concrete. The Romantics turn to conscience, or the "beautiful soul," to mediate between the dutiful individual and the laws of the State.[109] They determined the content of conscience, not by the otherness of specific duties, but by the interest of the consciousness knowing them.[110] But this attempt fails because the

---

[108] See Habermas, "A Reply," in *Communicative Action*, ed. H. Joas and A. Honneth (Cambridge, Mass.: The MIT Press, 1991), p. 220. Habermas argues that the ego is formed "equiprimordially as a subject in general, as a typical member of a social collective, and as a unique individual."

[109] *Phenomenology*, pp. 383ff./*Phänomenologie*, pp. 464ff. Earlier, Hegel had stated that the moral agent places the world and its ground within itself by means of conscience.

[110] *Phenomenology*, p. 385/*Phänomenologie*, p. 467.

actions that an individual conscience condones may not be consistent with reason's demand that they satisfy every conscience.

At this point in the *Phenomenology* spirit "returns" to an earlier
stage in the development of reason: language. Language is necessary
as the mode of expression through which self-consciousness can become universal. It is self-consciousness existing for others: "it is the
self that separates itself from itself, which as pure I = I becomes objective to itself."[111] But the language used for this universal identity
formation fails to achieve universal sameness, since each action it
determines is still reflected into the actor's own being-for-himself.
Habermas agrees that such a Romantic view of language is one that
views language as "an expressive whole that externalizes its essential
powers and assures itself of its creative subjectivity by contemplating
these objectifications."[112] Thus, language merely designates objective spirit. Habermas is correct in asserting that the *Phenomenology*
thus never acknowledges the possibility of a discursive use of language: its ability to enable speakers to reach agreement. He claims, I
think correctly, that this was also left for Humboldt to discover.

After realizing the failure of language to determine the mediation
of self-reflective universality, spirit finds that art and religion also fail
in this task. The historical forms of art fall prey to the objectivizing
problems Hegel had already pointed out in his critique of Schelling's
aesthetic intuition. And since the Christian Incarnation, the high
point of religious thinking, employs a representation that exists only
in the element of thought, it is still burdened with a diremption.
Spirit must become *existent* spirit, and can do so only through a
consciousness of duty that distinguishes itself *as other*. The Christian
resurrection does, however, make an advance by signaling a transition of a represented unity into actual self-consciousness. Each representation now receives a meaning opposite to what it previously
had: every duty fulfills itself by means of the other. The divine essence, embracing both human nature and death, is reflected into
itself and is thus spirit.[113] But even this does not achieve an absolute
being-for-self in the present moment, since the community's reconciliation remains projected toward a "beyond" in the future and the

---

[111] *Phenomenology*, p. 395/*Phänomenologie*, pp. 478–479.

[112] "A Reply," p. 216.

[113] *Phenomenology*, p. 472/*Phänomenologie*, p. 567.

God-man's reconciliation remains projected in the past. Thus, Hegel was forced to abandon his earlier view that representation in religious language and duty in religious practice are the final stages in the formation of self-consciousness.

Although by means of religion spirit becomes *self*-representational in the form of being in and for itself, it must still pass over into the final stage of the *Begriff* that "embraces within itself its own opposite."[114] Reaching the level of the *Begriff*, speculative reflection overcomes all the temporally and spatially representational aporias of Christianity's legacy of duties to others and to self. The absolute now is revealed, not as a static divine being in a temporal "beyond" or "before," but as *the process of self-reflective action*. But the process of absolute knowing must pass beyond even an inner consciousness that is a "moral self-consciousness."[115] Content passes from the representation of the God-man in religion to the concept of the action of a self that knows its action as all essence and existence. We now arrive at a science (*Wissenschaft*) of experience in which the ego becomes for itself both mediated and universal. As *differentiating*, the ego has a content and is consciousness; as *differentiated*, the ego is reflected into itself, and the content is made fully actual. We are left with an Aristotelian notion of the absolute as self-thinking thought, represented by religious images of reconciliation and punctuated by moral demands.[116] Reflection grasps subject as spirit: "The self-knowing spirit knows not only itself but also the negative of itself, or its limit: to know one's limit is to know how to sacrifice oneself. This sacrifice is the externalization in which spirit displays the process of its becoming spirit in the form of *free contingent happening*."[117] Thus, speculative reflection determines, not a surrender to an absolute subject that destroys differences, but limits unique for each free subject.

The "Preface" to the *Phenomenology*, however, begins to take this reflective grasp of limits in a direction that Habermas is justified in

---

[114] *Phenomenology*, p. 416/*Phänomenologie*, p. 503.

[115] *Phenomenology*, p. 481/*Phänomenologie*, p. 578.

[116] For Tugendhat, Hegel rests secure in his conviction that the subject behaves theoretically when it allows itself to be determined by the object, and practically when it determines the object: we do not know how the subject relates to itself *volitionally*.

[117] *Phenomenology*, p. 492/*Phänomenologie*, p. 590.

criticizing. Hegel argues that the true is the reflection of other-being into itself such that reflection's oppositions are overcome by a self-restoring sameness.[118] He rejects argumentation as negative and as a vain kind of thinking and takes a negative and destructive attitude toward the content it apprehends.[119] Science sees the *Begriff* turn back to its own innerness, and thus its activity is totally absorbed in the content: "This is the cunning which, while seeming to abstain from activity, looks on and watches how determinateness, in its concrete life, just where it supposes to strive for its self-contained and special interest, actually does the reverse: it dissolves itself and makes itself constitutive of the whole."[120]

One is reminded here of the way Adam Smith's "invisible hand" combines all individual acts of self-interest into the actual good of the whole. All the reflected differences—subject/object, self/other, subject/predicate, the act as expressed/the return of the act into self—decenter themselves by returning to the totality by which they are mediated. However, despite this cunning of reason, absolute reflection is not a fixed end point, but the quality of any synthetic reflection that achieves both a decentering and a return, via recognition, to its own limiting terms within an "immanent rhythm of the *Begriff*."[121]

Next I need to examine whether this alternative interpretation of reflection as a quality of self-reflection is consistent with Hegel's description of reflection in the *Science of Logic*.

Determining Reflection in the Doctrine of Essence in the Logic

In addition to the levels of recognition and moral thinking he developed in the *Phenomenology*, Hegel also explicated another discursive form of mediation in the *Science of Logic*: determining reflection.[122] This form of reflection is described as that which mediates between

---

[118] *Phenomenology*, p. 10/*Phänomenologie*, p. 23. Kojève calls reflection the labor of the negative that breaks the positivity of the immediate.

[119] *Phenomenology*, p. 36/*Phänomenologie*, p. 56.

[120] *Phenomenology*, p. 33/*Phänomenologie*, p. 53. The "cunning of reason" reappears in *The Philosophy of Right* when, in the very act of willing their own individual ends, persons "will the universal in the light of the particular" (§260).

[121] *Phenomenology*, p. 36/*Phänomenologie*, p. 56.

[122] I will refer to the *Science of Logic*, also known as the *Greater Logic*, by the term *Logic*.

opposites generated in "self-othering" reflective acts by guaranteeing the persistence of their dirempted terms.

Habermas claims that though the *Logic* should be able to form mediations among a large set of differences—the one and the many, the infinite and the finite, the universal and the temporal, and the necessary and the contingent—it ultimately fails to do so. The idealistic domination of the one, universal, and necessary remains in the totalizing and self-referential operations in the concept of mediation itself (PT 32). The absolute continues to be a telos that undercuts all particularly. But Habermas neglects to consider how the *Logic* explicates the ways in which absolute reflection, understood qualitatively in our alternative reading, requires the *persistence of the individuality that it reconciles with the universal.*[123] Reflection as analyzed in the *Logic* subsumes the difference that it realizes *it must be* in order to relate two terms. How does this function?

Hegel began the *Logic* by claiming that reflection is a power that can provide universal explanations through a dialectic between self-othering and a return into self.[124] He distinguished three successive levels of this form of reflection:

(1) the dissolving force of understanding (first reflection);
(2) the totalizing power of the speculative process (reflective determination); and
(3) one moment within that process (reflection as ground).[125]

In the *Differenzschrift* Hegel had distinguished between isolated and philosophical reflection. Isolated reflection was the "simple" reflection characteristic of the positings of the understanding (1). In Kant's philosophy isolated reflection had functioned as the power that delimited and posited opposites. In Schelling's philosophy, philosophical reflection had been related to the totality of the absolute (2). This level was more complex. As the primary determination of

---

[123] As Robert Pippin argues, while the *Phenomenology* considers the self-determination of the absolute, the *Logic* assumes that the self-determinaton itself becomes self-determined in being related to what appears. See his *Hegel's Idealism: The Satisfactions of Self-Consciousness* (Cambridge: Cambridge University Press, 1989), p. 212.

[124] See William Harris, *Hegel's Logic* (New York: Garland, 1984), p. 315.

[125] See Hegel, *Wissenschaft der Logik*, 2 vols. (Frankfurt am Main: Suhrkamp, 1985), 2.17 / *Science of Logic*, trans. A. V. Miller (Atlantic Highlands, N.J.: Humanities Press, 1969), p. 393. I will cite references from both texts.

reflection, essence was a threefold self-movement from immediacy, through the negativity of illusory being (*Schein*), to the realization that *this determinateness of illusory being is sublated in essence's own self*.[126] These determinations were the "essentialities" of reflection and the laws of all reflective thought.[127] Finally, the illusory being or "immediate appearance" which was described in the *Phenomenology* becomes a moment in the subject's self-determination (3).[128] The self-relation of a being's negative relation to the other now attains to a *form*. Hegel explicated this self-determination of reflection by using Kant against himself: Kant's unbridgeable gap between appearance and essence is overcome by the application of his reflective determinations of identity, difference, and contradiction *to appearance itself*.[129] Hegel will show how these reflective determinations reveal how what is negated, the term that limits the initial term, is preserved in a positive form. Reflection moves "from nothing to nothing" in three forms: first as positing, then as external, and finally as determining.[130] Each form has a specific function: positing reflection reveals the impossibility of a static "self-determining" reflection; external reflection reveals that reflection requires some kind of mediation; and determining reflection reveals the moment of synthesis between the two.[131]

In the *Logic*, positing reflection is the "absolute recoil" of a reflection that returns completely to itself. Fichte had described this type of reflection as the act of positing that reproduces the bad infinite of being and yet at the same time determines being as such. Starting from immediate being, it posits reflection *ex nihilo*. Like critical

---

[126] *Science of Logic*, p. 398/*Logik*, 2.22–23.

[127] Pippin, *Hegel's Idealism*, p. 210.

[128] Ibid., p. 211. Robert Holub draws out the socio-political results of this metaphysical claim. For Hegel, appearance and false consciousness are not always illusory, because they are both of essence. Thus, Adorno could claim that even false consciousness is part of social reality. See Holub's *Critic in the Public Sphere*, p. 25.

[129] As we have already seen, Kant has more reflective determinations than these, but Hegel chooses these three for the analysis.

[130] Hegel uses the gerundive forms *setzende* and *bestimmende* reflection, presumably to emphasize that both are activities.

[131] Pippin, *Hegel's Idealism*, p. 212. Werner Flach claims that each of these forms is a form of *thinking*: positing reflection is thinking as being, external reflection is thinking of being, and determinant reflection is thinking of meaning. See his *Negation und Andersheit: Ein Beitrag zur Problematik der Letztimplikation* (Würzburg: Ernst Reinhardt, 1959), p. 64.

practical reflection, positing reflection must presuppose an other that stands in a reflection of sameness to the original self. External reflection, on the other hand, immediately presupposes itself *as sublated*: as the negative of itself.[132] Kant had described this type of reflection as the movement of thinking that determines being as a product of cognitive activities in abstraction from immediate determinations of being. External reflection is thus the end point (*Schluß*) in which the immediate and reflection-into-self co-exist. Hegel characterized Kant's formulation of reflective judgment in the *Third Critique* as a form of external reflection: "the movement of the faculty of judgment that goes beyond a given immediate conception and seeks universal determinations for it or compares such determinations with it."[133] Kant's formulation assumes that the particular requires the positing of a universal; hence, external reflection determines both the universal and the particular. But Hegel argued that external reflection relates itself to the immediate as if to a given (PDM 48). He objected to the specification of the universal only in terms of subjective or regulative interests that are external to, and cannot be immediately derived from, *the particular itself*. Previous philosophers had external reflection in mind when they assigned to reflection "everything bad."[134]

While positing reflection sets forth the synthetic activity of understanding, and external reflection sets forth its analytic activity, determining reflection overcomes the one-sidedness of both forms by combining them in a *genetic moment of exhibition*. Determining reflection instantiates the dialectical determination of the realm of being as a totality. It starts from immediacy, from nothing, and posits a particular other "in such a manner that the quality of reflection is completely preserved."[135] The complete determination of a particular is possible only by referring to an immediate that is self-negat-

---

[132] Earlier in the *Logic* the infinite served the same function of external determination in the sphere of being.

[133] See *Critique of Judgement*, §I 28; *Science of Logic*, p. 404/*Logik*, 2.30.

[134] *Science of Logic*, p.405/*Logik*, 2.31.

[135] See *Science of Logic*, p. 406/*Logik*, 2.33–36. In the *Phenomenology* the individual achieved this reflectedness into self by means of "theoretical action": the language of the individual with itself about its action. The transition from what is now called external to what will be determinant reflection demands a pragmatic relation of the self to itself.

ing. Determining activity, therefore, is the activity of a return-into-self that both creates distinctions and particularizes.

Determining reflection brings the mediated moments of positing and external reflection back into a dynamic self-related immediacy: "reflection as immediacy."[136] This determines "the equality of reflection with itself" that still *enables the negative moment of its other-being to persist*.[137] It becomes the negative of the other of posited being.[138] Thus, only determining reflection acquires, in a qualitative moment, the completed copula of identity removed from the difference that is expressed in the terms of a proposition.[139] It achieves a reflectively grasped totality of the whole that contains diversity. By not allowing itself to be dominated by representation of external reflection, the determining reflection of speculative thinking holds the negation fast. It grasps and asserts contradiction in finite things and allows their *Begriffe* to appear. Speculative philosophy draws all positings into the reflective movement of consciousness coming to itself. This provides a form of mediation that allows both theoretical and practical differences to be sublated and yet persist. The interrelation of universality, individuality, and particularity instantiates a continuous *process*.

Is Hegel's systematization of reflection successful? Gadamer claims that Hegel's systemic formulation of reflection is impervious to division into further forms. Gasché argues that post-Hegelian theories of reflection generally accept Hegel's account of the relation between individual cognition and intersubjective action. But Hegel's logic of reflection, even under our variant reading, leaves unresolved two of Habermas's recalcitrant worries. First, Habermas is correct in pointing out that Hegel never confronted the possibility that language use contains a uniquely discursive kind of reflection. Though Hegel did argue that language gives the immediate existences of sen-

---

[136] Dieter Henrich, "Hegels Logik der Reflexion: Neue Fassung," in *Hegel-Studien* 18 (Bonn: Bouvier, 1978), p. 303.

[137] See ibid., p. 301.

[138] Ibid., p. 303. Henrich claims that since all self-relations are united to some form of otherness, Hegel ends up in an idealism, like Fichte's, which conceptualizes situated differences in the thinking of self-relation (p. 308).

[139] *Science of Logic*, p. 410/*Logik*, 2.37–39. Hegel concludes that reason cannot interweave the warp of identity and the woof of difference "from without." Gasché analyzes the ways in which these metaphors of weaving identity and difference began with Plato (*Statesman* 306a), and continue into Derrida.

sation, appearance, and representation a "higher" second existence, such a higher existence remains in a subject-centered identity.[140] Language use never attains to the second immediacy of a reflective act whose terms are distinct: speaker and hearer. Second, Hegel's absolute knowledge still underdetermines the contextualizing factors of time and space that must be accounted for in an analysis of reflection. He stipulates that spirit cannot become absolute knowledge unless the real lived time of human existence is decentered, reduced merely to the "thought of time."[141] Without the capacity of determining itself relative to time, reflection remains trapped in the idealist's absolute present.

Hegel's theory of reflection does effectively decenter the self relative to both itself and the concrete needs of the other, providing the recognitional grounds for a rational theory of intersubjectivity. Although our variant reading accounts for more determinant limitation of the self vis-à-vis the absolute than Habermas recognizes, he is right to maintain that the key linguistic turn needed for a complete discursive theory of reflection emerges only later, as we will see in the next chapter, in the works of Humboldt, Frege, and Mead.

HUSSERL: REFLECTION AND MONADOLOGICAL INTERSUBJECTIVITY

The story of the "philosophy of reflection" after Hegel becomes, although less interesting, more complex.[142] Post-Hegelian thinkers generally agree that although Hegel turned to Greek concepts of being and substance in order to overcome the reflexive aporias of Kant, Fichte, and Schelling, he ended up *subjectivizing* these concepts. Some deny that Hegel's reflection generates real oppositions (Husserl, Heidegger), while others grant that the oppositions are real

---

[140] See Hegel's *Enzyklopädie der philosophschen Wissenschaften*, ed. F. Nicolin and O. Pöggler (Hamburg: Felix Meiner, 1959), p. 459. See also *Phenomenology of Spirit*, pp. 486–487/*Phänomenologie*, pp. 583–584.

[141] See H. S. Harris, *Hegel's Development: Night Thoughts* (Oxford: Clarendon Press, 1985), p. 521.

[142] Gasché argues that the critique of reflection after Hegel takes three forms: (1) the overall rejection of self-relation due to its aporias (Russell, Whitehead, Henrich), (2) the ability of reflection to save itself from its own aporias (Tugendhat, Flach), and (3) a modification of the two positions (Husserl, Heidegger).

but cannot be reconciled in a totality (Dilthey, Nietzsche).[143] But all these critics shift the locus of reflection from Hegel's spirit to *pre-conscious structures*, such as "life" (Dilthey, Nietzsche), actual forms of material production (Marx), "Being" (Heidegger), or "transcendental subjectivity" (Husserl).[144] Husserl and Heidegger both resorted to pre-reflexive structures that circumvent the infinite regress of the idea of self-relation. Husserl ignored Hegel's concern for ethical life, developing instead a theoretical view of reflection closer to Kant's.

Husserl's phenomenology has had a profound influence on Habermas's thought. His early phenomenological work profoundly influenced Habermas's views on critical social science. Moreover, the second generation of phenomenology, inaugurated by Heidegger's critique of Husserl, influenced Habermas's views on hermeneutics and history.[145] Habermas also borrows a great deal from Husserl's method of scientific verification and from his phenomenological explication of the relation between the self and the other in a shared lifeworld.[146]

Habermas laid out his critical analysis of Husserl in his inaugural lecture of 1965. Here he accuses Husserl of adhering to a theoretical objectivism that links a Platonic kind of "pure theory" with the actual conduct of life. Husserl operated under the ontological assumption that the world is independent of the knower. His phenomenological point of departure was the "mediating ego" whose subjectivity is always the last possible horizon of legitimation for all relations over against an alien other.[147] Habermas concludes that Husserl failed to link linguistic use and sociation.

In *The Philosophical Discourse of Modernity*, Habermas intensifies

---

[143] My exclusion of Marx from these post-Hegelian philosophers requires some explanation. Marx embedded all relations, and thus all acts of reflection, within "material activity." See "The German Ideology," in *Karl Marx, Frederick Engels: Collected Works* V (New York: International Publishers, 1976), pp. 36–38. Thus, he basically regresses into a type of reflection in which spirit and nature remain opposed in a way resistant to the unity of a universal science of experience.

[144] Nietzsche, in *On the Genealogy of Morals*, observed that a "gap" had emerged between knowledge and self-cognition that rendered self-reflection decadent and mundane. See Gasché, *Tain of the Mirror*, pp. 81ff.

[145] See Rasmussen, *Reading Habermas*, p. 102; Roberts, *Logic of Reflection*, p. 216.

[146] I will take up Habermas's development of the lifeworld concept in Chapter 3.

[147] See Habermas, *Vorstudien und Ergänzungen zur Theorie des kommunikativen Handelns* (Frankfurt am Main: Suhrkamp, 1984), p. 56.

his critique of Husserl's theory of transcendental intersubjectivity: "The monadological start from the transcendental ego forces Husserl to reconstruct intersubjective relationships produced in communication from the perspective of the individual consciousness directed toward intentional objects" (PDM 169).[148] Since he equated the transcendental ego with "the existing consciousness of each individual phenomenologist," Husserl remained firmly grounded in the subject/object paradigm of a philosophy of consciousness (PT 41).

Following Luhmann, Habermas also criticizes Husserl's understanding of the lifeworld. Although conceived as a counter-concept to scientific objectivization, Husserl's lifeworld concept remained mired in apriorism (PDM 358).[149] Originally Husserl formulated the lifeworld as a response to commonsense philosophy's demand for an intuitive and subjective ground for ethics. His lifeworld embodied the "inner perspective" within which the subject both constitutes and is constituted by the world. But Habermas argues that a pretheoretical analysis of the praxis of life must include a theoretical and scientific analysis as well (TK 39). Though meant to mitigate the positivism of the social sciences, Husserl's uncritical pre-theoretical use of the lifeworld actually paved the way for Heidegger's existential ontology. Instead, Habermas argues for a non-transcendentalized communicative-theoretic view of the lifeworld whose idealizations are derived only from the various *language orientations*—ordinary, special, and expert—that are differentiated within it.[150] As we shall see in the next chapter, Habermas derives his life-

---

[148] Habermas points out that Schütz (hereafter, Schutz) also claims that Husserl did not solve the problem of intersubjectivity. See Alfred Schutz, "Das Problem der transcendentalen Intersubjektivität bei Husserl," in *Philosophische Rundschau* (1957), pp. 81ff. But Habermas also suggests that Schutz himself remains bound to Husserl's intuitive method. See TCA 2.138.

[149] See also Habermas's "Edmund Husserl über Lebenswelt, Philosophie, und Wissenschaft (1990)" in TK 34–48.

[150] Rejecting Husserlian despair in the face of science's encroachment upon the lifeworld's foundation of meaning, Habermas suggests that the systematizing contribution of the sciences can "correspond" with the lifeworld's projects. A philosophy that is able to remain conscious of its own dependence upon the lifeworld, and not "imperially" reach through it or over it, can at the same time lend the lifeworld its scientific-critical voice. See TK 48. Habermas is more optimistic than Husserl about the possibility of coordination between system and lifeworld. Bernard Flynn, however, sees a close parallel between Husserl's and Habermas's views of the crisis in the lifeworld. Husserl criticizes the deformation of the lifeworld; Habermas criticizes its colonization. Flynn also claims that Habermas borrows directly from Husserl's

world background, not from a theory of intentionality, but from a theory of communicative action.

Habermas contrasts the later Husserl's *Crisis of the European Sciences* with Horkheimer's "Traditional and Critical Theory," which was published at the same time. Horkheimer held that critical theory could resolve the tension that traditional "bourgeois" thinking, based upon the Cartesian dualism of thought and being, had produced between laborers and owners of means of production.[151] But Husserl, according to Habermas, never completely severed his ties to the traditional conception of critique as a contemplative search for first principles. Habermas claims that this foundationalist tendency, in which philosophy takes on the role of the "supreme judge" of all science, is present in all of Husserl's writings (MCCA 16). For Habermas, only Horkheimer's critical theory provides an emancipative and non-positivistic science of self-reflection.

Habermas thinks that several problems, endemic to any philosophy of consciousness, show up in Husserl's theory of intersubjectivity in the fifth *Cartesian Meditation*. There Husserl tried to explain how a universal perspective can arise from the pluralism of individual world-constituting monadic egos. But Habermas claims that the Husserlian ego encounters the other, not in the other's actual world-projecting spontaneity, but only abstractly as an objectifying counterpower. Husserl merely replaced transcendental synthesis with "the concrete yet structureless productivity of life" (see PT 41–42). Life-world practice remains a mere product of a transcendental subjectivity (see PDM 77–79). Though admitting that Husserl tries to make this production intersubjective, Habermas still claims that he never sufficiently clarified how the production is related to cultural forms of expression of subjects capable of speech and action. Husserl's transcendental reduction was a procedure by which the phenomenologist could clearly demarcate the world of beings given in the natural attitude from the spheres of "pure constituting consciousness which first lend beings their meanings" (PDM 138). Though this did build a bridge to formal semantics, it did not complete the

---

claim that when the rationality of the lifeworld is "occulted," irrational life-philosophies emerge. See Flynn's *Political Philosophy at the Closure of Metaphysics* (London: Humanities Press, 1992), p. 58.

[151] "Traditional and Critical Theory," p. 210.

linguistic turn. Husserl underestimated the role that discursive verification plays in intersubjective meaning.

Habermas's interpretation of Husserl demands some scrutiny. As
in the case of Hegel, the issue is again the extent to which an agent's
self-reflection is capable of decentering itself relative to others. Having criticized Hegel's absolute reflection for *de*centering subjects relative to itself, Habermas now criticizes Husserl for effectively
*re*centering subjects relative to themselves. Though some of Husserl's arguments do point in the direction Habermas alleges, Husserl's primary interest is in many respects similar to Habermas's. To
wit, both Habermas and Husserl value a systematic methodology by
which inquirers verify various truth-analogous claims. By ignoring
this similarity, Habermas undervalues his own indebtedness to Husserl's explication of modes of verification. Thus, I must analyze carefully the reflective processes upon which Husserl built his critical-
phenomenological analysis.

According to Roberts, Husserl's phenomenological method uses a
form of reasoning that "is not inferential, but *reflexive*. It does not
thrust abruptly into the dark secrets of causations, but simply looks
at itself. Reflection is the self-showing of reason."[152] But the self-
showing is inseparable from what is shown. Husserl defines a reflecting act as: "The reflecting act includes its object within itself to such
as extent that it is only by abstraction, as a moment incapable of
standing by itself, that it can be separated from it."[153]

But Husserl's theory of reflection went through a series of transformations. Like Kant, the early Husserl argued that reflection is unable
to posit a subject as either a constitutive principle or as an irreducible moment of consciousness.[154] But the later Husserl asserted that
self-reflection is a necessary condition of the constitution of the spiritual (*geistige*) world.[155] This self-reflection discovers its own intentionality in a kind of decentering scientific inquiry that mediates
between itself and the world.

---

[152] *Logic of Reflection*, p. 164.

[153] *Ideen zu einer reinen Phänomenologie und phänomenologischen Philosophie*, ed.
M. Biemel, 2 vols. (The Hague: Martinus Nijhoff, 1952), 1.86.

[154] See his *Logical Investigations*, trans. J. Findlay (New York: Humanities Press,
1970), pp. 47–51.

[155] Husserl, *Husserliana*, ed. M. Biemel, 23 vols, (The Hague: Martinus Nijhoff,
1954), 4.251–253. Roberts also speaks of this "turn" in Husserl' thought. See *Logic
of Reflection*, p. 216.

In the *Cartesian Mediations* Husserl developed one framework for this constitutional self-reflection in his analysis of the epoché.[156] He alluded to two different forms of the epoché: the first is the reflective act that "breaks" the natural attitude; the second is the act that reflexively determines universal structures of rationality. Both forms function, not as passive mirrorings of an ideal realm, but as active explications of self-evident meaning in the given.[157] While the first is a "retrogression" from the pre-given empirical world to the original lifeworld (empirical reflection), the second is the "regressive inquiry" which moves from the lifeworld to the subjective and originary logical operations from which it arises (logical and transcendental reflection).[158] Through the eidetic intuition of the second epoché, the phenomenologist uncovers a point of departure for a "systematic explication of human existence" within the apriori of the lifeworld.[159] Thus, the second epoché recovers not only a natural objective world as a particular mode of the transcendental life, but also an "objective verification of the objective" that governs praxis.[160] By providing the universal formulation lacking in the first epoché, the second epoché achieves a critical position-taking toward the truth or falsity of objective theoretical sciences.

This second epoché lays out the logic of the "absolute intersubjectivity" that mediates between the ego and all other subjects. Using a concept similar to the *Third Critique*'s maxim of enlarged thought, Husserl argued that such intersubjectivity results in "mankind's understanding itself as rational."[161] Husserl thus forged an inchoate link between intersubjectivity and rationality similar to that in Habermas's own theory of communicative action.[162]

---

[156] Husserl does deal with intersubjectivity in other later works. See especially Manuscript C 17 (1931); Hua XV, 334ff. But I will focus only on the *Cartesian Meditations* here. *Cartesian Meditations*, trans D. Cairns (The Hague: Martinus Nijhoff, 1960), §34.

[157] See Robert Sokolowski, *Husserlian Meditations: How Words Present Things* (Evanston, Ill.: Northwestern University Press, 1974), pp. 62–66, 244–249.

[158] See Husserl, *Experience and Judgment*, trans. J. Churchill and K. Ameriks, ed. L. Kandgrebe (Evanston, Ill.: Northwestern University Press, 1973), p. 50.

[159] *Meditations*, §59.

[160] Husserl, *The Crisis of European Sciences and Transcendental Phenomenology*, trans. D. Carr (Evanston, Ill.: Northwestern University Press, 1970), p. 176.

[161] "Philosophy as Mankind's Self-Reflection," in ibid., p. 341.

[162] David Carr argues that Husserl did not systematically deal with the problem of intersubjectivity in the first thirty years of his phenomenological writings. See Carr's *Phenomenology and the Problem of History* (Evanston, Ill.: Northwestern University Press, 1974), p. 82. Carr indicates that although Husserl mentions intersub-

Husserl then investigated the specific intersubjective structures that the second epoché reveals. He first argues that all problems of facticity and meaning occur *within* each subject's monadic sphere.[163] Thus, "the proposition that 'everything existing for me must derive its existential sense exclusively from me myself and from my sphere of consciousness' retains its validity and fundamental importance."[164] But despite this immanency of the ego's experience, the ego itself is not solipsistic. The relation between ego and other is characterized as a "monadological intersubjectivity": "within the limits of my transcendentally reduced pure conscious life, I *experience* the world (including others) and, according to its experiential sense, *not* as (so to speak) my *private* synthetic formation but as other than me, as an *intersubjective* world."[165]

Since the phenomenological method assures us that all transcendent knowledge is already included "without residue" in the transcendent ego, Husserl needed to determine only at what point the other can be determined as existent within the domain of the transcendental ego.[166] To do so he had to explain two things: (*a*) how the ego "which I am for myself" differs from the ego that the other is for itself, and (*b*) how both the ego and the other remain both "objects in the world" and "subjects for this world."[167] Husserl called these two aspects of the constitution of the other *empathy* and *practically executed reflection.*[168]

Empathy is the implicit intentionality in which the "being of oth-

---

jectivity in *Ideas II*, §§29, 43, this text was not published in Husserl's lifetime and thus his intersubjectivity theory remained essentially unknown until the 1930s. But Husserl did work on several essays that dealt with intersubjectivity in the period from 1910 to 1930, such as his Göttingen lectures of 1910–1911. See his "Zur Phänomenologie der Intersubjektivität," in *Husserliana*, 13.xvii.

[163] This criticism is found in his early writings. See *Husserliana*, 13.21. See also *Meditations*, §64.

[164] *Meditations*, §62. This is an entailment of Husserl's theory of constitution, another topic too vast to deal with in detail here. Michael Theunissen observes that two broad categories of interpretation of Husserl's constitution have emerged: some interpret it as basically "creation" (Fink, Schütz), others as "conceiving" (*empfangen*) (Bremel, Levinas). The former is the interpretation most congenial to my— and Habermas's—way of viewing Husserl.

[165] *Meditations*, §43.

[166] Husserl emphasizes that the ego does not emerge from experience, at least understood as an associative apperception constituted from a manifold, but rather from life itself. See *Ideen*, 2.252.

[167] Michael Theunissen, *Das Andere*, 2nd ed. (Berlin: de Gruyter, 1977), pp. 19, 103.

[168] The term he uses for the latter is *vollzogene Reflexion*. See *Husserliana*, 13.4.

ers for me" becomes constituted (*a*). Earlier, Husserl had argued that
in my experience of another, its ego can attain to being only "if it is
nature for me and thus in this way is its body, and vice versa."[169]
Now he argued that this experience of the other requires a reduction
to my ego's own transcendental sphere of "ownness." After dissolving the natural attitude in which the ego and the other are distinct
objects, an *otherness in the ego's own intending* is disclosed: "In this
pre-eminent intentionality there becomes constituted for me the
new existence-sense that goes beyond my monadic very-ownness;
there becomes constituted an ego, not as 'I myself,' but as mirrored
in my own ego, in my monad."[170]

What is the status of this ego-constituted other? Is it similar to
Fichte's not-I? Is it merely an unconscious or social part of the ego,
like Mead's "me"? Or is it an autonomous other? Husserl argued that
this other is, in the first instance, an *alter ego*.[171] This "mirrored"
relation of the alter ego to the originating ego bears a strong similarity to Hegel's positing reflection. The alter ego is paradoxically "an
analog of my own self and yet again not an analog in the usual
sense."[172] Michael Theunissen claims that through empathy the ego
literally transposes itself into the other subject.[173]

Husserl mitigated the solipsism of this simple positing of the other
by embedding both the ego and the other in the objective world
(*b*). In a "mundanizing apperception," or "appresentation," the ego
constitutes the world of the other and bears it intentionally within
itself. The act of practically executed reflection confers self-givenness upon all that is experienced and determines the universal structural forms of the ego and the other. Although the other is a
determining part of the ego's own concrete being, Husserl maintained that the other has an explicable essence of its own. This appresentation, or "making co-present," of the other transcends the
immediacy of the ego's original experience. In *The Idea of Phenome-*

---

[169] *Husserliana*, 14.274.

[170] *Meditations*, §44.

[171] *Meditations*, §43; *Husserliana*, 14.276. Husserl is not very exacting in some of
his use of terminology. He refers to the ego in some places as *absolute Ego* and in
others as the *eignenes transcendentales Ego*. He also refers to the other as an *andere
Ich, andere Ego, alter Ego*, and *fremde Subjekte* without clearly specifying the basis
for the different uses.

[172] *Meditations*, §44.

[173] Theunissen, *Das Andere*, p. 70.

nology Husserl had described the appresentation of a *physical object* in which the perceived "front" of a physical thing always and necessarily appresents its "back." Now he argues that the appresentations of an *other* and of a thing are identical, except that the fulfilling appresentation remains partially concealed in the case of the other. None of the appropriated meaning specific to the animate organism of the other becomes actualized in the ego's primordial sphere. Theunissen calls this Husserl's acknowledgment of an asymmetry between self and other.[174]

Having set forth the relation of sameness and difference between the self and the other, Husserl then described the structures of intersubjectivity as such. Criticizing Scheler's theory of empathetic constitution, Husserl argued for the need for a "supplement" (*Ergänzung*) in order to move from the empathetic constitution of the other to the transcendental constitution of the intersubjective world. The supplement is a cognitive "overlapping-at-a-distance" that occurs through an associative pairing and a "fusion" (*Verschmelzung*—the very term that Gadamer will use) of the meaning of one member to that of the other.[175] Earlier Husserl had claimed that the other is, in its own unique psychophysical experience, "given" in the same way to every other. Now he argues that in this form of mediation, "every successful understanding of what occurs in others has the effect of opening up new associations and new possibilities of understanding; and conversely, since every pairing association is reciprocal, every such understanding uncovers my own psychic life in its similarity and difference and, by bringing new features into prominence, makes it fruitful for new associations."[176] At first this new "objectivity" of the intersubjective world seems to contradict Husserl's earlier claim that the other is a synthetic unity constituted by the ego and inseparable from it. But this connection between monads is not only an intentional reaching of the other into the ego's primordiality, but also a form of background knowing that links all existents together. The ego and others form an "identity-meaning."[177]

---

[174] Ibid., p. 62.

[175] *Meditations*, §54.

[176] *Husserliana*, 13.443; *Meditations*, §54.

[177] *Meditations*, §55. Husserl points out that if there are *abnormalities*, they are constituted on the basis of an antecedent *normality*. Thus, even animals are consti-

How do ego and other interrelate to determine this meaning? In a way that resembles Mead's reciprocity of the behavior expectations of a generalized other, Husserl posits a *reciprocity of perception* in the relation between two organisms: "just as his animate bodily organism lies in my field of perception, so my animate organism lies in his field of perception and thus, in general, he experiences me forthwith as an other for him, just as I experience him as *my* other."[178] In a way reminiscent of Kant's formulation of the *sensus communis* Husserl expands this reciprocity to form the concept of an "intentional communion" of mankind in which each is able to take the place of an other.[179] Habermas adopts a similar principle of intersubjective connection among individual selves, though he replaces Husserl's perceptual grounding of it with a socio-theoretic one (PDM 314).

Husserl's reciprocity between ego and other requires—and with this Habermas agrees—a counter-factual "third": a shared world that grounds the intersubjective identification of an objective thing. This phenomenon anticipates the ego's ability both to change place with the other and to utilize language. But, as Habermas points out, Husserl fails to draw any linguistic or normative implications from this shared world. Though it does make intersubjectivity into an objective condition for the subject, the reflection that grasps it remains limited by the constitutional needs and capacities of a monological consciousness. Thus, the concrete other remains constituted from the epistemic limits of a single self-consciousness, not from the practical limits of discursive *will* formation.

In the *Crisis of the European Sciences* Husserl modified this view of mediation between self and world. Here he used his theory of intersubjectivity to develop a theory of inquiry. Though Habermas rejects the basic perceptual ground of Husserl's theory of intersubjectivity, he adopts Husserl's claim that a theory of intersubjectivity must lie at the core of any critique of science and culture.

Ironically, the European sciences Husserl criticized seem to have

---

tuted as variants of a more fundamental "humanness." Husserl thus evinces a radical anthropocentrism quite reminiscent of the early Heidegger.

[178] Ibid., §56.

[179] Ibid. The German phrase is *Wechselseitig-für-ein-ander-sein*. Theunissen argues that Husserl's reciprocity is based on, not a *Gleichstellung*, but a *Gegenüberstellung*. See *Das Andere*, pp. 82ff. Husserl speaks of the counterfactuality implicit in the capacities both to change pre-understandings and to forge agreement in *Ideen*.

adopted the objectivism of the second epoché while ignoring the subjectivism of the first. By exaggerating the need for a value-free "third-person" viewpoint, they were losing their original link to actual praxis and were developing an increasingly positivistic stance toward reality. In order to reclaim a proper practical grounding for science, Husserl devised a "methodological task of self-reflection" that could overcome the philosophical naïveté of objectivistic science. The philosopher can appropriate the history of inquiry and reconstruct the conceptual system that liberates him or her from prejudice through a kind of critical self-reflection. In order to elucidate this theory of inquiry, Husserl moved from an exclusive focus upon theoretical reflection on mutual *perception* of objects from a third-person perspective to a focus upon an analysis of the phenomenon of our mutual practical *interest* in objects.

Husserl then examined how scientists conduct their interest-guided inquiry within a "community of theory."[180] Discrepancies within the community of inquirers are overcome through a scientific criticism either openly discussed or unspoken. But he argued that the different methods of judging validity are in fact "taken from the same total system of multiplicities of which each individual is constantly conscious (in the actual experience of the same thing) as the horizon of the possible experience of the thing."[181] He tried to dynamize the reality of Kant's thing-in-itself by claiming that the world is a unity of the endless multiplicity of changing experiences *for consciousness*. Moreover, in *Experience and Judgment* Husserl contended that the conditions for the possibility of "predicative evidence" for judgment can be determined neither by psychology nor by logic, but only by a phenomenological clarification of the background origin of predicative judgment itself.[182] Thus the later Husserl left this egocentric aspect of his first epoché virtually unchanged. He still claimed that each ego becomes conscious of intending an

---

[180] *Crisis*, pp. 108–110. This reveals a more critical stance toward the grouping of individuals than in the *Meditations*, where Husserl maintained that the pre-delineation of the experience of an alter ego reveals an harmonious "community of monads" existing with each other and for each other. See *Meditations*, §49.

[181] *Crisis*, p. 163.

[182] *Experience and Judgment*, p. 47. Gasché argues that both of Husserl's epochés, or retrogressions, require a dismantling (*Abbau*) of the theoretical world. This dismantling is in fact a form of transcendental reflection. See *Tain of the Mirror*, p. 110.

other in the form of a particular other and "in an amazing fashion" this intentionality reaches into that of the other and vice versa.[183] The other is *pre-constitutively present in the ego's own experience*. Thus, even science must adopt a fundamental orientation consistent with the subjective experience in which all knowledge is constituted.

Habermas seizes on the persistent strains of subjectivism in Husserl's later work. Though acknowledging the progress signaled by Husserl's reference to a "community of theory," he maintains that the substance of the community is still limited by the constraints of the phenomenological experience of each particular member. Moreover, he is not alone in his characterization of Husserl's "final" version of reflection as monological. Quentin Lauer argues that Husserl's overall theory represents a regression from Hegel: "unlike the Husserlian phenomenology of intersubjectivity that first discovers the self and then seeks to 'constitute' a world of other selves, the Hegelian phenomenology finds that other selves are essential to the discovery of one's own self and that this 'discovery' is actually a producing of oneself in relation to others."[184]

Habermas concludes that although Husserl successfully undermined Kantian epistemological psychologism, he still ended up with his own form of Platonism (TK 15). All meaning is independent of time and place. His theory of truth lacks a pragmatic or communicative foundation.[185] As we shall see in the next chapter, Habermas stipulates that a community of theory can function only on the basis of publicly expressed speech acts and developmental learning processes. Thus, he will extend Husserl's theoretical interest more resolutely into the realm of the practical.

Is Husserl as hidebound with regard to subjectivistic formulations of reflection and understanding as Habermas thinks? In a 1923 text Husserl argues for a kind of communicative grounds for interaction: "as a pure ego I form an eidetic possibility context as a general context of efficacy, as an eidos: a possible pure ego generally remaining in relation to an openly infinite number of other egos alien to it, but as remaining relative to it in relations of sympathy and in I–Thou relations and in relations of *communicative altering effects*"(*kommun-*

---

[183] *Crisis*, p. 254.

[184] Lauer, *Reading of the Phenomenology of Spirit*, p. 101.

[185] Roberts agrees with this "idealist" reading of Husserl. See *Logic of Reflection*, pp. 165ff.

ikativer Wechselwirkung).[186] He insisted that the ego remains related to the factical givenness of others through *Mitsein*—the same term Heidegger will use in *Being and Time*—and communicative state of boundedness (*Verbundensein*).[187] Thus, truth is "supra-empirically" valid, independent of the perspective of a single empirical ego. Though he did not analyze the intersubjective structures of language, Husserl nevertheless grounded his transcendental subjectivity in the concrete needs of inquiring subjects. Inquiring subjects negate the radical otherness of the other by taking on a third-person viewpoint that assumes the other is also capable of determining itself as universal. In this respect Husserl's ego, like Heidegger's *Dasein*, is "always already intersubjectivity."[188] Thus, this third-person decentering of a subject always rooted in a lifeworld has a close affinity to Habermas's own theory of intersubjective validation.

HEIDEGGER AND THE TEMPORALIZING OF REFLECTION

The final stage of the development of reflection that Habermas considers still to be consciousness philosophy is found in Heidegger's early—and to a certain extent also his later—writings. Heidegger radicalized Husserl's theory of intersubjective monism by claiming that the subject, immersed in a pre-reflective intersubjective world, becomes authentic by projecting a world purged of its pre-reflective everydayness.[189] By this "destructive" move, Heidegger accounted for what he considered to be Husserl's neglect of the subject's concrete being-in-the world.[190]

The early Heidegger remained committed to the basic phenomenological turn achieved by Husserl's first epoché. But Heidegger re-

---

[186] Husserl, "Die intersubjektive Gültigkeit phänomenologischer Wahrheit," in *Husserliana*, 14.307.

[187] Ibid., 308.

[188] See Flynn, *Political Philosophy at the Closure of Metaphysics*, p. 72.

[189] Curiously, Heidegger rarely mentions Husserl in *Being and Time*. But Heidegger later admitted that *Being and Time* was written as a polemic against several of Husserl's arguments. See Theunissen, *Das Andere*, pp. 156ff.; and Heidegger's Foreword to William Richardson's *Heidegger: Through Phenomenology to Thought* (The Hague: Martinus Nijhoff, 1963), pp. 1–24.

[190] Heidegger ordinarily used the term *Destruktion* to describe this process. But in his debate with Cassirer at Davos, Switzerland, in April 1929, he used the even more forceful term *Zerstörung*.

jected the second epoché's method of transcendental verification. While Husserl exploited the objectifying power of consciousness in the form of a logic of transcendental subjectivity, Heidegger reverted to the non-objectifying experience of *Dasein*'s intentionality. While Husserl explicated the transcendental ego's constitution of being, Heidegger investigated the *mode* of being of *Dasein*'s constitution. In both his early existential analytic of *Dasein* in *Being and Time* and in his later critique of research and science in the *Letter on Humanism*, Heidegger rejected Husserl's claim that eidetic intuition mediates between the knower and essences (see PDM 138).[191] He distanced himself from traditional cognitive formulations of reflective acts that link subjects and objects. Thus, we find very few references to the terms "reflection" and "consciousness" in *Being and Time*, and even fewer in his later works.

Habermas argues that Heidegger completed the integration of historicism and *Lebensphilosophie* that Husserl had begun with his explication of transcendental subjectivity. Heidegger adhered to Husserl's distinction between the natural attitude and the meaning-constitution of consciousness. Habermas claims that even Heidegger's way of posing problems is Husserlian: he merely turned their epistemological status into an ontological one (PDM 138; PT 41–42). Under the rubric of *Dasein*, generative subjectivity is finally banished from the realm of the intelligible. The definitive figure of thought is the "thrown projection" caring for an existence that is one's own. Transcendental subjectivity finds itself subjected to the conditions of historical facticity.

Habermas asks, however, whether *Being and Time*'s destructive "letting-be" of being can be conceived as an activity at all. Like Husserl, Heidegger tried to resolve how an intersubjective world can arise in the pluralism of individual world-constituting monads. But Habermas insists that Heidegger ended up precluding this possibility, since *Dasein* authentically projects itself in response to its possibilities only in *solitude*. *Dasein* does not break out of the circle of the Fichtean I that makes itself into an object and thus fails to become a spontaneously generative subjectivity. Habermas sums up Heidegger's overall project as an initial explication of being-in-the-world "as a derivative mode of a more primordial practical loss of world" fol-

---

[191] Rasmussen, *Reading Habermas*, p. 102.

lowed by a defense of an objectivism as "the flipside of a subjectivity set on assertion" (PT 207–208). Thus, Habermas sees a curious kind of continuity between Heidegger's earlier and later works. With their positing of an overpowering and anonymous event of a temporalized originary power, Heidegger's later works place the subject beyond the reaches of the ontic history explicated in his early works. The later Heidegger treats language as an occurrence of truth. The world is comprehended as one event in an epochal discourse. But Habermas claims that "the later Heidegger conceives of language as the house of self-adaptive [*sich schickenden*] 'being'; hence, the various stages in the understanding of 'being' still retained for him a transcendent relation to a 'being' that always remains *itself*" (PT 209). This disintegration of transcendental subjectivity leaves only an anonymous occurring of language, according to Habermas, that "releases worlds from within itself and swallows worlds back up" (PT 209). It is based primarily on an aesthetic paradigm. The problem of intersubjectivity in the later works thus remains as irrelevant as it was in the earlier. Though language's power to create meaning becomes absolute, the overwhelming force of world disclosure devalues all innerworldly *learning processes*. The validity of a given horizon of meaning remains indeterminant.

Concerned with the absence of a theory of discursive language use in both the early and the later Heidegger, Habermas overlooks the contribution that Heidegger makes to an analysis of *temporal* forms of aesthetic and expressive forms of reflection we will discuss in the last chapter. Habermas spends little time analyzing Heidegger's development of the terms and relations of *Dasein*'s originary *pre-reflexive* relations: *Dasein* and the other, *Dasein* and the "they" (*das Man*), and *Dasein* and the world. By dispensing with traditional subject/object and self/other formulations, these "categories" set the stage for a new temporal conception of the terms of intersubjective reflection. Moreover, Habermas overlooks any emancipatory potential of the "category" of care (*Sorgen*) that Heidegger explicated as a guide for practical action.

The primary source of Heidegger's theory of temporally conceived expressive and aesthetic forms of reflection is found in Dilthey's hermeneutical theory. Through his concept of "lived experience," Dilthey had formulated a speculative version of Kantian reflective distinctions: "When we speak of what is real and its power, we mean first of all the facts of consciousness, as real lived experience—indeed as life itself—which constitute that realm."[192] Dilthey rejected the Kantian ideal of a special mode of consciousness that would determine "facts that lie behind what is observable."[193] He developed instead a "principle of phenomenality" based on the explication of the immediate. This principle provided the material for Heidegger's theory of the constitution of *Dasein*. Dilthey also developed a Husserlian kind of subjective constitution, arguing that "in reality, my self distinguishes itself from facts of my own consciousness, formations whose locus is in me."[194] Existence, reality, and being are only expressions for the way in which consciousness possesses its own impressions and representations. But, like Husserl, Dilthey broadened the domain of psychic life to include perceptions of things, persons, axioms, concepts, and feelings. Even acts of will are reducible to facts of consciousness; they are the lived experiences of "resistances" that point to a reality external to the subject.

Dilthey claimed that the principle of phenomenality, although oriented to the immediate, nonetheless requires a reflective act. He calls it a "becoming inwardly": an awareness that accompanies every perception. Without this reflexive break, consciousness places objects before itself only representationally. Although neither connected with every thought process nor empirically observable, this introspective awareness is *usually* connected with the emergence of the object and exhibits varying degrees of intensity.[195] It has an aesthetic dimension: "Feelings are inherently reflexive, and every feeling is accordingly a kind of reflexive awareness. Even a desire cannot be conceived without a reflexive awareness of the tension contained within it."[196] Dilthey attributed existence to all that we can experience in this reflexive manner. Although, like Fichte, he claimed that the ego exists only relative to the representation of a "thou," Dilthey

---

[192] Wilhelm Dilthey, "Introduction to the Human Sciences," in *Selected Works*, ed. R. Makkreel and F. Rodi (Princeton, N.J.: Princeton University Press, 1989), p. 251.

[193] Ibid., p. 258.

[194] Ibid., p. 245.

[195] Ibid., pp. 247, 254–256. Makkreel and Rodi note that the reflexive (self-given) is to be distinguished from the reflective (given to thought). As a result, first-order reflective awareness precedes second-order conceptual distinction into form and content.

[196] Ibid., p. 339.

insisted that the lived experience of self-consciousness *pre-exists the experience of a self outside of us.* The self-referential and existential quality of this awareness renders it a noetic form of reflection similar to Schelling's.

In addition to this reflexive awareness of a self, Dilthey also posited a second-order reflection on the *whole* within which the self knows facts of consciousness. Though this reflective act does not distinguish a subject from its cognitions, it does mediate between the self and its world. The world is the totality of experiential knowing that bestows continuity on self-consciousness. The self becomes the "point of transition" from outer perception to inner experience.[197] Dilthey argues that the world establishes the objective conditions of the psychic states that the subject knows. Heidegger will adopt this reflexive and pre-experiential aspect of the subject's embeddedness in the world. But by reformulating the question of Being and the role of hermeneutic reflection, Heidegger dissolved Dilthey's conflict between the psychology of understanding and the philosophy of history.[198]

In his existential ontology of *Being and Time,* Heidegger claimed that previous ontologies had explicated the ego only *essentially* as an atemporal supportive ground in either a substance or a subject. Although affirming both Kant's rejection of the ego as an ontically explained substance and his conception of the "I" as simply the "I think," Heidegger rejected Kant's positing of the ego as an isolated subject merely "present-at-hand."[199] He argued that Husserl's ego is similarly detached from existence and the world.[200]

Heidegger argued, instead, that the phenomenon of the world co-determines and delimits *Dasein*'s state of being. Borrowing from Dilthey, he investigated the mode of being of the everyday "interpretation" of *Dasein* already in-the-world.[201] This ability to project the

---

[197] Ibid., p. 269.

[198] *Being and Time* draws from many sources other than Dilthey, among them Brentano's claim that predication is not the essence of judgment, Husserl's regress from logic to the pre-predicative, Scheler's phenomenological analysis, and Jaspers's investigations into the psychology of worldviews.

[199] Heidegger, *Sein und Zeit* (Tübingen: Max Niemeyer, 1957), p. 320 / *Being and Time,* trans. J. Macquarrie and E. Robinson (New York: Harper & Row, 1962), p. 367. My citations will refer to both texts.

[200] See Theuissen, *Das Andere,* p. 158.

[201] Dilthey had explicated the different modes in which the givenness of a fact of consciousness occurs. See *Selected Works,* p. 253.

very world that engages it makes *Dasein* unique among beings. Nevertheless, *Dasein*'s being-in-the-world is always dispersed and fragmented in difference.[202] The "who" of *Dasein* can no longer be determined as a Husserlian or Kantian subject that "maintains itself as something identical throughout changes in its experiences and ways of behavior."[203] Rather, it is a "mineness" that does not relate ontologically to a "you" and a "we," but declares ontically its one mineness.[204]

In his Marburg lectures, presented shortly after the publication of *Being and Time*, Heidegger points out that *Dasein*'s self-relation is not a given, "as might be thought in adherence to Kant, in such a way that an 'I think' accompanies all representations and goes along with the acts directed at extant beings, which thus would be a reflective act directed at the first act."[205] Heidegger insisted that reflection does not set aside the facticity or situatedness of *Dasein* for a proto-ego or transcendental subject, but rather determines *Dasein* as given to itself before all reflection. Thus, reflection is not a self-disclosure, but a *mode of self-apprehension*.[206] Heidegger concluded that *Dasein*'s ontological constitution is defined, not through an analysis of self-consciousness, but only through a clarification of the temporal structures of existence. The structural modes of understanding proper to *Dasein* precede all thematic, propositional, and reflexive cognition. Husserl's explication of the empathetic relation between the ego and the alien "psychical life" of the other failed to uncover these deeper structures that reveal *Dasein*'s "being with" and "being toward" the other.

What exactly are these structures? Heidegger argued that *Dasein*'s being-in-the-world is essentially constituted through both the *Mitsein* of the self and the *Mitdasein* of others.[207] We encounter others

---

[202] *Sein und Zeit*, p. 56/*Being and Time*, p. 83. I will translate *Sein* as "being" instead of "Being" as Macquarrie and Robinson do.

[203] *Sein und Zeit*, p. 114/*Being and Time*, p. 150.

[204] *Sein und Zeit*, p. 42/*Being and Time*, pp. 67–68.

[205] Gasché, *Tain of the Mirror*, p. 83. See also Heidegger's *Basic Problems of Phenomenology*, trans. A. Hofstadter (Bloomington: Indiana University Press, 1982), p. 158.

[206] *Basic Problems of Phenomenology*, p. 159.

[207] *Sein und Zeit*, pp. 120ff./*Being and Time*, pp. 156ff. Since the translation of these terms is at worst impossible and at best clumsy, I will leave them untranslated. But it is important to note that the actual encounter with the other occurs in *Dasein*'s inauthentic *modes* of being-at-hand (*Vorhandenheit*) as a thing and being-ready-to-use (*Zuhandenheit*) as a tool.

principally through their work, which is their being-in-the-world. The being of the other possesses, not the mode of being of an external thing, as Husserl's empathy theory assumes, but the mode of *Dasein* itself. The other possesses the same character of "free-givenness" as *Dasein* itself. *Dasein* and the other exist in an originary entwinement (*Verfluchtung*). Like Husserl, Heidegger argued that the encounter with the other is oriented by that *Dasein* "which is in each case one's own." But unlike Husserl, he claimed that initially the other is one from whom "one does *not* distinguish oneself."[208] The issue is not *empathy with* but rather *differentiation from* the other which includes oneself. In Husserl's empathy theory the ego relates to the other through "a projection of one's own being-towards-oneself 'into something else.' The other would be a duplicate of the self."[209] But Heidegger argued that *Mitsein precedes* empathy. Thus, the self-relation to the other is the projection *of* one's being *to* one's self *in* an other. Since being-in-the-world has this "with" structure, the world is always already the one that *Dasein* shares with others. Heidegger concluded that "This *Mitdasein* of others is disclosed within-the-world for a *Dasein*, and so too for those who are *Dasein* with us, only because *Dasein* is in itself essentially *Mitsein*."[210]

Mitsein is an existential characteristic of *Dasein* even when an actual other is neither present-at-hand nor perceived: the absence of the other can be a reality only for a *Mitsein*. Even self-recognition is grounded in *Mitsein*. Heidegger thus saw *Mitsein* as the pre-condition for several tasks: the constitution of the other, the constitution of the consistency of the world, and even the constitution of the self. Nevertheless, *Mitsein* remains underdeveloped with respect to the extensive conceptual work it is supposed to accomplish.[211]

Heidegger's characterization of the relation between self and other thus departs significantly from Husserl's. While Husserl assumes that a certain harmony exists between self and other, Heidegger claims that the actual relation of *Dasein* to the other is plagued with discord. A "distantiality" (*Abständigkeit*) and subjection emerge in

---

[208] *Sein und Zeit*, p. 118/*Being and Time*, p. 154.
[209] *Sein und Zeit*, p. 124/*Being and Time*, p. 162.
[210] *Sein und Zeit*, p. 120/*Being and Time*, p. 156.
[211] See Tugendhat, *Self-Consciousness and Self-Determination*, pp. 246ff.

the relation between *Dasein* and the other.[212] Others can dispose of *Dasein*'s everyday projects as they please. Although anonymous and replaceable from *Dasein*'s point of view, the wills of others regulate *Dasein*'s everyday existence.[213] The "who" of these others is not a determinate "you," but the neuter "they." Publicness (*Öffentlichkeit*) is constituted, not by an Hegelian type of universal subject that unites a plurality of subjects, but by the "averageness" and "leveling down" of the "they."[214] Like Hegel, Heidegger thus recognized the need for autonomous recognition in order to overcome social disparity. *Dasein* achieves authenticity, not by a radical break from the "they," but by an "*existentiell* modification of the 'they': of the 'they' as an essential *existentiale*."[215] The objectivization into the "they" is overcome by modifying the givenness of *Dasein*'s own *modes of being-in* the "they."

At this point the differences between Husserl's and Heidegger's characterization of the mediation between self and other are quite pronounced. They differ, not in their claims about the role that the other plays in the constitution of the self, but in their mode of investigating the limits between self and other. They diverge principally in their formulation of the *given*. Husserl brackets the givenness of the ego and declares it indubitable. Heidegger rejects this form of transcendental bracketing as formal and empty, arguing instead that the given has a temporal structure uncovered by a phenomenological projection beyond interaction in the factical world permeated by *Mitsein*. While Husserl's mediation is accomplished by an harmonious empathy grounded in the subject's apperception of the other, Heidegger's is accomplished by *Dasein*'s struggle to detach itself from the everydayness of the "they" in which it is embedded.

How does *Dasein* formulate its practical day-to-day activity in the fallen world that limits its authenticity? Heidegger argued that the structural whole of our fallen mode of everydayness is revealed neither through a mere arrangement of its elements nor through a de-

---

[212] *Sein und Zeit*, p. 126/*Being and Time*, p. 164.

[213] Kathryn Brown argues that precisely this understanding of human alienation rendered Heidegger susceptible to Fascist ideology. See her "Language, Modernity and Fascism: Heidegger's Doubling of Myth," in *The Attractions of Fascism: Social Psychology and Aesthetics of the "Triumph of the Right,"* ed. J. Milfull (New York: Berg, 1990), p. 139.

[214] *Sein und Zeit*, p. 128/*Being and Time*, pp. 165–166.

[215] *Sein und Zeit*, p. 130/*Being and Time*, p. 168.

duction from an "idea" of the human being. He claimed, instead, that the fundamental *existentiale* of states-of-mind (*Befindlichkeit*) and of understanding (*Verstehen*) constitute the ontic being of the disclosedness of a way of being-in-the-world.[216] Heidegger thus adopted Dilthey's claim that states-of-mind are non-perceivable states revealed through an analysis of *Dasein*'s moods.[217] But these states of mind disclose neither a "state of a soul" nor a "lived experience" discovered through immanent reflection. Rather, the interpretation through which *Dasein* "appropriates" itself is derived from understanding and discourse (*Rede*). Being itself "is" only the understanding of beings.[218]

These *existentiale* reveal that *Dasein*'s being-toward-the-world is essentially practical. Heidegger termed this practical relation *care*. Care can be derived neither from the phenomena of will, desire, longing, or inclination nor from a specific set of actions. Through care, *Dasein* discloses its own future in a hermeneutical and non-reflexive state-of-mind.[219] The being of *Dasein* is explicable only in the interrelation between care, worldliness, ready-to-handedness, and at-handedness. *Dasein* is always already "beyond" itself, not acting toward other beings, but actualizing its ownmost possibilities. This being-ahead-of-itself (*Sich-vorweg-sein*) of *Dasein*'s bears little relation to Husserl's isolated, worldless ego. Heidegger flatly rejected the latent instrumentalism of Husserl's understanding of the fusion

---

[216] *Sein und Zeit*, pp. 133, 160/*Being and Time*, pp. 171, 203. The inauthentic modes of this disclosure are idle talk, curiosity, and ambiguity.

[217] *Sein und Zeit*, p. 134/*Being and Time*, pp. 172–173. Dilthey had already referred to the kind of consciousness involved in a "play of moods," as when one listens to a symphony. See his *Selected Works*, pp. 254ff.

[218] *Sein und Zeit*, pp. 160, 183/*Being and Time*, pp. 203, 228. One of the primary ways in which *Dasein* recovers itself is through awareness of its own death. Death does not just belong to one's own *Dasein* in a undifferentiated way, but lays claim to *Dasein* as individuated. Death is disclosed, not in a relation to a future object, but in the anticipation of "being-toward-death." Again we see the influence of Dilthey, who had proclaimed that "death is the great teacher from which we learn to differentiate the body from the living self-activity of the ego." See his *Selected Works*, pp. 351–352.

[219] The first phenomenon that is disclosed in this fundamental inquiry is that of anxiety (*Angst*). This anxiety emerges from *Dasein*'s flight from itself and its own possibilities. The possibilities of the "they" are actually of *Dasein*'s own construction. Nevertheless, anxiety discloses the very possibilities by which *Dasein* achieves its individuality. An interesting parallel can be drawn between the primordiality of Heidegger's *Angst* and Habermas's original "intuition" of vulnerability (*Verletzbarkeit*) of self and other that grounds all morality. See MC 199–200.

of the ego and the other: "The fact that this referential totality of the manifold relations of the 'in order to' has been bound up with that which is an issue for *Dasein* does not signify that a 'world' of objects which is present-at hand has been welded together with a subject."[220] The ontological whole of *Dasein* has, rather, the structure of being-along-side (*Sein-bei*) the beings it encounters in the world. But whether resolutions for specific actions can be instantiated in this kind of intersubjective matrix remains unclear. Care is neither a special relationship to oneself nor the practical action of the actor, but merely the opening of possibilities for *Dasein*.

It is difficult to exaggerate the radicality of Heidegger's introduction of care into the reflective apparatus of German idealism. Care is *Dasein*'s self-constancy and totality.[221] The structure of care is *always already* the structure of every factical behavior and situation of *Dasein*, and thus expresses no priority of practical over theoretical reason.[222] Thus, Heidegger single-handedly dismantles the tedious attempts of Kant, Fichte, Schelling, Hegel, and Husserl to work out the limits between theory and praxis. Heidegger then radicalized this "destructive" role of his existential project in his later writings.

After *Being and Time*, Heidegger outlined a deeper primordiality in the relation between *Dasein* and the factical. He argues that deconstruction must be historical: "Construction in philosophy is necessarily destruction, that is to say, a de-constructing of traditional concepts carried out in a historical recursion to the tradition."[223] He argued that philosophy must continue to challenge both *Dasein* and *Sein* pure and simple.[224] Thus, he set forth a new set of structures, such as *Zug*, *Fuge*, *Geviert*, and *Unter-Schied*, that "lay out" the manifold and contradictory in everyday temporal existence. These offer a kind of primal matrix for the irreducible differences of subject and object, and of self and other. By generating a vocabulary based on

---

[220] *Sein und Zeit*, p. 192/*Being and Time*, p. 236.

[221] *Sein und Zeit*, p. 323/*Being and Time*, p. 370.

[222] *Sein und Zeit*, p. 193/*Being and Time*, p. 238. Solicitude (*Fürsorge*) is another non-instrumental form of being-with-others in care through which an "explicit disclosure of the other" occurs.

[223] *Basic Problems of Phenomenology*, p. 23.

[224] Heidegger, *Introduction to Metaphysics* (New Haven, Conn.: Yale University Press, 1958), pp. 8ff.

poetic, social, and political metaphors, Heidegger purified his philosophy of all vestiges of Husserlian self-reflective science.[225]

The later Heidegger took a retrogressive "step back" to the primal origins of thought. Discarding rational thinking, he argued that recollective thinking (*Andenken*) and reflective thinking (*Besinnung*) differentiate between the disclosure and the unveiling of things. Bereft of a constructed ideal, recollective thinking brings us face to face with thinking.[226] Reflective thinking is a recollective temporal return to a pre-given "letting be." The ground that these forms of thought reveal cannot become an object of theoretic reflection, since "as one reaches out for it reflectively, it withdraws."[227] Hegel had synthesized reflective differences in an absolute present; the later Heidegger returned to a primordial past that can project emancipative possibilities.

The later Heidegger's deconstruction, however, can be conceptualized as a form of temporally contextualized reflection. It thematizes the moment of difference in the relation between the limits of a *present* inauthentic mode of being and a *future* state informed by a *past* primordiality. The aim of such destructive thinking is an emancipatory *Gelassenheit*. This "letting go" does not sublate the difference between self and other in a speculative proposition, but preserves the difference in the equivocations of poetic speech. It is no coincidence that French philosophers of alterity have embraced Heidegger with such enthusiasm. His temporal analysis of thinking has profound ramifications for any theory of emancipation.

Habermas, however, has little interest in the later Heidegger's concerns for deep temporal structures and for his project of "destruction." He claims that Heidegger merely raised the being-in-the-world

---

[225] See Rorty, *Philosophical Papers*, 2:17, 27. Rorty is, however, less ambivalent about the positive value of pragmatism than Heidegger was.

[226] Heidegger, *Identity and Difference*, trans. J. Stambaugh (New York: Harper & Row, 1969), p. 64.

[227] See Gasché, *Tain of the Mirror*, pp. 118–120. Derrida argues that even the later Heidegger actually remains faithful to metaphysics, because his *Abbau* and *Destruktion* alike possess the goal of attaining the "ultimate foundation" of concepts. Gasché is more ambivalent about Heidegger's deconstruction of metaphysics. On the one hand, Heidegger overcomes metaphysics by avoiding metaphysical concepts and making a more practical application of reflection. On the other, Gasché admits that "it may well be that deconstruction cannot be termed non-reflexive, in the sense that I have applied this term to *Abbau* and destruction."

of a "mundane I" to a transcendental level. As a result, Heidegger was forced to posit his anonymous *Seingeschichte* to fill the emptiness of this "vacated" subjectivity (TK 40). No longer breaking new ground, Heidegger's deconstruction remained firmly embedded within a foundationalist philosophy. He merely provided a new formulation for the old distinction between the transcendent and the empirical. Habermas claims that the "heroic" understanding of the early formulation of *Dasein* led inevitably to an isolated and decisionistic view of human action in the later works.[228]

CONCLUDING SUMMARY: HABERMAS AND HIS PREDECESSORS

It remains unclear exactly to what extent Habermas's theory of communication, though rejecting much of Husserl's model of structural thematization and verification of implicit knowledge and Heidegger's model of a "deconstructive construction" of ontic possibilities, was nonetheless heavily influenced by them.[229] He does acknowledge that Heidegger nullified the metaphysical distinctiveness that Husserl had given to methodological self-reflection (PDM 146). But Heidegger considered rationality "the most stiff-necked adversary of thought."[230] On the one hand, Habermas accepts Husserl's emphasis on a scientific verification of truth and rejects Heidegger's denial of the need for rational verification. On the other hand, he rejects the perceptualist roots of Husserl's understanding of verification and

---

[228] Habermas's interpretation is difficult to square with Heidegger's denial of the "exceptional condition" of *Dasein* vis-à-vis the other. Habermas nevertheless links even Heidegger's seduction by National Socialism to his decisionistic notion of human action. See TK 60ff. Robert Scharff strongly criticizes Habermas's claim that Heidegger remains firmly within a decisionistic philosophy of consciousness. Scharff argues that *Mitsein*—a principle that to his mind continues to have tacit force even in Heidegger's later writings—expresses a primordial intersubjective givenness that is "more deeply implicated in our existence" than can be represented in any concept derived either from Husserl's transcendental intersubjectivity or Habermas's protest against modern philosophies of the subject. See Scharff's "Habermas on Heidegger's *Being and Time*," *International Philosophical Quarterly*, 31, No. 2 (June 1991), 191–193.

[229] Tugendhat defines evocative thinking as the revelatory power of the single word over that of a proposition. He also presents a critique of Heidegger's use of it. See *Self-Consciousness and Self-Determination*, pp. 145ff.

[230] Heidegger, "Nietzsche's Word: God Is Dead," in *The Question Concerning Technology*, trans. W. Lovitt (New York: Harper & Row, 1977), p. 112.

adopts Heidegger's desire to challenge everyday fallenness. In a recent text, Habermas even affirms the world-disclosive orientation of Heidegger's project: "Pragmatism, genetic structuralism, and epistemological anthropology have highlighted in their respective ways the phenomenon described in an ontological fashion by Heidegger as 'being-ahead-of-oneself' in a 'thrown projection.' The anticipatory character of understanding is universal: the moments of projection and discovery complement each other in *all* cognitive activities" (JA 31). Habermas grants that a subjective projection provides at least a partial form of mediation between the self and the world.

Can Habermas have it both ways? Can he adopt a phenomenological concern with subject's situatedness in the lifeworld while dispensing with a phenomenological adherence to the subject's constituted "mineness"? In what follows, we will examine how Habermas's rejection of the self-disclosedness of being-in-the-world—the point to which the philosophy of reflection had developed in Heidegger. We shall also see that this rejection weakens Habermas's ability to contextualize the temporal structures of discursive argument. In the next chapter we shall examine his own early formulation of reflection: the discursive mediation between the self and its world through language and interaction. Though he rejects the objectivization of his predecessors' consciousness-based theories of self-reflection, Habermas nonetheless borrows freely from them, particularly from Hegel's self-formative processes of recognition and Husserl's intersubjective community of inquiry. Adding elements of pragmatism, speech act theory, and theories of social interaction, he blends both the theoretical and the practical levels of reflection we have examined into a unique critical discursive reflection embedded in everyday interactive praxis.

2

The Early Habermas and the Development of Psychoanalytic Reflection and Normative Discourse

Having completed a conceptual analysis of reflection and an historical analysis of the genesis of the various modes of reflective acts, we can now analyze how Habermas modifies the philosophy of reflection so that it can function without a consciousness-based theory of truth. We shall examine the early development of Habermas's theory of reflective interaction in this chapter, and its later development in the next. My thesis is that Habermas's early work is made coherent only if it is read as a new theory of reflection that emerges from his immanent critique of the theories of reflection we examined in the last chapter and of other theorists he examines, particularly Peirce, Freud, and Gadamer. Habermas's unique contribution to reflection theory is his development of a reflection capable of determining the validity of claims relevant to the individual and social *interests* of practical agents.

The strain of post-Hegelian theories of reflection that most influenced Habermas can be traced, not to analytic philosophy's—particularly Russell's—rejection of *any* form of self-relation, but to phenomenology's relocation of self-relation in various *objective* constructs, such as experience, being, and, in particular, the lifeworld.[1] Wary of the positivism of analytic theories, Habermas begins his analysis of truth determination, not from the point of view of logical or metaphysical categories, but from the critical perspective of indi-

---

[1] Gasché points out that analytic philosophy generally has demonstrated the "formal antinomies that characterize the idea of self-reference or reflexiveness." See *Tain of the Mirror*, p. 68.

vidual and social emancipation from systemic distortions unique to the modern world. Like other critical theorists, he focuses on language, domination, and labor as the universal media in which the social life of the human species evolves.[2] His early theory of truth combines phenomenological descriptions of these intersubjective structures with theories of self-formative processes (Hegel, Marx), critiques of positivism (Peirce, Dilthey), psychological methodologies (Freud, Piaget), and hermeneutics (Gadamer). He derives a theory of knowledge from the structures of rational communication against a background of interests. We will thus examine, first, how he uses the reflective tools of psychoanalytic method to re-align linguistic disturbances that occur within the descriptive framework of everyday interactions. We will see, secondly, his move from psychological to political and social applications of his theory of self-reflection. In the next chapter we will examine his later additions of speech act theory and functionalist sociology to his theory.

REFLECTION AND TRUTH

In his inaugural lecture of 1965, Habermas acknowledges that any re-alignment of dysfunctions and distortions of life activity requires some type of reflection. He proposes to set forth a methodological self-reflection that could carry out such a task.

Habermas first considers Schelling's description of the concept of reflection that had defined philosophy since its Greek beginnings. Schelling argued that the Greek philosophers applied the term *theoria*, originally a term with religious connotations, to the "looking on" that one utilized when contemplating the cosmos. They concluded that only a reflective attitude that frees the subject from practical interests can properly orient human action. In this framework, reflection established the demarcation between being and time that became the foundation of traditional ontology. *Logos* became the realm of constancy and certainty; *doxa*, the realm of the mutable and perishable. The philosopher brought himself into accord with the *logos*'s proportions of the cosmos by reproducing them internally and conforming himself to them through *mimesis*. Through this relating

---

[2] See Thomas McCarthy, "Translator's Introduction," LC xiii.

of the soul to the ordered motion of the cosmos, a purely theoretic reflection entered into the conduct of life. Habermas claims that this ideal of theoretical reflection remained ensconced in philosophy for more than two millennia, forming the background of even Hegel's theory of reflection.

Habermas argues that Marx's social critique occasioned a fundamental shift away from this contemplative view of reflection. Inspired by Marx's social theory, Horkheimer distinguished between a *traditional* positivistic notion of theory, characterized by Descartes's exclusively theoretic method of reflection, and a *critical* theory which takes both material and theoretic interests into account. Horkheimer thus offered a viable alternative to Husserl's "pre-scientific unity of experience" that, although no longer positivistic, was still a contemplative "pure theory" that abandoned interest.[3] Horkheimer developed a type of dialectical critique of ideology that refers every thought back to the historical situation in which it arose and to the real context of interests behind it (see LC x).[4] Moreover, Horkheimer remonstrated Hegel for "forgetting" the significance of the time-bound interest which influences the direction of thought, specifically the interest in the *future*. But Habermas criticizes Horkheimer for underdetermining the hermeneutic element of the critique needed to account for the "complex relation" between knowledge and interest.[5] He claims that Horkheimer never completed a "philosophical elucidation of thought on materialist presuppositions."[6] Like Adorno, Habermas thinks that the hermeneutic tradition, which analyzes the changing understanding of subjectively intended meanings (*Sinnverstehen*), must be integrated into critical theory.[7] Thus, Habermas investigates the possibility of developing a critical and hermeneutical self-reflection that is *both aware of its own interest and able to determine critically the validity of knowledge claims*. In effect, he reformulates the foundations of historical materialism on the basis of a social-theoretic epistemology. His theory of reflection will

---

[3] Axel Honneth, *Kritik der Macht: Reflexionsstufen einer kritischen Gesellschaftstheorie* (Frankfurt am Main: Suhrkamp, 1986), p. 231.

[4] Habermas is referring to Horkheimer's "Zum Problem der Wahrheit," in *Kritische Theorie*, ed. A. Schmidt (Frankfurt am Main: Suhrkamp, 1968).

[5] See Honneth, *Kritik der Macht*, pp. 248. He argues that this hermeneutic buffer protects Habermas from the charge that he ignores Foucault's critique of power.

[6] McCarthy, "Translator's Introduction," LC xiii.

[7] Honneth, *Kritik der Macht*, p. 115.

form the limits an agent must set on his own interests relative to those of other agents.

In *Knowledge and Human Interests*, Habermas lays out this social-theoretic project. He first assumes that the truth of all statements is linked to the intention of the good life (KHI 312–313). He then develops the theoretic framework for a critical self-reflection able to determine legitimate human interests that promote the good life. His original breakthrough is reflected in the very title of the work: knowledge of the good life can be valid and emancipative if, and only if, it reflexively takes account of its own specific objectivizing and instrumental interest.[8] Interest is no longer merely the self-awareness of the drive to theorize essences, as Husserl claimed, but the very force that mediates knowledge and the real. If knowledge and its *own* interest are joined in self-reflection, the proper limits of an emancipatory "knowledge-constitutive interest" are determined (KHI 211). By introducing this interest-laden self-reflection of knowledge, Habermas sees himself as bringing a consciousness-based philosophy of reflection to a definitive close.

Habermas argues that a mere historicizing of the philosophy of reflection fails to rehabilitate this interest-specific dimension of knowledge. Following Benjamin and Horkheimer, Habermas contends that the hermeneutic and intersubjective "experience of reflection" outlined in Hegel's early works achieved a unity of the practical and the theoretical that neither previous nor subsequent attempts rivaled.[9] Most of *Knowledge and Human Interests* is a critique of post-Hegelian theories of knowledge that approximated, but did not reach, this self-reflection of knowledge. After beginning with the early Hegel's critique of Kant's philosophy of reflection, Habermas critically examines the ways in which Marx, Dilthey, and Peirce articulated the relation between knowledge and interest. Then he examines Freud's attempt to formulate a science of self-reflection. But instead of developing his own complete, systematic theory of

---

[8] Max Weber had already stressed the importance of considering the relationship between ideas and interests in the social order, but Habermas was perhaps the first to look at the epistemological consequences of the inclusion of interests. See BFN 66ff.

[9] Henrich criticizes Habermas for basing his paradigm shift to communication on insights that took a century to have an effect on modern research methods. See "Was ist Metaphysik—was Moderne?" p. 29.

self-reflection to replace these theories, Habermas relies upon his immanent critique of these other theories to *exhibit the very critical self-reflection he proposes.*

THE FAILURE OF THE PHILOSOPHY OF REFLECTION TO FORMULATE AN INTEREST-BOUND THEORY OF REFLECTION

Habermas acknowledges that both Kant and Fichte grasped an inchoate union between knowledge and interest by analyzing the role of reason in knowing and acting. Kant defined interest as the satisfaction that we bind with the representation of the existence of an object or an action. But Kant left the practical and theoretical aspects of interest disjointed. He located practical interest in moral intuitions, and theoretical (speculative) interest in regulative knowledge. Thus, he explicated a practical pure reason, but one that does not know *how* it is practical. Fichte, on the other hand, conceived self-reflection as a practical—and therefore interest-laden—action in which the ego reflexively turns back on itself. But like Kant, he failed to coordinate the practical and theoretical aspects of this theory of action. Neither Fichte nor Kant realized the implicit circularity of their assumption that we "know" the criteria for validity of knowing before we "know" some actual thing.

Habermas acknowledges that Hegel's system of abstract negation developed the idea of an emancipatory practical reflection whose "negation," as we have seen, destroys the dogmatism of life forms. Thus, negation is not an empty form, but a truth-determinate result of each previous stage of spirit's manifestation. Habermas claims that Hegel's experience of critical reflection is self-reflective, since it enables the subject to perceive that the transcendental relation between subject and object "alters itself behind its back" (KHI 20).[10] The key problem for Habermas is to show how this critical experience of reflection can be applied to knowledge-constitutive interests.

As we have seen, Habermas argues that the later Hegel abandoned

---

[10] Rorty characterizes Habermas's appropriation of Hegel's concept of reflection as an "idea of an analytical emancipation from objective illusions." See Rorty, "Epistemological Behaviorism and Analytic Philosophy," in *Hermeneutics and Praxis,* ed. R. Hollinger (Notre Dame, Ind.: University of Notre Dame Press, 1985), p. 115.

his early insights regarding the self-formative processes of interaction, language, and work. But Habermas argues that they can be reappropriated if we understand that spirit does not manifest itself in each of these mediations separately, but emerges only through a *dialectical interrelation* of all three.[11] Habermas claims that although Cassirer's dialectic of symbolization, Lukács's dialectic of labor, and Theodor Litt's dialectic of recognition each attempted to formulate an interrelation among these levels of self-formation, each remained one-sided.[12] Although Habermas also finds Marx's attempt to work out a dialectical theory of labor apart from both language and interaction one-sided, he does acknowledge the importance of Marx's link between self-formative processes and the concept of the historical development of the species. Habermas develops his own version of the interrelation of the three levels of formative processes in his later systematization of the objective, subjective, and social worlds.

THE SOCIAL-THEORETICAL THEORY OF KNOWLEDGE: HEGEL AND MARX

Habermas claims that Hegel's early writings provided Marx with the tools to "materialize" Hegel's later speculative philosophy. Marx inverted Hegel's two "relations of reflection"—the self-reflection of a solitary subject and the reciprocal relation of self and other in interaction—by linking reflection neither to a subject nor to a predicational linking of symbols, but to the social life processes of material

---

[11] "Arbeit und Interaktion," p. 10. The early Hegel did speak both of the interplay of language and interaction in the concept of the "language of a people," and of the interplay of labor and interaction in the development of norms which regulate instrumental behaviors (pp. 32–33). Even in the *Phenomenology* Habermas finds the beginnings of a turn away from the dialectic of labor and interaction. In the *Encyclopedia* language and labor completely lose their respective dialectical workings; only ethical relationships retain it (p. 37). Oliva Blanchette claims that Hegel's early study of contemporary economics was responsible for his Jena-period conviction that the movement of real spirit was not the triumphal sacrifice of one's life to the absolute, but the structure of spirit as a linking of symbolically mediated word and interaction. Blanchette notes that Habermas claims that such a reduction shows that the patterns of language, labor, and interaction were heterogeneous only in appearance under the presuppositions of what was already a philosophy of identity. See Blanchette's "Language, the Primordial Labor of History," 325–382.

[12] "Arbeit und Interaktion," p. 31.

production and consumption. Rejecting Hegel's nature/spirit distinction, Marx argued that subjective nature and objective nature, although conceptually distinct, are joined in the social labor of the self-reproducing species. Marx dispensed with symbolic interaction and cultural traditions as forms of mediation between the species and reality. Labor alone becomes the epistemological category that sets forth the transcendental conditions of the subject's relation to objects of experience.[13]

While acknowledging the value of Marx's "socialization" and concretization of Hegel's system, Habermas claims that Marx's theory of social labor forfeits all possibility of theoretically guided critique. Since Marx based his social theory solely on the paradigm of production, he could no longer distinguish between a science subjected to the transcendental conditions within which a species self-consciously produces itself and a critique that reflects upon the process of production. Thus, he restricted the scope of reflection to the level of instrumental action alone. He took Fichte's philosophy and undermined it with materialism: "Here the appropriating subject confronts in the not-I not just a product of the I but rather some portion of the contingency of nature. In this case the act of appropriation is no longer identical with the reflective reintegration of some previously externalized part of the subject itself" (KHI 44). Without an interaction-bound form of mediation, the subject's thought and will are completely determined by natural processes. Marx's system thus conceals the dimension of self-reflection in which it nevertheless moves. Marx's neglect of the theoretical side of social relations eventually reappears in later forms of positivist sociology.

Habermas acknowledges that although Marx's theory of social relations failed to achieve an effective synthesis between objective and subjective nature, his dialectic of class antagonisms did provide tools for such a synthesis. Marx modeled class struggles on the basis of the early Hegel's struggle for recognition. Habermas argues that, without reading the Jena manuscripts, Marx somehow "divined" the early Hegel's relationship between labor and interaction and applied it to his distinction between powers and relations of production.[14] The class dialectic is instantiated through power relationships between

---

[13] See Blanchette, "Language, the Primordial Labor of History," 348.
[14] "Arbeit und Interaktion," p. 44.

social classes. Social classes reflect class consciousness materially on the grounds of the objectivization of external nature alone. Nevertheless, Habermas claims that, in *The German Ideology*, Marx reduced both relations to the unspecified notion of mechanistic "social practice," thus losing the force of the synthesis (KHI 62). Marx represented the material side of interest within his theory of the development of the species. Habermas criticizes, not the critical element of this theory, but only its exclusion of the theoretical "self-reflection of the knowing subject" needed to interpret and form interests linguistically (KHI 63). But he makes the case that Peirce and Dewey developed an alternative form of cognitive synthesis through social labor that Marx did not envision.

The Reflective Structure of Inquiry

The Development of a Logic of Inquiry

In the years prior to the publication of *Knowledge and Human Interests* Habermas, along with Popper, had taken a leading role in the German debate about positivism in the social sciences. Both criticized positivist sciences for defining knowledge, not on the basis of a self-reflexive determination of conditions of critical knowledge, but by means of a closed relational system that generates its own definitions and relations with an assumed isomorphism of statements and facts. Habermas claims that such sciences operate by means of a picture theory of truth. These systems relegate the problem of the subject—whether understood as consciousness, ego, spirit, or species—to empirical psychology alone (KHI 68). Habermas argues that both Dilthey and Peirce attempted to break the force of positivism by developing scientific methodologies that could transcend their own empirical limits by means of a critical self-reflection. Both expanded this analysis by examining the *genesis* of both empirical and human sciences in the context of the objective life of the species.

Peirce argued that science must be grounded on the theoretic principle that the constitution of an object of possible experience is determined, not through the categorical "equippings" of a transcendental Kantian consciousness, but through the mechanism of a self-

regulated process of inquiry.[15] He held that every experience is mediated through inferential interpretations that are in turn bound to
representational signs. He thus shifted from the epistemological paradigm of a subject's direct psychological perception of an object to a
paradigm in which thinking is mediated by signs that have a threefold relation to an object, an interpreter, and a quality.[16] Habermas
notes that this determines a belief on the basis of "uncompelled and
intersubjective recognition" (KHI 92). This is not, however, recognition in Hegel's sense. Rather, Peirce combined the traditional analysis of formal relations between symbols with Kant's transcendental
analysis to form a methodology that defines rules according to which
true statements about reality are not simply understood, but *won*
(KHI 94).[17] Truth is ultimately linked to problem solving, and specifically to the overcoming of doubt, rather than to intersubjective
recognition of a belief.

Habermas claims that Peirce completed the turn from a transcendental critique of consciousness to a logic of language and inquiry.
Peirce's logic of language held that all elements in human thought
correspond to mediating signs. Every sign is directed to two "minds":
a "quasi-utterer" and a "quasi-interpreter" (PT 88). This link of
thought to signs guarantees the proper limits and objectivity of
meaning. Each sign has three relations:

(1) as a symbol, it relates *to* a thought which interprets it;
(2) as an index, it is a reference *for* an object for which it keeps
    the same meaning for every thought;

---

[15] See Charles Sanders Peirce, *Collected Papers of Charles Sanders Peirce* I–VI, ed.
Charles Hartshorne and Paul Weiss (Cambridge, Mass.: The Belknap Press of Har-
vard University Press, 1931–1935);VII–VIII, ed. Arthur Burks (Cambridge, Mass.:
The Belknap Press of Harvard University Press, 1958), 7.322.

[16] Peirce, *Writings of Charles S. Peirce: A Chronological Edition*, ed. Nathan
Hauser et al., 5 vols. to date (Bloomington: University Indiana Press, 1982), 3.67.

[17] The German term is *gewonnen*. Habermas draws several parallels between the
symbol theories of Cassirer and Peirce. Both claimed that "there is no element in
human consciousness that does not have something corresponding to it in word"
(KHI 331n13). Both resolve the need for continuity in experience by a semiotic
interpretation of consciousness. Habermas notes that Peirce even provided the very
"spectrum" of symbolic forms—images, indexes, expressive gestures, relations of
similarity, and signs—that Cassirer later enumerated. See TK 146. But unlike
Peirce, Cassirer grounded the process of mediation by signs in a transcendental
unity of consciousness. Cassirer read the transcendental unity of consciousness
completely into the process of the mediation of signs. Peirce grounded it in practical
learning processes.

(3) as an icon, it refers *in* or through its own material quality, as an image of the object (KHI 103).[18]

(1) refers to a sign's sense, and (2) to its reference. (3) refers to the material quality of the sign itself (the sign "cat," for example, is a written word materially composed of three letters). Habermas is wary of the unmediated, and thus potentially positivistic, aspect of (3). He argues that (3) is only a special case of (1), since linguistic signs have a "quality" only insofar as they represent meaning relative to the immediate, non-intentional content of experience. Each representation is linked with other thoughts, forming a proposition which represents a fact. What is crucial for Habermas is that each sign has a *force* (or, as Austin later terms it, an "illocutionary power") relative to the thought of an interpreter.[19]

Habermas criticizes Peirce's logic of language on two grounds. First, it derives from itself an ontological concept of reality limited to itself. Second, it remains satisfied with the observation that reality is constituted under conditions of the grammatical forms of universal propositions. Peirce thus conceptualized the interpretation of signs abstractly, detached from a model of linguistic communication between speaker and hearer. In the end, the logic of language is replaced simply by a doctrine of categories that abandons any transcendental conditions (KHI 111).

Though rejecting this theory of signs as a proper ground for a social-theoretic theory of knowledge, Habermas finds Peirce's logic of inquiry more promising for such a task. According to his logic of inquiry, each statement can be transformed into other statements through rules of inference.[20] Peirce claimed that the finality, "the why," of intersubjective inquiry, cannot be determined in a Kantian

---

[18] Peirce, *Collected Papers*, 5.283. Peirce develops a theory of the real as the sum of the signification of all predicates occurring in true statements. The totality of all of these statements, however, is a facticity that we formulate not directly in a linguistic content, but only mediately through the index function of speech.

[19] Peirce, *Chronological Edition*, 1.477.

[20] There are three forms of inference: the determinant *deduction* (the voluntary element), the factual *induction* (the habitual element), and the hypothetical *abduction* (the sensual element). See *Collected Papers*, 5.171–181. Deduction is the least important form of inference. Abduction enlarges our knowledge, which then is verified by inductive facts. Habermas claims that the validity of abduction and induction can be deduced not by formal logic, empirical means, or an ontological structure of reality, but only transcendentally. See KHI 116–117.

synthetic apriori. He claimed simply that *if* we in fact use these inferential procedures, we come nearer to the truth.[21] He linked these procedures of inquiry to real life activities, such as the stabilizing of opinions, the elimination of uncertainty, and the fixation of true belief.

Though endorsing this modification of a logic of inquiry, in *Knowledge and Human Interests* Habermas criticizes Peirce's failure to see that only in the circle of instrumental action can initial conditions be set so as to produce an observable reaction that exhibits a universal effect. If Peirce had taken seriously the communication of inquirers as a subject that transcendentally formed itself under empirical conditions, then he would have been forced to a self-reflection which would have exceeded its own limits as a fixed inquiry. Instead, Peirce made the contradictory assertion that an *intersubjective* inquiry regarding meta-theoretical problems is a condition for purposive rational action that remains *solitary* in principle. Habermas suggests that this later led Peirce to adopt a form of universal realism that ontologized the process of attaining an ever more accurate representation of the world through inquiry (PT 92–93; KHI 131). Thus, the problem of Kant's unknowable "thing-in-itself" reappeared in Peirce's claim that the immediate taken up in the interpretations of our inferential thinking cannot be represented *as* immediate.

It is important to note, however, that Habermas later modifies his early interpretation of Peirce. In "Peirce and Communication" (1989) he presents a more sanguine view of the categories of representation present in Peirce's logic of language. Habermas now acknowledges the intersubjectivity implied in Peirce's claim that every sign has both a "quasi-utterer" and a "quasi-interpreter" (PT 88–89). He admits that Peirce expanded the realm of sign usage into the realm of linguistic forms of expression by showing that the indexical and iconic functions refer to "analogous" actuality and object-relations independent from mere propositional representation. For Habermas these two functions open up Peirce's theory of meaning to the realms of the aesthetic and social. But Habermas continues to

---

[21] *Collected Papers*, 5.354.

criticize Peirce for ignoring the broader "world-disclosing" function of signs.[22]

Habermas continues to level the criticism, however, that Peirce attempted to anchor the chain of signifiers in reality and, like the later Husserl in *Experience and Judgment*, "descend[ed] from the method of a logical genesis of judgments of perception into the realm of pre-predicative experience" (TK 98). Such semantic realism insufficiently accounts for the distinction between first- and second-person discourse, a claim that Habermas develops more fully after *Knowledge and Human Interests*. Habermas argues that learning processes must be grounded, not in a metaphysical concept of na-ture, a position which the later Peirce adopted, but in *actual argu-mentation with others about practical conflict*. Habermas claims that we cannot break out of the sphere of language and argumentation: "we can only establish the relation to reality, which is not equivalent to 'existence,' by projecting a 'transcendence from within'" (PT 103).[23]

For Habermas this view of inner transcendence both respects the "objectivity" of the intersubjectivity of understanding that has be-come reflexive and avoids the ontologization of reality. He argues that if the learning processes of the human species are limited to mirror only what is already contained in nature, they lose the con-vincing power of the better argument, and he espouses instead a kind of "intersubjective realism": agreement always occurs *between* ego and alter *about* something in the world. Both the topic of the agreement and the other with whom agreement is reached give the intersubjective dialogue an objectivity. Habermas claims that the later Peirce abandoned the very moment of "secondness" that limits and distinguishes the self from the other (PT 110–111). Peirce thus could not account for the fact that an actor maintains the facticity of his difference and uniqueness (*Eigensinn*) even in the process of successful communication with the other.[24] But we will later see that

---

[22] Apart from these other realms, Habermas agrees with Manfred Frank that world-disclosure becomes a "syndrome" that spreads to various forms of irratio-nalism.

[23] Habermas also takes up this new view of transcendence from within in "Trans-zendenz von Innen, Transzendenz ins Diesseits." See TK 127–156.

[24] We will see elsewhere how Habermas argues that such *Eigensinn* cannot be absolutized. Despite its deficiencies, Habermas claims that the richness of Peirce's theory is "not yet exhausted." See TK 146.

Habermas's prioritizing of argumentation also poses some threats to the uniqueness of each arguer.

The Need for a Hermeneutic Understanding of the Context of Inquiry

Peirce claimed that intersubjective agreement serves as a medium between knower and reality. But his ontologizing of the representation of the facts determined by the agreement betrayed a kind of positivism, according to Habermas. Habermas thus considers whether Dilthey's hermeneutic methodology of the social sciences overcomes the "dulled reflexivity" of a pre-scientific conception of communication and social integration.[25]

As we have seen, Dilthey set forth the principle that the inquiring subject in the social sciences both observes his cultural world from a distance and remains embedded in it. A subject's experience is two-fold. On one level the ego synthesizes its own manifold of experiences: its world is radically egocentric. But, on another level, the ego's world is intersubjective, because the ego expresses itself only by means of symbols that are intersubjective by nature. The subject moves reflexively through a life history within the medium of linguistic understanding with other subjects.[26] Dilthey thus avoided the difficulty Husserl had in bridging the gap between the ego and the other. For Dilthey the subject has both a horizontal relation to the whole of its linguistic community and a vertical relationship to its specific life history. Hermeneutics provides the universal categories that can decode an otherwise inexpressible and contextualized meaning for the individual.

Although Habermas respects such hermeneutic contextuality, he criticizes the ideal of pure description implicit in Dilthey's concept of re-experiencing (Nacherleben). But he argues that Dilthey's "objectivizing" concept of a reconstruction of meaning-constituting acts fails to mitigate the psychologizing effects of this re-experiencing (KHI 180). By requiring a detached observation, re-experiencing still embodies the kind of interest-free contemplation and picture theory of truth characteristic of positivism. But Habermas does acknowl-

[25] See Dilthey's Selected Works, pp. 462–463; Gesammelte Schriften, 12 vols. (Leipzig and Berlin: Teubner, 1927), 7.79–89.

[26] Dilthey, Gesammelte Schriften, 7.73.

edge that Dilthey avoided the idealism of the later Peirce's final grounding of reality. For Dilthey, the conditions for the possibility of symbolic interpretation require that the object domain is not constituted under the transcendental conditions of the methodology of inquiry, but is confronted as something *already* constituted. We already have seen the influence this had on Heidegger's view of *Dasein*'s temporal situatedness. This detachment achieves a synthesis in which "an interpretation can only grasp its object and penetrate it in a relation in which the interpreter reflects on the object and himself *at the same time* as moments of an objective structure that likewise encompasses both and makes them possible" (KHI 181). Dilthey binds the possible objectivity of human knowing to the condition of the "virtual simultaneity of the interpreter with his object" (KHI 182).[27] The early Habermas adopts this same hermeneutic relation between reflection and simultaneity, but later stipulates that the thing interpreted can be analyzed from the three interpretative perspectives that correspond to the three forms of address in performative use of language. We shall take up this triple speech-theoretic perspective in the next chapter.

Habermas concludes that the difficulty in finding a terminus for thought led Peirce to resort to an ontological flight into universal realism and Dilthey to cling to a thought model of an empathetic psychologism. Peirce proposed a transcendental framework that "pre-forms" experience into a framework of possible technical control; Dilthey proposed a hermeneutic framework that pre-forms meaning into a life history of universal, repeatable effects based on the "reproductive feeling of the psychic states of others" (KHI 182). But neither provided sufficient grounds for knowledge's critical awareness of its own interests.

Habermas claims that the objectivism of either idealism or psychologism is overcome only when *reason itself becomes aware of its interest in the fulfillment of self-reflection.* Here we clearly see Hegel's influence. Habermas proposes that the validity of a statement derives only from knowledge-constitutive interests reproduced under determinant cultural conditions in a life context. This occurs only in the

---

[27] Dilthey speaks of the simultaneity on the level of physical science as a *Zusammenhang* and at the level of the subject as a *psychische Zusammenhang*. See ibid., 82–83.

reflective process of a self-constituting species that realizes that it has a cognitive interest in analyzing the conditions of its emancipation. This is the "interest of reason" (KHI 198). The interest of reason articulates its content in the concept of a formative process in which reason and will are identified to such an extent that reason becomes forceless. The conditions under which the species is reproduced are posited, not through an absolute movement of reflection, but through the conditions of both subjective and objective nature. In Habermas's view—closely linked to Horkheimer and Adorno at this point—reflection depends on the conditions of the individuating socialization of interacting individuals (subjective nature) and the conditions of the material exchange of communicatively acting persons within an environment that must be made technically controllable (objective nature) (KHI 210).

Habermas then turns to Freud's attempt to elucidate scientifically the interplay between the objective and the subjective natures of a subject. He makes the case that Freud's meta-psychology is a genuine science of self-reflection. As a science, it places empirical observations of self-formative processes—the reflexive medium, derived from Hegel, that Habermas has established as legitimate—within invariant *theoretical* structures that can serve to critique human actions.

A Science of Self-Reflection

Unlike Peirce and Dilthey, Freud refrained from interpreting experience through established social and psychological disciplines. Instead he developed the entirely new self-reflective science of psychoanalysis. As a science, his psychoanalysis provides universal rules for a subject's knowledge of the mediating symbolic complexes constituted by both his motives and his instincts. As a self-reflective science, psychoanalysis explicates the structures of conscious and unconscious limits of meaning. Habermas will develop his own science of self-reflection on the basis of his appropriation and critique of Freud's theory.

Freud developed psychoanalysis in part from his early work in dream analysis. In *The Interpretation of Dreams* (1900) he developed a hermeneutic method modeled on a philologically guided interpretation of the "texts" of dreams. He later formed a similar interpretative scheme for the psychoanalytic decoding of the "texts" of neurotic behaviors. Habermas is interested principally in the fact that Freud reconstructed not only the structural distortions in the text of a dream or neurotic behavior, but also *the very structures of text corruption itself* (KHI 217).[28] Since dreams confront the author himself as alienated and incomprehensible, the structures must be elucidated, not by hermeneutics, but by a science of self-reflection (KHI 220).[29]

In chapter 6 of *The Interpretation of Dreams*, Freud listed the structures of the "dream work" that distort the symbolization of instincts initially repressed at childhood.[30] The conscious ego continually represses the unwanted motivations and need dispositions of the id, transforming them into unconscious non-linguistic states. Ordinarily these repressed parts of one's life history remain forgotten in the unconscious. But sleep weakens repression mechanisms, causing the id's unruly instincts to threaten to wake the dreamer. Dream work "guards" sleep by attaching the instincts to various symbolic representations that defuse their force. A similar weakening of repressive mechanisms allows repressed instincts to emerge in neurotic and psychotic behaviors. But since they obey neither the grammatical rules of everyday language nor cultural norms of behavior, the symbolic complexes of both dreams and overt neurotic behavior initially are indecipherable. They manifest themselves as symptoms that persist until they are replaced by a functional equivalent.

Habermas interprets such Freudian symptoms as signs of the self-

---

[28] Lorenzer also uses the analogy of the psyche as a text. He claims that the "textual flaws" that form the subject matter of psychoanalysis are conceived of as the result of repressed motives and privatized needs which in turn lead to the severance of symbols from the realm of public communication. See his *Sprachzerstörung und Rekonstruktion* (Frankfurt am Main: Suhrkamp, 1970).

[29] For a good definition of the distinction between "structure" and "content" applicable at both the individual and the societal levels, see Korthals, "On the Justification of Societal Development Claims." Structures deal with legitimation and justification; content, with actual institutions or ways of solving conflict.

[30] Sigmund Freud, "The Interpretation of Dreams," *The Complete Psychological Works of Sigmund Freud* IV–V, trans. J. Strachey (London: Hogarth Press, 1953). The analytical categories are condensation, displacement, representation (including symbolization), and secondary revision. In the realm of action they are rigidity and repetition compulsion. Freud gives a very comprehensive analysis of the repetition compulsion in *Beyond the Pleasure Principle*, trans. J. Strachey (New York: Norton, 1961), pp. 13–17.

alienation of a subject whose communication *with himself* has been disrupted. The symptoms reveal that the ego has deceived itself about its own identity in its attempt to keep the forces of the id at bay.[31] Such *structural* psychical self-deception is dissolved when the patient recovers the forgotten content of the repressed instincts. The patient must reflexively gain access to the "genetically important phases of life history" in its own excommunicated language (KHI 228).[32] Habermas uses the term "excommunicated" to emphasize the linguistic nature of both the patient's reinterpretation and the therapist's possible linguistic construction of the repressed content. The patient then either affirms or denies the validity of the construc-tions.[33] Habermas stresses that such a construction aims, not at the understanding of symbolic structures, but at the structures of the act of self-reflection itself (KHI 228). This same relation between symbolic content and the act that understands it is found in Haber-mas's later distinction between the content of a sentence and its reflexive relation to the claim formed from it.

How does the patient find a cure for himself? Freud was aware that neither the disappearance of symptoms nor the patient's affir-mation of an analyst's interpretation of the cause of the symptoms is sufficient ground for the verification of a cure.[34] Habermas agrees that a psychoanalytic interpretation's conditioned prognosis can be falsified, not through controlled observation of the disappearance of

---

[31] Bernard Flynn sharply disagrees with Habermas's claims about Freud's view of the relation between ego and id. Habermas assumes that, although the id is the alienated form of the ego, in principle the ego can eventually reconcile itself with the id. Flynn argues that Freud sees no possibility of such reconciliation; the ego emerges from the id and continues to obey the suggestions that arise from the id. See Flynn's *Political Philosophy at the Close of Metaphysics*, p. 51. Lacan, in a similar vein, lauds Freud's discovery of "alterity in the heart of ipseity" and the "uncon-scious as the discourse of the other." See Lacan, *Écrits: A Selection*, trans. A. Sheri-dan (New York: Norton, 1977), pp. 307–308.

[32] Ricoeur builds his semantics of desire from these traces that repressed instincts leave behind in their symptoms. See his *Freud and Philosophy*, trans. D. Savage (New Haven, Conn.: Yale University Press, 1970), p. 387.

[33] Ordinarily a linguistic interpreter can mediate directly between two speakers of different languages through some kind of transcendent level of interpretation. There is no such level in psychoanalysis. Freud notes that the patient's affirmation or denial of the analyst's construction usually takes place indirectly through produc-ing new memories and associations that complete and fulfill the construction. See his "Konstruktionen in der Analyse," in his *Gesammelte Werke* XVI, 3rd ed. (Frank-furt am Main: Fischer, 1968), pp. 44–53.

[34] See ibid., p. 49.

symptoms, but only through the patient's "experience of reflection" upon the success of its formative processes. For Habermas, the patient's "yes" must produce an "act of recollection and agreement" that completes the verification of the construction (KHI 270). Even in his later writings, Habermas holds to this possibility of *internal* agreement of a subject with himself. But what exactly is the standpoint from which a subject can perform a reflexive self-critique of his own distortions?

Habermas bases self-critique on the early Hegel's phenomenological experiences of reflection and recognition.[35] To heal himself, the patient must see himself *through the eyes of another* and reflexively learn the origin of its self-caused symptoms (KHI 235–236). The patient must identify with his own "alienated self" as the early Hegel's criminal did: both "selves" must recognize a damaged ethical totality and, *precisely through this recognition,* be restored to the totality. Thus, analytic dialogue attempts to instantiate a mutual struggle for recognition between the self of the ego and the alienated objectivization of itself in the id (KHI 258). The use of language in this dialogue bestows two distinct powers on the ego. First, the ego can "stabilize" itself by fastening symbols to what is internal to it, thus achieving intersubjective "existence." Second, it can test the reality of objective culturally-interpreted needs and interests through intersubjective public dialogue (KHI 238). Habermas insists that any instinct theory that views instincts apart from the linguistic and intersubjective "meaning-structure of the lifeworld" falls prey to objectivism and positivism (KHI 256).[36]

Habermas also considers the structures of id, ego, and superego that Freud derived from observing patients who successfully overcame their own strategies of repression through analytic reflection. Freud argued that the ego is the "authority" that decides which de-

---

[35] Ricoeur agrees with Habermas's claim that Freud's psychoanalytic theory is very Hegelian, pointing to an obvious parallel between the master/slave dialectic and the Oedipal complex. Ricoeur claims that Freud rejects an Husserlian "perceptual intersubjectivity" in favor of an Hegelian threefold process of intersubjective recognition: the "reduplication of desire in desire," the education of desire in the struggle for recognition, and the inauguration of the struggle in a non-egalitarian situation. See *Freud and Philosophy*, pp. 387–388.

[36] It is noteworthy that here Habermas is using the phenomenological concept of the "lifeworld" well before he systematically develops it in the second volume of *Theory of Communicative Action*.

sires and demands of the id are to be repressed.[37] The ego has a mediating function that operates not only between the desires (both the drives and the id) and reality, but also between the desires and the superego's internalized norms. The superego, an agency of defense unknown to the ego, is formed through the open-ended identification with the expectations of the primary object.[38] Freud argued that psychological development is coextensive with the strengthening of the ego against the assaults of both superego and id. Habermas adopts the same basic scheme, claiming that the ego carries out its repression through a "flight" that substitutes a symptom for the unwanted drive (KHI 240). But Habermas "socializes" this structure by insisting that this flight is carried out only within the "drive-representing" capacity of *language*. Neurotic symptoms are caused by ego "desymbolizations" and "delinguistification."[39]

Habermas also adopts Freud's claim that self-reflection and moral responsibility are linked. For the Freudian therapist, "analytic knowledge is also moral insight, because in the movement of self-reflection the unity of theoretical reason and practical reason has not yet been undone" (KHI 236). Freud argued that a patient must take responsibility for his psychological illness.[40] Habermas modifies this by arguing that the patient's moral development can be realized only in an emancipated society in which there is a non-authoritarian dialogue and a frame of reference in which the truth of statements is based on "anticipating the realization of the good life" (KHI 314). Although Habermas later abandons this substantive emphasis on the good life in favor of a more procedural and deontological approach to social responsibility, he continually maintains that individual emancipation requires the existence of social institutions which have internalized a certain level of rational self-reflection.

Habermas's Meta-psychology

Although Habermas adopts the basic outline of Freud's psychoanalytic science of reflection, he criticizes the inconsistency of its under-

---

[37] See Tugendhat, *Self-Consciousness and Self-Determination*, p. 130.

[38] See John Thompson, *Critical Hermeneutics: A Study in the Thought of Paul Ricoeur and Jürgen Habermas* (New York: Cambridge University Press, 1981), p. 200.

[39] For more on how Habermas understands this "desymbolization," see his and N. Luhmann's *Theorie der Gesellschaft oder Sozialtechnologie: Was leistet die Systemforschung?* (Frankfurt am Main: Suhrkamp, 1971), pp. 120–121.

[40] Freud even claimed that we must take this same responsibility for our dreams. See "Interpretation of Dreams," p. 620.

determination of the very reflective processes that produced it. Habermas claims that Freud omitted the very movement of reflection that overcomes the pathological states of compulsion from the ego functions on the meta-psychological level (KHI 245). In fact, Freud always envisioned psychoanalysis as a natural science. He never discarded his early energy-distribution model of the psyche and even held that psychoanalysis could in principle eventually be reduced to the natural science of pharmacology. Habermas thus characterizes Freud's theory of self-reflection as "physicalistic," because it never fully specified its operational assumptions (KHI 253).

Habermas construes a proper meta-psychological theory as a "general interpretation of self-formative processes" (KHI 254). Meta-psychology first assumes that every therapeutic self-narrative takes on the inherent self-reflexivity and universality of the ordinary language it uses. Borrowing from Lorenzer, Habermas argues that meta-psychology operates on two methodological levels: the level of universal interpretations accessible to empirical verification, and the level of meta-hermeneutical assumptions about communicative behavior. Meta-psychology represents motives, not as blind forces, but as subjectively guided, symbolically mediated, and reciprocally limited intentions. All irrational and unconscious motives are considered part of a first nature that can be subjected to the second nature of cognitive and linguistic rational formulation.

By bringing unconscious intentions and motives under the conscious control of a second nature, meta-psychology operates on the level of Hegel's reconciling "causality of fate" (KHI 256). Psychoanalysis attempts to reconcile irrational motives with rational life. In a rare reference to a theologian, Habermas later compares this process of reconciliation to Klaus Heinrich's idea of a religious covenant. Heinrich argues that the Jewish covenant did not exclude those who disobeyed its precepts, but continually sought reconciliation with them (PDM 324). Habermas argues that all social actors are, in a similar way, members of the "covenant" of communicative reason. Those who follow communicative reason are not free to form a detached elite, but are compelled to seek reconciliation with those who resort to instrumental methods of resolving conflict.[41] Many psychologists, Freudian and non-Freudian alike, reject such a reconciliatory

---

[41] See Sander Griffioen, "The Metaphor of the Covenant in Habermas," *Faith and Philosophy*, 8, No. 4 (October 1991), 525–526.

hypothesis on the grounds that not all unconscious or irrational psychic content can be made conscious. But Habermas, following Wittgenstein, assumes that all mental states can in principle be made "public." Habermas's claim that all meaning content can be formulated in meaningful propositions rings consistent with his intersubjective understanding of meaning and truth.

Habermas's formulation of the meta-psychology of self-reflection in his early work is thus based on three reconstructed principles:

(1) there is a structure to everyday undistorted communication;
(2) language distortion emerges from the confusion of the prelinguistic and linguistic stages of the organization of symbols; and
(3) these distortions can be traced to deviant processes of socialization extending back to childhood.[42]

Habermas argues that the proper interrelation of the ego, id, and superego is established, not through a Diltheyian hermeneutic circle, but through the reconstruction of actual personal histories identifiable by consistent and unique "horizons of expectation" (KHI 262). The historical meaning of these expectations constitutes both the ego-identity of a unified life history and the group identity of a collective life history. These two identities form the basis of an invariant developmental structure within which the human sciences can make empirically testable predications about human behavior.[43] The empirical verification of a general interpretation is thus carried out, not through the presuppositions of instrumental analysis, but through the self-verification of *all who recognize themselves in an interpretation.* When formulated systematically, these validated generalized interpretations provide both causal explanations and conditioned prognoses. Thus, psychoanalysis makes causal claims not only in em-

---

[42] See Thompson, *Critical Hermeneutics*, pp. 194–195. Although agreeing with Lorenzer that there are structural aspects of psychological distortion, Habermas does not adopt his "depth hermeneutic" reconstructive appropriation of Freud's analysis of specifically incomprehensible expressions and neurotic symptoms. Lorenzer draws up a lexicon of the meanings that are formulated in private languages. Habermas criticizes his "scenic understanding" for relying on theoretical assumptions, not on the skilled application of communicative competence.

[43] See Habermas, "The Hermeneutic Claim to Universality," in *Contemporary Hermeneutics*, ed. J. Bleicher (Boston: Routledge & Kegan Paul, 1980), p. 201.

pirical, but also in *intentional* contexts "understood and reconstructed according to grammatical rules" (KHI 272).[44] By means of a verified prognosis, a subject can overcome his attachment to the causal forces behind a symptom.

Although Habermas's explication of the procedures by which these meta-theoretic rules are formed is clear, his delineation of the rules themselves and their application to human behaviors is rather opaque. Are they patterns of behavior found in a large set of empirically observed behaviors? What are the corresponding conditions for falsifying such a prognosis? How are all these intentions intersubjectively accessible? Moreover, his meta-psychology is hindered both by his insistence that subjects are the ultimate arbiters of psychoanalytic interpretations and by his adherence to phenomenological concepts, such as "intention" and "horizon." Several commentators have pointed out the insufficiencies of these claims. Axel Honneth calls Habermas's equating of self-reflection and reconstruction of ego structures "simplistic."[45] Rorty claims that Habermas's notion of self-reflection follows the path of Russell, C. I. Lewis, Ayer, and the logical positivists who adopted a transcendental standpoint completely divorced from the domain of empirical psychology.[46]

Adolf Grünbaum has made an extensive critique of Habermas's psychoanalytic claims. He holds that Habermas's meta-psychology misconstrues the verification methods of an empirical science. He criticizes Habermas for establishing the patient as the epistemic arbiter of the validity of a general interpretation, since no other medical science bestows such a privilege on the patient. For Grünbaum the verification of a psychoanalytic construction requires the affirmation not only of the patient, but also of both the analyst and an objective

---

[44] Susanne Langer locates grammar on the level, not of symbols, but of discourse that deals with relations among symbols. See her *Philosophy in a New Key*, 3rd ed. (Cambridge, Mass.: Harvard University Press, 1957), p. 66.

[45] Honneth points out that Habermas understood the task of ideology critique on the model of a hermeneutic self-reflection that would overcome the self-misunderstanding of either an individual's or a society's formative processes. See *Kritik der Macht*, p. 309.

[46] See "Epistemological Behaviorism and Analytic Philosophy," in *Hermeneutics and Praxis*, ed. R. Hollinger (Notre Dame, Ind.: University of Notre Dame Press, 1985), p. 114. But Rorty immediately qualifies this accusation: "I cannot claim to have grasped his project well enough to be sure that this criticism is to the point" (p. 115). Holub also argues that the "quasi-transcendental" status of Habermas's notion of self-reflection is problematic. See *Critic in the Public Sphere*, p. 9.

analytic observer.[47] Habermas's self-verification procedure thus excludes the possibility that epidemiological studies could falsify a general interpretation. But Grünbaum makes two unsubstantiated claims about Habermas's interpretation of Freud. First, due to what seems to be an oversight of Freud's later writings, Grünbaum claims that Freud himself held for the priority of the therapist's interpretations over those of the patient. Much evidence indicates, however, that the later Freud did in fact bestow a large degree of interpretative power on the patient himself.[48] Second, Grünbaum claims that Habermas failed to account for the auxiliary hypotheses regarding both initial conditions and theoretical frameworks that any empirical experimental procedure must take into account. He claims that Habermas's linking of psychoanalysis with the natural sciences is a "pseudo-asymmetry."[49] He also criticizes Habermas for arguing that the treatment setting is the sole arena for all validation or disconfirmation of universal propositions.[50] Although Grünbaum is correct about Habermas's neglect of the some of the assumptions about causality and inference in psychic processes, he is incorrect in assuming that a hermeneutic self-verification has to follow the same metatheoretical assumptions as an empirical science. For Habermas, the crucial difference is that a science of self-reflection is aware of its own limits as a science.

Although Habermas does not deal extensively with psychoanalytic theory after *Knowledge and Human Interests*, he does not give up on the psychoanalytic method entirely.[51] Even in *Philosophical Discourse of Modernity*, he still maintains that the analytic conversation

---

[47] See his *The Foundations of Psychoanalysis: A Philosophical Critique* (Berkeley: University of California Press, 1984), pp. 23–26. Grünbaum calls Habermas's characterization of Freud's psychoanalysis as a scientistic misunderstanding a "myth."

[48] See specifically Freud's "Konstruktionen in der Analyse," pp. 45–53.

[49] *Foundations of Psychoanalysis*, p. 36. For a formulation of this principle see Duhem's *The Aim and Structure of Physical Theory*, trans. P. P. Wiener (Princeton, N.J.: Princeton University Press, 1954), p. 187.

[50] *Foundations of Psychoanalysis*, p. 38. In the rat-man case, for instance, Grünbaum argues that what falsified the diagnosis was not the rat-man's experience of reflection, but his mother's extraclinical testimony.

[51] He deals with psychological issues again in "Moralentwicklung und Ich-Identität," *Zur Rekonstruktion des historischen Materialismus* (Frankfurt am Main: Suhrkamp, 1976), pp. 63–92; and in a work coauthored with Rainer Döbert and Gertrud Nunner-Winkler entitled *Entwicklung des Ichs* (Cologne: Kiepenheuer & Witsch, 1977), especially in "Zur Einführung," pp. 9–28.

between doctor and patient offers a suitable model for employing narrative tools in a dialogically conducted self-critique.

> This self-critique, which is aimed at eliminating pseudo-nature, that is, the pseudo-aprioris made up of unconsciously motivated perceptual barriers and compulsion to action, is related to the narratively recollected entirety of a course of life or way of life. The analytic dissolution of hypostatizations, of self-engendered objective illusions, is due to an experience of reflection [PDM 299].

Habermas stipulates that although psychoanalytic self-reflection can liberate the patient from some psychic illusions or anonymous rule-systems, it is limited in its scope. It can neither provide liberation for the *totality* of a course of life nor completely illuminate what is experienced in the lifeworld. Habermas concludes that there are two types of self-reflection that overcome the limits of the philosophy of consciousness: rational reconstruction and methodologically guided self-critique.

Social Legitimation and Truth: The Expansion of Reflection Beyond Psychoanalytic Dialogue

In 1962, Habermas published *The Structural Transformation of the Public Sphere*, in which he analyzed the processes by which social structures are modified and changed. By 1973, with the publication of *Legitimation Crisis*, he was already in the process of applying his newly minted structures of critical reflection to problems of social integration. He stipulated that conflicting social norms be understood as hypothetical norms of action "on whose competing validity claims judgment could be passed in practical discourse" (LC 28).

Habermas thus develops a form of social rationality which *theoretically* refigures social and systemic distortions, now termed "conflicts" or "crises." This theoretical model construes many modern economic dysfunctions as crises that have lost the character of events accessible to self-reflection and merely acquired the objectivity of natural events (LC 30). But Habermas argues that if a crisis is described as an empirical phenomenon independent of either communication theory or systems theory, it loses its relation to *truth* (LC 28). The values and norms in accordance with which any motives are formed have an immanent relation to truth. Thus, the moral and political crisis tendencies in advanced capitalism can be analyzed, on the assumption that moral and scientific systems follow "inner logics" (LC 88). Such conflicts are resolved only if the validity of all norms is linked to discursive will formation. Social norms should be regulated through compromise or formal norms of action that can be made the subject of discussion (LC 89).

Habermas uses Piaget's levels of ontogenetic development to define the stages of reflective consciousness. The highest stage is a universalistic morality "which can be traced back to fundamental norms of rational speech" (LC 95). Thus, a person's compliance with a norm on the basis of its legitimacy represents a higher level of development than a compliance based on the latent force of sanctions. The higher levels of development link the motivational function of compliance with norms more closely to the norms' truth value.

Habermas argues that discursive reflection can overcome generalizable interests that have been suppressed either by individuals or by groups (LC 113). The reflection involved here imagines oppressive "limit cases" to be overcome:

> it is meaningful and possible to reconstruct (even for the normal case of norms recognized without conflict) the hidden interest positions of involved individuals or groups by counterfactually imagining [*fingieren*] the limit case of a conflict between the involved parties in which they would be forced to consciously perceive their interests and strategically assert them, instead of satisfying basic interests simply by actualizing institutional values as is normally the case [LC 114].

After social scientists propose conflict-free hypothetical norms, those to be affected by the norms confirm them as true or false.

Then Habermas returns the application of the theory of discursive legitimation from the society back to the individual. He realizes that the institutionalization of such an intersubjective demand for the legitimation of action would effectively signal the "end" of the bourgeois, or conventional, individual. But he argues that "the reflexivity of the person grows in proportion to his externalization" (LC 91, 128).[52] By decentering its own interests in adherence to intersubjec-

---

[52] Habermas then highlights the phenomenon of the "adolescent crisis" which occurs when universalistic values systems and countercultural experiential complexes clash.

tively determined norms, the ego stabilizes itself. Yet, as this occurs, the post-conventional ego is exposed to more and more contingencies and vulnerabilities, and thus the possibility of alienation remains a constant threat. Continual vigilance is needed to safeguard both individual and social emancipation.

A CRITICAL SCIENCE OF SELF-REFLECTION:
THE DEBATE WITH GADAMER

Even as Habermas shifted his focus back and forth between individual and social critique, his basic adherence to a *scientific* form of reflection remained constant. In his inaugural lecture, Habermas had located the power of emancipation, not in historical-hermeneutic sciences, but in sciences of self-reflection. Thus, only a self-reflective science can properly be termed *critical*. In so doing, Habermas set himself against hermeneuticists, like Gadamer, who claimed that the critical power of hermeneutic methods is sufficient for emancipation. But only in the context of his later debate with Gadamer does Habermas further spell out just how discursive procedures are needed to supplement hermeneutic interpretations.

Gadamer claims that an historical and tradition-bound hermeneutic theory can be emancipative without a methodological self-reflection upon its own knowledge-constitutive interest. Like Habermas, Gadamer rejects Chomsky's claim that one can construct a theory of meaning from ordinary language apart from an analysis of its reflexive and transcendent operations. But Habermas claims that Gadamer overlooks the fact that ordinary language contains two unique reflexive capacities: the reflexivity by which it can express its own limits, and the reflexivity by which a language user can translate from one ordinary language to another.[53] Habermas criticizes theories of formal languages that understand ordinary language as merely a "last meta-language."[54] He argues that such formalism excludes the fact that speakers can determine *ad hoc* rules of application for individual sentences. However, both he and Gadamer agree that or-

---

[53] Habermas, "A Review of Gadamer's *Truth and Method*," in *Hermeneutics and Modern Philosophy*, ed. Brice R. Wachterhauser (Albany: State University of New York Press, 1986), pp. 244–245.
[54] "Hermeneutic Claim to Universality," p. 182.

dinary language forms a system that is not closed like a formal language, but transcends the limited perspectives of each user. Ordinary language can communicate simultaneously both a manifest universalizable message and a latent message as to its particular application. Both agree that this reflexive quality of ordinary language is the basis for metaphor and other indirect uses of language.

Habermas also shares Gadamer's suspicions regarding the narrowness of the later Wittgenstein's rule-bound conception of language.[55] In the *Philosophical Investigations*, Wittgenstein refers to the problem of thought and its rules only in the actual use of expressions such as "understanding," "meaning," and "thinking." Rule and rule application are inseparable.[56] But Gadamer argues that linguistic understanding is not a passive absorption of rules, but an active application of rules to specific situations. Although Wittgenstein showed that the rules of linguistic communication imply the conditions of possibility of their own application, he failed to observe that they also include the condition of possibility of their interpretation *over and against other forms of life.*[57]

Habermas and Gadamer, however, diverge in their views of how rule-guided interpretations apply to particular situations. Gadamer

---

[55] Since the grammar of language games cannot be reconstructed according to general rules at the symbolic level, Wittgenstein held that linguistic understanding must be derived from the virtual repetition of the training through which "native" speakers are socialized into a form of life. Every language game is completely ordered by formal rules. Gadamer argues that this understanding of language neglects the practical reality that the accompanying reflection on the application of linguistic rules "emerges only when a language game becomes problematic." See Habermas, "Review of *Truth and Method*," p. 338.

[56] For a discussion of the problem of rules, see Herbert Schnäldelbach's "Bermerkungen über Rationalität und Sprache," in *Kommunikation und Reflexion*, ed. W. Kuhlmann and E. Böhler (Frankfurt am Main: Suhrkamp, 1982), pp. 347–368.

[57] Gadamer claims that an interpreter of a text produces a new language which adequates itself to the original text. The interpreter can in principle "fuse horizons" with the otherness of the text. See *Truth and Method*, p. 340. Borrowing from Collingwood, Gadamer claims that the interpreter initiates a dialectic of questions and answers in a "conversation" with the text's possible meaning. The interpreter is part of the text's own tradition of interpretation and regards himself as "addressed by it." Contextual application is *always already* a structural dimension of all understanding. Gadamer's strong version of contextualism, however, still acknowledges the temporal distance from the interpreter which both the text and its tradition of interpretation maintain. For a good description of Gadamer's position, see Werner Jeanrond, *Text and Interpretation as Categories of Theological Thinking* (New York: Crossroads, 1988), pp. 24ff.

argues that one interprets, not from the point of view of an ideal theoretical observer, but through a kind of *phronesis* with a view to a possible action. We have a transcendental necessity to *project* the provisional "end-state" of a system of reference out of our immediate horizon in order that our interpretations become applicable to life practice. In *Truth and Method* Gadamer argues that our natural "linguisticality" (*Sprachlichkeit*) already guarantees that we make this transcendent application. We have no need of scientific methods of application.[58] He refrains from applying a method of critical reflection to any "objective" structure, such as tradition or authority.[59] Following Heidegger, he assumes that a tradition supplies a "supporting consensus" that *precedes* all understanding and misunderstanding.[60] Even the use of a psychoanalytic treatment is supported by a prior social consensus.

Habermas rejects Gadamer's claim that the moment of application is intrinsic to linguisticality. He claims that Gadamer's theory of innate linguisticality fails to furnish a critique of the *brokenness* of intersubjectivity and the systemic distortion of communication.[61] Gadamer's emphasis on the skill of rule application leads him to a theory of meaning that is overly context-bound. His hermeneutical analysis "automatically" corrects a misunderstanding by uncovering the previous consensus.[62] Habermas does not dispute Gadamer's claim about the importance of a preceding consensus in any present

---

[58] Gadamer sees the beginnings of linguisticality in Plato's phrase, "everything that exists is reflected in the mirror of language." See his "Rhetorik, Hermeneutik, und Ideologiekritik," in *Kleine Schriften* I (Tübingen: Mohr, 1967). See also Thomas McCarthy, *The Critical Theory of Jürgen Habermas* (Cambridge, Mass.: The MIT Press, 1978), p. 170.

[59] Gadamer assumes that authority within a tradition is mutually *recognized* by the individuals served by it, and thus cannot be an instrument of domination. He fails to see any kind of conflict between authority and reason. Borrowing from Hegel, he claims that since authority is sustained by dogmatic recognition, it is superior to other types of dogmatism. See Habermas, "Hermeneutic Claim to Universality," p. 207.

[60] Ibid., p. 203.

[61] Rüdiger Bubner agrees with Habermas's criticisms. Bubner finds a "resignation" in Gadamer's affirmation of praxis. Since *doxa* indeed characterizes our knowledge and rhetoric in everyday life, we simply have to acknowledge that there are no objective standards that enable us to judge between good and bad usage. We are simply left with no better standard than the Aristotelian practical ideal of the good life. See Bubner's "Summation," *Cultural Hermeneutics*, 2, No. 4 (February 1975), 360–361.

[62] Gadamer, "Die Universalität des hermeneutischen Problems," in *Kleine Schriften* I (Tübingen: Mohr, 1967), pp. 104, 124.

conflict, but only *how the consensus is defined*. Habermas argues that the truth of a consensus derives, not from its *de facto* occurrence, but from its ability to meet certain meta-linguistic criteria. Gadamer assumes that we legitimate problematized action through discovering a given consensus that supports it; Habermas argues that we must enter into a dialogue with the actual participants here and now in order to confront a proposed norm with transcendent truth claims. Habermas adopts Apel's requirement, derived from Mead, that the consensus must be established with a meta-theoretical "unlimited community of interpreters."[63]

Habermas concludes that one must apply critical reflection not just to unjust practices, as Gadamer claims, but also to the *genesis of traditions that maintain them*.[64] Habermas builds a critical hermeneutics that can step outside the dialogical structure of everyday language in order to use language "in a monological way" to formally construct theories that guide the organization of purposive rational action, as he did in *Legitimation Crisis*.[65] He thus criticizes, not Gadamer's critique of the false objectivistic aspects of scientific thinking, but only his dismissal of all methodological procedures. Such procedures are required to uncover the interests behind the thinking.[66]

Concluding Summary: The Meta-linguistic Structures of Emancipation

As a result of his debate with Gadamer and his construction of a critical theory of social science, the early Habermas formed a critique

---

[63] "Hermeneutic Claim to Universality," p. 205. See Apel's "Szientismus oder transzendentale Hermeneutik?" in *Hermeneutic und Dialektik*, 2 vols. (Tübingen: Mohr, 1970), 2.48; *Transformation der Philosophie*, 2 vols. (Frankfurt am Main: Suhrkamp, 1973), especially Volume II. Habermas will later transform Apel's ideal community into an "ideal speech situation."

[64] "Review of *Truth and Method*," p. 359. Borrowing from his earlier critique of Marx, Habermas claims that reflection reveals that symbolic conditions of language depend upon non-normative influences which stem from social labor. Changes in the modes of production engender new linguistic interpretations which restructure world-views.

[65] "Hermeneutic Claim to Universality," p. 188.

[66] But in a 1975 article responding to accusations of his "rejection" of scientific methodology, Gadamer adopts a more critical perspective. He argues for a philo-

of ideology that is a kind of psychoanalytic reflection writ large: "The structures of linguistically originated intersubjectivity, which can be prototypically differentiated in elementary speech acts, are equally constitutive for both social and personality systems."[67] By determining the collective interpretation of needs within historically defined conditions, critical theory remains bound to the human contextuality of actions.[68] We meet the same "consciousness structures" both in social institutions and in individual socialized action competencies.[69] Habermas locates both the formation of just social action and the critique of unjust social action within the inner rational perspective of ordinary language users.

At this point Habermas has worked out the following principles for an emancipative theory of reflection:

(1) every knowledge, even of one's private states, must be reflexively aware of how it is limited by its own practical interest,

(2) an interest, whether empirical, social, or psychological, is limited by its possible lack of generalizability relative to the interests of others,

(3) valid knowledge must transcend the limits of what can be projected hermeneutically from its context, and seek a further theoretically explicated validity.

---

sophical form of critique that would include a modern ideal of method and maintain a "condition of solidarity with and justification of our practical living." Gadamer now admits that "immediate and natural interaction in the course of daily life is no longer the unique source and the dominant mode for the elaboration of common convictions and normative ideas." See his "Hermeneutics and Social Science," *Cultural Hermeneutics*, 2 (1975), 313. Did Habermas's criticisms induce this modification?

[67] Habermas, *Zur Rekonstruktion*, p. 12.

[68] Thompson, *Critical Hermeneutics*, p. 95.

[69] Habermas, *Zur Rekonstruktion*, p. 12. Michiel Korthals criticizes Habermas's facile equating of individual and social structures. He claims that Habermas bases social structures on principles of law and morality derived from ontogenetic development of levels of morality and right. But he argues that Habermas fails to take into account the fact that although individuals cannot justify *personality development* from different points of view given different audiences, a collective can justify *societal development* in the presence of an external audience which does not belong to the collective. Without this distinction, Habermas's social critic lacks the flexibility needed to critique a social development claim while still remaining in the discourse of his or her own society. See "On the Justification of Societal Validity Claims," p. 36.

(1) will remain unchanged and unexplicated in his later work. As for (2), Habermas later develops a more empirical understanding of the social context of interest validation, based on an analysis of the work of Mead and Parsons. At this point in Habermas's early works, (3) is the most problematic. He has not made salient exactly what constitutes the structures by which a consensus can be determined as universally valid. On the one hand, he wants to construct his entire theory of meaning from the reflexivity of context-bound ordinary language. Like Hegel, he wants to distance himself from the Romantic's illusion of an absolute, self-grounded autonomy detached from "the soil of contingency on which it finds itself."[70] On the other hand, like Apel, he wants a kind of transcendent viewpoint from which one can critique unjust structures.[71] This means that he must refer to some kind of idealization that transcends the contingent interests of the participants.

In the next chapter I shall take up how Habermas uses speech act theory and empirical studies of functional individual and social competencies to develop structures of argumentation that determine validity of claims. After criticizing Max Weber's claim—which also influenced Adorno and Horkheimer—that the Enlightenment failed to provide a non-instrumental method for rational critique, Habermas develops a comprehensive theory of communicative action that determines how subjects can rationally coordinate their interests with other subjects.

---

[70] "Review of *Truth and Method*," p. 357.
[71] See Thompson, *Critical Theory of Jürgen Habermas*, p. 184.

3

Habermas's Development of a Reflective Acceptability Theory of Truth

Richard Bernstein claims that the early Habermas failed to distinguish properly between two "classical" forms of self-reflection:

(1) the context-bound self-reflection of reason on the universal and necessary conditions of its employment, which Kant explicated in the *First Critique*; and

(2) the context-free self-reflection that emancipates a subject from dependence upon hypostatized powers, which Kant explicated in "What Is Enlightenment."[1]

(1) is the synthetic form of transcendental reflection that determines the limits of possible experience and (2) is Kant's later synthetic form of emancipatory reflection that determines the proper limits of an individual or a social will.[2] It also forms the basis of Hegel's theory of reflection. The early Habermas used (1) in his formulation of knowledge-constitutive interest and (2) in his analysis of the emancipatory theories of Freud and Marx. But Bernstein claims that Habermas neither fully explained the normative foundations nor adequately elucidated the dialogical character of (2). Bernhard Heidtmann also criticizes the narrow view of reflection implicit in Habermas's early formulation of reflection. Although he affirms Ha-

---

[1] See Bernstein's "Introduction," in *Habermas and Modernity* (Cambridge, Mass.: The MIT Press, 1985), p. 13.

[2] Like Bernstein, Apel also claims that Habermas failed to distinguish between Kant's transcendental self-reflection on the general conditions of the possibility of knowledge, and Hegel's critical self-reflection on the unconscious restraints that inhibit self-formative processes. See Apel's "Wissenschaft als Emanzipation? Eine kritische Würdigung der Wissenschaftskonzeption der kritische Theorie," in *Materialien zu Habermas' "Erkenntnis und Interesse,"* ed. F. Dallmayr (Frankfurt am Main: Suhrkamp, 1974), pp. 318–348.

bermas's attempt to overcome the one-sidedness of Luhmann's analytically derived systems theory, he claims that Habermas erred by adopting a synthetic view of speech based on a social grounding of individuation. Heidtmann concludes that while Luhmann analyzes society *realistically* from the point of view of the dominated class member, Habermas analyzes society *nominalistically* from the point of view of the bourgeois subject. In Hegelian terms, Habermas rejects determining reflection in favor of positing reflection. Heidtmann concludes that Habermas's exclusive reliance on individual reflection robs his analysis of all possibility of systems critique.[3]

After the publication of *Knowledge and Human Interests*, Habermas soon acknowledged his need to explain more clearly his uses of these two types of reflection. He admitted that

> it occurred to me only later that the traditional use of the term "reflection," which goes back to German Idealism, covers (and confuses) two things: on the one hand, it denotes the reflection on the conditions of potential abilities of a knowing, speaking, and acting subject as such; on the other hand, it denotes the reflection on unconsciously produced constraints to which a determinate subject (or a determinate group of subjects, or a determinate species subject) succumbs in its process of self-formation.[4]

He describes the first type as reconstructive reflection on the conditions of the intuitive know-how of various sciences and the second type as self-reflection on unconsciously produced individual and social constraints.[5] In order to find a coherent account of both senses of reflection, in the early 1970s he abandoned his project of analyzing psychoanalysis and critical hermeneutics and turned to an analysis of theories of language use and sociology. He argued that both types of reflection obtain in speech act theory, since it assumes that all

---

[3] This critique, though unabashedly Marxist, is instructive. See Bernhard Heidtmann, "Systemwissenschaftliche Reflexion und gesellschaftliches Sein: Zur dialektischen Bestimmung der Kategorie des objektiven Scheins," in *Marxistische Gesellschaftsdialektik oder "Systemtheorie der Gesellschaft"?* (Berlin: Marxistische Blätter, 1977), pp. 85–86. Heidtmann argues that only Marx achieves true critique by adopting—then materializing—Hegel's dialectical determining form of reflection.

[4] Habermas, "Nachwort (1973)," in *Erkenntnis und Interesse* (Frankfurt am Main: Suhrkamp, 1973), p. 411.

[5] "Some Difficulties in the Attempt to Link Theory and Practice," in *Theory and Practice*, trans. J. Viertel (Boston: Beacon, 1973), pp. 22–24.

knowledge claims (1) are also claims about the legitimacy of the way in which actions are *coordinated* (2). The two types of reflection thus interpenetrate each other. Thus, Habermas's early concern with the theoretical grounds of knowledge-constitutive interest gave way to a linguistically guided critique of all claims to truth.[6] Using Mead's theory of social interaction, he then analyzed these reflexive processes on the basis of their use in actual social interactions, particularly in the interactions required for reaching understanding. He thus constructed a theory of discursive reflection that specifies the means by which subjective limits of thinking and willing are overcome.

In this chapter I shall outline and analyze the way in which Habermas explicates the reflective background conditions of this discursive theory of truth. I shall focus most specifically on the structures of rational or reflective acceptability implicit in argumentation about contested validity claims (see OPC 356–357). To accomplish this analysis, I must examine his critique of semantic theories of meaning and truth, his appropriation and modification of speech act theory, his theory of critical self-reflection, and finally his systematic formulation of a theory of discursive rationality. In the course of this analysis, the originality of his linguistically derived "solution" to the traditional problems of reflection should become clear. However, I will also note how some of the contextual background conditions of his discursive theory of truth, particularly its temporal features, remain underdetermined.

HABERMAS'S CRITIQUE OF SEMANTIC THEORIES OF MEANING AND TRUTH

Before turning to Habermas's appropriation and modification of speech act theory, we need to look at how he criticizes several semantic theories of meaning and truth. He classifies semantic theories as

---

[6] See Honneth, *Kritik der Macht*, p. 310. Honneth maps out how Habermas systematically enlarged his theory of social evolution in the 1970s, progressively moving from a phylogenetic to an ontogenetic analysis. As a result of his debate with Luhmann, Habermas applies the reconstructive process borrowed from universal pragmatics to the internal logic of social development. He also criticizes the "reflexive compulsion to objectify" present in all forms of analysis that conceive of a subject who constructs objects out of a "manifold of de-substantialized individual matter." See PDM 323ff.

those that view language as a combination of individual names or words that refer to intended objects. He criticizes various inadequacies found among four different types of semantic theories: intentionalist semantics, reference semantics, semantic "ontology," and truth semantics.

Husserl's theory of language exemplifies a type of semantic ontology. In the "Origin of Geometry," for example, Husserl argued that language represents ideal states of affairs: "Language itself, in all its particularizations (words, sentences, speeches), is, as can easily be seen from the grammatical point of view, thoroughly made up of ideal objects."[7] What exactly are these "objects"? Idealizations of real objects? Or merely ideal "states of mind"? Aristotle held the latter position, claiming that the structures of these ideal objects are both ontologically independent from linguistic structures and identical for all knowers.[8] Like Aristotle, Husserl claimed that whenever something is asserted one can distinguish the thematized meaning of the ideal object from the unthematizable assertion itself. But Husserl stipulated that even a claim publicly expressed in language maintains its unexpressed independent ideal in the form of its own self-evidence.

How does this semantic embodiment of an intrasubjective mental structure make it an objective structure? Husserl argued that the process of contingent creation of signs that refer to mental entities presupposes a pre-established harmony of possible meanings of ideal objects.[9] Language belongs to the "horizon of civilization" constituted by the community of interpreters.[10] The world is, in turn, the universe of linguistically expressible ideal objects. But although in principle every ideal object can be named, for Husserl each specific name remains, as it did for Aristotle, merely a *convention*.[11] The contingent productions of language reproduce their likenesses from person to person such that, by a kind of epistemological invisible hand, "the repeatedly produced structure becomes an object of conscious-

---

[7] *Crisis*, p. 357.

[8] See Aristotle, *De interpretatione*, 16a3.

[9] For Habermas's critique of these "timeless ideal beings," see BFN 13.

[10] *Crisis*, p. 358.

[11] See Apel, "Transcendental Conception of Language-Communication and the Idea of a First Philosophy," p. 36.

ness, not as a likeness, but as the one structure common to all."[12] The repetition itself universalizes the structure.[13]

Despite this intrinsic relation between language and ideal objects, Husserl acknowledged that speakers can use language improperly. He proposed that improper expressions can be corrected by a recon- structive process of *explication* that operates in both the mathemati- cal and the human sciences. Explication is the logical activity that transforms the passive self-evidence of a sentence structure into an active production of meaning. But the explicative judgment about an object remains itself an ideal object capable of designation in the domain of logic. This means that we can form critical ideas about critical ideas *ad infinitum*. Whether or not the tools of a critical philosophy of consciousness can bring this possible regress to a halt remains uncertain.

Gadamer also adopts a kind of semantic ontology. Like Husserl, he assumes that the articulation of *logos* expresses the structure of being. But, unlike Husserl, he holds that language neither mirrors the pre-given order of being nor constitutes an objective universe of beings. He claims, rather, that language *mediates the historical rela- tion between the subject and his world*. Each linguistic interpreter "belongs" to the linguistically constituted world in such a way that he no longer views reality metaphysically as a teleologically struc- tured subjective mind oriented to an ontologically understood objec- tive world.[14] We view reality from *within* language: language is the point where the self and the world manifest their original unity.

Gadamer concludes that the actual operation of language lets grammar vanish entirely behind what is actually said.[15] But in this paradigm does the situatedness of the speaker and the hearer also vanish—as the structuralists claim—behind what is said? Like Hus- serl, Gadamer maintains that a theory of language must include an emancipatory element: it must provide for a critique of false mean-

---

[12] *Crisis*, p. 360.

[13] For a good description of Husserl's phenomenological theory of repetition, see John D. Caputo, *Radical Hermeneutics: Repetition, Deconstruction, and the Herme- neutic Project* (Bloomington: Indiana University Press, 1987), pp. 1–59.

[14] *Truth and Method*, p. 419.

[15] *Philosophical Hermeneutics*, trans. D. Linge (Berkeley: University of California Press, 1976), p. 64.

ing and ideology. Although rejecting the need for any form of *meth-odological* critique, he claims that consciousness can "draw itself into its own reflection" and thus perform a kind of *self*-critique within the whole of language.[16]

Gadamer develops an evocative theory of meaning in which each word elicits multiple dimensions of meaning: "every word breaks forth as if from a center and is related to a whole. . . . Every word causes the whole of the language to which it belongs to resonate and the whole of the view of the world which lies behind it to appear. Thus every word, in its momentariness, carries with it the unsaid, to which it is related by responding and indicating."[17] Every linguistic disclosure of finite possibilities of meaning within the whole of language becomes a hermeneutical event. Borrowing from Hegel's distinction between external and speculative reflection, Gadamer declares that the meaning of an event results not from the active application of a method to the object, but from "the act of the thing itself."[18] The law of the subject matter dialectically elicits statement and counterstatement and "plays them into each other."[19] "We can now see that this turn from the activity of the thing itself, from the coming into language of meaning, points to a universal ontological structure, namely, to the basic nature of everything to which understanding can be directed."[20] He concludes that being that can be understood is language. In *The Rule of Metaphor*, Ricoeur similarly claims that language possesses the reflexive capacity to place itself at a distance and consider itself as related to the totality of what is. The knowledge that accompanies this self-referential function is "the knowledge of its being-related to being."[21]

Although granting language use a priority over all other rational

---

[16] Ibid., p. 93.

[17] *Truth and Method*, p. 415.

[18] Ibid., p. 431. Hegel's speculative reflection, as we have already seen, demanded the destruction of the two terms of a proposition in order that the unity of the concept emerge. Gadamer argues that in the speculatively reconstructed proposition, words are not related to each other as in a criticizable proposition, but individually "express a relation to the whole of being" (p. 426). Each meaning event is absolutely open; and each interpretation, speculative.

[19] For a further analysis of Gadamer, see Jeanrond, *Text and Interpretation as Categories of Theological Thinking*, pp. 26ff.

[20] *Truth and Method*, p. 431.

[21] *The Rule of Metaphor*, trans. R. Czerny (Toronto: University of Toronto Press, 1977), pp. 300–304.

media, Habermas rejects the ontological conclusion that being *itself* is a linguistic reality. Rorty similarly decries all attempts to make language into a "transcendental topic."[22] Even though Habermas adopts Gadamer's view that language use always remains embedded in actual reproductive processes, he insists that a linguistic *claim* has a nature that transcends its ontic meaning. He argues that speech use is both context-dependent *and* able to make valid normative claims that transcend the space and time in which it is uttered (PT 139). He situates the transcendent element, not in the evocatory power of language itself, but in both the inner perspectives of the *users* of the language and the external perspectives of the claims themselves. The "teleological language game" of communicative action is directed not toward instrumental ends, but toward illocutionary aims "that do not have the status of innerwordly purposes to be realized" (TCA 2.125).[23] These transcendent illocutionary aims require the unforced cooperation of other participants in a linguistic community. Thus, Habermas's instrumentality aims, not to realize the ends of discrete actors, but to establish *relations of ends* among these actors.

Habermas is thus skeptical of a semantic ontology's ability to provide the reflective tools needed to critique false claims and unjust social structures. His most forceful criticism of the inability for a phenomenological or hermeneutic theory to provide a theory of

---

[22] Rorty bases this on Ian Hacking's critique of the "death of meaning" theories. See Rorty's "Wittgenstein, Heidegger, and the Reification of Language," in *Philosophical Papers*, 2.50.

[23] Habermas and Apel have already worked out how a transcendental power resides in a validity claim which ensures for every speech act a temporally transcendent future reference. See TK 147. Fred Dallmayr criticizes Habermas's notion of transcendence on both logical and epistemological grounds. He claims that Habermas merely replaces a transcendental subject with a quasi-transcendental intersubjectivity. He labels Habermas's theory a "humanism" in which the distinction between empiricism and hermeneutics, system and lifeworld, and propositional and reflexive speech can, without undue violence, be reconciled with the basic framework of metaphysics. Dallmayr concludes that Habermas simply ontologizes the bifurcation between the self and the other. See Dallmayr's *Polis and Praxis* (Cambridge, Mass.: The MIT Press, 1984). But Habermas responds to Dallmayr by arguing that transcendence must be viewed within the parameters of the paradigm change to pragmatics and language outlined in the *Philosophical Discourse of Modernity*. For another critique of Habermas's notion of trancendence, see Bernstein's "Introduction," in *Habermas and Modernity*, pp. 13–14; for Habermas's response, see *Habermas and Modernity*, pp. 193–195.

truth adequate for rational critique occurs in his evaluation of MacIntyre's method.

Though refraining from making ontological claims about his method, MacIntyre claims that social and moral development analysis is confined to the parameters of a given tradition. He does not share Gadamer's view that *any* text can be sufficiently translated by *any* interpreter who engages in the logic of question and answer with the text. He rejects the Enlightenment principle of what he calls ideal "international languages" by which one can translate, regardless of context or tradition, between all forms of expression.[24] Rather, he argues that "when texts from traditions with their own strong, substantive criteria of truth and rationality, as well as with a strong historical dimension, are translated into such languages, they are presented in a way that neutralizes the conceptions of truth and rationality and the historical context."[25] MacIntyre does not ground the reflexivity of modern interpretations of the world in an abstract universalism. He claims, rather, that *traditions themselves* engage in a dialectical truth-orienting struggle about their conflicting understandings of practical reason, life-ideals, and concepts of the good. By means of this dialectic process, traditions "learn" about, and even at times adopt, each other's patterns of behaviors.

Habermas denies that MacIntyre's hermeneutics of traditions successfully combines contextualist with anti-relativist principles of meaning and truth. He argues that any translation, either from one language to another or from one tradition to another, requires not a truth-orienting struggle, but a "zone of rational overlap" (JA 101). Though acknowledging that a critical hermeneutics can in some cases overcome misunderstandings between traditions, Habermas argues that a dialectic among traditions fails to provide the tools for overcoming *systemic* distortions. The improper limits traditions impose on meaning cannot be corrected simply by hermeneutic means.

While semantic ontology emphasizes the production of meaning by language generally, intentionalist semantics restricts its domain

---

[24] Benjamin also criticized the possibility of complete translation, describing the nucleus of writing as "the element that does not lend itself to translation." See Mark C. Taylor, "Foiling Reflection," in *Tears* (Albany: State University of New York Press, 1990), p. 102n17.

[25] Alasdair MacIntyre, *Whose Justice, Which Rationality?* (Notre Dame, Ind.: Notre Dame University Press, 1988), p. 384.

of analysis to the object of each specific semantic assertion. It assumes that the meaning of each symbolic expression x requires that a hearer understand the purposes that the speaker means or intends in a situation by the utterance of x. It analyzes, not the coordinating mechanisms of linguistically mediated interaction, but only the content of the consequence-oriented aim of the utterance.

Habermas finds no justification for this restriction that intentionalist semantics imposes on the analysis of meaning. He characterizes as counterintuitive the claim that what an expression means is derived solely from the purpose a speaker intends to achieve by using it (TCA 1.274–75). Intentionalist semantics thus fails to account for the reason the speaker communicates a specific intention to a specific hearer in the first place. From the viewpoint of intentionalist semantics, language "loses the autonomy of having its own internal structure" (PT 60).

Referential semantics, on the other hand, is a kind of formal semantics that analyzes, not the intentional, but the representational and literal function of symbols. It formulates a system or structure of syntactical and semantic rules governing the relation of symbols or signs to a signified (or referent). It determines the meaning of an expression by the class of objects to which it can be applied in true sentences (WUP 30). Frege realized that the reference of a descriptive statement "x is y" differs from the reference of the assertion "that x is y." To account for both types of reference, he argued that meaning is based, not on the way that the words stand for an object, but on the way the facts to which a sentence refers make it true. He concluded that the primary element of the meaning is not the conceptual representation of an object, but the thoughts that refers to states of affairs expressed by propositions (BFN 10). These thoughts follow from the formal properties of expressions and their generative rules (PT 60).

In *Knowledge and Human Interests*, Habermas argued that it is possible to *reconstruct* meta-linguistic rules of constitution in order to understand the meaning of formal relations within language (KHI 162). He also later formalized a set of speech acts, called *operatives*, that signify the application of generative semantic rules but have no genuine communicative intent (TCA 1.326). But Habermas maintains that Frege's advance still could not account for assertions involving non-existent or counterfactual states of affairs. He concludes that the determination of the validity of these types of assertions must account for the formal properties and generative rules not only from the perspective of the utterer but also from the perspective of the recipient of the assertion. This requires an analysis of the *intersubjective praxis* of verification. Thus, he will turn formal semantics of predication into a formal pragmatics of discourse about claims.

Truth semantics, the fourth type of semantics that Habermas discusses, accounts better than reference semantics for the complexities of the relation between statements and the objective world of which they themselves are a part. It emerges from Frege's insight that to understand a sentence is equivalent to knowing the conditions under which it is true. It considers truth a "syncategoramatic notion" that enables us to talk about sentences themselves instead of about their references to objects alone.[26] It led both Austin and Searle to distinguish between the meaning of the sentence and its *force*.

The early Austin divided speech acts into two separate categories: locutionary acts that assert something about the world and illocutionary acts that attempt to bring about an interpersonal relation. But later he argued that the two acts are only *analytically* distinguishable since every speech act can be judged as to whether it is both "right" as an illocution and "in order" as a locution (PT 70). Assertions can be just as infelicitous as illocutionary acts: one can make such a mess of a story that it is no longer really a story, or discuss a delicate matter so bluntly that those present will not tolerate discussion of it further. Searle later explicated this validity dimension, not as a diversity of truth values in the same speech act, but as the establishment of conditions for standardized contexts that must obtain if the speech act is to be meaningful and successful.

On Habermas's account, truth semantics still reduces the validity dimension of meaning to representational formulations that admit of variation solely according to the direction of a "fit" between language and the world. Thus, it is too narrow for distinguishing the several illocutionary forms that express the authorized imperatives and commissive speech acts with which a speaker sincerely binds its own will to a normative obligation.

---

[26] See Hilary Putnam, "Why Reason Can't Be Naturalized," in *After Philosophy*, ed. Kenneth Baynes, James Bohman, and Thomas McCarthy (Cambridge: The MIT Press, 1987), p. 240.

Though he criticizes elements of each of these four forms of semantics, Habermas does not abandon semantic considerations altogether. He stresses the necessary role that semantic analysis plays in determining the comprehensibility of any claim, and he argues that speech act offers can have an action-coordinating effect only if one understands the obligations implied in the acceptance of a claim. These obligations arise from the semantic contents of the utterance.[27] But truth determination requires a further reflective process that can explicate fully the intersubjective conditions of meaning. This is achieved by analyzing language use relative to its conditions of verification within the shared contexts of its actual use. Truth determination thus requires some reference to the perspectives of the agents that use the language.

HABERMAS'S TRANSFORMATION OF TRUTH SEMANTICS

Habermas's Development of Formal Pragmatics[28]

Unlike a semantic theory, a pragmatic theory analyzes language not only on the basis of the genesis or logic of sentences, but also on the basis of the success of utterances used by competent speakers. Habermas offers a formal pragmatic analysis which rests on the fundamental principle that in every speech act a speaker comes to an understanding *with* another person *about* something. In *Knowledge and Human Interests* his theory of truth required that a subject discover the unconscious symbolic complexes presupposed in his conscious acts. Now he reconstructs the generative structures underlying the production of symbol formation in intersubjective communication (see WUP 13).[29] This reflexive reconstruction makes explicit generalizable rules that a speaker, regardless of his particular intentions, employs in every successful speech act.[30]

---

[27] "Actions, Speech Acts, Linguistically Mediated Interactions and the Lifeworld," in *Philosophical Problems Today* I, ed. G. Fløistad (Dordrecht: Kluwer, 1994), p. 52.

[28] Habermas uses the terms "universal pragmatics" and "formal pragmatics" interchangeably. He previously used only the former in order to stress the consensus-demanding character of the theory. But in later writings he uses primarily the latter.

[29] "Hermeneutic Claim to Universality," p. 186.

[30] "Hermeneutic Claim to Universality," p. 188. Habermas is aware that, in uncov-

Habermas's formal pragmatics is derived from his conviction that the abandonment of the concept of the transcendental subject does not entail the renunciation of all transcendental investigation into the constitution of experience. But he rejects Apel's claim that this reconstruction of a theory of truth requires transcendental first principles (see WUP 22). The analysis is not transcendental, but *formal and empirical*. Like Wittgenstein, Habermas argues that speakers can identify linguistic expressions only by reference to the *actual* situations in which they are used. The speaker aims, not to conceptualize his experience of objects, but to reach intersubjective agreement about what can be asserted about and expected from the objects.

Habermas exhibited traces of a formal pragmatics even in his early writings. In *The Logic of the Social Sciences* (1967) he adopted Wittgenstein's claim that, in the context of a language game, action and speech interpret themselves linguistically.[31] In *Knowledge and Human Interests* he argued that the grammar of ordinary language determines proper usage relative not only to standards of internal consistency, but also to standards of external consistency between an utterance and the situation in which it is uttered (KHI 172).[32] He argued that since ordinary language, unlike a formal language, has an action orientation, it can employ informal signs whose meaning must be explicated *reflexively*, since its unique limits are determined relative to the situation in which it is used (KHI 168).

Habermas's later reconstruction of speech act competencies is, for the most part, derived from Austin's claims about the reflexivity in-

---

ering the non-linguistic roots of operative thought, Piaget determined that much intelligence is pre-linguistic and many uses of language are simply instrumental. We have already seen how Rorty holds to such an instrumental view of language. But Habermas argues that if this were the case, the universality thesis would be applicable only in non-scientific or non-purposive realms.

[31] *Zur Logik der Sozialwissenschaften*. Philosophische Rundschau Beiheft (Tübingen: Mohr, 1967), p. 124.

[32] Habermas notes that for Dilthey there are three data of life-expression. The first are obviously the symbolic expressions of ordinary language. The second are communicative or intentional actions by which understanding objectifies itself. These actions require a hermeneutic decoding, since the actor who follows universal norms needs to communicate through non-linguistic universals. The third are "life-expressions," such as gestures, laughing, and crying, which do not have direct cognitive content. These have a privileged ability to show a latent meaning within manifest communications. They can legitimate, empower, deny, interpret ironic mutations (*Brechungen*), and unmask deceptions.

trinsic to speech acts.[33] Rejecting a Russellian critique of self-reference, Austin argued that self-referential statements first establish limits around which they are circumscribed and then *place themselves outside of the boundaries.* They "outstrip their constituent situations."[34] Such statements thus intrinsically refer to the performative context in which they are uttered. Austin had to develop a new terminology for this performative analysis of language. He defined a *constative utterance* as any expression that can be judged true or false on the basis of its meaning-content alone, without regard to its context. A *performative utterance*, on the other hand, does account for the interpersonal and contextual elements. Performatives, such as warnings and threats, are judged on the basis of whether they are expedient and opportune, not true or false.

Although performative utterances cannot be judged true or false, Austin claimed that they can be determined as felicitous or infelicitous.[35] Their felicity depends upon their conformity to

(1) the conventional procedures of a group; and
(2) the sincerely expressed intention of the speaker.

Austin noted the wide divergence of opinions as to how (1) is determined. He thus sets forth the principle that all linguistic procedures or codes must in principle remain open to revision. This fails to describe, however, exactly *how* this process of group consensus formation resolves a disputed convention. (2) involves the "total situation" in which the utterance is issued: the total speech act.[36] It must include entailments, implications, and presuppositions of the performative act. For example, the claim "I promise *x*" entails "I am committed to do *x* in the future."[37]

---

[33] See J. L. Austin, *How to Do Things with Words* (Cambridge, Mass.: Harvard University Press, 1962). Habermas does acknowledge that the origin of speech act theory goes back to Frege.

[34] See Roberts, *Logic of Reflection*, p. 43.

[35] Austin brings up some extreme cases in which a constative utterance seems to be *both* true and false. (1) "France is hexagonal" is generally true, but false for a geographer; (2) "Lord Raglan won the battle of Alma" is true, but false insofar as many of his orders were never transmitted to his subordinates; (3) "All snow geese migrate to Labrador" brings up the problem of whether any statement with "all" can be true. See *How to Do Things with Words*, p. 143.

[36] Ibid., p. 52.

[37] Ibid., p. 138.

To describe the functions of a speech act, Austin analyzed not only its locutionary and illocutionary aims, but also its perlocutionary effects. The perlocutionary effect of a performative act is what is changed or brought about by virtue of the utterance itself. Austin noted that "saying something will often, or even normally, produce certain consequential effects upon the feelings, thoughts, or actions of the audience, or of the speaker, or of other persons: and it may be done with the design, intention, or purpose of producing them."[38] Thus, a perlocutionary effect need conform neither to social conventions nor even to the original intentions of the actor. An external observer can determine a speech act's locutionary and illocutionary components even if unable to determine its perlocutionary aims. This is consistent with both Kant's rule regarding the separation of intention and consequence as well as Hegel's acknowledgment that the consequences of an act are "prey to external forces" we do not intend.[39]

Habermas agrees with Austin's claim that philosophers and semanticists have focused for the most part only on the locutionary and perlocutionary components of speech, neglecting the illocutionary. To redress this deficiency, Habermas stipulates that the illocutionary component must be analyzed from the sides of both speaker and hearer. From the side of the speaker, he distinguishes between speech competence and speech performance.[40] Speech competence is a speaker's ability to master an abstract system of linguistically generated rules; speech performance modifies this competence under certain restricted conditions that emerge in actual situations of speech use. Habermas agrees that Austin's speech acts determine a speaker's employment of pragmatic universals. A successful speech act has aspects of both competence and performance: it must be both a well-formed proposition and a competently used statement. From the side of the hearer, speech act theory stipulates that the aim of a speech act is to make a hearer both understand and *recognize* or accept the legitimacy of a claim. This requires both the achievement of a shared intersubjectivity between speaker and hearer and their

---

[38] Ibid., p. 101.

[39] See Hegel, *The Philosophy of Right*, p. 116.

[40] See *Technik und Wissenschaft als Ideologie*, pp. 101–103. Habermas is referring to Chomsky's speech act analysis as set forth in *Aspects of the Theory of Syntax* (Cambridge, Mass.: The MIT Press, 1965).

agreement about the specific topic of the communication.[41] Habermas later specifies that mutual understanding (*Verständigung*) is, when underpinned by the same reasons, a process of reaching agreement (*Einigung*). To do so, the participants must have a collective like-mindedness (*Gleichstimmtheit*) to reach a "propositionally differentiated" agreement (*Einverständnis*). Unlike a de facto accord (*Übereinstimmung*), such an agreement fulfills the conditions of rationally motivated assent (*Zustimmung*) (see TCA 1.286–287; OPC 320–321).

Following Chomsky, Habermas then equates speech competence not simply with the correct application of the content of symbols, but also with the correct following of reconstructed rules for competent speakers. But he argues that speech act theory must reconstruct not only the rules to be followed, but also the reflexive "evaluative accomplishment of rule consciousness" itself (WUP 13). A successful speaker does not merely follow rules; he also has at his disposal the basic qualifications of the symbolic interaction required for rule following generally. In other words, the speaker must have *reasons* for it and the hearer to follow rules (PT 74). The semantic universals that a speaker uses must be understood not merely as pre-existent rules that are learned, but also as constituents of an intersubjectively reproduced cultural system. A speaker thus communicates the locutionary content of an utterance not only on the basis of an anticipation of the rules the hearer will understand, but also by means of the utterance's illocutionary force to *form, orient, and change the attitudes of a hearer* if he has reasons for doing so. A speaker and a hearer know that their interpretations of the meaning and legitimacy of a claim are identical, and thus normative, when they accept both the same reasons given for the claims and the same procedures by which the reasons were generated.

Habermas then specifies the crucial relation between Austin's locutionary and illocutionary aspects of communication. First, he argues that the distinction is valid only within an analysis that takes into account the relative independence of sentence meanings relative to the contingent changes of meaning that they can undergo in

---

[41] *Technik und Wissenschaft als Ideologie*, p. 105. Speech acts are able to be judged true or false inasmuch as they express statements that describe facts. Later Habermas attributes the identification of this property of statements to Strawson. See WT 128.

different contexts. Thus, the distinctions regarding a speech act's meaning, force, and effect are based precisely on the speaker's attitude or disposition relative to possible learning contexts. Second, the sentence not only specifies a claim, but also specifies in what sense the propositional context is to be understood, "Mp." While the speaker forms his illocutionary intent in the performative attitude of establishing interpersonal relations, he forms its meaningful sentences through the objectivizing or representational attitude of an observer (WUP 48).[42] Third, the locutionary component has two forms of expression: nominalized propositions of the form "that p" refer to states of affairs and are thus linked to the illocutionary mode of asserting; propositions of the form "p" represent facts (WUP 36). But Habermas also realizes that the truth of non-constatives, or performatives, can be made explicit through transforming their "that p" propositional content into a propositional sentence "p." In his early work, Habermas claimed that the illocutionary component can be expressed only in "that p" sentences. But in his later analysis of Mead's theory of reciprocal behavior expectations, he argues that a speaker implicitly takes up an illocutionary relation to a hearer even by means of a "p" locution alone.

Thus, rationality resides not only in the accurate representation of the locutionary realm, but also in the legitimate contextualization of the illocutionary realm.[43] A statement can be judged not only as *true* when it accurately represents a state of affairs, but also as *truthful* when the speaker's conviction in expressing it is authentic and *right* when the demand it makes on another is legitimate. Habermas situates these three types of truth conditions within the ontology of a phenomenologically derived "system of worlds" (TCA 1.278).[44] Any statement takes on three world-relations within this system. A speaker *simultaneously* demarcates itself

---

[42] Habermas reiterates this stress on the rationality of the illocutionary in TCA 1.288–295.

[43] Habermas finds the grounds for this distinction in Bühler's distinction between the three functions of language: the cognitive function of the representation of a fact, the expressive function of the report on the experience of a speaker, and the appellative function of a demand it makes on the hearer. See PT 57–58.

[44] Moreover, in *regulative* speech acts, the participants raise normative claims that appeal to something in the social world; in *imperative* speech acts they raise claims that appeal to some state of affairs in the objective world. The distinction between the truth of statements, the truthfulness of expressions, and the rightness of norms is already found in his *Theorie der Gesellschaft oder Sozialtechnologie*, p. 123.

(1) from a world that it objectifies in the third-person attitude of an observer;

(2) from a world to which it conforms in the "ego–alter attitude of a participant"; and

(3) from its own subjectivity to which it is related in a first-person attitude.[45]

Each of the three worlds is a "totality": the external world is the totality of states of affairs, the social world is the totality of all normatively regulated interpersonal relations, and the inner world is the totality of intentional experiences. Language is *the reflexive medium in which the three relations are systematized*.[46] Language thus remains "in a peculiar half-transcendence" relative to how communicative action presents itself to the speaker and the actor as a segment of reality *sui generis* (WUP 67). Communicative actions are not reducible to any one of the three levels, but are *reflexive*: utterances are relativized against the possibility that their threefold validity will be contested by other actors. Thus, communicative acts presuppose that there is a "linguistic medium that reflects the actor's relations to the world as such" (TCA 1.94).

In their standard form, illocutionary aims are carried out by performative sentences that coordinate acts in various ways. But Habermas distinguishes three kinds of performative effects a speech act can have. The first are those that arise simply from the meaning of the speech act itself; the second are those that do not follow from the grammatical rules of the act but occur, depending on the context, contingently. The latter are usually public components of the interpretation of a given situation such that they could be declared without jeopardizing the action. The third are more problematic: they are the effects that follow only if the speaker *conceals* his actual intended aims from the hearer. Habermas calls these "latent-strategic"

---

[45] Internal nature consists of all wishes, feelings, and intentions to which the speaker as first person has privileged access and can express publicly as his own experiences. The "I" knows itself in this expressive attitude (3) both as subject *and* as someone who transcends the limits of subjectivity through cognition, language, and interaction. Habermas will later drop the inner/outer nature distinction operative in (1) and (3). He used it in "Wahrheitstheorien" to contrast that to which we have privileged access from that which requires normative formulation. See WT 172.

[46] In *Theory of Communicative Action* Habermas calls the levels teleological, normative, and dramaturgical/self-presentational. See TCA 1.99.

actions.[47] It is Habermas's contention that these latent-strategic acts live parasitically off normal communicative actions. On this basis he claims that communicative acts have a primacy relative to all strategic acts. Communicative acts achieve action coordination by fulfilling *generalized* interests, since they link a first-order interest in bringing about a specific state of affairs with a second-order interest in achieving a mutual agreement with other subjects regarding the legitimacy of the first-order interest. So, while strategic acts achieve coordination by exerting influence, communicative acts gain the same end by reaching mutual understanding. All moral argumentation is embedded in this context of communicative action.

Having rejected intentionalist semantics, as we saw earlier, how exactly does Habermas explain the way in which actors are *motivated* to use speech acts communicatively? In other words, how are speech acts related to the performative intentions and ends of a speaker that they both express and coordinate? Habermas maintains that although an observer can understand a nonlinguistic act only when it grasps the performative intention that is supposed to be satisfied through the act, a speech act identifies itself by an intrinsic self-reflexive property: the speaker *says* in the illocutionary mode what he is *doing*. When the illocutionary property of speech acts is fully determined, a communicative act results. Moreover, these communicative acts in turn neutralize the egoistic aspects of the performative intention of any act coordinated through them. Habermas thus insists that in a properly mastered language game speech acts sustain the interactive practices "in a completely different way" than they support the instrumental intentions that are first coordinated through them (PT 64).[48] This grounds a developmental social theory that views the maximization of communicative action as its goal. Speakers are motivated to use communicative acts because they

---

[47] See "Actions, Speech Acts, and the Lifeworld," pp. 52–53. For a good description of these aspects of speech acts, see Georgia Warnke, "Communicative Rationality and Cultural Values," in *The Cambridge Companion to Habermas*, ed. S. White (Cambridge: Cambridge University Press, 1994), pp. 121–122.

[48] Habermas adopts Apel's justificatory claim that a claim's presuppositions of argument must always be recognized if the language game of argumentation is to have any meaning. But Habermas denies that this appeal to performative contradiction provides a final foundation for all truth. He maintains only that every argument contains an *unavoidable* pre-theoretical intent to find universal agreement, even if the skeptic denies it. See MCCA 81.

achieve the realization and coordination of their interests in a way most consistent with the structures of action itself.

Though these structures of action are intersubjective, Habermas argues that the theoretical activity that reconstructs them is mono-logical. A kind of theoretical reflection, which takes place in an "objectivizing attitude," reconstructs these structures of actual speech competencies (WUP 43). Although the theoretical reconstruction relies upon the reflexive property of natural language, "the language of explication is *at the same level* as the explicandum language" (WUP 13). Thus, reconstructive science, unlike empirical-analytic science, reconstructs the pre-theoretical knowledge of an intuitive competence *it cannot falsify*. The report of an intuition can be false, but not the intuition itself. Habermas acknowledges the circularity of the "maeutic method of interrogation" that verifies an intuition about a competence. But he claims that such circularity is found in all research processes, since they continuously move between theory formation and precise specification of the object domain. As Thomas McCarthy puts it, this model of universal rational reconstruction has an "assumed pre-reflective/reflective asymmetry."[49] This means that no reasons can be given to justify the reconstructive method itself.

The Reflexive Elements of Formal Pragmatics

Having sketched the basic rationale behind formal pragmatics, I now need to target more closely its fundamental reflexive processes. Reflexive processes emerge in three loci: in the second-order "objectivizing" of ordinary language use, in the discovery of identical meaning, and in the idealizations required for rational argumentation about the validity of claims.

Habermas claims that the locutionary and illocutionary constitute the double structure of the "inherent reflexivity" of language. In ordinary language, a speaker can choose to take on an objectivizing attitude about the very illocutionary "content" of his speech act (WUP 42–43).[50] For example, a speaker can utter the claim "I hereby am addressing you about this matter." But this second-order

---

[49] See McCarthy's "Rationality and Relativism," in *Habermas: Critical Debates*, ed. D. Held and J. Thompson (Cambridge, Mass: The MIT Press, 1982), p. 75.

[50] If the subject reflexively adopts an objectivizing attitude toward himself, this "alters the sense in which intentions can be expressed" (WUP 67).

objectivizing process cannot go on *ad infinitum*. Habermas insists that the objectivation can be expressed only in a new speech act *in which the illocutionary content is not objectified*. Thus, although speakers cannot simultaneously perform and thematize an illocutionary act, every performance utterance reflexively transcends its locutionary limit through its objectivizing illocutionary aim. This asymmetry between the locutionary and the illocutionary leads many to conclude that language can only describe objects or exchange information. But Habermas avoids this "descriptivist fallacy" by stipulating that an illocutionary aim is implicit in every well-formed speech act.

Another use of reflection in formal pragmatics is found in the determination of identical meaning. The universality of meaning depends on the linguistic idealizations that enable speakers to recognize the same sign type in individual sign tokens and the same grammatically structured sentence in different claims. But this kind of identity is not the same as the identity of an object that can be identified by different observers. Meanings establish identity in the same way as rules establish unity in the multiplicity of their exemplary embodiments. Thus, as Wittgenstein argued, identity in meaning is derived from conventional regulations. Habermas argues that a subject can follow a rule only by following the *same* rule under changing conditions of application (see TCA 2.17). Irregular behavior is determined not relative to empirical regularities, but relative to intersubjective validity. Thus, the translation of a linguistic meaning or a social practice from one situation to another requires *pragmatic* judgments guided by idealizations. These identity-determining idealizations emerge from a reflexive act by which speakers can impartially evaluate the *generality* of rule-following (PT 55).[51]

Reflexive acts are required for a speaker's ability to overcome not only the limits of ungeneralizable meaning, but also the limits imposed by uncoordinated action (TCA 1.293). Following Austin, Habermas claims that speech acts can untangle cases in which a speaker and a hearer find themselves in the "gray areas" of incomprehension,

---

[51] In regard to idealization, Habermas is explicitly referring to Mary Hesse's critique. See her "Science and Objectivity," in *Habermas: Critical Debates*, ed. D. Held and J. Thompson (Cambridge, Mass: The MIT Press, 1982), pp. 277ff.

intentional and involuntary untruthfulness, and conflict (WUP 3). These truth distortions can manifest themselves either as individual pathologies or as social ideologies. Habermas holds that specific idealizations are required to deal with such distortions. As McCarthy points out, "Habermas relocates the Kantian opposition between the ideal and the real within the domain of social practice itself. He argues that communicative interaction is everywhere permeated by idealizing pragmatic presuppositions concerning reason, truth, and reality."[52] Habermas finds inadequate both Husserl's claim that the repetition of individually constituted acts of meaning forms a universal structure of meaning and the hermeneuticist's uncritical faith in a dialectical fusion of differing traditions. Instead he explicates idealizations that can ground *all* mediation between the differences in meaning, interpretation, and truth. Specifically, these include a speaker's capacity both to attach context-transcending significance to validity claims and to ascribe rational accountability to other speakers (PT 55). These idealizations determine the critical resources by which the perspectival limits of a speaker's well-formed assertion can be overcome through formulating reasons that can be accepted by all participants in argumentation (OPC 308).

The "Methodology" of Reflective Acceptability: Discourse

On the basis of these various reflexive idealizations, Habermas reconstructs the actual procedure of discursive truth determination. He analyzes first the various features of claims able to be determined as true or false, and then reconstructs the formal procedures of *discourse* by which validity claims about them are raised and redeemed by means of taking a hypothetical attitude toward them.

Habermas defines the "standard form" of a speech act that is able to be determined as valid or invalid. First, it must be a propositionally differentiated speech act. Though many non-linguistic gestures and actions, for example, a facial expression or even the act of arriving at work at a certain time, implicitly raise claims, propositionally

---

[52] Thomas McCarthy, "Philosophy and Social Practice: Avoiding the Ethnocentric Predicament," in *Zwischenbetrachtungen in Prozeß der Aüfklarung* (Frankfurt am Main: Suhrkamp, 1989), p. 209.

differentiated linguistic acts carry with them "more degrees of freedom in relation to a recognized normative background" for the claim
(WUP 38). Second, it must be a speech act free of "shifts of meaning." This incorporates Searle's principle of expressibility which stipulates that all speech acts can be specified by a complex sentence
intelligible to all hearers. Third, the speech act must be comprehensible relative to at least one of three "analytic viewpoints":

(1) the *third-person* representation of a fact or state of affairs
    through an elementary proposition,
(2) the expression in *first-person* speech of an internal reality of
    the intentions a speaker wants to express before a public,
    and
(3) the formation of *second-person* intersubjective norms recog-
    nized as legitimate by means of the rationality of an illocu-
    tionary act (WUP 28).[53]

Fourth, a speech act must be able to produce effects at more than
one level of interaction. Although Austin analyzes speech acts in
their contexts of interaction, he focuses primarily on institutionally
bound acts such as betting, christening, and appointing. He fails to
account adequately for the perlocutionary effects that these speech
acts can achieve at different levels of interaction. Habermas thus is
concerned primarily with institutionally unbound utterances in order
to see how they bring about a *coordination* of perlocutionary effects
at different levels of interaction (TCA 1.294). He defines perlocu-
tions as "a special class of strategic interactions in which illocutions
are employed as means in teleological contexts of action" (TCA
1.293). This reflexive property of perlocutionary acts, by which they
bring about a state of affairs *and* coordinate actors' intentions and
actions in the process, mitigates their instrumentality.

Habermas next considers the range of objects to which a claim can
refer. A speaker can formulate statements that refer to subjects or
objects, private or public entities, and real or apparent objects. The

---

[53] Habermas argues that while (1) has been well developed in reference semantics
from Frege to Dummett, (2) and (3) require further pragmatic specification. Propositionally differentiated speech acts (1) offer the actor "more degrees of freedom in
relation to a recognized normative background" (WUP 38). This differentiation
becomes the basis for his analysis of the subjective, social, and objective speaker-
world relations.

speaker distinguishes between real and apparent objects by means of the structures of sense, reference, and context. A speech act can refer to objects that are not only common and generalizable, but also "inalienable and individual."[54] The speaker expresses the individual and particular, not by general interpretations, but only by "meta-communications" that encode our direct message in metaphors or symbols. This meta-communicative process utilizes two kinds of symbols: paleo-symbols and "created" symbols. Paleo-symbols are affect-laden and unconscious symbols that resist integration into a system of logic or grammatical rules. The subject must resort to them in order to express certain repressed or censored needs. But they remain at a level where the speaker operates neither with the distinction between himself and a hearer nor with the distinctions among symbolic sign, semantic content, and referent. The second level, which Habermas calls "linguistic creation," integrates paleo-symbols into a grammatically guided and publicly accessible system. He later refers to this kind of innovative and hypothesis forming language as "world-disclosive" language (PT 105).[55] Both these indirect uses of language are required for the determination and development of identities, whether ego or social.

Having explicated the referential structure of a speech act claim, Habermas then looks at the intersubjective mediation that grounds the ability of speakers to communicate. To convince a hearer of a claim, a speaker first must rely upon his membership within a language community. The "intersubjectivity of the world" that is the background for meaning and truth is not a generality under which individuals are subsumed as elements under a class, but a non-analytic and reflective structure of the limits a self has relative to itself and to other participants in an interaction.[56] This identification between self and other moves within this lifeworld context.

Within this intersubjective context, speakers identify themselves with two mutually incompatible dialogical roles. One role secures their identity with themselves; the other, with the groups to which

---

[54] See "Hermeneutic Claim to Universality," pp. 196–198.

[55] Husserl also spoke of a world of conceptual possibilities which can "be fixed in univocal language as the essence constantly implied in the flowing, vital horizon." See *Crisis*, p. 375. Both Heidegger and Gadamer also see language as that which discloses new horizons and possibilities.

[56] "Hermeneutic Claim to Universality," p. 196.

they belong. But Habermas insists that the roles by which the identifications take place are *universalizable*. Unlike Austin, Habermas defines successful interaction as the moment, not when the hearer understands the meaning of the sentence uttered, but when the hearer actually *enters into* the relationship intended by the speaker. Habermas's bestowal of universality upon these identity-formation processes allows him to overcome what he sees to be the solipsism in Husserl's empathetic account of the relation between the self and an "alien" other. Habermas thus accounts for intersubjectivity by relying upon an *identitarian grounding* of the linguistic structures of all language users.[57] The act of reflection in the "struggle" for intersubjective recognition overcomes the limits of the alien status of the other by *realizing that rules that speaker and hearer follow in successful communication are identical*.

Next we must examine what kind of truth claim a speech act can make. Austin rejected the pragmatist's claim, based only on the evaluative analysis of the perlocutionary effect of an utterance, that the true is what works. With Strawson, Habermas claims that the truth of a speech act is based not only on utterances understood as contingent historic events or "speech episodes," as Austin claimed, but also on statements understood as constative speech acts validated through argumentation.[58] Thus, Habermas defends the pragmatist theory of truth, but only on the condition that "what works" harmonizes with *the communicatively determined agreement of all affected by the particular act*.

This agreement can be determined from three formally distinct viewpoints: its constative truth, its normative rightness, and its intentional authenticity. Thus, Habermas agrees neither with the descriptivist's claim that normative statements are true or false in the same way constative statements are, nor with the empiricist's claim that normative statements are incapable of verification altogether. He also rejects "decisionistic" positions (Weber, Popper, Hare)

---

[57] For a further analysis of this "identitarian" aspect of Habermas's theory, see Martin Jay's "The Debate over Performative Contradiction: Habermas versus the Poststructuralists," in *Zwischenbetrachtungen in Prozeß der Aüfklarung* (Frankfurt am Main: Suhrkamp, 1989), pp. 181ff. Jay argues that Habermas's shift to identitarian reflection followed from Austin's rejection of the mentalistic fallacy.

[58] P. F. Strawson, "Truth," in *Logico-Linguistic Papers* (London: Methuen, 1971), pp. 190–213.

which hold that normative statements lack truth value since they express only beliefs or convictions. Habermas claims that the pluralism of individual ethical ends can be transcended, not by recourse to an external moral principle, but only by the expectation of the discursive redemption of a normative validity claim to rightness (see LC 110ff.). Thus Habermas's formal pragmatics avoids the instrumentalizing tendency to which other pragmatic theories are prone.

But what happens when communicative actors, even when they are aware of these intersubjective structures, find that their interpretations of a speech act situation *conflict*? When confronted with a situation in which coordination of action is blocked, communicative actors have two options. They can either attempt to rectify the situation by resorting to strategic acts that aim to bring about new effects in the world, or they can suspend the claims that "govern" the situation and take a hypothetical viewpoint from which they engage in argumentation about the legitimacy of the claims themselves. This latter validity-determining form of communication is called *discourse*. In discourse each actor coordinates his illocutionary intentions with other actors and argumentatively evaluates a "suprasubjective" or transcendental validity claim (WUP 4). The actors take on a third-person attitude in which they impartially consider whether the conditions for the generalizability of the disputed claim obtain (WUP 62).[59] The discourse itself requires neither an exchange of information about whether or not the claim is disputed nor a determination of the genealogy of the claim in question.

Habermas distinguishes three "categories" of discourse:

(1) "therapeutic discourse," which produces the conditions of discourse through a methodological self-reflection,
(2) the "normal case" of discourse, which serves to provide the grounding of problematized validity claims, and
(3) "innovatively aimed" discourse, which produces new hypothetical claims.[60]

---

[59] Habermas warns that previous attempts to formulate intersubjective validity claims have tended to restrict themselves to the instruments developed in logic and grammar which are inadequate for capturing pragmatic relations. Other approaches—such as those of Grice and Lewis—have started from the model of an isolated, purposive-rational actor and fail to understand the reciprocity of intersubjective validity claims. See WUP 8.

[60] *Theorie der Gesellschaft oder Sozialtechnologie*, p. 121. There are two additional

All three categories of discourse aim to achieve a *particular* agreement guided by the counterfactual ideal of a *universal* speech situation.[61] (1) involves the theoretical activity that reconstructs competencies of reflection within a certain discipline. Theoretical reconstruction determines both the universal structures of speech acts and the structures of moral and practical argumentation. (2) is the process of reflection that analyzes grounds for a claim. In later writings, Habermas develops different types of "normal" discourse: empirical, moral (both justificatory and applicatory), pragmatic (hermeneutic), ethical-existential (clinical), aesthetic, expressive, and democratic (political) (see JA 5–17; BFN 104–107).[62] He also distinguishes discourses on the basis of the kind of claims they ground: theoretical discourse determines cognitive claims to truth, and practical discourse determines the impartial justification of norms and interests "common to all" (TCA 1.19). In the next chapter, I shall analyze the moral and ethical-existential forms of normative discourse more closely. (3) is the discourse that forms, even in cases in which present norms are not perceived as problematic, new hypothetical inductive formulations of claims that can then be subjected to (2). These discourses are guided by a kind of induction that Piaget claimed generates progressive stages of learning how to adapt to one's environment (see WT 168–169).

Schnädelbach claims that Habermas's embedding of reflection in language rather than in consciousness significantly reduces the difficulty of formulating how reflection functions. He correlates the elements in Habermas's theory of discourse to those in cognitive, or "traditional," theories of reflection:

Cognitive Reflection	Reflexive Discourse
subjective consciousness	speaker
reflexive activity	objectivizing speech act
object of consciousness	problematized claim.

But Schnädelbach argues that, in addition to these elements, a theory of discourse must explicate the *meta-communication that pre-*

---

cases of discourse: discourse as a means of communicative action, and "apparent" discourse which is misused to justify ideologies.

[61] See ibid., pp. 117–122.

[62] The pragmatic, ethical-existential, and moral constitute three types of practical discourse.

cedes the instantiation of discourse.[63] He criticizes Habermas for underdetermining the pre-conditions needed for discourse. Since discourse can thematize only *part* of the totality of a claim or norm, Schnädelbach argues that actors must *choose* which parts are to be admitted to discourse. But what are the conditions for this choice? Does the discourse simply gravitate to the most problematic element of the norm in question? Habermas claims that our choice of a "speech system" determines what will serve as evidence—such as observational data or need interpretations—for or against a claim (WT 166). He also specifies that a special set of speech acts, which he terms *communicatives*, determine reflexively second-order considerations that concern speech acts themselves (distributing conversational roles, the order of conversation, when a point is being affirmed, and so on) (TCA 1.326). But Schnädelbach is interested in the evidence that determines the choice regarding how the entire norm or claim is problematized in the first place. He argues that actors make this choice, not by direct intuitions into the problematic elements of the norms, but by engaging in "descriptive" discourse in which they exchange information about the situational factors relevant to their choice.[64] Actors must reach consensus about which partial claims are to be thematized in discourse *before* they can begin any type of discourse. In the last chapter I shall take up this problem of the descriptive contextualization of discourse.

Once it is clear to discourse participants that a claim is indeed problematized, they take up a reflexive hypothetical attitude with regard to the disputed cognition or interest. They begin by subjecting the claim to a series of speech acts expressed by different participants in the discourse. Despite criticisms of his earlier science of self-reflection, Habermas thus continues to assume that needs and interests are in principle able to be formulated in speech acts. Then the actors form rational inferences about the generalizability of the claim from the pragmatic units of speech that refer either to these claims or to the actors' own interests. But these inferences can be derived neither from statement logic, which provides rules for the transformation of statements, nor from transcendental logic, which investigates relevant grounding concepts for the constitution of ob-

---

[63] See *Reflexion und Diskurs*, pp. 139–144.
[64] Ibid., p. 185.

jects of possible experience. Simply put: Habermas claims that neither statement nor transcendental logic can reflexively account for
its rationality "within its own framework" (TCA 1.24). Only an informal logic can specify this kind of reflexive acceptability.

Habermas develops his theory of informal inference principally
from Toulmin (see WT 161–65; TCA 1.22–37).[65] Toulmin argues
that claims are provided with rational grounds to motivate their acceptance by a combination of three factors:

		Theoretical discourse	Practical discourse
(D)	Data	causes, motives	grounds
(W)	Warrant	uniformities, laws	rules, norms
(B)	Backing	observations	interpreted needs (WT 164).

The grounds for a given claim are established primarily through the
warrants (W). The backing (B) is a variable form of evidence used
to back (W). Both (B) and (W) *motivate* our acceptance of the
grounds for holding the claim. What is distinctive in Toulmin's analysis is that the relation between (W) and (B) is based, not on a
deduction from principles, but on a non-deductive inference that
serves as a bridging principle to justify the transition from descriptive
references to norms.

Habermas applies Toulmin's theoretical and informal argumentation scheme specifically to the way in which normal discourse determines validity. He criticizes Klein for applying argumentation to the
analysis of the validity of social praxis without making the critical
distinction between a social norm's de facto validity (*Geltung*) and
its argumentationally demonstrated validity (*Gültigkeit*).[66] This distinction is required in order to distinguish between the rhetoric of a
conventional consensus and the universal argumentation of a valid
consensus. Bereft of a transcendent point of view for distinguishing
between the determinate validity of opposing standards, Klein is left
with a rhetorical relativism. Toulmin, on the other hand, both allows
for a plurality of de facto validity claims *and* offers a notion of argu-

---

[65] In "Wahrheitstheorien" Habermas refers to Toulmin's *The Uses of Argument*
(Cambridge: Cambridge University Press, 1958); in *Theory of Communicative Action*
he refers to Toulmin's *An Introduction to Reasoning*, coauthored with R. Rieke and
A. Janik (New York: Macmillan, 1979).

[66] Habermas refers to Klein's "Argumentation und Argument," which appears in
Zeitschrift für Literaturwissenschaft und Linguistik, 38/39 (1980), 9ff.

mentational validity. Like Hegel, he argues that the impartial stand-point of a rational judgment is not based on mere arbitrary presuppositions, but emerges through the actual historical undertak-ings of the speech community. He distinguishes field-invariant struc-tures from field-dependent rules needed to apply argumentation to specific problems in medicine, science, politics, etc. But Habermas maintains that impartiality derives not only from the functional use of argument in specific cases, as Toulmin suggests, but also from the conditions of the discursive redemption of validity claims them-selves. Habermas argues that the various argumentation forms that Toulmin proposes are *recognized* in the distinct arguments forms, but not *constituted* through them. For Habermas actors determine grounds that not only determine the rationality of the claim, as Kant's grounds do, but also *motivate* actors to accept the claim as rational.

Habermas does hold that a claim, even when verified by actors in discourse, is still falsifiable. Ordinarily, when a newly validated claim "nullifies" a previously validated claim, we can explain what occurs in one of two ways:

(1) the new claim renders the original claim false; or
(2) the new claim does not falsify the original claim, since the original claim never claimed to be "true for all time."

It seems as if Habermas wants to accept (2). He stipulates that the discursive redemption of assertoric validity claims is subject to the fallibilistic qualification that "we cannot know definitively whether the assertion taken to be true will withstand all future objections" (JA 38). But if so, the truth status of any verified claim becomes difficult to assess. If a truth claim transcends space and time, how can it be "altered" by later spatial and temporal conditions? Haber-mas maintains that his claims about transcendence imply neither a foundationalism nor an infallibilism.[67] The meta-theoretical inter-connection between the theoretical analysis of autonomous disci-plines and spheres of knowledge is ensured by *coherence*, not by a correspondence type of grounding (JA 83). This no longer requires verification by means of evidence presented to an isolated self-con-

---

[67] See his "Questions and Counterquestions," in *Habermas and Modernity*, ed. R. Bernstein (Cambridge: The MIT Press, 1985), p. 193.

sciousness. He concludes that his reconstruction of universal and necessary structures of knowledge, derived from the very reflexive act Kant used to analyze the constitutive achievement of the subject, is no less fallible than other learning processes (MCCA 119). Thus, he offers an alternative account of fallibility:

> (3) The fallibility that characterizes all knowledge claims amounts to the acknowledgment of the critical potential of superior future knowledge, that is, of history in the shape of our own unforeseeable learning processes (JA 39).

This fallibility is based, not on a "cognitive provinciality" in view of the better future knowledge, but rather on an "existential provinciality" resulting from historical transformations in the objects themselves. In other words, the contexts in which future actions will be determined are governed by interactive rules accepted at present. This gives his postmetaphysical philosophy a new impartiality and objectivity. He argues that as "communicative actors, we are limited [*ausgesetzt*] by the conditions of a transcendence which allows of linguistic reproduction, without being subjected [*ausgeliefert*] to them" (TK 155). Since linguistic intersubjectivity is not simply a higher-level subjectivity, Habermas dispenses with the concept of absolute transcendence of truth—found in both Hellenistic Christianity and right-wing Hegelianism—without abandoning the concept of a transcendence of truth "from within." I shall deal more specifically with the contextuality problems related to this inner transcendence in Chapter 5.

The Domain of Discourse

Habermas argues that all problematized claims, including even the expressive claims of speech acts in first-person discourse, can be subjected to validity claims. But he points out that not all validity claims in communicative utterances have a direct connection with corresponding forms of discursive argumentation (see TCA 1.40–41). In earlier works Habermas was unclear about the validity status of expressive claims. In "Wahrheitstheorien" he distinguished between the discursivity of normative and truth claims, and the non-discursivity of truthfulness claims. He claimed that the truthfulness of an expressive claim, such as an avowal, can be stressed at the same level of communicative action as the truth of a proposition and the rightness of an interpersonal relation (WUP 57). An illocutionary claim is required of all expressive claims except for acts that are not merely symbolic.

In the *Theory of Communicative Action*, Habermas modifies the set of conditions needed for the determination of expressive claims. In expressive claims the most a speaker can do is "show in the consistency of his action whether he really meant what he said" (TCA 1.41). The sincerity of an expressive claim cannot be grounded, but only *shown*. A therapist's evaluation of his patient's self-deception, for example, is verified only when the patient can interpret his expressive claims through a "therapeutical dialogue by argumentative means" relative to his own interests (TCA 1.334). But Habermas insists that the argumentation about expressive claims in a therapeutic setting differs from discourse about other claims in several respects: "the validity claim is not regarded as problematic from the start, the patient does not take up a hypothetical attitude toward what is said; on his side, it is by no means the case that all motives except that of cooperatively seeking the truth are put out of play; the relations between the partners in dialogue are not symmetrical, and so on" (TCA 1.41). He thus calls the arguments regarding the truthfulness of an expressive claim *critique* instead of discourse.

To elucidate further the ways in which subjects determine truthfulness of expressive claims, Habermas adopts Goffman's dramaturgical model of everyday self-representation (*Selbstdarstellung*). Goffman argues that the expressive actor reveals his intentions, wishes, and feelings before a public while maintaining a reflexive relation to its own inner world. Thus, Goffman analyzes the ways in which an actor presents himself to his audience by bringing something of his subjectivity to appearance. Though agreeing that the actor reflexively expresses his inner self in this way, Habermas insists that this trait must be regarded "only under the aspect of persons encountering one another" (see TCA 1.90–91). Thus, Goffman fails to account for the actor's ability to behave toward the social world with a norm-conformative attitude. Self-presentation is limited by the expectations of others. Thus these subjective experiences cannot be seen as mental states or inner episodes, for we would thereby assimilate them to elements of the objective world. Though the subject has a privileged access to his inner states, he does not "have" or "possess" desires and feelings that he can express simply "at will" before a public.

For Habermas dramaturgical expressive acts presuppose two worlds: the internal (subjective) and the external (objective). Though cognitions, beliefs, and intentions belong to the subjective world, they stand in an internal relation to the objective world. The actors can treat the audience in the external world as either a public or an opponent. Moreover, the strategic success the dramaturgical action has in the objective world always remains analytically separate from its subjective claim to truthfulness. Expressive acts have a "paradigmatic status" relative to the objective world (TCA 1.91).

What exactly is the validity status of the inner experiences of feelings and needs that the subject presents to others in expressive claims? Habermas argues that speakers can determine the validity of evaluative expressions—expressions about our predilections such as wanting to go on vacation or opposing military conscription, etc.— relative to certain "evaluative standards" (TCA 1.16–17). Though not universally generalizable, these evaluative claims are nonetheless subjected to the rationally motivated power of the better argument. Their component of justification "is the bridge between the subjectivity of experience and that intersubjective transparency that experience gains in being truthfully expressed and, on this basis, attributed to an actor by onlookers" (TCA 1.90). Therefore these claims are validated when others *recognize these interpretations in their own needs*. Habermas thus guarantees individual and cultural particularism without value relativism.[68]

A Discursive Theory of Truth

Is it plausible for Habermas to reduce all validity determination— even with these slight variations we have seen—to the power of reflective acceptability? Rorty agrees with Habermas's conviction that philosophy ought to be argumentative. He also agrees with Habermas's claim that neither the "transitions" in Hegel's *Logic* nor the "new conditions of possibility" in *Being and Time* are arguments. He

---

[68] The relative paucity of Habermas's references to "aesthetic" rationality has been widely noted. Unfortunately, further discussion of aesthetic claims lies beyond the limits of this study.

even accepts Habermas's principle that a speaker must use propositions in arguments.[69] But since Rorty—along with Wittgenstein, Tugendhat, Quine, and Davidson—holds that language is primarily a *tool* used to "get what we want," he rejects Habermas's claim that language is the unique *medium* in which truth is discovered and interests are evaluated. This relativistic account of language offers a pragmatic kind of voluntarism that, if warranted, poses a serious challenge to Habermas's theory of reflective acceptability.

In response to such voluntarist arguments, Habermas insists that we resolve conflicts among competing versions of "what we want" only through argumentation aimed at validity. Rejecting the need to determine thin pragmatic grounds for the coherence among one's beliefs—the cornerstone of the Davidsonian view of truth that Rorty adopts—Habermas's truth theory relies upon an assumed *coherence within a speech system*. The coherence is established, not between cognitive entities (schemes, concepts, or predicates) and reality, but between statements and facts. Nonetheless, the existence of a fact expressed in the statement is determined, not by the appropriateness of a speech system, but by the truth of the statement itself (WT 172). Successful discourse re-establishes "behavioral certainties" (OPC 363).

To recapitulate: Habermas specifies the following procedures for discourse. First, he specifies the domain of what can be subjected to a criticizable validity claim, as we have seen. Validity claims are contained not only in communicative utterances, but also in wishes, feelings, and even moods. Second, he insists that the basic predicates of linguistic systems express these cognitive schemata in such a way that the relation between language and reality is regulated, as Piaget noted, through a dynamic but nevertheless formal process of learning and development. The rationalization of communicative action is reflected in progressive forms of social integration and ego-identity formation. But Habermas rejects Piaget's claim that the schema formed in actual interaction processes systematize experience with-

---

[69] See *Philosophical Papers*, 2:124–126. Rorty claims that Habermas derived this principle from Tugendhat's appropriation of Wittgenstein. Rorty agrees with Tugendhat's claim that the phenomenon of justification and the question of justifying what is considered true is nowhere to be found in Hegel, since *Aufhebung* is a form of "pseudo-argumentation" in which the unit of speech is the word, not the sentence.

out any reference to inferential processes. Instead he argues that if we "de-mystify" inference, then we can use it to determine the validity of statements within a theory of cognitive development. Third, Habermas assumes that there is an internal relation between a speech system and the statements referred to it. The appropriateness of a speech system can be proved indirectly by true statements *which we can form in it* (WT 170).

How plausible is this universalistic and reflexive account of speech use? How can a formal pragmatic analysis both picture reality accurately and critique it relative to standards of truth? How metaphysical is Habermas's employment of terms such as "totality" and "system"? I shall present a further critique of Habermas's post-metaphysical communicative rationality in the next chapter when I evaluate how his theory of communicative action applies to the problems of ego-identity and discourse ethics. Before that, it will be helpful to examine how his systemic theory of truth accounts for the particularities of the *speaker* of language. I need to examine the relation between the procedure of reflective acceptability and the *self*-reflection of those employing the procedure. In other words, how does Habermas understand this speech act-theoretic theory relative to his earlier concerns about the emancipation of the subject?

The Problem of Self-Reflection

Habermas argues that all validity-determination requires reflexive processes embedded exclusively in language and argumentation. But *who* is the participant in discourse? How are these participants to understand themselves? To specify the self-understanding of speakers, Habermas must first confront a potential dualism that lingers in his formal pragmatics.

Habermas's formal pragmatics views the individual both as an autonomous speaker *and* as one participant among others in the interaction objectively viewed. In Schnädelbach's terms, the subject is described on two separate levels of explication. In traditional metaphysics this same dualism has taken forms as diverse as the body/soul distinction (Descartes), occasionalism (Malebranche), the denial of matter (Berkeley), and so forth. So, for Habermas, what guarantees the *unity* of the speaker, given his bifurcated relation to inner and outer worlds?

Habermas turns to proposals offered by Kant and Fichte to avoid this potential fragmentation of the decentered subject.[70] Although under the influence of a dualism of the phenomenal and the noumenal, Kant argued that the intelligible ego is a spontaneous unity of recognition and action *addressed by universal moral laws*.[71] Applying a genetic analysis to Kant's claim, Fichte concluded that the ego is both a practically completed and a reflexively fulfilled *actor*, thus preparing a way for a pragmatically unified theory of intersubjectivity. For Fichte the very conception of self-activity requires that the ego be conditioned by the force of the other's free will. Thus, the individual realizes his freedom not through the power of its own essence, but only through a kind of paradoxical *self-limitation by the other*.

Habermas "solves" the dualism by uniting the inner and outer worlds of the subject by means of his use of language. Linguistically, the subject has a first-person relation to his inner world, a third-person relation to the outer world, and, most important, a second-person relation to the social world of interaction. By adopting this triangulated interactive view of the subject, Habermas avoids the liability to which most contemporary theories of language, especially post-structuralist ones, are prone: the denial of the autonomy of subjects, or speakers, of language. Habermas explicates the individual and moral identities of speakers in his performative analysis of their progressive adaptation to their environment. His theory of individuality views the speaker as a complex combination of

- (*a*) self-expression in first-person address,
- (*b*) self-description relative to a third-person observer perspective, and
- (*c*) self-explication relative to a second-person interlocutor.

---

[70] In *Knowledge and Human Interests* Habermas contrasted Kant and Fichte with Peirce and Dilthey. Now in *Postmetaphysical Thinking* he contrasts them with Hegel and Leibniz.

[71] Again we are faced with the puzzling fact that Habermas omits any mention of the *Third Critique* in his discussion of Kant's unification of practical and theoretical reason.

These three levels are unified in the performative activity of a communicative actor. A competent actor achieves a kind of rational accountability (OPC 310).

Habermas describes how Rousseau and Kierkegaard made the turn from a descriptive to a performative analysis of individuality. Rousseau portrayed individual authenticity as an actor's ability to make a secular confession of his own life practices subject to the judgment of a "public" (see PT 166–167). Kierkegaard argued that an isolated soul achieves individuation and justification for its existence only through a conversation with God (PT 165). Habermas argues that both these performative "self–other" relations broke through the reigning metaphysical dualism that predicated individuality on the basis of a combination of substance (essence) and accidents alone. Habermas argues that the performative theory of self-identity must include not only autonomous self-description, but also self-explication to an other. But he admits that, by requiring confirmation by a second person, the justification of self-identity remains an arduous task. Nevertheless, he refrains from avoiding the difficulties posed by the socialization of self-understanding by resorting—as Fichte, Kierkegaard, and Tugendhat do—to "decisionistic" formulations of intersubjective performance.[72]

The resources needed for a non-decisionistic understanding of speaker performance Habermas finds in Mead's theory of symbolically mediated interaction. Mead understood performance, not as the processes of coordination that previously was guaranteed by a "common instinct repertoire" and normatively generalized expectations, but as symbolically mediated interaction. Habermas adopts Mead's requirement that the actor perceive itself as the social object of an other and, in a "reflexive instant," make the behavior expectations of the other *its own*.

Mead's Theory of Individuation

In *The Theory of Communicative Action*, Habermas situates Mead's analysis within the broad phylogenetic shift that took place in mo-

---

[72] In "Werk und Weltanschauung" Habermas also levels this charge against Heidegger. Even Heidegger's later development of *Seinsgeschick* does not mitigate the effects of decisionism. See TK 70.

dernity, specifically toward norm-guided behavior. Durkheim foreshadowed this shift by breaking free of metaphysical individualism and focusing on the role that social norms play in the formation of individuals. He argued that the emerging rationalization of world views—which paralleled the increasing societal acceptance of the authority of a secularized science—engendered a critical "reflexive attitude" that dissolved the symbol-based authorities of taste, tradition, and even the sacred. A new "system based on reflection," evident in the emergence of democratic politics, autonomous science, and autonomous art, overthrew the domination of traditional norms (TCA 2.82). The development of a reflexive view of normativity led to a more widespread generalization of values, the universalization of law and morality, and the development of individual autonomy. Although affirming this developmental process of social rationality, Durkheim argued that at times the individual could fully safeguard his autonomy only through deviance from the social milieu. This capitulation to "institutionalized individualism" (Parson's phrase), posed a threat to the development of true individual autonomy (PT 149).[73] Mead took a different approach to the problem of the development of individual autonomy within a society. Unlike Durkheim, he formulated an ontogenetic theory of social interactionism through an analysis of an actor's self-perceptions and subsequent behavioral expectations in the context of *actual processes of differentiation*. Mead claimed that an individual differentiates himself by learning to internalize controls over his own behavior. The "self" of the practical self-relation is no longer the locus of an original or reflexive self-consciousness, but rather the instance of *self-control over its own action*. Self-reflection thus takes on the specific task of marshaling motives for action (PT 179). When situations of conflicting expectations arise, the inner control of self-serving impulses allows the actor to develop new forms of role coordination with others. Thus, individuation depends, not on the possession of specific roles, but on the skill of *coordinating* one's own role expectations with

---

[73] Habermas uses Gehlen and Foucault to reinforce this claim. Gehlen emphasizes the importance of institutions in individual formation processes, and even claims that the individual is one case of an instituition. See his *Die Seele im technischen Zeitalter* (Hamburg: Rowohlt, 1957), p. 118. Habermas points out that in some cases Foucault defended the need for institutional restraints on the self. See PDM 279.

those of others: "It is by means of reflexiveness—the turning back of the experience of the individual upon himself—that the whole social process is thus brought into the experience of the individuals involved in it."[74]

What reflective limit determination does the individual require in order to effect this coordination? Mead spelled out a theory of reflexive coordination of action in "The Definition of the Psychical" (1903). He first criticized the narrow cognitivist confines of the psychical theories of reflection of his day.[75] Most psychical theories held that, by providing some kind of physical or material structure for behavior, reflection functions only to unify and to orient psychic experience. According to Mead, although these psychical theories tried to combine theories about the perception of outer objects with theories of immediate experience, they negated the subject altogether. Mead found it curious that although "the long struggle of modern reflection has brought the world of knowledge into the experience of the self, the theory of the peculiar experience of that self should have no place in the doctrine of reflection."[76]

Mead saw a logical contradiction in this objectivizing use of self-reflection: self-reflection provided the very terminology that the psychical required to explain itself as a system without a self. Mead avoided this contradiction by turning the psychical *in on itself*—making it aware of its own limits—and thus focusing on the way it represents ideas for its own possible action.[77]

Defining reflection as an inner deliberation that terminates in action, Mead distinguished between the non-reflective immediacy of habitual actions and the reflective deliberation required for actions that reconstruct disintegrated action coordination. Reflection deliberates about future behavior in two ways: through *analysis* it indi-

---

[74] *Mind, Self, and Society*, p. 134. Mead's theory of language is also reduced to the instrumental tasks of problem solving. Language is a process of indicating certain stimuli and changing our responses to them in a system of behavior. Through language, the individual picks out responses and holds them in his organism, so that they "are there in relation to that which we indicate" (p. 97).

[75] Mead, "The Definition of the Psychical," in *Selected Works of George Herbert Mead*, ed. Andrew Reck (Chicago: The University of Chicago Press, 1964), p. 25. Mead still operated very clearly within a philosophy of consciousness, claiming that the only common characteristic of all definitions of subjectivity is that they equate identity with "the consciousness of individual as individual" (p. 26).

[76] Ibid., p. 35.

[77] Ibid., p. 26.

cates novel features of the object that give rise to conflicting impulses, and through *representation* it organizes its reactions toward the object *from itself in exactly the same way as it would be from an other*. These processes embody the analytic and synthetic forms of reflection we have already seen. What is new is Mead's claim that this reconstructive activity arises out of an original projection of an "I." The reflection of the "I" not merely subsumes the coordinating behavior of the self under scientific laws, but controls its own impulses during the coordination process in a "phase of experience within which we are immediately conscious of conflicting impulses that rob the object of its character as object-stimulus, leaving us in an attitude of subjectivity; but during which a new object-stimulus appears due to the reconstructive activity which is identified with the subject 'I' as distinct from the object 'me.' "[78] This "I" retrospectively discovers innovative content for new hypotheses. The retrospective determination of a possible act takes place by means of an *image*.

Though granting a role for images in reflection, Mead was aware of the uncritical usage of images common in most associationist and attention-process theories. Associationist theories link images with memory. Even Peirce had argued for a weak form of associationism in which we know the effect of a chain of thoughts by its producing some image or "idea" in us. Mead modified the quality of this association by specifying that an image interprets *conditions* for a forward-looking "state of reflection" in the same way as a predicate interprets a subject in a proposition. This formation of hypothetical images commences once actors thematize a breakdown in behavior coordination. The formation operates much like Kant's reflective judgment: "It is evident that in this phase of reflection it is impossible to present the elements out of which the new world is to be built up in advance, for disintegration and analysis of the old is as dependent upon the problem that arises as is the reconstruction."[79] The logical determination of this synthetic determination of subject and predicate Mead called the "copula phase" of judgment. Symbolic representations of these dispositionally oriented images are derived from logical abstractions of thought-objects and justified by the interpre-

---

[78] Ibid., p. 55.
[79] Ibid., p. 58.

tation of *actual* physical processes and conflicts. Habermas adopts this same pragmatic ground of innovation.

In "Social Consciousness and the Consciousness of Meaning" (1910), Mead described the role of gestures in the communication of behavior expectations.[80] He defined a gesture as "a social act" that serves as a stimulus to elicit a response from another individual. An actor's consciousness of meaning arises only in this mutual coordination of social stimulation with an other. Anticipating Austin, Mead claimed that this consciousness of meaning consists primarily in the *attitude* of the individual toward the object of his intended action. The actor's attitude determines the coordination between the processes of stimulus and response: the better the adjustment between stimulus and response, the less conscious we are of the response itself. Successful social conduct brings the actor into a field within which consciousness of his own attitudes can control the conduct of others. It is in this "field of gesture" that the interplay of social conduct turns precisely upon changes of attitude. Meaning entails knowing one's own attitudes of response in order to control and interpret the gestures of others.[81]

The logic of this process of self-control takes the linguistic form of the interrelation between the first-person performative expressions "I" and "me." Mead claimed that although the self always appears in consciousness as a "me," the "I" "is, of course, not the Hegelism of a self that becomes another to himself in which I am interested, but the nature of the self as revealed by introspection and subject to our factual analysis."[82] The "I" is not the observer that accompanies our actions, but the reflective self who is yet another "me," criticizing, approving, suggesting, and planning responses. The "I" stands over against other selves and "thus becomes an object, an other to himself, through the very fact that he hears himself talk, and replies."[83] Introspection follows upon the prior social self-distance we already have learned to assume toward ourselves. Mead insisted that this introspection is not a solipsistic struggle within the

---

[80] "Social Consciousness and the Consciousness of Meaning," in *Selected Works*, pp. 123–133. This article's overall aim is to determine the genetic conditions under which self-conscious life emerges.

[81] Ibid., p. 133.

[82] "The Social Self," in *Selected Works*, p. 122.

[83] Ibid., p. 146.

individual, but rather a way of reconstructing situations so that more adequate behaviors and personalities may emerge. Introspection constitutes an emancipatory and spontaneous path for the "I" to follow.

Although Habermas clearly adopts the pragmatic thesis of Mead's self-reflexive internalization of behavior controls, he criticizes some of its key assumptions. First, he criticizes Mead for neglecting the distinction between an "originary self-relation," which makes the transition from gestures to real communication, and "reflected self-relation," which is established only in the conversation with oneself that presupposes linguistic communication (PT 178). The reflected self-relation is de-linguistified and made ultimate in philosophies of consciousness. Second, Habermas criticizes the implicit behaviorism of Mead's stimulus/response analysis. This model assumes that agreement between two actors exists *in itself*, not *for them*. Mead does not adequately distinguish between the organism's reaction to its own gesture and the addressing of its gesture to an other (TCA 2.13). The traditional subject/object model is manifest in Mead's claim that the individual introspectively makes itself *an object to itself*.[84] Third, Habermas claims that Mead regulates interests, not by propositionally differentiated forms of linguistic communication, but only by norm-regulated actions. Mead's theory thus bestows self-relation upon the conditions of interaction *before* a linguistic medium for speaker and hearer perspectives is formed. Habermas voices the same kind of "knowledge before knowledge" objection about Kant's cognitional theory (MCCA 2). Thus, Mead operated essentially at the pre-linguistic level of gestures that embody an intentional relation of the subject to himself (PT 175). In Tugendhat's terms, Mead insufficiently distinguished the epistemic self-relation of the knowing subject from the practical self-relation of the acting subject. He never developed a theory of meaning capable of analyzing the distinction between assertoric and imperative moods in an interaction.

Despite these reservations, Habermas demonstrates how the structures of first-, second-, and third-person performative attitudes are present in Mead's model of behavioral interactionism. Mead used the symmetry of the performative *Du–Mich* relation as the basis for

---

[84] See Tugendhat, *Self-Consciousness and Self-Determination*, p. 232.

his critique of the hitherto "mirror-model" of self-relation. The self of Mead's original self-relation is a *generalized other* emerging not out of the anonymous objectifying perspective of a third-person observer, but out of the constituting perspective of a second-person addressant. Self-consciousness is thus "decentered," though not as radically as it is for later post-structuralists. The "me" appears as the higher "reflective form of spirit" and is thus neither a product of a past ego withdrawn from consciousness nor an entity dependent on the self-consciousness of an other. The "me" of the practical self-relation reveals itself as a conservative power that mirrors the life forms and institutions of a particular culture. Habermas concludes that Mead actually had two distinct forms of the "me": the "me" of self-reflection that correlates with the performative attitude of a third-person observer, and the "me" of social participation in interaction in which the actor encounters *itself* as a second person (PT 172; OPC 308). The "I," on the other hand, is the locus of the subject's affective and creative impulses (see TCA 2.98–100). This serves as the basis for the "pathic" self. But Habermas criticizes Mead's failure to properly explicate one important practical dimension of the "I," specifically its "impulse of creative fantasy" that creates new language by which we can see the world with new eyes (PT 180).

Habermas concludes that the subject's reflexive self-relation can be thematized not only as self-determination (*Selbstbestimmung*) based on its identification with certain social roles, but also as self-*realization* (*Selbstverwirklichung*) based on its unique differentiation from certain social roles (PT 183). Although the concrete life forms and institutions of a particular collective find expression in the "me," conventional identity can splinter under the force of conflicting "me" expectations. Habermas argues that a "post-conventional ego-identity" is thus attained not by others' *agreement* with my judgments, but by their *recognition* of my life history's claims to uniqueness (PT 186). The "I" not only has a direct access to its spontaneous action through mediated acts of self-recognition, but becomes autonomous and individuated through its own *return to itself*. Habermas thus acquiesces to a determining (in Hegel's sense) reflective act. Nevertheless, he insists that this self-realization of our particular life history remains only a *regulative ideal* relative to actual interaction: "The self-critical appropriation and reflexive continuation of life history would have to remain a non-binding or even indeterminate idea as long as I could not encounter myself before the eyes of all, i.e., before the forum of an unlimited communication community."[85]

In the next chapter, I shall analyze in greater detail the way in which Habermas systematizes these two self-performative perspectives in his theory of personal identity. At this point, Habermas's reading of Mead has clarified the reflexive relation of the self relative to the *other*. Habermas's debate with Dieter Henrich and Tugendhat brings the self's relation relative to *itself* more clearly into focus.

The Debate with Henrich

Although Habermas takes pains to provide a practical theory of the self, as we have seen, Henrich argues that the cognitional side of his theory is woefully inadequate. He claims, *pace* Mead and Habermas, that all subjects possess a natural and spontaneous epistemic self-relation that is independent of any implicit reference to interaction with an other. Like many of his fellow Heidelberg school theorists, he assumes that within self-consciousness the ego is equivalent to its own conscious states or experiences. Self-relation can be formulated without recourse to dialectical argumentation with other subjects. Tugendhat points out a certain "de-linguistification" implicit in this claim: "Henrich adheres to the traditional conception of self-relation as a kind of 'being acquainted' with oneself, but he believes that it is necessary to transfer this from self-consciousness into a phenomenon of consciousness which no longer expresses itself as an 'I.' "[86] For Henrich the puzzles and paradoxes of self-actualization and self-determination theories can be dissolved by explicating this cognitive aspect of self-relation. Since his theory clashes directly with Habermas's theory of a pragmatically unified self-consciousness, an intense debate has ensued between the two.[87]

---

[85] Ibid.

[86] Ibid., p. 42.

[87] Henrich started the debate with claims raised in *Fluchtlinien* (Frankfurt am Main: Suhrkamp, 1982) and in a column written in *Merkur* 430 (December 1984). Habermas responded in his "Rückkehr zur Metaphysik: Eine Tendenz in der deutschen Philosophie?" in *Merkur*, 439–440 (October 1985), 898ff., later published in *Nachmetaphysisches Denken*, pp. 267–279. Henrich then replied in "Was ist Metaphysik: was Moderne?" pp. 11–43. Habermas responded in turn in the essay "Metaphysics After Kant," in PT 10–27.

Henrich interprets the problem of the relation between the individuality and the universality of the self in terms of the distinction between transcendental and empirical self-apperception. Fichte pointed out the inability of Kant's transcendent viewpoint to deal effectively with the inherent circularity of such an epistemic self-reflection. In order for the self to know itself when it reflects on itself, it must know in advance that the object reflected will be itself. Thus, reflection upon origins of the self-relation fails to explain self-consciousness.[88] Fichte explicated the self's relation to itself, not by a reflexive derivation from a given manifold of experience, but *in the simple originality of its spontaneous and intimate self-relation.*[89] Fichte explicated this self-identity as the act of a "self positing itself absolutely *as* positing itself."[90] The "as" represents a process of uniting the self's individuality and universality in an intentional self-knowledge or "attending to oneself."[91] This phenomenon makes self-determination a universal phenomenon of nature in which life displays a self-reverting activity.

Habermas affirms Henrich's Fichtean attempt to find a theory of the self immune from both naturalism and analytic materialism (see PT 10–11).[92] He also respects his desire to find an epistemic self-

---

[88] See "Fichte's Original Insight," p. 20. Gasché concludes that Henrich ends up in a non-Hegelian mode of speculation "in which the demand for unity and deduction is to be achieved on non-reflective grounds." See *Tain of the Mirror*, p. 72.

[89] "Fichte's Original Insight," p. 22. But Tugendhat points out that Fichte's critique of Kant's philosophy of reflection rests on the erroneous assumption—nonetheless adopted by Henrich—that the object of the reflection is something "whose essence consists in the identity of knowing and what is known" such that self-consciousness exists in the identity of its relata. See *Self-Consciousness and Self-Determination*, p. 52.

[90] See "Fichte's Original Insight," pp. 25, 32.

[91] Ibid., p. 51. But in a later article, Henrich is less optimistic about the success of Fichte's pragmatic unification of self-consciousness. See Henrich, "Selbstbewußtsein: Kritische Einleitung in eine Theorie," in *Hermeneutik und Dialektik* I, ed. R. Bubner (Tübingen: Mohr, 1970), pp. 257–284. Henrich moves closer to a practical unity by using the term "acquaintance" (*Kenntnis*) with oneself. For Tugendhat acquaintance is always propositional. Henrich also admits that the circularity of reflection is not removed, as Hegel thought it was, merely by bestowing the quality of immediacy upon it. But he still concludes that self-consciousness is unintelligible and that we must return to consciousness understood as a "dimension" in which acquaintance with oneself is included (p. 277).

[92] Habermas notes that Robert Spaemann has formulated a return to metaphysics more plausible than Henrich's. Spaemann takes modern forms of consciousness as a point of departure; Henrich remains bound by them. See *Nachmetaphysisches*

relation that will challenge claims that the self is oriented only to instrumental self-preservation.[93] Nonetheless Habermas contends that Henrich's claim that an ego-less consciousness can ground self-consciousness by means of a self-intimacy fails to overcome this instrumentalism. He compares Henrich's "subject" to the impersonal and reductive "system" of a systems theory: both are identities that preserve their identities regardless of the environmental factors that confront them. Henrich's spontaneous self-relational account of the individual is neither developmental nor practical, but merely descriptive of a metaphysical unity.[94] Thinking posits the immediate familiarity with oneself that answers the question "Who am I?" We derive self-interpretations and self-descriptions out of this transcendental "grounding relation" of our life. Habermas argues that this metaphysical self-interpretative view of the subject, though legitimate, is incomplete. Its self-interpretations employ a disclosive "deciphering of the inconceivable" that is detached from any relation to criticizable discursive validity claims.[95] Henrich's category of thinking fails to present rational means of resolving conflicts among self-interpretations.

In "Was ist Metaphysik—was Moderne?" Henrich tries another tack. He argues that the metaphysical thinking that Habermas criticizes is both essential to modernity and a fact of reason. He claims that Kant himself linked metaphysics to the spontaneity of a conscious life engaged in self-understanding. Self-reflection plays an essential role in metaphysical thinking by allowing us both to "break"

Denken, p. 271; Spaemann's and Reinhard Löw's *Die Frage Wozu: Geschichte und Wiederentdeckung des teleologischen Denkens* (Munich: Piper, 1981).

[93] Adorno described the irony that every heroic and cunning attempt of the individual to preserve itself (*Dialectic of Enlightenment*) and to identify and distinguish itself from others (*Negative Dialectics*) ends up in a marginalization of the individual and a loss of identity. For Henrich individual subjectivity aims for, but is never reducible to, its own attempts at self-preservation. See TCA 1.393–395.

[94] See *Fluchtlinien*, p. 19; see also pp. 99–110.

[95] See *Nachmetaphysisches Denken*, pp. 273–275. Habermas argues that Theunissen follows much the same line as Henrich. See Theunissen's, *Selbstverwirklichung und Allgemeinheit* (Berlin: de Gruyter, 1982). Without the aid of speech act analysis, Theunissen tries to transform Hegel's concept of the concrete universal into an intersubjective theory. Rejecting a theory of truth as rational acceptability, Theunissen persists in the metaphysical conviction that "the demand that things are rational in themselves or that reason can be read out of itself defends against the danger of a subjectivizing to which truth falls prey if one simply broadens subjectivity into an intersubjectivity." See *Nachmetaphysisches Denken*, p. 279.

from given forms of agreement and to "gain distance" from them in order to find new forms of stability for conscious life. Henrich claims that we derive stability, not from Habermas's phenomenologically accessible intuitive lifeworld, but from our own spontaneous reflection on life. He calls Habermas's lifeworld concept a "theory language" that avoids the problem of illusion and opts for an immediacy in which the resources are always reliable.[96]

Henrich then criticizes Habermas's theory of discursive rationality in general. He claims that it relies on the "reduction" of meaning to the use of signs. Since signs are subject to the laws of the successive situating of spatial and temporal points in the material world, Habermas's sign-use theory is a form of naturalism. When the usage of signs itself is suspended and analyzed, all its claims to knowledge and agreement are empty. It is quite puzzling that Henrich would thus consider social norms, the determination of which speech act usage is always implicitly oriented toward, to be empty. His critique assumes that Habermas's theory of meaning involves *only* sign usage. Habermas, in fact, argues that sign usage is oriented toward coordination of actions.

Despite his critique of the naturalism of Habermas's sign usage, Henrich does not dispense with the value of naturalism altogether. He points out that Aristotle developed metaphysics out of the natural realities of physical objects and motion. But although condoning a naturalistic *starting point* for philosophy, Henrich adopts a neo-Kantian view that metaphysical thinking is required to account for the limits only to which an analysis or use of a set of natural entities can extend. He points out that even Habermas's critical theory predecessors analyzed these limits.[97] On his account, Habermas shifts the focus of self-consciousness from thinking to relating to an other without considering the problem of the limits of the self as such. Thus Habermas devalues the self's natural ability to *ground* its relation to the other in its own contemplative reflection (*Besinnung*) and obediential respect (*Einhaltung*).[98] Echoing his earlier criticism of the emptiness of the reference of a speech act, Henrich calls Habermas's view of the subject–world relation—expressed in his theory

---

[96] "Was ist Metaphysik—was Moderne?" p. 19.

[97] See ibid., pp. 23–29. Henrich claims that Benjamin served as the inspiration for Habermas's appropriation of the early Hegel.

[98] *Fluchtlinien*, p. 39.

of dramaturgical action and expressive utterances—a concept without content.

In "Metaphysics After Kant" Habermas gives a calm and measured response to these potent criticisms of the very core of his communicative project. He focuses on the differences between his and Henrich's understandings of the subject. He sees a dualism of spirit and matter in Henrich's claim that the subject can validate itself within a "world-forming horizon" detached from contingent things and experience. This dualism, which had taken an *empirical* form in the tradition from Hume until Quine, now takes a *transcendent* form in Henrich. Henrich's transcendent ontology views communicative action theory as an idealism that relies on a transcendence beyond the immediacy of the self-givenness of the other. Habermas agrees with Henrich's claim that a semantic analysis of first-person linguistic expressions alone cannot satisfactorily explain self-consciousness. But he rejects Henrich's claim that self-relation and language use are equiprimordial (PT 23).[99] Meaning is derived, not from the monological reflexive understanding of sentences, but from the analysis of expressions used to forge agreement. "If, namely, the self is part of a relation-to-self that is performatively established when the speaker takes up the second-person perspective of a hearer toward the speaker, then this self is not introduced as an *object*, as it is in a relation of reflection, but as a subject that forms itself through participation in linguistic interaction and expresses itself in the capacity for speech and action" (PT 25).[100] Henrich's pre-linguistic subjectiv-

---

[99] Henrich assumes that because a single, identifiable person is in fact referred to by "I," the person is identified *without the possibility of error*. Tugendhat attributes this erroneous belief to Henrich's adoption of three assumptions derived from traditional theories of reflection: (1) self-consciousness is grounded upon a substance ontology based upon the subject/predicate model; (2) self-reflection is grounded upon the subject/object relation as a representational structure; (3) absolute reflection is an identity of knower and known such that all immediate knowledge is rooted in perception, and thus self-reflection is inner self-perception. See *Self-Consciousness and Self-Determination*, p. 70.

[100] There are other ways of interpreting this "other" of the self. In *Sickness unto Death* Kierkegaard argued that although the self is accessible only in self-consciousness, the self must relate itself to itself since reflection cannot go behind the back of this self-reflection. Second, such a relation must either (a) posit itself, or (b) be posited through another. He rejects (a) and argues that the other of (b) is the Christian God. Henrich considers God the "pre-reflexive trusted anonymity of a conscious life." See Henrich's "Dunkelheit und Vergewisserung," in *All-Einheit: Wege eines Gedankens in Ost und West* (Stuttgart: Klett-Cotta, 1985), pp. 33ff.

ity absolves itself from the need to analyze the self-relation posited either through the structure of linguistic intersubjectivity or through the reciprocal relation of ego, alter, and neuter. Thus, the self's expression and action forgo all possibility of intersubjective verification, the very touchstone of rationality for Habermas.[101] Henrich wants an epistemic self-reflection to determine the limits of the subject relative to the totality of reality external to it; Habermas wants a pragmatic self-reflection to determine the limits of an actor's contribution to actions that can be coordinated with and recognized by others.

The Critique of Tugendhat's Linguistic Self-Relation

The debate with Henrich reveals the critical importance of a theoretical formulation of the relation between the epistemic and the pragmatic elements of the performatively understood self. Communicative action theory assumes that linguistic mediation between self and other occurs through interaction in which either a content about something in the world is communicated to an other or an agreement between two or more actors is reached. This theory of reflective acceptability accounts for the determination of both the propositional form of the meaning and its specific performative use in an utterance.

The later Wittgenstein criticized formal semantics for its inability to account for linguistic expressions, such as prayers, jokes, and thanking, that do not refer to empirical facts. This led to his development of a linguistic pragmatics in which the conditions of propositionally expressed meaning are linked to the use of the utterance in a given "game." In *Self-Consciousness and Self-Determination* Tugendhat takes up and develops the ramifications of Wittgenstein's linguistic pragmatic approach to meaning for the self.

Tugendhat claims that the explication of the epistemic side of the self-relation is based upon an analysis of the phrase "to know oneself." Formerly such a proposition could be understood within one of three possible paradigms:

---

[101] Gasché concludes that because Henrich does not explain the nature of the non-reflexive relation that constitutes the fundamental fact of such an original identity, his approach remains basically skeptical. See *Tain of the Mirror*, p. 70.

(1) *subject/predicate*, which was the earliest and, as Tugendhat says, the most unproblematic because it is based on the subject's "having" states;

(2) *subject/object*, which is much more problematic because it entails the subject's "representing" objects (and thus to relate itself to itself, the subject must represent itself as an object); and

(3) *inner perception*, or a "state of being directed."

Kant rejected (2) but was left with a transcendental ego much like (3). Tugendhat succinctly dismisses Husserl's version of (3), since it is merely a metaphor. Rejecting all three forms, Tugendhat offers his own epistemic model of self-relation based on

(4) the grammatical analysis of the epistemic relation in terms of sentences of the form "I know that p" ("p" referring to psychical, or ø, states).[102]

(4) assumes that a self-referential assertion has a predicate, separated by the "that," distinct from the subject. Thus, for a first person "I" self-report to be true, its translation into this equivalent third-person expression must be true.

How does this epistemic formulation of self-consciousness relate to practical self-determination? Tugendhat sees the unity of the epistemic and practical aspects of the self in a "volitional relationship" of oneself to oneself that completes the self-relation. The transition from the epistemic to the practical is necessitated by Freud's indication that subjects "have" certain *unconscious states* that cannot be fully rendered in attributive propositions. Thus, the practical relation is determined by the relation of the subject, not to itself, but to *its future states of behavior*. Kierkegaard noted that the relation to anticipated behavior actually is a relation, not to one's self, but to one's own existential self-relation.[103] For Tugendhat the relation to oneself is achieved not merely by formulating descriptive sentences about oneself, but also by adopting a yes/no position toward the nor-

---

[102] See *Self-Consciousness and Self-Determination*, p. 10.

[103] Although such a relation could be the relation of the finite and the infinite, the temporal and the eternal, or freedom and necessity—all of which Kierkegaard considered—Tugendhat argues that it ultimately refers to a "relation of synthesis": one's very existence. See ibid., pp. 140–141.

mative consequences of this position for one's life.[104] This practical reflection, in the sense of deliberation about the normativity of action, is emancipative.[105]

Although Habermas is sympathetic with Tugendhat's inquiry into both the semantic and the performative dimensions of self-reference, he criticizes some of its ramifications. First, he objects to Tugendhat's insistence on the utter voluntaristic uniqueness of the person. Habermas finds no need to resort to a solely existential characterization of an individual's act if one analyzes its semantic elements performatively. For Habermas, the self of a performative self-understanding is not "an absolute possession of individuality": the ego does not *belong* to "me" (PT 170).[106] Thus, he insists on Mead's socialized view of individuation. Second, he argues that Tugendhat's claim that formulations of first-person self-reports must be translatable into third-person assertoric statements is based on an untenable "assimilation thesis." Tugendhat claims that a first-person self-report

(*a*) "I have a pain"

has a "veritative symmetry" to the equivalent third-person assertion

(*b*) "He has a pain."

Habermas attributes this symmetry to Tugendhat's claim that a speaker can *refer* to itself with the term "I" without at the same time *identifying* itself as such. Since for Habermas every proposition must assert a constative claim, he distinguishes (*a*) and (*b*) on the basis that (*a*) refers to a claim of *truthfulness* about the "I" that is not directly derived from the constative claim of *truth* in (*b*). Tugendhat analyzes self-reports only on the level of third-person factual claims, not on the expressive level of performative usage. Thus, he cannot distinguish between the validities in first-person reports about oneself (in which validity demands sincerity) and first-person reports about another person (in which it does not) (TCA 1.315).

Habermas's critique of Tugendhat requires some qualification. One can clearly see some similarities between Tugendhat's *volitional* relation of the self to itself and Habermas's *pathic* self-relation. Tugendhat's claims about the ego's uniqueness have more to do with

---

[104] Ibid., p. 235.

[105] Ibid., p. 307.

[106] According to Habermas, Tugendhat's claim *"das Eigenste einer Person ist"* is decisionistic.

truthfulness than Habermas will allow. On the other hand, both strongly defend the claim that the self is other-directed. Tugendhat criticizes basing truth theories on monological theories of freedom, truth, and knowledge; Habermas criticizes basing theories on subjectively grounded theories of respect, world-disclosure, and insight.

Habermas's formulation of the pragmatic and epistemic elements of the self's reflexive relation to itself leaves us with a self-reflection whose explication and justification relies upon structures that are *analogous* to structures of intersubjective argumentation. Though the self is "accessible" only through language, part of the language must be that of a first-person report. These reports cannot be systematized in the same way as third-person reports can be. Nonetheless, the sincerity and expressibility of first-person reports must be rational, and thus subject to warrants and reasons. But the reflexive processes that determine these grounds must be oriented to determining, not the limits of one's thinking or of one's will, but the limits of one's relations to others (both as individual others and as a social *system*). This is why Habermas's insistence on a decentered self is so crucial to his theory of truth.

THE LIFEWORLD BACKGROUND OF REFLECTIVE ACCEPTABILITY

The "Decentering" of Both Self and World

Habermas applies his reconstructive method of linguistically based formal pragmatics, as we have seen, to the problems of social relations and the self. He builds these theories on presuppositions that no longer submit to the constraints of the traditional categories of metaphysics, particularly those that concern thinking and willing. These assumptions form a kind of post-metaphysical "logic" that contains two fundamental parts. The first part is composed of the phenomenologically grounded background *structures* in which communicative action moves: speaker-world relations and the lifeworld. The second part elucidates the post-metaphysical thinking that interrelates these structures into a *system*.

In ordinary language, the term "world" generally refers either to the inner world of the subject or to the outer world of events and things. Although all actors have equal access to the outer world, only the individual has a privileged access to its inner world. Habermas derives this notion of "world" from Husserl's phenomenological understanding of the horizon within which a subject understands the self-givenness of objects. The world in this sense "does not exist as an entity or object, but every singular drawn from it presupposes it."[107] Husserl further stipulated that this concept of the world holds to an "essentially lawful set of types" to which all life and science are bound.[108] Claiming that this essentialist aspect of Husserl's idea of the world renders it vulnerable to an objectivistic misinterpretation, Habermas instead develops a decentered concept of the world that correlates directly to the rationality of communication.

This decentered understanding of the world is derived from a validity-theoretic self/world relation. Habermas argues that language use reveals a world that is not monological and stable, but dynamic and developmental. Popper had differentiated three types of worlds: the physical, the mental, and the world of the products of human spirit (culture). But Habermas claims that Popper's three-world theory never shed its empiricist grounding, remaining an instrumental and ontological concept linked to a correspondence theory of truth (see TCA 1.78–79). Habermas argues that a proper formal division of worlds requires a "reflexive contact" with actuality that exhibits the conditions of the linguistic process of understanding.[109] He bases the division of worlds on Weber's social-theoretic differentiation of the subjective, intersubjective, and objective worlds pre-reflexively assumed in all linguistic interactions.

Habermas stipulates that the self/world relation decenters not only the world but also the self. Habermas describes this decentered self in Hegelian terms: "From the structure of language comes the explanation of why the human spirit is condemned to an odyssey—why it first finds its way to itself only on a detour via a complete externalization in other things and in other humans. Only at the greatest distance from itself does it become conscious of itself in its irreplaceable singularity as an individuated being (Wesen)" (PT 153).

But language not only distances the self from itself, it also provides the bridge by which the decentered actor "returns" to itself. This return is effected by the language use of intersubjective agreement.

---

[107] Crisis, p. 143.
[108] Crisis, p. 173.
[109] See Honneth, Kritik der Macht, p. 318.

From a theoretical point of view, speakers have the ability to take on either an objectivizing attitude about an existing fact, a norm-conforming attitude about a social norm, or an expressive attitude about an experience. From a practical point of view, speakers have the ability to take on first-, second-, and third-person perspectives in order to come to an agreement about something in the world. These intersubjective structures form a "logic" consisting of the first-, second-, and third-person attitudes (or perspectives) of speakers. "The 'I' simply affirms his absolute non-identity *vis-à-vis* the 'You'; but at the same time both recognize their own identity by accepting one another as irreplaceable individuals. In this process they are connected by something they share (the 'We')."[110] These structures determine intersubjective interaction both among individuals and within groups.[111] Oriented to intersubjective agreement, communication is constituted only under the conditions that determine the level of intersubjectivity under which meaning is communicated.[112] We call analytic the speech use that deploys meta-communication only as a means to achieve the understanding about the object; we call reflexive the speech use that employs the communication about the object as a means to achieve an understanding about the "meaningful use" of propositions.

Habermas correlates these speaker/world perspectives to a grammatically equivalent structure of perspectives of speaker roles and attitudes (see MCCA 138–139). There are four elements to this structure of perspectives:

(1) the teleological, in which either a solitary actor or a group aims at decisions (it is strategic when at least one additional

---

[110] "Hermeneutic Claim to Universality," p. 196.

[111] Habermas modifies his claim that individuals and groups attain reciprocity in parallel ways. He notes that although the expressions "I" and "You" have the same performative relation as "We" and "You" (plural) there is also an asymmetry. Although "We" not only is used in a collective speech act over and against an addressee who takes on the communicative role of "You" (plural) under the conditions of reciprocity, it also can be used so that a corresponding sentence is not the complementary relation to an other group, but one presupposed for other individuals of one's own group. Thus, "We" has not only a self-referential, but also a self-identificatory sense. Although the "I" also can be used for purposes of self-identification, it always demands intersubjective recognition of an other, "You." But the self-identification of a group does not *require* recognition by other groups. See "The Development of Normative Structures," CES 107–108.

[112] *Theorie der Gesellschaft oder Sozialtechnologie,* p. 106.

actor's success enters into the original actor's own anticipation of success);

(2) the normatively regulated, by which a social group shares
"common values";

(3) the dramaturgical, in which each of us, as a solitary actor,
presents to our public a certain image (*Bild*) that is our
"reflective character of self-presentation before others";

(4) the communicative, in which at least two subjects establish
interpersonal relations and use *interpretation* to negotiate
the definitions of the situation through consensus (see
TCA 1.85–89).

The teleological (1) is correlated solely with the objective world
shared by all actors; the normative (2), with both the objective and
the social worlds; and the dramaturgical (3), with both the objective
and the subjective worlds. But Habermas insists that this objective
viewpoint is not an extramundane ideal language that is context-free
and could make infallible statements (see PT 138–138). (4) is the
reflexive level, missing in Popper, that mirrors the actor's relations
to the worlds *as such* (TCA 1.94).[113] In (1), (2), and (3) language is
used as a medium, but functions only one-sidedly. But (4) presupposes language *use*: "Only the communicative model of action presupposes language as a medium of uncurtailed communication
whereby speakers and hearers, out of the context of their preinterpre-
ted lifeworld, refer simultaneously to things in the objective, social,
and subjective worlds in order to negotiate common definitions of
the situation" (TCA 1.95).

Thus, a communicative act simultaneously expresses propositional content, offers an interpersonal relationship, and expresses an
intention. Speakers take up a relation to the world not only directly
in teleological, normatively regulated, or dramaturgical acts, but indirectly in the reflective way they *relativize* these acts against possible
challenges from other actors. A communicative action is, therefore,
a symbolic expression not reducible to a grammatical analysis alone.
Although from the perspective of the speaker's performative attitude
its actual speech uses remains "behind its back," the speaker can

---

[113] Habermas had already claimed that our symbol formation both represents an
object and distances us from the object. Thus, spirit is neither an inner nor an
outer, but a *medium*, the *logos* of the world. See his "Arbeit und Interaktion," p. 25.

never reach an extramundane position relative to the actual context of a specific communicative act. This is the half-transcendence of the medium of understanding.

In addition to decentering both self and world through the plurality of speaker/world perspectives, Habermas also decenters them relative to a pre-reflexive intersubjectively shared *lifeworld*. The lifeworld includes the ethical and aesthetic sensibilities of the individual. Habermas develops his lifeworld theory from the "unprethinkable" of Schelling and the constitution theories of Husserl and Schutz.[114] He tries to balance these phenomenological approaches to the lifeworld with his own critical requirements.

In *Crisis* Husserl argued that the *onta* of things can be considered either from the objective perspective of "the manner of being of an object in the world" or from the lifeworld perspective of "the world itself."[115] The objective world is a theoretical construct; the lifeworld is the world as actually and intuitively experienced by subjects.[116] Since the lifeworld concept emerges from our common sense and pre-scientific certainty about spatial and temporal appearances, Husserl used it to refute the positivistic objectivity of the European sciences of his day.[117] Their scientific naïveté could be overcome only by an "occasional reflection" on the life interest each science was originally intended to serve.[118] Husserl thus expanded the domain of objectivity from its narrow anonymous consciousness structures to the broader field of transcendental sociation.[119]

---

[114] See Roberts, *Logic of Reflection*, p. 279; TCA 1.82. Habermas clearly states that the lifeworld concept is derived from a *konstitutionstheoretischen* tradition, or, as McCarthy translates it, "phenomenological tradition." By this translation McCarthy perhaps forges a stronger link between the lifeworld and phenomenology than Habermas may have intended.

[115] *Crisis*, p. 143.

[116] Ibid., p. 127.

[117] See also Habermas's "Edmund Husserl über Lebenswelt, Philosophie, und Wissenschaft," in TK 34–48. Husserl argued that science was originally tied to the lifeworld context. The Egyptians, for example, had developed the science of geometry to serve the practical need to reconfigure their agricultural plots after the Nile's annual floodwaters abated. But with Galileo and the beginnings of European science, mathematicians *forgot* their link to the real world of needs "actually given through perception." See *Crisis*, p. 49.

[118] *Crisis*, p. 96. Husserl even pointed to a reciprocal relation between knowledge and interest: the "interest" of the lifeworld itself sets into play the analysis of its formal structures through a general reflection (p. 141).

[119] Habermas actually uses the term "particular worlds" (*Sonderwelten*) to de-

Although acknowledging its success in countering positivism, Habermas criticizes some of the presuppositions of Husserl's lifeworld theory. First, because Husserl granted the last horizon of legitimation in the lifeworld to the "mediating ego," he failed to construe a complete reciprocity of linguistic use and sociation in the lifeworld.[120] Despite its claim to respond to both theoretical and practical demands, Husserl's lifeworld concept thus remained one-sidedly theoretical and firmly linked to its *perceptual* origin.[121] This explains why Husserl's notions of both self and world continued to be permeated by idealism. Second, Husserl subordinated language to thought. Although Habermas agrees with his claim that all verification depends upon an original mode of self-evidence of the lifeworld, he strongly disagrees with Husserl's claim that language is a "substruction" of thought incapable of providing the original evidence for verification.[122] Husserl even claimed that language seduces us into an objectification that dims the clarity of objects of the lifeworld.[123] Habermas argues, *pace* Husserl, that a speech act theoretic view of language is the only means we have of attaining to a non-objectivizing view of the lifeworld.

Habermas also examines Schutz's view of the lifeworld, specifically its function as a spatio-temporal coordination system. Schutz argued that the lifeworld can be understood in two ways: either naïvely, as always already constituted, or intentionally, as constituted anew in the stream of my enduring ego "of which I become aware by a reflexive glance."[124] But Schutz claimed that the problem of meaning is not only a passive awareness of myself as opposed to the world, but an active determination of how I am to *act* in the world. Habermas claims that Schutz's more existential view of the lifeworld, although not derived from the abstract quality of the epochè, nevertheless

scribe Husserl's broadening of the notion of world. See Habermas's "Vorlesungen zu einer sprachtheoretischen Grundlegung der Soziologie," in *Vorstudien und Ergänzungen zur Theorie des kommunikativen Handeln*, p. 38.

[120] Ibid., p. 56.

[121] See "Edmund Husserl über Lebenswelt, Philosophie, und Wissenschaft," TK 36–37. Habermas insists that phenomenology generally remains tied to a "psychology of perception."

[122] See *Crisis*, p. 128.

[123] See Kevin Paul Geiman, "Habermas's Early Lifeworld Appropriation: A Critical Assessment," *Man and World*, 23 (1990), 79.

[124] Schutz, *Phenomenology of the Social World*, trans. G. Walsh and F. Lehnert (Evanston, Ill. Northwestern University Press, 1967), p. 35.

inherited the overly abstract quality of Husserl's transcendental phenomenology from which it developed. Habermas claims that Schutz ends up replacing the value system of daily practice with the scientific objectivity and resolute *decision* of a theoretical observer (TCA 1.123).[125]

From his critique of Husserl and Schutz, Habermas develops his own socio-theoretic concept of the lifeworld conditioned by the constitution of both a speaker's self-relation and its relation to the social world as a whole.[126] He first specifies that the lifeworld concept appeals neither to an undifferentiated existential immediacy nor to a Romantic *Lebensphilosophie*. Instead, he adopts Schutz's differentiation between the communicative and social "forms" of the lifeworld:

(L1) objectively viewed, the lifeworld is a formal-pragmatic concept that complements the internal structures of communicative action and reveals the network of communicative actions through which it reproduces itself,

(L2) socially viewed, the lifeworld characterizes social life as a network of symbolically structured interactions among social actors.

Habermas rejects, however, the "egological consciousness" implicit in Schutz's claim that the (L1) lifeworld is a necessary subjective condition of *experience* (TCA 2.129). He insists that the lifeworld is the unthematically given horizon within which participants in communication move in common when they refer thematically to something in the world. This reference horizon consists in the interrelation of the three speaker/world relations and the lifeworld. The differentiation between lifeworld and world, completed in the ontogenesis of speech and behavior competencies, repeats itself in every consciously instantiated act of communication aimed at agreement. The (L2) lifeworld is a more complex totality of interrelated

---

[125] Habermas uses the forceful term *"Entschluß"* for this decision. But he does admit that theoretical determinations remain under the determinant condition of the control of others.

[126] See Geiman, "Habermas's Early Lifeworld Appropriation," p. 63. But Geiman makes the erroneous claim that Habermas's pragmatic understanding of language permits him to ignore theories of judgment and predication (p. 73). Habermas's theory of *comprehensibility* takes into account a theory of predication; his theory of *discourse* takes into account a theory of judgment.

and permeable symbolic structures that constitute the social world. It provides social theory with an immediate and unified background knowledge. Although "co-given" in every experience, it is a "totality of what is taken for granted" that defies conceptual formulation (TCA 2.132). This lifeworld concept functions not only as a passive moment of the coordination of actions, but also as an active moment for the constitution of the unity between self and world. It explains how the social actor is both an *initiator* of new actions and a *product* of previous actions of others (MCCA 135).

Axel Honneth claims that, with the addition of the (L2) aspect of the lifeworld, Habermas has shifted from his earlier model of labor and interaction to a model that opens the possibility of viewing socio-cultural development as both a material and symbolic totality.[127] Robert Holub describes how this social totality derives from reflection: "Totality therefore entails the notion of self-reflection: if the researcher works dialectically he must reflect upon his own research as part of the social totality. In a dialectical totality the parts are not related to the whole in an additive fashion; nor is there a mutual implication of parts and whole. Rather, it appears that "totality" in the sense that Adorno and Habermas use the word is something to be intuited."[128] The lifeworld provides the social actor with both a situational horizon-knowing and a thematic context-knowing. The lifeworld "supplies" the resources—attitudes, competencies, ways of perceiving, and identities—by which the social world reproduces itself. This constitutive function of the lifeworld guards the

---

[127] *Kritik der Macht*, p. 321. Habermas admits that the maintenance of a material substratum is a necessary condition for the maintenance of the symbolic structures of the lifeworld itself. See TCA 2.151. David Rasmussen points out that the differentiation between material and symbolic reproduction is crucial for understanding the distinction between system and lifeworld. This in turn goes back to Habermas's appropriation of the early Hegel's dialectical linking of labor and interaction. See *Reading Habermas*, p. 52. Honneth argues that Habermas reduces material and symbolic reproduction to a "simple" methodological distinction between participant and observer perspectives.

[128] *Critic in the Public Sphere*, p. 30. As noted above, Habermas does not refrain from referring to totalities. He even condones Robert Spaemann's claim that "every philosophy makes a practical and a theoretical claim to totality and that not to make such a twofold claim is to be doing something which does not qualify as philosophy." See "Der Streit der Philosophen," in *Wozu Philosophie?*, ed. J. Lübbe (Berlin: de Gruyter, 1978), p. 96. But Habermas refrains from asserting that these totalities have any metaphysical status.

social actor against the fragmentation and contingency of everyday experience.

Habermas then differentiates three different kinds of symbolic processes that function within the lifeworld on the basis of Parsons's three aspects of social action: personality, society, and culture.[129] On the level of personality, the individual actor recognizes that the sequence of its own actions forms a narrative life history and provides resources for his or her actions; on the level of society, a group thematizes its identity in the narrative history of the collective; on the level of culture, it provides members with interpretative schemes regarding technologies, theories, and actions.[130] The lifeworld concept thus takes into account both the continuity of tradition and the coherence of knowing sufficient for everyday praxis.[131] The structural differentiation of the lifeworld corresponds to the functional specification of the reproduction processes of discursive will-formation and learning. These provide the "reflexive refraction" of the symbolic reproduction of the lifeworld (TCA 2.147).

The lifeworld concept presupposes the grasp of two reflective limits. The (L1) lifeworld presupposes that actors can verify their linguistically expressed claims only on the basis of other linguistically expressible claims. The (L2) lifeworld presupposes that successful lifeworld functioning has evolved to require *system* coordination that is not linguistically mediated and thus stands in a dialectical relationship to the lifeworld that nonetheless requires it.

Habermas recognizes the important contribution that Parsons made to social theory by making a technically rigorous concept of system fruitful for social-theoretical reflection. But Habermas claims that Parsons failed properly to reinterpret and assimilate action theory to fit this systems approach. Thus, Habermas uses system analysis to provide a coherent and systematic explanation of nonlinguistic coordination of development within the lifeworld (see TCA 2.199– 203). He analyzes how cultural symbolism functions within an expanded perspective of symbolic interaction. Because the theoretical presuppositions which society can identify with the lifeworld are lim-

---

[129] See, for example, Parsons's *The Social System* (Glencoe, Ill.: The Free Press, 1951), pp. 6ff.

[130] It was Durkheim who overcame the phenomenological understanding of the everyday lifeworld that was restricted to culture alone.

[131] See Honneth, *Kritik der Macht*, p. 318.

ited, Habermas suggests that society be conceptualized by an interplay of what he calls the "higher reflexive levels" of both lifeworld and system.

The system/lifeworld model can account for the fact that we encounter intersubjective situations already determined according to the confines of nature, society, and inner nature (TCA 2.132). The lifeworld embodies the institutional frameworks that govern symbolic interaction; system embodies the interactions of purposive rational action within a given set of empirical interrelations. In the system/lifeworld model, the reproduction of normative structures within a society remains dependent upon evolutionary challenges posed by economically conditioned systems functioning.[132]

Habermas views system and lifeworld as the historical result of a differentiation process through which social evolution reveals itself as a whole.[133] This process takes place in the struggle to achieve adequate communication procedures within spheres of normatively conceived institutions and among social groups. Although Habermas can now incorporate "group specific" action coordination in his social critique, Honneth claims that initially he operated only from the levels of communicative acting subjects and fully organized social systems, ignoring the middle level of praxis of socially integrated groups. Habermas only later recovers these "middle elements" of social organization in his appropriation of Parsons's steering mechanisms of money and power.

The system/lifeworld model's theoretical notion of a dialectical totality differs markedly from Luhmann's concept of a social totality whose parts are related to the whole and analyzed according to the deductive connections of mathematical functions.[134] Habermas discards system theory's concept of the environment (*Umwelt*) which forms the background against which an individual's acts are functionally directed. While Luhmann's systems theory depends on the model of the individual as an organism within a collective environ-

---

[132] "Development of Normative Structures," p. 98.

[133] See Honneth, *Kritik der Macht*, p. 324. Honneth thinks that Habermas succeeds in working his way up from the levels of development of his social theory to a diagnosis of the age able to account for Adorno's and Foucault's critique of power complexes. Habermas situates power relations between system and lifeworld and their steering mechanisms (p. 332).

[134] See Holub, *Critic in the Public Sphere*, p. 30.

ment, Habermas's theory views the individual as a participant in an interplay (*Zusammenspiel*) of cultural reproduction. Though Habermas does admit that a systems approach is legitimate insofar as it analyzes what Marx called the "metabolism" of a society from the point of view of external nature, he warns that system theory's exclusive focus on this "outer perspective" results in a reduction that obscures the "inner perspective" of symbolic interactions among individual actors. Though systems analysis played a central role in Habermas's early functional principle of the "world" of linguistic interaction, he rejects its claim that a language user is a macrosubject of an anonymous system of action, and claims instead that a participant in interaction utilizes group-specific experiences to work out new emancipatory insights. Thus, the reflexive relation to the lifeworld that Habermas posits is generated not only with respect to its dialectical relation to systemic structures, but also with respect to actors' own self-interpretations. For this reason Habermas can speak of a proper rationalization of the lifeworld as an achievement of communicative actions.

Communicative Rationality and the Theory of Reflective Acceptability

Having differentiated the structures of speaker/world relations and the lifeworld, Habermas then sets forth more clearly their interrelation. He wants to avoid both the fragmentation of the individual actor relative to the various world relations as well as the over-particularization of meaning and truth in the lifeworld. Habermas thus systematizes these structures of self, lifeworld, and world not by using traditional metaphysical methods, but by developing a *post-metaphysical* rationality.[135]

Habermas transforms the relation of a subject vis-à-vis the world into a model of the ethical self-ascertainment of a responsible person acting in an intersubjectively shared world. In this paradigm the ego understands itself, not through the formulation of an indefinite number of self-referential descriptions, but only through the *recognition* of its self-referential claims by a second person. Thus, an indi-

---

[135] Habermas finds post-metaphysical thinking in Davidson, Putnam, MacIntyre, Gadamer, Apel, and Ricoeur.

vidual achieves self-identity, not by its skill in self-articulation or self-description, but by its ability to communicate rationally. This intersubjective requirement renders the achievement of self-identity a daunting task. It assumes that all aspects of the person—its motives, interests, and even instincts—are linguistically expressible. This is, as we have seen, a weighty assumption in itself.[136]

Habermas acknowledges that Humboldt, not Hegel, was the originator of a linguistic-performative account of rationality. Hegel had concluded that although language use is a necessary moment in dialectical thinking, it is not as essential as the word: a name or *Begriff*.[137] But Humboldt argued that the intersubjective address of language use itself is an *ontological necessity*: "thinking is essentially ordered to social being, and men require, apart from their bodily and sensible relations, a simple unity between the 'I' and its corresponding 'You' through pure thinking."[138] This social aspect of being is revealed through the second-person performative address of language. Language forcelessly subsumes a manifold under its universal rules, much as a substance subsumes its accidents in traditional metaphysics. Humbolt argues that the grammatical and performative aspects of language form a self-reproducing system: linguistic praxis creates the very linguistic community through which it renews and maintains itself.[139]

Habermas claims that this unifying power of second-person address reveals that language is a manifestation of reason. Reason embodies itself in the self-sufficient universality of the structures of language. The universality manifests itself in the fact that all speech communities have the same grammatical roles of truth, rationality, and justification, even if they are applied and interpreted differently (PT 138). Although this medium of speech evinces only a weak unity

---

[136] Habermas rarely deals with the problem of the unconscious. He assumes that what cannot be propositionally expressed is private language, outside the parameters of rationality.

[137] For Hegel's description of the priority of name-giving, see *Enzyklopädie der philosophischen Wissenschaften*, p. 452.

[138] Wilhelm von Humbolt, *Werke* III (Darmstadt: Wissenschaftliche Buchgesellschaft, 1963), p. 201.

[139] Ibid., p. 160. Humbolt was the first to differentiate performative rules into the various references of personal pronouns. But because of the "subjectless" characteristic of discourse, the existential status of the first person speaker in Humboldt's scheme remained problematic. It also is problematic in Mead's.

of reason, Habermas maintains that it escapes the idealistic spell of a metaphysical concept of unity of world or self which triumphs over the particular and the individual. The reciprocity and impartiality inherent in language use manifests its inherent rationality.

Habermas's postmetaphysical paradigm envisions a model of the rational speaking subject who uses language to determine act coordination. The speaker's individuality emerges when the performative meaning of the "I" synthetically interprets its role as both *unique* within a network of third-person social relations and *normative* relative to the perspectives of the particular second person addressed. The *alter ego* is thus addressed, not as Mead's or Husserl's kind of representative other, but only *in propria persona* (PT 190). Individuality is no longer formulated on the basis of a set of anonymous third-person descriptions; all three perspectives are necessary for a complete understanding of the speaker as an acting and moral self. Moreover, these structures are *universal*: "The universal pragmatic presuppositions of communicative action constitute semantic resources from which historical societies create and articulate, each in its own way, representations of mind and soul, concepts of the person and of action, consciousness of morality, and so on" (PT 191). It is significant that the pragmatic need for communication *precedes* the formation of the semantic rules.

Communicative rationality rests upon the assumption that a kind of intersubjective symmetry exists, at least in principle, among all linguistic actors. Habermas points out that "all languages offer the possibility of distinguishing between what is true and what we hold to be true. The *supposition* of a common objective world is built into the pragmatics of every single linguistic usage. And the dialogue roles of every speech situation enforce a symmetry in participant perspectives" (PT 138). Lorenzer explicated this kind of symmetry that exists in argumentation procedures, specifically in formalized dialogue where the roles of proponent and opponent are clearly defined.[140]

Critics have raised objections to this symmetry required for communicative rationality. Roberts argues that a formalized symmetry cannot support the much greater intersubjective symmetry of perspectives that Habermas requires for his discourse theory.[141] In a sim-

---

[140] For Lorenzer's theory of dialogue, see his *Konstruktive Wissenschaftstheorie* (Frankfurt am Main: Suhrkamp, 1974).

[141] *Logic of Reflection*, p. 279.

ilar vein, David Rasmussen criticizes Habermas's theory of communicative rationality for relying on the problematic assumption that illocutionary acts, which are the acts that forge the symmetry of perspectives needed for understanding and agreement, embody the "originary" communicative mode of linguistic usage, while perlocutionary acts are only "parasitic" upon them. He expresses a strong reservation about the discursive theory of truth that such a prioritizing of communicative action creates: "Presumably, there is a difference between discoursing about the nature of things and arriving at the truth about the nature of things. In other words, the nature of theoretical truth is not necessarily found in discourse while the nature of practical truth is in discourse but not in discursive consensus."[142] Hugo Meynell echoes Rasmussen's reservation. He claims that Habermas ignores the metaphysical principle that the world exists "as it is, prior to and independently of anyone's getting to know about it by means of such a system of validity claims."[143] In Meynell's view, to deny this realism of the world undermines any kind of rationality. In the next two chapters we will examine more closely whether Habermas's assumptions about this symmetry of perspectives determine a plausible account for the verification of certain truth-analogous claims.

CONCLUDING SUMMARY:
LEVELS OF REFLECTION IN FORMAL PRAGMATICS

To summarize, we have seen how Habermas employs several different forms of reflection in his theory of reflective acceptability. Each posits a unique kind of limit needed for formal pragmatics. In the order of his development of them, they are:

(1) *Therapeutic self-reflection.* This reflection determines the hermeneutical retrieval of meaning for a subject. It is the subject's anticipation of a possible *future* state that transforms the limitations of its *present* systemically distorted meaning.

---

[142] *Reading Habermas*, p. 44.
[143] "Habermas: An Unstable Compromise," *American Catholic Philosophical Quarterly*, 65, No. 2 (Spring 1991), 195.

(2) *Rational reconstruction (Nachkonstruktion)*. This analytic reflection reconstructs structures of competencies, such as the threefold world relations of rule-following competencies.

(3) *The self-reflexivity of ordinary language*. In ordinary language a speaker posits the limits of *instrumental* and isolated action relative to *communicative* action by concurrently communicating a locutionary content and an illocutionary claim offer to a hearer.

(4) *Argumentational perspective-taking*. This form of reflection functions in the argumentation and discourse employed to determine the validity of a problematized norm intersubjectively. The limited *egoistic* perspective of each actor is hypothetically generalized relative to *rule* following, and then particularized relative to the procedures by which it can affirm or deny a specific problematized claim.

(5) *"Inner transcendent" self-reflection*. This refers to the reflection by which every actor determines the limits of its *own* isolated perspective relative to the perspectives and interests of *others* by means of the recognition implicit in "second person" speech use.

(3), (4), and (5) are new forms of reflection not found among the forms we examined in Chapter 1.

Habermas's postmetaphysical theory of reflective acceptability recognizes the difference between self and other but reconciles it relative to idealizations implicit in the illocutionary component of speech act address. The theory is thus Hegel's "cunning of reason" in new garb; it overcomes reason's inability to rid itself of the limitation of the self vis-à-vis the other by acknowledging that illocutionary force reconciles the self/other difference by means of interpersonal agreement. The rational illocutionary force of language both posits and overcomes the difference in the relation between self and other.

Though several key foundations of Habermas's theory of truth have shifted in the process of its development—analytic philosophy replaced German Idealism as the source of philosophical grounding and Mead's theory of social interaction replaced Marx's as the locus of social critique—his fundamental aim has remained squarely set upon the investigation of the structures of critical reflection and social emancipation. But by shifting his analysis from the self-formative processes of the species to "supra-subjective" learning processes borne by language users, Habermas mitigated the idealistic implications of his earlier theoretical concept of a unified subject of history.

The fundamental question that remains is how his theory of reflective acceptability works in actual *practice*. The success of Habermas's theory of emancipative forms of reflection depends upon whether it can apply to concrete cases in which either taking on the perspectives of others or determining one's own perspective is crucial. Thus, in the next chapter, I shall critically examine how Habermas employs his theory of reflective acceptability in two realms where this praxis of "decentering" reflection is tested most severely: in his moral theory and in his theory of ego-identity development.

4

Reflective Acceptability in Discourse Ethics and Ego-Identity Development

Since Habermas argues that a rule-guided *agreement* among participants in discourse is the middle term of all validity determination, the most crucial role for reflection in his theory is to determine the proper limits of the various perspectives, particularly the interests, of the participants in the discourse. Habermas thinks that all actors, by properly utilizing the intersubjective power of the illocutionary component of the speech acts they employ, are able reflexively to determine these limits in such a way that they retain their autonomy (as individuals with unique perspectives) while determining a norm that obligates each of them. Thus, even though the illocutionary component of speech acts does not have a significant role in language acquisition or in the comprehension of identical meaning, it grounds Habermas's entire system of communicative action.

Habermas applies his theory of reflective acceptability to various types of claims, as we have seen. The claims can involve determinations about empirical matters, ethical-existential ways of life, moral norms, need interpretations, aesthetic claims, and the ethical-political clarification of collective self-understanding. Those claims which, when understood, oblige actors to *act* in determinant ways are the most difficult to specify, since the terms of practical reflection are the acts of perspective-taking of individual subjects.[1] These perspectives involve what is normative for a group of subjects (in moral discourse), for a political community (in political discourse), what an individual actor ought to do (in ethical-existential discourse), and what are the best means to achieve a given practical goal (in prag-

---

[1] For an good analysis of the difficulties of the "common space" assumed in a consensus, see William Rehg's *Insight and Solidarity* (Berkeley: University of California Press, 1994), especially pp. 233–237.

matic discourse). This chapter will analyze moral and ethical-existential discourses, since, in contrast to theoretical discourses, they
do not simply *explicate*, but *constitute* truth content for the participants.[2] Moral discourse involves the intersubjective *agreement* that
grounds "the role in which other subjects are encountered" as individuals (JA 15). It must synthesize the twofold contingency under
which an individual will confronts the reality of another will. Ethical-
existential discourse confronts the *clinical advice* one receives concerning the correct conduct of life to form its resoluteness toward
the realization of one's life project (JA 9). Ethical-existential discourse aims to free one from an idiosyncratic way of life.

Just as Habermas earlier developed a form of psychoanalysis as a
method of reflection applicable to the problems of individual communication distortions, so in the early 1980s, inspired by Apel's work,
he develops a form of discourse ethics applicable to the problems of
collective will-formation. Habermas derives his version of discourse
ethics from Kant's principle of universalization, Hegel's theory of
recognition, Kohlberg's stages of moral development, and Selman's
theory of perspective-taking. By means of such a hybrid cognitive
theory of moral reflection, he hopes to avoid the dilemmas of the
theories of the good life found in MacIntyre and Taylor. They determine the good merely on the basis of "an order of constitutive goods
as a publicly accessible reality" (see JA 72–74). Ethicians who restrict
morality to evaluative questions of the good life tend to deny the
possibility of generalized or common interests. They argue that interests are legitimate only if they are accepted within the confines of
a specific ethical community. But for Habermas moral reflection in
a postmetaphysical paradigm determines, not a set of goods constitutive for a particular community, but only a procedure of progressive regulative idealizations that guide actors to the proper
justification and application of all norms.

Habermas narrows the domain in which discourse ethics functions
to include only the "reflective analysis of the procedure through
which ethical questions *in general* can be answered" (JA 75). Thus,
his primary concern is how moral norms are justified. This reflects

---

[2] For a good discussion of the difference between truth claims and moral claims,
see Maeve Cooke, *Language and Reason* (Cambridge, Mass: The MIT Press, 1994),
pp. 156–157.

his conviction, evident since his earliest writings, that emancipation is linked to truth. But when applied to the moral realm, the theory of reflective acceptability encounters several difficulties. What does it mean for an interest, embodied in a norm, to be generalizable? How can the wills of diverse actors be determined to conform to a single general norm? Are the justification procedures for a moral norm and for constative claims exactly the same? Does this theory allow for flexibility in the application of a general norm by particular individuals to particular situations?

To analyze these problems, I shall present in relatively short compass a sketch of the background of Habermas's discourse ethics, its general procedures, and then his response to its critics.[3] Then I shall look at how reflection functions in the reciprocal perspective-taking that underlies moral discourse. Moreover, since Habermas claims that identity formation is to a large extent a function of an individual's acquisition of a competence in moral and ethical reasoning, I shall conclude the chapter with an examination of how he understands the relation between the theory of reflective acceptability and the development of *ego-identity*. I shall examine the therapeutical ethical-existential discourses (as well as the background assumptions assumed in their function) that serve to form one's identity. My thesis is that the applicability of reflection to the practical realm demands a greater systematization of *temporal* background conditions of validity determination than Habermas provides. Temporal considerations are particularly crucial in the achievement of the *symmetry of perspectives* that Habermas requires for intersubjective agreement on norms.

Reflective Acceptability and the Moral Realm: The Development of Discourse Ethics

When a social norm is problematized, Habermas argues that an ethical agent is faced with a choice. Either he can disregard the norm and operate on an instrumental level of strategic action, or he can move to a reflexive level of action that seeks consensus with others

---

[3] Habermas's replies to his critics occur principally in JA 19–111; MCCA 172–188; and TK 148–156.

about the norm's validity. The latter is the level of discourse. By determining the rightness of the norm that is universal for all participants, discourse ethics directly addresses the lack of action-coordination that instrumental action can cause. Thus, discourse is the cornerstone of proper lifeworld functioning.

Habermas notes that a confusion arises when communicative action and discourse are not properly distinguished.[4] While an ordinary communicative act involves *any* exchange of meaning, including even non-linguistic context-bound gestures, discourse is the communication that discursively verifies propositions or norms.[5] While in ordinary communication an actor understands himself as a participant in concrete interactions with a set group of others, in discourse each actor agrees on the *reversibility* of his perspective relative to all other possible participants. In discourse the participants allow the "unforced" power of the better argument—and not merely a de facto consent—to motivate their internal change of attitude relative to the claim in question. Although in communicative action actors tacitly presuppose validity claims, in discourse the actors reconstruct a problematized validity claim into an hypothesis that can be subjected to the normative content of pragmatic presuppositions of argumentation (see MCCA 201). Providing the possibility of an orientation toward validity claims, discourse gives no content-determined orientation for the carrying out of practical tasks: it is *not* immediately practical (BFN 5). The rightness that discourse ethics determines merely draws practical consequences from a general action, though it does motivate us to behave consistently in the future in light of the anticipated consequences (TCA 1.15).

In discourse, impartial argumentative decisionmaking becomes the warrant of the rightness of a normative agreement about a claim. Discourse is, therefore, a rarefied form of communication: we neither exchange information about the claim nor engage in "meta-

---

[4] *The Past as Future*, pp. 111–112. Recently, Habermas has distinguished between communicative action in the weak sense (when the aim is finding mutual understanding regarding one-sided expressions of will) and communicative action in the strong sense (when the understanding extends to normative reasons for the selection of goods themselves). See OPC 326.

[5] See *Theorie der Gesellschaft oder Soziologie*, pp. 115, 121. In this section I am dealing only with the "normal" case of discourse that thematizes validity claims. I shall analyze the other two types of discourse, the "therapeutic" used in self-reflection and the "innovatively aimed" used in learning processes, in later sections.

discourse" about the choice between different forms of argumentation (JA 16). While ordinary communicative praxis embeds itself in all everyday routine, the arguments in discourse are "islands in the sea of praxis."[6] Discourse thus extends the context-bound nature of communicative action beyond the limits of one's individual form of life.[7] Through discourse, communication achieves its full rational and emancipatory power.

How does discourse resolve a dispute regarding a norm? Habermas first stipulates that, although "unencumbered by action," discourse ethics transforms norms that guide action into hypothetical states of affairs that may or may not exist. He calls this break a "temporary decoupling" of an ordinary speech act's ability to bind socio-cultural levels of development (WT 131). This "hypothetically broken perspective" has two systematic components:

(1) it thematizes a problematized interest from the point of view of a "hypothetically broken world perspective"; and

(2) it brings forth a coordination of the participants' individual perspectives.

(1) enables speakers, acting within the horizon of the pre-interpreted lifeworld, to thematize a problematized norm within the social world. The actors must distance themselves from their everyday understanding of the lifeworld. This suspension allows for an attitude change that breaks down the naïveté that surrounds a normative pattern of behavior in the lifeworld (JA 24). (2) allows participants to move from the reciprocal linking of behavior perspectives and the coordinating of observer perspectives to the acquisition of a second-person *performative attitude* which allows them to crossover to each other's perspectives (JA 12).[8]

---

[6] *The Past as Future*, pp. 111–112. Schnädelbach, as we have seen, rejects Habermas's strict division between communication and discourse. He claims that discourses are always "regional" and form a unity of action and experience. See his *Reflexion und Diskurs*, p. 145.

[7] Habermas has worked out his theory of discourse ethics in conjunction with Apel. Apel claims that it was Habermas's influence that made him turn to political and social concerns. See Apel's "Zurück zur Normalität?" in *Diskurs und Verantwortung* (Frankfurt am Main: Suhrkamp, 1990), pp. 378ff.

[8] Husserl similarly argued that each ego becomes conscious of intending others in the form of a particular other and "in an amazing fashion" a simultaneity of perspectives is reached in which this intentionality reaches "into" that of the other and vice versa. See *Crisis*, p. 254.

All participants thus achieve a reciprocal perspective-taking through which they can simultaneously focus on the same problematized norm. This relation between reflection and the achievement of a simultaneity of perspectives is evident in Habermas's description of Dilthey's hermeneutics: "An interpretation can only grasp its object and penetrate it in a relation in which the interpreter reflects on the object and himself *at the same time* as moments of an objective structure that likewise encompasses both and makes them possible" (KHI 181) Habermas stipulates that such a definition of a common situation requires a common interpretive task. The task consists in the incorporation of the other's interpretation of the situation into one's own such that "in the revised version 'his' external world and 'my' external world can—against the background of 'our' life-world—be relativized in relation to 'the' world, and the divergent situation definitions can be brought to coincide sufficiently" (TCA 1.100). This demands that each actor suspend all his own perlocutionary motives that normally follow from a speech act except the motive to achieve cooperative agreement (WT 131).

In moral argumentation the success orientation of the "competitors" aims for a higher-level suprapersonal imperative in which the intersubjective authority of a common will is assimilated into a form of communication for reaching understanding. But the competitors are, not personal points of view, but arguments (MCCA 160). Reflexively "broken" world and speaker perspectives become linked to the critical roles of proposing and opposing validity claims. In discourse ethics the participants rely on the complete reversibility of their relations with other participants and simultaneously attribute the perspective of their will to the force of the better argument. This provides the cognitive grounds for Habermas's ethics.[9] What results is a growing ability to "coordinate perspectives" that used to exist in isolation (MCCA 158–160).

---

[9] Though including an analysis of consequences and side effects of a norm on all those affected by it, discourse ethics is clearly a deontological theory. In a deontological paradigm, the truth of an ethical claim or prescription is judged on the grounds of logically consistent rules. Kant held to a kind of mixed deontological position. On the one hand, he argued that logically consistent laws ground the validity of both natural and moral claims. On the other, he held to a strict separation between the sensible realm of nature and the intelligible realm of morality. Habermas adopts the first deontological claim, with some modifications, but rejects the second.

Discourse ethics achieves, by *coordinated* acts of reflection, an overcoming of an actor's lifeworld naïveté and isolated perspectives in order to determine for them a new world-relation within a simultaneity of perspectives.[10] The suspension achieves an intersubjective *present* moment in which participants can impartially determine a *future* behavior expectation embodied in a norm. I shall take up the specifically temporal consequences of this suspension, or break, in the next chapter, concentrating in this chapter on how Habermas understands the conditions and structures involved in the achievement of this reciprocal perspective-taking.

The Phenomenological Background Conditions of Discourse Ethics

Before describing further the reciprocal perspective-taking needed both to thematize a social norm as problematized and to project an intersubjective idealization of agreement about it, I need to examine two phenomenological intuitions that Habermas claims ground practical reason generally.

The first intuition rests on an existential insight into the *vulnerability* of the individual moral actor:

> The more the subject becomes individuated the more he becomes entangled in a densely woven fabric of mutual recognition, that is, of reciprocal exposure and vulnerability. Unless the subject externalizes himself by participating in interpersonal relations through language, he is unable to form that inner center that is his personal identity. This explains the almost constitutional insecurity and chronic fragility of personal identity [MCCA 199].

This intuition into the fragility of the moral actor links intersubjective moral development with ego-identity development, which I shall take up below.

The second intuition rests on the phenomenological insight that an individual's interests are not isolated and subjective, but always already embedded, interpreted, and interrelated in a social world.

---

[10] Following Apel, Bubner argues that an act of reflection must break the continuity between subjects and their agreement about the world in order to determine the conditions of possibility of speech use. Rüdiger Bubner, "Selbstbezüglichkeit als Struktur transzendentalen Argumente," in *Kommunikation und Reflexion*, ed. W. Kuhlmann and D. Böhler (Frankfurt am Main: Suhrkamp, 1982), pp. 328–329.

Compare this with Husserl's view of individual and society in "Philosophy as Mankind's Self-Reflection":

> Human personal life proceeds in stages of self-reflection and self-responsibility from isolated occasional acts of this form to the stage of universal self-reflection and self-responsibility, up to the point of seizing in consciousness the idea of autonomy, but there is an inseparable correlation here between individual persons and communities by virtue of their inner immediate and mediate interrelatedness in all their interests—interrelated in both harmony and conflict—and also in the necessity of allowing individual-personal reason to come to ever more perfect realization only as communal-personal reason and vice versa.[11]

Thus, Husserl held to the reality of both sociation and the generalizing of interests. Heidegger also argued for the primacy of one's situatedness in the social world of others over one's own isolated interests. Habermas, it seems, is in good phenomenological company here.

Unlike his phenomenological predecessors, however, Habermas contends that the conditions his two fundamental moral intuitions impose on moral subjects can be rationally coordinated in a process of collective will-formation. This process of will formation assumes the Hegelian principle that there is an internal relation between the justice that protects the individual's human autonomy and the principle of solidarity that protects the web of intersubjective relations in which the individual is embedded (JA 1). But Hegel argued both that justice cannot be guaranteed solely by the abstract universality of Kant's categorical imperative and that solidarity does not emerge simply from the concrete particularism of an Aristotelian common good. He claimed instead that the demand of normative solidarity must be balanced with the justice of rational obligation.[12] Habermas agrees with Hegel, though stipulating that our rationally formed agreements form the basis of our obligations (MCCA 201). The illocutionary power we possess, when oriented toward the social order, fosters both justice and solidarity.

---

[11] *Crisis*, p. 338.

[12] David Ingram claims that solidarity, "in conjunction with the instrumental constitution of a field of objects and the subjective expression of basic needs, comprises one of three prelinguistic roots of communicative action." See his *Habermas and the Dialectic of Reason* (New Haven, Conn.: Yale University Press, 1987), p. 106.

How are these principles of justice and solidarity viewed theoretically? On the one hand, Habermas rejects a constructivist view of them. He characterizes Hobbes's view of actors who must "create" solidarity through forming a contract based upon their contingent interests and preferences as completely "artificial" (JA 27).[13] On the other hand, Habermas himself uses some constructivist principles implicit in the praxis of argumentation to forge solidarity and social justice.[14] Discourse ethics requires that each actor compensate for his isolation and his vulnerability by forging agreements with others about social norms. He then tries to mitigate the ambiguous position he takes toward constructivism by insisting that discourse ethics constructs, not a set of individual interests or universal anthropological premises, but only an impartial moral point of view already presupposed in argumentation about norms. Although the interpretation of any one specific element of practical reason always remains unpredictable, Habermas maintains that each is as much *constructed* through communicative acts as it is *discovered* by them (JA 30). Nevertheless what is primary for discourse ethics is not whether its elements are constructed or discovered, but the fact that its procedure is reconstructed from actual communicative competencies.

The Cognitive Foundations of Discourse Ethics

Habermas insists that discourse ethics is a cognitive ethics. The rational determination of a social norm's validity is what determines its obligatory force upon the will. Once a norm is problematized, actors attempt either to revalidate it or to validate a hypothetical replacement they have constructed for it. In either case the putative norm is then subjected to a formal principle of universalization (U) reconstructed from the procedures implicitly used in successful argumentation. (U) specifies a procedure of collective will-formation:

(U) *All* affected can accept the consequences and the side effects [the norms'] *general* observance can be anticipated to have for the satisfaction of *everyone's* interests (MCCA 65).[15]

---

[13] See also *The Past as Future*, pp. 101–102.

[14] See Schnädelbach, *Reflexion und Diskurs*, p. 275.

[15] For a good analysis of the ramifications of (U)'s inclusion of interests, see Joe Heath, "The Problem of Foundationalism in Habermas's Discourse Ethics," *Philosophy and Social Criticism*, 21, No. 1 (January 1995), 90–94.

This "structural reduction of perspectival bias" of (U) results in an ego-less projection of the expected side effects of norms.[16]

Habermas developed (U) from Kohlberg's explication of the stages of post-conventional morality. Acknowledging that differences in the content of actual moral claims exist, Kohlberg argued, not for the universality of a given moral procedure, but for the invariance of certain stages in the development of moral competence. Kohlberg's sixth stage required, as (U) does, the reversibility of standpoints, the inclusion of all affected by the moral claim, and the reciprocity of recognized claims. Habermas essentially links the reflexive "prior to society perspective" the actor achieves in Kohlberg's sixth stage to the hypothetical attitude of his discourse participant who aims to generalize interests through argumentation.

How is this procedure of universalization justified? Habermas justifies (U) not simply by demonstrating its actual use by mature moral actors, but also by demonstrating, through a transcendental-pragmatic derivation, the inconsistency involved in the denial of a need for it in moral reasoning. Even to deny that we are subject to the universalizing procedures implicit in discourse places one in the very "circle of conditions" needed to make the denial recognized by others in the first place. But he rejects Apel's claim that this argumentational principle secures "an unavoidable Archimedean point of self-reflection" that is itself a norm.[17] Habermas claims that (U) is not an apriori and infallible "final ground," but only a falsifiable grounding principle.[18] He thus restricts the central concern of philosophy to the establishment of universal presuppositions of argumentation (JA 83).[19]

---

[16] William Rehg, "Discourse Ethics and the Communitarian Critique of Neo-Kantianism," *Philosophical Forum*, 22, No. 2 (Winter 1990), 123.

[17] For Habermas's discussion of the problem of "final grounds" see MCCA 86–90, 95–96; JA 54–57, 79–82, 84–87. For Apel's response, see "Normative Begründung der kritischen Theorie durch Rekurs auf lebensweltliche Sittlichkeit?" in *Zwischenbetrachtungen im Prozeß der Aufklärung*, ed. Alex Honneth et al. (Frankfurt am Main: Suhrkamp, 1989), pp. 15–65. Habermas claims that Apel's adherence to final grounds actually contradicts Apel's own description of the paradigm change from consciousness to linguistic philosophy. See MCCA 96.

[18] See Rasmussen, *Reading Habermas*, p. 61.

[19] A vigorous debate has emerged regarding how principles of universalizability can be justified. Several claim that this principle is only a product of an advanced Western society in a certain stage of development. Others criticize the circularity of such a claim. Habermas argues, not for a logical proof of universalizability, but for its performative consistency.

Discourse ethics utilizes (U) to validate claims about the coordination of the perspectives of a set of actors embodied by a norm. Echoing an earlier argument in *Knowledge and Human Interests*, Habermas claims that following (U) guarantees that the "interests of individuals are given their due without cutting the social bonds that intersubjectively unite them" (MCCA 202). How exactly are these subjective interests limited in order to be properly coordinated? Earlier Habermas used the principle of unity between labor and interaction to specify the way needs are interpreted intersubjectively through language use. He assumed that linguistic conceptualizations of our interests "dovetail" with lifeworld intuitions shared by other participants. But the early Habermas left this process of need-interpretation underspecified. How are interests able to be propositionally formulated so as to enter into discourse in the first place? How do we represent needs that resist expression in constative assertions, and ordinarily are expressed only in symbols?[20] We shall examine how interests are expressed through language in our discussion of ego-identity later in the chapter. For now our focus is on the way an individual's interest, once it is expressed in a propositionally formulated claim, does or does not become generalized in discourse.

Habermas holds that the coordination of interests is achieved by an interplay between material and ideal components. Modifying insights of Marx's, Horkheimer had developed a materialism based upon the link between all social relations and *production* (see MCCA 211). For Habermas the material component of interests derives from the sheer fact that my interests make *claims* on other persons' interests within the context of a lifeworld oriented to reproducing itself both materially and socially. But Habermas is aware of the challenge that an increasingly pluralistic and instrumentally oriented world imposes on this materialist view of needs (JA 90). Thus, he also views interests ideally, stipulating that the purpose of morality, and the point at which synthetic reflection is employed, is to formulate and justify universal norms that regulate interests.

In early works, Habermas spoke of finding a "common interest ascertained without deception" (LC 39). Later he speaks of a "general interest" that gives equal consideration to the interests of each

---

[20] For a good description of non-discursive expressions, see Langer, *Philosophy in a New Key*, pp. 61–66.

individual (MCCA 203). The interest is generalized, not when it becomes every actor's interest, but when it can be *coordinated* with the legitimate interests of all actors. For example, even though each person has a general interest in fire protection, each person must contribute toward the fire protection without having to have an interest in becoming a fireman. If a norm cannot embody a general interest, then it is excluded from discourse ipso facto as incapable of consensus. It can yield to prudential compromises, but cannot be validated by discourse (WT 173). Habermas concludes that common interests are not simply *discovered* by introspection and procedures of will-formation, but also *created* in the process of communication itself (see LC 108).[21] Objective generalizable interests develop within actual social and historical conditions. But Habermas claims that discourse, unlike communication, cannot make interests generalizable; it can only determine when an interest is generalizable.

Seyla Benhabib is critical of this restriction of the shaping of interests to communication and coercion alone. She argues that, in order for Habermas's theory of interest to be distinguishable from theories such as Rousseau's general interest or Rawls's least advantaged interest, *discourse itself* must be capable of generalizing or shaping interest and need interpretation.[22] She calls discourse a "moral transformatory process" that can change and modify the very hypothesized interests it considers. In the last chapter we will take up Benhabib's suggestion.

In addition to the problem of the way generalizability is determined, one can ask whether some legitimate interests simply resist generalizability altogether. Habermas's political writings abound with descriptions of such interests. To a large extent this phenomenon is due to the strong pluralizing of life forms and to the individualizing and de-sacralizing of life histories in modernity. Thus, Habermas claims that sanctions must be imposed when interests conflict with the "stability of behavior expectations" (BFN 24). A society can legitimately impose sanctions that promote social integration, as long as they flow from the presuppositions for intersubjectively recognized normative validity claims (BFN 26).

---

[21] See also "Reply to My Critics," in *Habermas: Critical Debates*, ed. David Held and John Thompson (Cambridge, Mass.: The MIT Press, 1982), p. 253.

[22] *Critique, Norm, and Utopia: A Study of the Foundations of Critical Theory* (New York: Columbia University Press, 1986), p. 312.

Criticisms of Generalizability in Discourse Ethics

Critics of discourse ethics have charged that Habermas fails to account adequately for the way in which its formalized procedures account for substantive conceptions of the good. As William Rehg argues, Habermas claims that at both the formal and the material levels we "find the justificatory power of discourse ethics dependent on or tied to something approximating a notion of the good or a telos. The procedural forum must suppose the approximate realization of an 'ideal communication community.' "[23] But Robert Pippin makes the stronger claim that the procedures of discourse ethics are derived *directly* from social values regarding the public status of reason, reciprocity, and self-consciousness. He argues that if Habermas were to explain how a society as a whole could come to be interested in such an intersubjective agreement about a specific coordination of interests, he would realize that discourse theory itself rests on a prior ethical intuition of the good life.[24] But Rehg cautions against taking such an admittedly teleological aspect of discourse ethics too far. Habermas maintains that the common good implicit in discursively validated norms remains "thin," containing only those structural aspects of the good life which, from the universal viewpoint of communicative sociation, can be skimmed off the concrete totalities of particular forms of life. Though Habermas claims that these moral procedures become "substantive," thus defying Hegel's contention that a procedural morality can make only tautological statements about morality, he still maintains that the ultimate determination of a norm rests not upon its status as a collective good, but upon its validation as a universal norm (MCCA 204).

Benhabib points to another problem inherent in discourse ethics's claims about the generalizability of interests. She argues that discourse ethics is more a critical test for *uncovering non-generalizable interests* than a means of generating universal ones.[25] Following MacIntyre, she suggests that the universalizability principle used to de-

---

[23] "Discourse Ethics and the Communitarian Critique of Neo-Kantianism," 134.

[24] "Hegel, Modernity, and Habermas," 347.

[25] *Critique, Norm, and Utopia,* p. 312. Benhabib claims that the possibility of interest generalization has been a consistent theme in Habermas's writings since *Legitimation Crisis.* On the problem of generalizable interest in Habermas, see Paul Lakeland, *Theology and Critical Theory: The Discourse of the Church* (Nashville: Abingdon Press, 1990), pp. 54–60.

termine non-generalizable interests is at best inconsistent and at worst tautological. The tautological charge would run something like this: "a valid norm requires the consensual agreement of all because the successful norms that have been reconstructed by theoreticians required the consensual agreement of all."

This brings up the crucial issue of whether Habermas's appeal to a performative contradiction is a proper way of justifying the reconstruction of discourse competence, a topic that is unfortunately beyond my present scope. More incisive to my argument is Benhabib's specific inconsistency charge. She claims that participants bring the universalization principle into play only in situations in which an existing background consensus has *broken down*. A paradox then arises: although discourse functions only when the intersubjectivity of ethical life is endangered, "the very project of discursive argumentation presupposes the ongoing validity of a *reconciled* intersubjectivity."[26] Thus, she concludes that (U) is unnecessary.[27]

David Rasmussen argues that this inconsistency can be traced back to the fundamentally different ways in which Kant and Hegel viewed moral reason. For Kant, reason is not a "motive for action"; but comes into play only when action is thwarted by conflict.[28] For Hegel, on the other hand, reason shapes and gives content to desire. Habermas tries to bring together these two conflicting interpretations of moral reason. As Benhabib indicates, this fusion of Kant and Hegel is not an easy task. On the one hand, Habermas solidly upholds the deontological universalism of Kant's project. But he does modify it by shifting the justification of a moral claim from a brute "fact of pure reason" to the universal presuppositions of argumentation.[29] He also mitigates Kant's moral solipsism by placing its highly abstract universalizing requirement within an intersubjective context. On the other hand, Habermas finds many of Hegel's criticisms

---

[26] *Critique, Norm, and Utopia*, p. 321.

[27] *Situating the Self* (New York: Routledge, 1992), p. 37

[28] *Reading Habermas*, p. 67.

[29] Douglas Rasmussen claims that discourse ethics can thwart legitimate individual ends. Although allowing that one's formative process is always social and that the discursive testing of one's needs is part of the very process of establishing one's identity, he maintains that discourse ethics at times requires a person to ignore his own needs or interests and thus "abandon certain central understandings of himself." See his "Political Legitimacy and Discourse Ethics," *International Philosophical Quarterly*, 32, No. 1 (March 1992), 33.

of Kant plausible. While Kant had to assume that all empirical egos have a kind of Leibnizian pre-established harmony, discourse ethics follows the Hegelian insight that traces social harmonization back to "intersubjectively mounted public discourse" (MCCA 203). By its inclusion of side effects and subjective attitudes in the very process of a norm's validation, discourse ethics sides with Hegel's moral formation processes against Kant's moral rigorism. But these Kantian and Hegelian elements clearly remain in a tension in Habermas's discourse theory.

MacIntyre applies some of Hegel's critique of Kant to Habermas himself. We have already seen his criticism of the Enlightenment belief that all cultures and traditions are part of a universal language of interpretation and translation.[30] In *After Virtue*, he takes up Hegel's charge that a universalizing procedure like Kant's could in some cases justify a counterintuitive norm. He claims that discursive actors can avoid this counterintuitive aspect of universalization only if their discourse remains bound to the specific tradition in which it is situated.[31] Discursive verification occurs only within and among actual ethical traditions. MacIntyre concludes that the Enlightenment's misguided trust in the impartiality of discourse stems from an erroneous belief about the range of universalizability.

Habermas responds to MacIntyre by claiming that it is not only empirically but *logically* impossible for discourse to verify norms counterintuitive to members of subgroups. The very capacity to identify a supposedly agreed upon norm as counterintuitive is prima facie evidence for its *lack* of validity.[32] Habermas maintains that moral reflection leaves intact the social bond to a tradition even though the consensus required of all concerned "transcends the limits of any actual community" (MCCA 202). He then criticizes three

---

[30] Michael Kelly claims that Habermas insists that practical reason ultimately is pure, while MacIntyre makes the Gadamerian claim that practical reason is always situated. See Kelly's "MacIntyre, Habermas, and Philosophical Ethics," *Philosophical Forum*, 21 (1989–90), 88. For a defense of MacIntyre's position, see John Doody, "MacIntyre and Habermas on Practical Reason," *American Catholic Philosophical Quarterly*, 65, No. 2 (Spring 1991), 143–158.

[31] MacIntyre, *After Virtue*, p. 222.

[32] Another common communitarian objection to discourse ethics is that it fails to address the question of motivation. Habermas is simply content with a minimalist theory of motivation: there is indeed no reason to assume that a moral theory should motivate people to act rationally. I will take up the problem of motivation in the next chapter.

aspects of MacIntyre's understanding of traditions. First, his description is too selective: MacIntyre is really proposing a method of self-learning among traditions which applies only to a Western tradition. (Ironically, this is very similar to objections that have been raised against Habermas's own theory of communicative action.) Second, MacIntyre logically contradicts himself by positing universal structures regarding the development of any tradition, while claiming that these structures remain particular to each tradition. Third, Habermas characterizes as inconsistent MacIntyre's claim that, on the basis of a "zone of rational overlap," each tradition can "learn" from another tradition in a kind of self-conversion. For Habermas the rational consideration of another tradition can modify one's own tradition only if "the learning subject can compare the explanatory force of both traditions in respect to the *same* problems" (JA 101). Habermas concludes that MacIntyre ends up in a narrow ethical interpretation in which he assimilates the understanding of any symbolic expression to "processes of self-understanding" (JA 104).[33]

Aware of his critics' attempts to place discourse ethics on one or the other extreme of the Kant/Hegel spectrum, Habermas clings to the belief that he has found a procedure that tempers the abstraction of the Kantian ideal of generalization with the concreteness of actual intersubjective practices. Our question is whether the reflective "mechanics" of this procedure make this claim plausible.

Reflection in Moral Discourse

The reflective process involved in discourse ethics is a function of *idealizations* implicit in arguments that redeem validity claims raised by actors regarding social norms. Habermas argues that if—as in Rawls's theory of justice—individuals agree on a norm without af-

---

[33] MacIntyre argues, against critics of his own communally centered relativism, that formal pragmatic notions of truth are actually more open to the Nietzschean relativist critique than his view is. See MacIntyre's *Three Rival Versions of Moral Enquiry* (Notre Dame, Ind.: Notre Dame University Press, 1990). Doody claims that MacIntyre offers a "realistic" as opposed to "consensual" interpretation of truth by reference to the communal practices of crafts. Doody concludes, *pace* Habermas, that MacIntyre is not the strict communitarian he has been portrayed, because he maintains that the standards by which we judge truth remain independent of any local community. See his "MacIntyre and Habermas on Practical Reason," *American Catholic Philosophical Quarterly*, 65, No. 2 (Spring 1991), 151.

firming or denying validity claims in the process, their consent is grounded by the guarantee of their acquisition of a particular set of primary goods, but not by the universal structures of communication.[34] Thus, discourse ethics does not just generate a de facto consensus about a norm; it also reflectively determines the norm's validity relative to the moral point of view. A claim is valid when the interest it legitimates is coherent within a "universally valid form of life" (JA 8). The (U) principle expresses this idealization implicit in all successful coordination. It is derived neither from the projection of a future utopia nor from a pre-established harmony of interests, but from each member's implicit use of argumentation in every successful discourse. Borrowing from Kohlberg's concept of "ideal role-taking," Habermas accounts for this ideal role-taking assumed in practical discourse by specifying a specific formalized procedure of moral discourse about a problematized norm:

(D)   Only those norms can claim to be valid that meet (or could meet) with the approval of all affected in their capacity *as participants in a practical discourse* (MCCA 66).[35]

What are these idealizations implicit in practical discourse?

In Rawls's original position, the participants decide on principles of justice by putting aside their own particular advantages under a "veil of ignorance" in order to reach an impartial point of view.[36] For Habermas such a constructive idealization is unnecessary; in practical discourse participants simply *do in fact make* ideal counterfactual presuppositions (MCCA 198).[37] To claim that anything must be "put aside" to achieve this moral point of view indicates a pre-reflective

---

[34] For a recent interaction between Rawls and Habermas on the public use of reason in political discourses, see Habermas's critique of Rawls's *Political Liberalism* and Rawls's reply to Habermas in *The Journal of Philosophy*, 92, No. 3 (March 1995), 109–180.

[35] Habermas proposes a new formulation for (D) in *Between Facts and Norms*. He gives it a more general formulation: "Only those norms of action are valid to which all those possibly affected by them could assent in their capacity as participants in rational discourses" (BFN 138). But for our purposes, the early formulation suffices for moral determinations.

[36] For a good description of this "non-metaphysical" veil of ignorance, see Rawls's *Political Liberalism* (New York: Columbia University Press, 1993), pp. 24ff.

[37] Rasmussen claims that although Rawls has acquiesced to the critiques of the communitarians, Habermas has remained firmly committed to the universalization principle of the theory of communicative action. See *Reading Habermas*, p. 62.

attitude: for Habermas the point of view of the generalized other is not beyond the limit of my everyday communicative perspective. Two intuitions into ordinary communicative competence confirm the presence of these idealizations. First, Habermas claims that the very fact that we can lie and distort communication indicates that we possess some kind of idealizing capacity over and above what we actually express.[38] Second, common sense reveals that speakers are indeed capable of transcending the limits of their personal preferences in response to public demands (JA 23). In discourse ethics this idealizing capacity functions as a "regulative idea" (JA 51).[39] This reciprocal perspective-taking is not what participants agree *to* attain, but it is an antecedent condition *for* any agreement. Yet it is not "achieved" spontaneously, since it requires a deliberate reflective act on the part of all participants.

Discourse ethics thus posits an analogy between the rightness of moral claims and the truth of assertoric statements: both are subject to discursive redemption through argumentational procedures. The argumentation in a moral consensus is based, not on a strict deductive necessity, but on a logical coherence between statements and facts.[40] But Habermas argues that the way a speaker relates to the intersubjective world of morality differs from the way he relates to the objective world of science.[41] By the redemption of a objective truth claim, an existential fact becomes "theoretized"; by the redemption of a social claim to rightness, an ordering of social relations becomes "moralized" (MCCA 161). The question "why be moral" forces one to confront the problems of human vulnerability and lack

---

[38] *The Past as Future*, p. 102.

[39] Despite this aim of ideal consensus, Habermas does allow "morally justified procedures for compromising." See MCCA 205. This also protects discourse ethics against a charge of rigorism. For more on his theory of compromise, see BFN 165–166.

[40] For Lakeland, the claims involve, not the relation between a particular speech act and a norm, but the rationality of the norms themselves. "It is important to distinguish his position [discourse ethics] from the abstract universality of formal ethics, which establishes a hypothetical universalizability (the categorical imperative) in order to justify a highly individualist ethical position." See *Theology and Critical Theory*, p. 52.

[41] Bernard Flynn criticizes Habermas's implicit assumption that reason, in its moral form, is subject to interest. Such a claim falls into a naturalism, and, correlatively, an irrationalism. See *Political Philosophy at the Closure of Metaphysics*, pp. 45, 75.

of motivation in a way that questions about the empirical world do not.

Discourse ethics's normative justification procedure thus utilizes both theoretical and practical insights. The theoretical component of the idealization overcomes what Habermas claims to be the one-sidedness of both Bernstein's and Rorty's pragmatic approaches to ethics. Nevertheless, Habermas adopts an admittedly "weak" idealization, denying that there is one set viewpoint to which the theoretician has direct access: "Neither social collectives nor society as a whole can be regarded as a subject writ large. For this reason, I'm rather careful these days about using the expression 'emancipation' beyond the realm of biographical experiences."[42]

In discourses there are only *participants*. The practical component, on the other hand, is able to identify social practices that suppress legitimate interests, such as the denial of legal safeguards or the systemic exclusion of certain groups from the political agenda.[43] This practical component requires verification from studies of actual social and political competencies. The theoretical and practice are combined in the act of perspective-taking.

Perspective-Taking in Discourse Ethics

Among those who have analyzed and criticized discourse ethics—such as Williams, Tugendhat, Günther, Wellmer, Taylor, Honneth, White, Jay, MacIntyre, Rasmussen, Fraser, and Benhabib—few have dealt specifically with the problem of the intersubjective perspective-taking needed for successful discourse. The key task for this reflective accomplishment implicit in discourse ethics is to determine the limits of a moral actor's individual will or interest vis-à-vis the wills and interests of others. To explicate this act of moral reflection, Habermas combines the theoretical analysis of the validity determination of a moral norm with the practical analysis of the facticity of the social environment to form a model of the *ontogenetic development of reflective moral competence*.

Before developing this ontogenetic theory, Habermas lays out two

---

[42] See *The Past as Future*, p. 104.
[43] See Steven Lukes, "Of Gods and Demons: Habermas and Practical Reason," in *Habermas: Critical Debates*, p. 138.

background assumptions. First, Habermas first indicates that what a discourse determines as true are not predicates, concepts, or language systems, but statements that are legitimated by the force of a better argument (WT 171). These states of affairs that discourse confirms, then, are not real in the sense that they "exist" as represented to a "mind" (see BFN 10–13). Habermas thus avoids characterization as an ethical realist.[44] Second, Habermas formulates a theory of social evolution from empirical observation of the way individuals interact with each other through time. Kant articulated the impartial moral point of view a moral actor can achieve, but did not specify its origin or evolution.[45] But Kohlberg formulated, as we have seen, stages of moral development that *include* the moral point of view.[46] Following Kohlberg, Habermas claims that social evolution culminates when the moral point of view becomes reflexively grasped and encoded in social institutions and political systems. The reflexivity achieved in discourse is a result of the growth of rationality itself.

Habermas has thus set the stage for describing the *development* of the individual actor's ability to take on the perspectives of others. He derives the stages of this ontogenetic development primarily from Robert Selman's empirical studies of perspective-taking.[47] Selman's research is based on two theoretical assumptions. Not surprisingly, he first includes Mead's theory of role-taking in his description of the background assumptions of his research methodology:

> The essential ingredient in this integration is conveyed by Mead's dialectical distinction between the self as a subject (Mead called this the "I," or the perspective taker), and the self as object (the "me," or perspective being taken). It is the integration of these two compo-

---

[44] For a good description of the ethical realist position, see Bruce Brower, "Dispositional Ethical Realism," in *Ethics*, 103 (January 1993), 221–225. Brower calls Habermas a dispositional ethical realist, since the ideal speech situation, unconstrained by domination, is the disposition that determines whether a moral response ought to obtain.

[45] See Rasmussen, *Reading Habermas*, p. 68.

[46] For an analysis of the material and formal aspects of the moral point of view, see Lutz Wingert, *Gemeinsinn und Moral* (Frankfurt am Main: Suhrkamp, 1993).

[47] Robert Selman, *The Growth of Interpersonal Understanding* (New York: Academic Press, 1980). Selman notes that the theoretical background of his "structural-developmental" approach comes from James Mark Baldwin, Mead, Piaget, and Kohlberg. A good deal of his empirical procedure comes from John Flavell.

nents that makes perspective-taking truly social, and not simply the application of a developing reflexive or recursive thinking ability to some arbitrary social content area.[48]

Mead had assumed that social meaning arises from the interactional contexts in which an individual finds himself. Given this initial assumption about the social conditioning of all action, one wonders whether Selman's subsequent empirical observations can be sufficiently theory-neutral. But his frequent disclaimers regarding the limitations of his empirical methods make the "objectivity" of his observations plausible. Second, he argues that the social researcher must take account of "chronological time-released, cognitive capacities" within each individual in a given study.[49] Changes in the understanding of coordination between persons through time causes changes in what each person expresses about his feelings and motivations. Selman thus contextualizes his observations by taking into account the temporal dimension of the subject's perspective-taking.

Postulating a link between social development and perspective-taking, Selman's research derives the structures of the latter from an empirical determination of the former. To determine a subject's social competence he employs Kohlberg's method of "reflective interviews" in which subjects are asked to respond to a set of questions about a hypothetical moral dilemma.[50] From an extensive set of

---

[48] Ibid., p. 34.

[49] Ibid., p. 66.

[50] Ibid., p. 35. One could argue that there is some circularity in this method: the interviewer must assume that the dilemma involves a moral issue *before* there is any consensus with the respondent as to whether or not it does. Selman admits that there are also problems with any study of "pure" perspective-taking: "any model that aspires to deal with the relation between inferred or underlying social-cognitive processes and directly observable manifestations must try to define correspondences between the two without denying the potential role and contribution of other cognitive and perceptual abilities" (p. 49). The "reflective interview" method admittedly confronts the subject with hypothetical situations abstracted from the "natural conditions" of everyday interactions (p. 210). This confirms the general observation that "real life situations generally constrain an individual's ability to utilize his or her full social cognitive capabilities" (p. 233). Selman concludes that the reflective interview can provide the data for a formal analysis that descriptively characterizes the outputs which compose an ontogenetic sequence, but not a functional analysis that determines the way individuals actually apply a given formal scale (p. 215). Selman also realizes that the two theoretical models—the clinical focus on the symbolic meaning of the content of experience and the developmental focus on the

these interviews Selman derives five ontogenetic levels of perspective-taking:

- Level zero (ages 3 to 6): undifferentiated and egocentric perspective-taking. The child cannot differentiate physical and
  psychological characteristics of persons. Differences are only
  physical and *perceptual*.
- Level one (ages 5 to 9): differentiated and subjective perspective-taking. The agent distinguishes physical from psychological characteristics. But the relating of perspectives is
  conceived of in one-way unilateral terms.
- Level two (ages 7 to 12): self-reflective, second-person, and
  reciprocal perspective-taking. The agent realizes that both he
  and the other can take on a self-reflective stance. But the
  agent sees as actual only the self and the other, not the relationship system between them.
- Level three (ages 10 to 15): third-person and mutual perspective-taking. The actor can step not only outside his immediate perspective but also *outside the situation as a totality*. The
  actor sees itself as both actor and object, simultaneously acting and reflecting upon the effects of action.
- Level four (ages 12 to adult): societal-symbolic perspective-
  taking. The agent can abstract multiple mutual perspectives,
  whether societal, conventional, legal, or moral. Feelings, actions, and thoughts are understood to be psychologically determined, but not necessarily self-reflectively understood.
  The agent becomes aware of motivations that are *unconscious*
  and "resistant to self-analysis by even the most introspectively functioning mind."[51]

The stages represent a linear development in social competence.

Habermas justifies his adoption of this basic sequence of perspective-taking on the grounds that it was developed from empirical research. But he modifies it slightly. He first classifies levels one
through three as an actor's threefold process of increasing differentiation: the differentiation between outer world and inner person, the

---

structure of understanding—often end up providing two very different explanations
for the same behavior (p. 247).

[51] For a complete description of these five stages, see ibid., pp. 37–40, 104.

differentiation of intentions and need orientations, and the distinction between intentional and non-intentional action. On level one, the child lacks the cognitive grounds for the world of social norms, since he is unable to perceive the perspectives of others (MCCA 145).[52] Though the child can use third-person pronouns correctly, he fails to reach a third-person objectivity *with respect to himself.* On the second level, the reciprocal speaker/hearer relations become extended to the relation among actors who share the situation. This is the level of communicative action. At the third level, the actors use a third-person perspective within an interaction situation such that the actor achieves the "neutral attitude" of a disinterested person even toward himself. For Habermas this entails that the ego can no longer attribute to the other an "attitude that is stable over time" or ascribe a determined set of preferences to it (MCCA 150).

In collaboration with Rainer Döbert and Gertrud Nunner-Winkler, Habermas examines the logical relations of universality and particularity that function within Selman's levels. On the first level, all meaning is context-dependent and there exists only particulars. On the second level, at which individual actions are set over and against norms, the "symbolic structures of universal and particular become differentiated."[53] On the third level, actors thematize the determinate norms on the basis of their capacity for universalization. Actors use this moral point of view to depart from strictly role-based identities and consider themselves as individuals who possess a unique life history. Now the other has the position, not of a neutral opponent, but of a second person, "you." This level is crucial for Habermas, since its reciprocity of perspectives *has itself been made into an object* and internalized by the subject. Both interaction partners at this level *know* that their own perspectives are reciprocally limited, but nonetheless linked, with those of others.

Thus, we can now see three unique features that reflection acquires when seen from the point of view of a perspective-taking competence. First, the background for cognitive moral reflection is a dynamic learning process: it follows a definite pattern or sequence of stages. Second, moral reflection has a definite telos: it is linked to

---

[52] See also Selman's article in *Entwicklung des Ichs*, ed. Rainer Döbert, Jürgen Habermas, Gertrud Nunner-Winkler (Cologne: Kiepenheuer und Witsch, 1977), p. 111.

[53] "Zur Einführung," ibid., p. 26.

actual *problem solving*. The moral subject improves his ability to take
on the perspectives of others for effective management of conflict
and social functioning. Third, the terms of reflection change in each
stage of moral development: in the first, the actor determines the
limits of its own needs relative to those of others; in the second, it
determines the limits of what is assertible about interests relative to
what is not; in the third, it determines the limits of interests that
can be coordinated relative to those that cannot.

It is important to note that Habermas's theory of perspective-taking excludes two of Selman's levels. Understandably, Habermas
omits level zero because it fails to differentiate between self and
other. But he omits level four, presumably because it presupposes
the concept of a norm of behavior that requires complex intentional-
ities and social-cognitive concepts he considers to be outside the
parameters of publicly expressible meaning. He thus leaves the roles
of contextual factors such as unconscious motives and affective demands entirely out of the developmental process of perspective-taking. He omits the case studies in Selman's research that reveal, for
example, that "affective mechanisms can prevent application of reflective understanding and the related social-cognitive function in
children who are normally capable of higher levels of conceptualiza-
tion."[54] This is again a consequence of Habermas's conviction that
moral action is motivated, not by conscious or unconscious psychological motives, but by the rational force of the better argument. But
by excluding psychological sources of motivation, Habermas leaves
underdetermined the complexity of moral motivation that Selman
captures at level four. In the next chapter, I shall analyze the way
some of these contextual factors can be made part of the discourse
about a norm.

Habermas concludes that the development of perspective-taking
conforms to the progressive decentering of one's understanding of
the world.[55] From the point of view of intersubjectivity theory, autonomy entails not the subject's right of self-actualization, but its
derivation of its own independence in conjunction with the independence of others (see JA 43). One's vulnerability as an individual in

---

[54] *Growth of Interpersonal Understanding*, p. 261.
[55] Habermas then forms his own Kohlbergian six levels of moral development. See
MCCA 166–167.

society is overcome by recognizing that one transcends the limit between self and other *in the very act of acknowledging that in order to communicate successfully both self and other must determine the same limits relative to each other.* Habermas's faith in the possibility of a simultaneous decentering of participants' perspectives in discourse runs directly counter to the fixated subject-centeredness of both Adorno's negative dialectics and the early Wittgenstein's world-disclosure analysis.[56]

DISCOURSE ETHICS AND THE PROBLEM OF APPLICATION

Having justified a social norm, how do participants determine how to *apply* a norm to a particular situation? Though affirming the primacy of justification in morality, Habermas claims that discourses of application are needed because actors cannot determine in advance all the salient features of future ethical situations. Thus, the application of a norm to a situation demands a unique kind of discursive competence.

> In this case, the impartiality of judgment cannot again be secured through a principle of universalization; rather, in addressing questions of context-sensitive application, practical reason must be informed by a principle of appropriateness [*Angemessenheit*]. What must be determined here is which of the norms already accepted as valid is appropriate in a given case in the light of all the relevant features of the situation conceived as exhaustively as possible [JA 14].

This appropriateness is determined by discourses of application.

Carol Gilligan had indicated some difficulties entailed by discourse ethics's initial underdetermination of questions of application. She claimed that ontogenetic theories of "reflective thought" have generally failed to take into account the uniqueness of the moral agency of women.[57] She argued that both the justification and

---

[56] Surprisingly, Habermas acknowledges that Heidegger, although burdened by a flawed model of world-disclosure, managed to avoid such extreme subject-centeredness. See "Ludwig Wittgenstein als Zeitgenosse," in TK 89. This world-disclosure is threefold: *weltklärende, welterschließende, weltverändernde.* None of the forms focus on innerwordly praxis or problem solving.

[57] Nancy Fraser also criticizes Habermas for his failure to take into account women's issues, particularly the problems of subordination to men and child-rearing.

the application of moral norms ought to be gender-specific. Based on her empirical research into the ethical decision-making of women, she argues that women evince a unique "reflective understanding of care."[58] Men analyze moral dilemmas in terms of justice; women, in terms of a logic of relationships. For men the moral imperative appears as an injunction to respect the rights of others and thus avoid interference of their rights to life and self-fulfillment. Given their proclivity for hypothetical reasoning, men tend to abstract from the concrete realities of other persons. But Gilligan argued that women see a "violence" in this abstract reasoning.[59] As an alternative, Gilligan offered an "ethics of responsibility" that requires that the moralist identify and define developmental criteria that encompass the categories of women's perspectives. But, like Habermas and Selman, she also holds that moral reflection functions primarily in the resolution of actual conflicts, not in the ethical formation of theories of the good life.[60]

In his response to Gilligan, Habermas agrees that moral reflection must take into account not only the abstract, but also the concrete

---

She argues that in order to be truly critical, Habermas must account for not only the symbolic sphere, but also the power relations that take place in the private sphere of the family. See Nancy Fraser, "What's Critical About Critical Theory: The Case of Habermas and Gender," in *Unruly Practices* (Cambridge, Mass: Polity Press, 1989), pp. 113–143.

[58] Carol Gilligan, *In a Different Voice* (Cambridge, Mass: Harvard University Press, 1982), pp. 72–73, 105.

[59] Ibid., p. 100.

[60] Stuart and Hubert Dreyfus follow many of Gilligan's insights by proposing a model of "ethical coping" based upon "caring intuitions" that one develops in handling ethical situations. They contend that "ethical expertise" is learned from experience in the same way as any other expertise; thus, moral philosophers such as Habermas have the burden of proof to show how their ethical expertise differs from other expertises. The Dreyfuses claim that "skilled people know how to act justly in specific situations" so that we can "drop the appeal to rules or principles to guide action in the first place." See Hubert and Stuart Dreyfus, "What Is Morality: A Phenomenological Account of the Development of Ethical Expertise," in *Universalism vs. Communitarianism*, ed. D. Rasmussen (Cambridge, Mass: The MIT Press, 1990), p. 257. Lenny Moss criticizes the Dreyfuses, claiming that their monological model misinterprets Habermas's understanding of the role of intersubjective understanding in morality. The Dreyfuses' category of ethical coping would clearly fit on Habermas's level of the psychological categories of interactive competence and ego-identity rather than on the higher level of reflective moral rationality. Thus, the "ethical coping theory" fails to account for the unique role that conflict plays in moral reasoning. See Lenny Moss, "Ethical Expertise and Moral Maturity: Conflict or Complement?" *Philosophy and Social Criticism*, 16, No. 3 (1990), 231–232.

other. But he still maintains that questions of justification and application must be kept distinct. While justification considers the individual as an "illustrative example" in a demotivated and decontextualized situation, application considers the individual as bearing a particular identity, gender, and life history in concrete social relationships (TK 150). Moreover, Kohlberg showed that moral agents are indeed quite capable of distinguishing the two levels.[61] Habermas argues that only the hypothetical attitude of the participants in discourse raises social actors out of their embeddedness in pre-reflective, naïve forms of life. But he also agrees that evaluative questions about specific forms of the good life, which are accessible only within the horizon of a concrete form of life, form the identity of groups and individuals. But since ethical ways of life preclude their participants from asking questions that would "gamble away" their dominant goods, justificatory discourses are always required as a corrective.

Given this defense of the impartial justification of norms, how does Habermas explain the way in which impartial application relates to specific situations and persons? Valid norms owe their abstract universality to the decontextualization of the conditions in which they are determined. Thus, they can be applied only in a "standard situation" whose distinguishing characteristics have been taken into account from the start in the "conditional component" of a rule (JA 13). In non-standard and unanticipated contexts, Habermas allows for a hermeneutic kind of discourse of application: "Since moral norms do not contain their own rules of application, acting on the basis of moral insight requires the additional competence of hermeneutic prudence (*Klugheit*) or, in Kantian terminology, reflective judgment" (MCCA 180).

Habermas earlier stipulated that Gadamer's one-sided application of the hermeneutic model, in which we determine only what the author *meant for us*, has to be reciprocally broadened to include what the author could *learn from us* (TCA 1.134). Habermas advocates the employment of this kind of hermeneutic procedure in the application of norms to specific situations. The norm is concretized in light of the details of the salient features of the situation, *and* the situation is revealed in light of the norm (JA 37). This hermeneutic

---

[61] See Rasmussen, *Reading Habermas*, p. 70.

application is carried out in an historically finite outlook that is "provincial in regard to the future" (JA 13).[62] Habermas even claims that actors can learn application competence that is guided by the universalistic content of the norm. But he insists that this need for hermeneutic interpretation in the discourse of application in no way denies the priority of the discourse of justification.

Is Habermas proposing a kind of faculty of prudence for the problem of application? Although he strictly rules out the adoption of an Aristotelian form of reflective judgment that relates rules to cases, he does speak of the acquisition of a "feel" (*Gespür*) for the "sorting out" of moral problems. Although a "good" form of life generally does not contradict moral demands, Habermas insists that it cannot be justified from a moral point of view (TCA 2.100). But he refrains from reducing reflective judgments to "opaque" constructions comprehensible only in phenomenological terms (JA 17). Reflective judgments are needed in order to keep morality linked to local conventions and the "historical coloration" of a particular form of life (MCCA 109). Above all, he maintains the need for impartiality in judgments about application of norms. Moreover, he insists that the cognitive operations of application processes are demanding. Perhaps in deference to Gilligan, he also argues that these operations are internally linked with emotional dispositions such as empathy. In cases where socio-cultural distance is a factor, concern for the fate of one's neighbor "is a necessary emotional prerequisite" (MCCA 182).

Given this sensitivity to application, Habermas's discourse ethics takes on further reflective tasks. First, the other in discourse is understood to be neither radically different from the self nor simply a generalized other cognitively identical to the self. Thus, he rejects the alterity claims of both MacIntyre's intranslatibility of traditions and Gilligan's gender specificity, on the one hand, as well as the identitarian claims of Gadamer's fusion of horizons, on the other. Second, Habermas seeks a balance between a strong and a weak view

---

[62] On these grounds, norm application requires the argumentative explanation of its own legality (*Recht*). Habermas himself does not go into great detail about the way an application procedure refers to rights at this point, deferring instead to Klaus Günther's *The Sense of Appropriateness: Application Discourses in Morality and Law* (Albany: State University of New York Press, 1993). He does take up this problem later. See BFN, chap. 5.

of reflective acceptability in justificatory discourse. A discourse theory could be based on either a strong version of acceptability that emphasizes the non-fallible universality of truth for all times and cultures, or a weak view that emphasizes the particularity of each actor's unique perspective. He admits that Rawls's concept of overlapping consensus does provide a cogent interpretation of the way for the universal and particular mutually to presuppose each other in social coordination processes (JA 105). But, as we have seen, Habermas's sympathies clearly lie in the direction of a strong universalizability, and thus for the presupposed symmetry of all actors' perspectives in a situation of argumentation.

My contention, however, is that the weakness of Habermas's discourse ethics as a theory of reflection lies, not in its privileging of justification over application, but in its assumption that morality is primarily a device for solving conflicts that are already recognized as such. Habermas contends that *if* a problematization occurs, *then* discourse can provide justificatory procedures to determine the validity of a replacement. He thus provides no impartial procedure for the determination of the problematization of deeply ingrained or strongly habituated sets of interlocking norms whose temporal contexts have changed since their validation. Can't discourse ethics "trouble shoot"? Can't moral actors apply "preventative" discourses to norms that do not *appear* problematic, but nevertheless *could be*? It would seem that discourse would have to address these second-order claims to problematization if it is to overcome systemic distortions that stem from following norms *which normally do not appear as problematized*. I shall take up this problem of the problematization of norms further in Chapter 5.

REFLECTION AND EGO-IDENTITY DEVELOPMENT

As we have seen, Habermas argues that moral development is a function of the cognitively guided interaction between actors and the social world. By means of principle-guided moral judgments and internalized motive-formed convictions, an individual actor learns to guide his action relative to a system of normative behavior controls. Habermas links the actor's capacity to play a competent role in a rule-governed society to its very status and role-identity as a person.

But, in addition to *coordinating* its interests with others, the social actor also requires *recognition* of its interests by others. Since one's very identity as a person requires this recognition, the reflective activity associated with recognition determines one's ego-identity development. Ego-identity develops not only within the social world, as moral discourse does, but within a more complex connection of communicative action and the structures of the objective, social, and subjective worlds. When his moral development reaches a post-conventional level, an individual agent moves from a role-determined identity to a mature ego-identity (see MCCA 169–170).[63]

Two difficulties immediately present themselves. First, if individual identity-development parallels moral development, what happens when an individual actor cannot gain social recognition because he does not conform to a certain set of universal roles or normative expectations? Can the individual rationally "dissent" from a set of norms? Would the inability to conform to a norm entail a "loss" of identity? Second, if norms are validated only through public discursive procedures, how are we to understand Habermas's stance toward the Enlightenment's vision of individual autonomy? Has Kant's hope for the freedom of the individual as a moral lawgiver for himself completely vanished? Does Habermas gain a Pyrrhic victory by freeing modernity from Adorno's and Horkheimer's specter of instrumental reason, only to forfeit individual autonomy in the process?[64]

Habermas addresses these difficulties by reconstructing processes of individual will-formation similar to, but also in some respects distinct from, the collective will-formation of discourse ethics. Both are rational forms of reflective deliberation about the validity of norms

---

[63] "Zur Einführung," pp. 16, 26. Habermas first argued for the link between moral and ego development in "Moralentwicklung und Ich-Identität" in *Zur Rekonstruktion der historischen Materialismus.*

[64] Eugene Gendlin argues that Habermas for the most part ignored his critical theorist predecessors' theories of ego development. Adorno and Horkheimer, for example, explicated a series of ego stages. The first stage was the role identification of the "bourgeois" ego. The bourgeois actor was a "false subjectivity," because it attributed its strength to its role, not to society. The second stage was the weakening of the family in the postwar society. This stage witnessed the increasing growth of narcissism. The third stage, starting in 1968, was characterized by a rebellion against consumerism and other social conventions. For a further description, see Gendlin's "A Philosophical Critique of Narcissism," in *Pathologies of the Modern Self: Postmodern Studies on Narcissism, Schizophrenia, and Depression*, ed. David Levin (New York: New York University Press, 1987), p. 254.

that obligate us. Individual will formation determines roles that guarantee autonomy and authenticity for an individual actor; collective will-formation determines social norms that guarantee autonomy for a group. Each also is a mechanism for resolving dysfunctionality, because each is instantiated only when a social norm or individual role has been problematized.

Habermas admits that the reflective processes of individual will-formation are particularly difficult to define. As McCarthy points out, in a post-conventional paradigm, "the subject's thought is now marked by the decentration, differentiation, and reflexivity which are the conditions of entrance into the moral theorist's sphere of argumentation. Thus the asymmetry between the pre-reflective and the reflective, between theories-in-action and explications, which underlies the model of reconstruction, begins to break down."[65] Nevertheless Habermas stresses that higher-level processes depend on the lower levels whose operations of reflexivity they reconstruct and universalize at a more abstract level (MCCA 169). Just as discourse represents the highest level of intersubjective communication, ego-identity development represents the highest level of individual maturation. But what happens if others refuse to reciprocate my projection of a symmetry of perspectives? What if, as a consequence, my individual will-formation *conflicts with* collective will-formation? Which takes priority? I shall use this tension between the subjective and intersubjective levels of reflective acceptability to guide my analysis of Habermas's theory of ego-identity development.

Ego-Identity Theory

The development of ego-identity reveals a dimension of the reflexivity of the illocutionary act more complex than required by discourse ethics. Discourse ethics demands a decentering relative to a *generalized other*; ego-identity development demands a decentering relative to *one's very self*. How exactly does this self-relation to oneself develop so as to determine one's identity? To answer this, I must first define this identity relation generally, then analyze its background conditions, and finally indicate how Habermas applies it specifically to the self.

---

[65] "Rationality and Relativism," p. 74.

Ego-identity is a perplexing reality: the self must relate to itself without reducing itself to an object. As we have seen, Habermas avoids Fichte's reduction of the self to an object by adopting an Hegelian solution to this dilemma. Hegel argued that an individual is related, not to its immediate self, but to a future self it strives for through its performative actions. Moreover, one's role-identities, as expressed through these acts, must be recognized as legitimate by others.

From a logical point of view, identity is *an equivalence between two related terms*. The terms of any identity relation can be related in two different ways:

(1) *Qualitative identity*. This occurs in cases when the two or more terms are exactly alike. The comparison is made relative to a *tertium quid*.

(2) *Numerical identity*. This occurs in cases when a term is unique, even if it is also exactly like another term.[66]

Peter Geach speaks of (1) when he claims that the identity predicate can be used meaningfully only in connection with the general characterization of a class of objects (TCA 2.103).[67] Henrich calls (1) generic identification and (2) identity as such. He distinguishes between conditions and criteria of generic identity: conditions divide off types of objects from one another, while criteria individuate within the domain of a type of object which can change over time (TCA 2.103–104).[68]

How are these two types of identity applied to the person? Qualitative theories base self-identity upon the self's possession of a set of predicates. Thus, one's identity is expressed by means of indicators such as date and place of birth, nationality, religion, social class, etc. Numerical identity, on the other hand, deals with uniqueness criteria. Strawson argues that numerical identity demands that the "I" be a self-referential expression with which the speaker identifies him-

---

[66] For a description of this distinction, see Derek Parfit, *Reasons and Persons* (Oxford: Clarendon, 1984), pp. 201–202.

[67] See also Peter Geach's "Ontological Relativity and Relative Identity," in *Logic and Ontology*, ed. M. Munitz (New York: New York University Press, 1973) pp. 287–302.

[68] See also Dieter Henrich, "Identität," in *Identität, Poetik, und Hermeneutik* (Munich: Fink, 1979), 8.371ff.

self as distinct from others.[69] Tugendhat claims that the grammatical role of the first person in "experiential sentences" expresses a speaker's privileged access to its projected future.[70]

Habermas bases his theory of ego-identity on a *pragmatic* model that includes three types of identity: numerical, generic, and qualitative (see TCA 2.105).[71] Numerical identity is one's *self-determination* as a unique individual. Generic identity is one's identity as a speaking and acting autonomous subject. But one's qualitative identity is a "predicative self-identification"; it represents an identity that is achieved through one's development as an individual. Qualitative identity emerges in answering the question "Who do I want to be?" Thus, one develops a qualitative identity throughout one's life history by linguistic acts of symbolic self-expression and by moral acts of responsibility. These acts form the basis for the person's *self-actualization*. Any theory of identity that lacks this qualitative dimension Habermas considers decisionistic and subjectivistic.

To avoid either a formalistic or a decisionistic ego-identity, Habermas stipulates that the qualitative aspect of identity demands that the person also be identified, or recognized, by others (TCA 2.102). Yet, on the other hand, he maintains that an other's failure to recognize the validity of a person's particular self-claims does not *ipso facto* erode the person's identity and autonomy (PT 189–190). So, how are we to understand the other's recognition as a necessary but not sufficient condition of identity? To get at this phenomenon of recognition, I need to examine some of the background assumptions of Habermas's ego-identity theory.

The Hegelian Elements in Ego-Identity Theory

In his early work, Habermas analyzed the development of both social and individual identity from an Hegelian perspective. His theory of

---

[69] See P. F. Strawson, *Individuals: An Essay in Descriptive Metaphysics* (London: Methuen, 1959).

[70] See also Carlos Thiebaut, "The Complexity of the Subject, Narrative Identity, and the Modernity of the South," *Philosophy and Social Criticism*, 18, Nos. 3–4 (1992), 313–332.

[71] The distinction between the numerical and the qualitative can also be applied to a political paradigm. Liberal theorists tend to emphasize the qualitative aspects of identity, sometimes resulting in atomistic notions of the self. Communitarians, on the other hand, tend to follow the numerical model and identify the individual

identity adopted three Hegelian principles. First, Hegel argued that each society *develops* an identity that gives its particular form of spirit a normativity. Thus, identity is not inherited, but acquired and developed in the course of its particular history. Second, Hegel maintained that self-identity requires some form of *recognition* from the other. At Hegel's level of self-consciousness, the subject relates itself to itself by both recognizing and being recognized by the other. From Hegel and Piaget, Habermas adopted the conviction that this universalizing self-consciousness is mediated by a form of objective spirit, embodied in a family or nation, by which "the subject can grasp hold of itself only in relation to and by way of the construction of an objective world" (CES 100). Third, Hegel claimed that, at the level of reason, self-consciousness meets *conflicting* norms and expectations. Hegel argued that, by subjecting these norms to principles of universalizability, the moral agent himself becomes both an absolute universal and an absolute individual.

Adopting these Hegelian principles in his early work, Habermas later modifies them by placing them in a postmetaphysical framework. First, he claims that each person progressively develops its identity within the continuity and unity of both a life history and, as we will see below, a personality system. Second, he argues that ego-identity requires that behavior expectations form around the person's ego ideal that are stable and recognizable by others. Third, he claims that identity has both a universal and a particular aspect. The individual employs both universalizing criteria to formulate future action and particularizing criteria to organize its past action into its invariable life history. In *Knowledge and Human Interest* Habermas held that this life history functions within Hegel's causality of fate (KHI 272). Although this causality of fate is also responsible for the individual's repression and formation of pathological symptoms, the individual's own power of self-reflection remains capable of dissolving these repressions and distortions.

Is this assumption regarding universal developmental stages of identity coherent? Robert Pippin argues that Habermas fails in his attempt to reconstruct universal social norms—and thus *a fortiori*

---

with the group, often to such an extent that they render virtually impossible an individual's critical distance from the community. See also Rainer Forst, "How (Not) to Speak About Identity," *Philosophy and Social Criticism*, 18, Nos. 3–4 (1992), 293–312.

ego-identity theory—from Hegel's narrative account of developing forms of consciousness. He claims that Habermas cannot show how his communicative action theory is universally valid, not merely a product of his own cultural milieu. Thus, he argues that Habermas needs to do a genealogical analysis of *the development of the theory of communicative action itself.* Pippin also suggests that the achievement of the embodiment of reciprocity and mutual recognition in modern social norms stems, not from the development of the structures of linguistic interaction, but from the more basic social achievement of the self's *struggle* for recognition.[72] Pippin is thus making two separate claims:

(1) the structures of language are independent from the way intersubjective recognition is achieved through struggle; and

(2) Habermas relies on these linguistic structures alone for his determination of recognition processes.

Claim (1) can be challenged if one holds, as I think Habermas does, that the structures of language have an *internal relation* to the achievement of recognition. Borrowing from Bühler, Habermas argues that all language use involves the inner formation of a claim, the addressing of the other, and the expression of the claim. No linguistic claim can be expressed apart from the mediation of these structures. Since recognition requires communication, it is always mediated by the invariant structures of this communication. Claim (2) is contested by Habermas's conviction that following communicative structures is a necessary but not sufficient condition for the achievement of recognition. Recognition also requires the communicative processes within the lifeworld background of a social world. Habermas holds that structures guarantee only the universality of the ego's identity, not the actual recognition of it. In effect, Pippin and Habermas differ as to the parameters within which one understands recognition to occur.

Empirical Studies of Ego-Identity Development

From these Hegelian presuppositions, Habermas reconstructs the universal levels of "ego structure" that emerge in an individual's de-

---

[72] "Hegel, Modernity, and Habermas," 348.

velopment of identity (see CES 70–73). His developmental structure combines a Freudian structural model with insights from developmental psychology.

Habermas works out an empirically grounded theory of ego-identity development in conjunction with the research of Döbert and Nunner-Winkler. Studying the formative behavior of adolescents, they examine links between levels of moral consciousness and life-orientation in a personality system. Defining identity as the symbolic structure that allows the ego "to secure a personality system in the changes of biographical conditions and over the continuity and consistency of various positions in social space," they claim that the psychological concept of the ego is closely linked to the sociological concept of identity.[73]

Döbert and Nunner-Winkler maintain that identity theory explicates levels at which the ego develops certain cognitive *skills*. An agent claims his ego-identity both *for itself* and as *distinct from others*. But self-identification also requires a *symmetry with the other's expectations*. The reflexive relation of the individual who is identified with himself depends upon the intersubjective relation that he establishes with the other. But in addition to this threefold *horizontal* stage of recognitional structures, identity requires the *vertical* dimension of the individual's maintenance of identity through his various stages of life. The individual and social structures together constitute an identity. Döbert and Nunner-Winkler conclude that the actual formation of identity occurs genetically in three stages, only slightly modified from what Habermas presented in his earlier writings:

(1) the natural identity of young children,
(2) the role identity of older children, and
(3) the ego-identity of young adults.[74]

(3) is achieved when the self-reflective actor realizes that norms it learned in earlier stages are not mere givens, but *have grounds*

---

[73] "Zur Einführung," p. 9. See also Döbert and Nunner-Winkler's *Adoleszenzkrise und Identitätsbildung* (Frankfurt am Main: Suhrkamp, 1975).

[74] In Habermas's third stage there is (*a*) the capacity to remain consistent with oneself in contradictory role systems, (*b*) the readiness to question pre-existing norms and thus achieve autonomy, and (*c*) the capacity to place oneself in the context of a unique life history. Habermas's earlier discussion of the three levels is found in his "Notizen zum Begriff der Rollenkompetenz (1972)," in *Kultur und Kritik* (Frankfurt am Main: Suhrkamp, 1973), pp. 208–210, 226–230.

and justifications. The actor no longer identifies himself only with particular roles and given norms, but with special roles and norms which he both creates and integrates. At this level the previous role identities are transformed into the "biographical traces" of a learning process that has become reflexive. But ego-identity forms a post-conventional identity only by means of the articulation of its life orientation within a cultural system of interpretation. I shall return to this problem of the interpretation of one's life history below.

How plausible is such an ontogenetic analysis for a theory of identity development?[75] Pippin labels it naturalistic, arguing that Habermas begs the question by assuming that one stage of moral argumentation is empirically superior to the others *before* setting out to prove it. He also claims that no theorist has ever successfully applied developmental theory to the actual history of a social community.[76] Although Pippin's circularity charge has some cogency, it is doubtful whether Habermas intends empirically based research to carry the *justificatory* weight in his ego-identity theory and discourse ethics that Pippin assumes it does. Habermas uses this empirical research, as he also used Selman's, only to explicate the invariant performative attitudes that underlie *all* intersubjective communication and, *mutatis mutandis*, ego-identity development and discourse ethics. For Habermas these developmental stages are to be understood as reconstructed background conditions, not explanations, of competencies.

In addition to explicating stages of moral identity development, both Habermas and Döbert and Nunner-Winkler also analyze

---

[75] Habermas, Döbert and Nunner-Winkler note that other research has also produced a cognitive and developmental understanding of ego-identity. Piaget's research observed the outer nature of manipulable objects and strategically reified social relationships. His cognitive development of operations forms a "structured whole" which is formally explicated in a rational reconstruction. Mead focused on the symbolic reality of behavioral expectations, cultural values, and identities experienced in a performative attitude. Freud examined the inner nature of intentional experiences and the uncommunicable drives of the body. In all three theories the actor learns progressively to transform outer reality into inner processes and structures. Habermas, Döbert and Nunner-Winkler argue that the convergence among these three theories, especially between Mead's and Freud's, is becoming more pronounced. They maintain, however, that empirical theories of identity development are still only provisional. They conclude that a principle-guided morality must be anchored in an identity-formation that is ultimately independent of socially acceptable role behaviors.

[76] See "Hegel, Modernity, and Habermas," 346.

sources of ego-identity that involve motives and instincts. They begin by analyzing the culture-invariant structures—specifically the ego, id, and superego—that shape an individual's identity. These structures help to explain an individual's history of "motive formations," such as defense mechanisms or neurotic behaviors.[77]

Children are normally under the domination of parents in the normatively guided relationships of the family. By forming a superego, the child learns the "motive behavior" of roles by which he can avoid pain and gain pleasure. The child represses certain instincts in order to acquire protection and security. Freud accounts for the motive formation at this early level. Adolescents, however, normally develop a self-reflection that distances them from the domination of both outer authorities and inner instincts. The adolescent learns that he or she can choose either a strategic or a norm-guided path to interact with others. Echoing the conclusions of Selman's research, the actor can both differentiate and systematically join a performative attitude of first- and second-person linguistic roles with the neutral attitude of a third-person observer perspective. "The system of personal pronouns brings to expression the decisive linking of the crossover perspectives of self and other with the possibility of transformation between participant and observer attitudes: the reciprocal crossover perspectives can now be perceived from the perspective of a third."[78]

The interpersonal relationship that ego achieves with the other in this process is not immediate, but reflexive. A meta-communicative level of understanding emerges in which "all rational answers to situations concerning distorted communication demand a reflexive thematizing of what is stated, done, or intended."[79] Actors have the possibility of achieving a relationship that is *completely symmetrical*: "both sides can communicate in the consciousness that each of them has before their eyes the complementary linking of behavior expectations and fulfillment."[80] As soon as these conditions are ful-

---

[77] Piaget does not account for this level of "critical self-reflection," which consists of a critical distancing from the unconsciously lived experience of one's own unique course of life. See Habermas, "Zur Einführung," pp. 17–18.

[78] Ibid., p. 22.

[79] Ibid., p. 23.

[80] Ibid. The use of the term "consciousness" here should be interpreted simply as "awareness," not as a private kind of insight.

filled, the two reciprocal behavior expectations form not a *modus vivendi* of instincts, but a system of reciprocal motivation. The id's instincts become socialized. Thus, Habermas claims, just as he did in regard to collective will-formation as we saw above, that the ego's inner coordination of instincts can bring about *changes in instincts and drives themselves.*[81] The ego can construct enduring motives for behavior independent from recognition by reference persons and authority figures, but dependent upon its own *self-recognition.*

Ego-Identity and Communicative Rationality

This theory of self-recognition, or self-actualization, stands in marked contrast to Habermas's earlier theory of self-reflection. He no longer maintains a utopian view of a reflexively achieved intersubjectivity that regulates the exchange of both the meaning and the instincts "behind" the meaning. He now develops a theory of symmetry of interest recognition among mature social actors. He explicates identity formation, not in psychological terms, but in terms of a theory of communicative rationality.

Borrowing from Durkheim and Mead, Habermas argues that a person's identity is predicated not merely upon semantic self-description, but also upon the fact that he or she can *address* another person by speech acts: "The symbolic structures constitutive for the unity of the collective and of its individual members are connected with the employment of personal pronouns, the deictic expressions used to identify persons" (TCA 2.99). Habermas speaks of three dimensions of first-person usage. First, it can be used affectively (*pathische*) to express wishes and feelings. Second, it can be used *practically* to act in conformity with norms. Third, it can be used *critically*, Habermas proposes, to raise and redeem validity claims. At the third level the "I" and "me" return in a reflective form (TCA 2.100). This self-critical level, as we have seen, requires an observer perspective—the point of view of the ideal communication community—that embeds the I–Thou relation within a system of speaker perspectives. Now a speaker has a *choice* about how to communicate: he can use either

---

[81] Benhabib argues that linguistic self-reflection manifests an interesting phenomenon. The more we develop the ability to articulate the needs and drives that we have discovered through reflection, the more we are freed from the power of that which drives and motivates us. See *Critique, Norm, and Utopia,* p. 335.

an expressive mode to report about feelings, wishes, intentions, and opinions, or an observational mode in which experiences are objectified from a third-person perspective.

Can this system of first-, second-, and third-person performative attitudes ever allow for an individual to dissent from a valid social norm? Although Habermas's earlier writings are at times quite optimistic regarding the course of individuation "apart" from sociation, his later writings are more ambiguous. On the one hand, he suggests that in some cases an actor can licitly distance itself from conventions which "have no more meaning" (TCA 2.97). But, on the other hand, this sanctioned distancing still must submit to the stabilizing forces of intersubjective recognition: "The identity of the ego can then be stabilized only through the abstract capacity to satisfy the requirements of consistency, and thereby the conditions of recognition, in the face of incompatible role expectations and in passing through a succession of contradictory role systems" (TCA 2.98). In the final analysis, communicative rationality demands that actors be able to anticipate and expect certain behaviors from other actors. Since dissent and innovation limit the stability of these expectations and the possibility of rational coordination, they must be restricted in a system of communicative action.

A Reflexive Self-Relation

An analysis of identity from the point of view of the performative usage of language and interpretation of one's life history provide, as we have seen, a restricted degree of individual autonomy in a self-critical attitude. But Habermas offers another level of analysis that ensures a greater degree of individual autonomy: the reflexive self-relation. This is the reflection operative in ethical-existential discourse.

Habermas develops his view of reflexive self-relation primarily in light of his discussion of Tugendhat's work on identity. Tugendhat stresses the importance of explicating qualitative identity by determining who the person "wants to be." He criticizes Habermas's early theory of ego-identity on the basis of its uneven distribution of numerical and qualitative determinations of self-reflection.[82] He claims that, like Mead, Habermas fails to provide a sufficient account of one's *volitional* relationship to oneself. Tugendhat argues for a reflexive self-relation that culminates in one's willed *choice* of a unique future.

In *Theory of Communicative Action*, Habermas takes up this volitional aspect of self-choice and decision-making. Habermas formulates a self-relation based on the ego's actualization of who it wants to be. He first points to the paradox that although we do not choose (*wählen*) the particular life form in which we become socialized, we can existentially decide (*entscheiden*) who we want to be (TCA 2.109).[83] But the question of who we want to be remains partially "irrational," because the choice of a life project always involves a certain moment of arbitrariness. An individual cannot take an impartial or hypothetical attitude relative to his own life history in the same way as he can in relation to a social norm or a scientific claim.

So, how exactly does one achieve this existential self-relation? Tugendhat posits a twofold self-relation: the self's epistemic relation to its predicatively formulated "states" and its practical relation to its own future "projects." Habermas subsumes this double relation into a threefold *critical* self-relation. The self relates simultaneously to three different realities: its statements, its actions, and its own self-presentation. This determines the self as:

(1) an epistemic subject, who is capable of learning and has already acquired knowledge in dealings with reality (*Realität*);

(2) a practical subject, who is capable of acting and has already formed a certain character or superego in interaction with others; and

(3) an affective, or pathic, subject, who is "passionate" and has already determined a subjectivity marked by privileged access and intuitive presence (TCA 2.75).

---

[82] See *Self-Consciousness and Self-Determination*, pp. 256–265. Tugendhat makes the confusing assertion that Habermas posits qualitative identity in his second stage of role identity, and generic or numerical identity in the first and third stages. On my reading, Habermas posits numerical identity in all three stages, and qualitative only in the third.

[83] Curiously, Habermas says that he had endorsed this existentialistic way of speaking "earlier," but without specifying exactly when and where.

At first glance this seems astonishing: Is Habermas returning to a subjective and consciousness-based theory of the self? How subjective and private are these immanent objects to which the self relates? Not very. As for (1), Habermas claims that identity formation takes place not only in moral-practical and expressive realms of experience, but also in cognitive contact with objective reality. The subject's relationship to the objective world is always already embedded within the everyday *intersubjectively* shared lifeworld. As for (2), the self's superego is also clearly an intersubjective reality, since it represents internalizations of primary relationships, such as parents or authority figures. One's own sensibility and self-presentation, (3), is not as clearly intersubjective. Although Habermas has not dealt extensively with the affective realm, he consistently denies the possibility of making this private and privileged space normative. Even the experience of pain must yield to the demand of *expressibility*: a third-person objective characterization comprehensible by both oneself and others. So, exactly what kind of affective state is Habermas considering here? He obliquely refers to, but does not elaborate on, Feuerbach's notion of "passion."[84] In later writings he also mentions, rather surprisingly, the role that guilt feelings play in individuation processes. He claims that although guilt indicates a violation of duty, it also reveals the consciousness that we "could not have done otherwise." We feel pangs of conscience when violating social norms. Guilt thus indicates an internal division of the will (JA 14). Despite these brief mentions of the private affective states of the individual, Habermas still maintains that individual will-formation must be analyzed against the public background of the intersubjectively shared lifeworld.

In "On the Pragmatic, Ethical, and Moral Use of Practical Reason," Habermas further elucidates the role that ethical-existential discourse plays in identity and individual will-formation. He maintains that the fundamental ethical question—"What ought I do?"—

---

[84] The German term is *Leidenschaft*. Habermas does not cite this reference to Feuerbach. The only place I could find where Feuerbach speaks of passion is in his "Der Ursprung des Bösen nach Jakob Böhme" in his *Gesammelte Werke*, ed. W. Schaffenhauer (Berlin: Akademie Verlag, 1981), 1.519–531. According to Böhme—whom Feuerbach does not criticize at all here—the principle of evil determines the *Entzweiung*, derived through the "fire of *Ichheit* and *Selbstheit*," needed for the bringing forth of God's own self-consciousness and goodness (p. 523).

can be answered in three ways: pragmatically, ethically, and morally. Pragmatic reasoning determines what means or strategies I ought to carry out to gain a predetermined end. Ethical-existential reasoning determines the kind of person I want to become. While the ethical determines the ends best *for me*, the moral reasoning determines the ends best *for all*. Each of these "strong preferences" is bound with one's own identity (JA 4).

Ethically viewed, the self determines its ends based upon both individual and social projections of an ideal (*Vorbild*). For Habermas this existential self-understanding is *evaluative*, determining the authenticity of both the life-historical genesis of the ego and the possible future norms of the ego-ideal. Ethical evaluation of these ideals possess a certain degree of critical and therapeutic power: "If illusions are playing a role, this hermeneutic self-understanding can be raised to the level of a form of reflection that dissolves self-deceptions" (JA 5). Habermas thus appears to have mitigated his earlier skepticism regarding Gadamer's claims about the critical power of hermeneutics. Habermas even admits that the answer to the question of one's identity is worked out between a study of an economy of drives and a theological education.[85] But the roles of agent and participant in ethical-existential discourses overlap: those who belong to the individual's lifeworld are the participants who can "assume the catalyzing role of impartial critics" for the agent himself (JA 11). But Habermas fails, however, to specify fully the kinds of *idealizations* by which such clinical and therapeutic argumentation functions.

Despite this critical component it possesses, Habermas insists that ethical-existential discourse fails to mediate sufficiently between conflicting versions of the good life. Each ethical form instinctively protects its own interest. Habermas argues that only the moral point of view can overcome the limited and egocentric perspectives of both the pragmatic and the ethical levels. Although Aristotle correctly saw that individual ends are embedded in the ethos of the polis, Haber-

---

[85] Habermas does lapse into theological musings from time to time. At one point he claims that the importance of life history in identity formation is "the direction pointed in by the Western (i.e., articulated in the Judeo-Christian tradition) concept of the immortal soul of creatures who, in the all-seeing eye of an omnipresent and eternal creator, recognize themselves as fully individuated beings." See TCA 2.106.

mas maintains that the ethical level is unable to resolve interpersonal conflicts among these individual ends. Only moral-practical reflection (*Überlegung*), the very term Kant used to describe his transcendental reflection, can determine whether an individual's maxims are suitable for common life.

Moral discourse nonetheless always remains attached to the ethical level of practical discourse. Habermas stresses that only the ethical-existential aspect of practical reason provides grounds for moral decisions about values. Moreover, the individual achieves a reflexive distance relative to its own life history only in the horizon of an ethical project formed in conjunction with others. A person can critically reconstruct the evaluative aspects of his or her life history into a descriptive account of formative processes. This provides a reconstructive viewing of one's past in view of what one can become in the future.

In his 1987 Copenhagen lecture Habermas takes up the specifically existential dimension of ethical-existential discourse. He explicitly commends Kierkegaard's defense of the existential individual against the strong centralizing tendency of Hegel's state.[86] Although Habermas tends to prioritize collective over individual will-formation, he concedes that Kierkegaard's concept of individual will-formation is valid even if "read in a somewhat more secular way."[87] But although Kierkegaard's concretization of Kantian ethics through a turn to radical inwardness moves toward a post-conventional ego-identity, Habermas contends that it fails to account fully for recognition by the other. But Habermas rejects the accounts of recognition provided both by the later Hegel's appeal to the absolute and by Kierkegaard's appeal to the other of the Christian savior. He offers, instead, a third self-*reflexive* recognition based on a performative understanding of grammar: "If, namely, the self is part of a relation-to-self that is performatively established when the speaker takes up the second person perspective of a hearer toward the speaker, then this

---

[86] Habermas, "Historical Consciousness and Post-Traditional Identity: The Western Orientation of the Federal Republic," in *The New Conservatism: Cultural Criticism and the Historians' Debate*, trans. S. Weber Nicholsen (Cambridge, Mass.: The MIT Press, 1989), p. 260. For a good discussion of Habermas's Copenhagen Lecture, see Martin Matustik, "Habermas's Reading of Kierkegaard: Notes from a Conversation," *Philosophy and Social Criticism*, 17, No. 4 (1991), 313–323.

[87] "Historical Consciousness and Post-Traditional Identity," p. 260.

self is not introduced as an *object*, as it is in a relation of reflection, but as a subject that forms itself through participation in linguistic interaction and expresses itself in the capacity for speech and action" (PT 25). Habermas concludes that this linguistically structured self-relation achieves stabilization through the anticipation of a "symmetrical relation" of forceless reciprocal recognition from an other (PT 188).

From his systems perspective, Luhmann provides a suggestive, though unconvincing, critique of Habermas's theory of reflexive self-relation.[88] Conceiving society as a functionally differentiated social system, Luhmann claims that only a "hidden relation" mediates between the functional differentiation of the societal system and the individual's self-designation as a subject.[89] Since he rejects the constructs of a *subiectum* or a transcendental consciousness, Luhmann conceives of the individual only as an empirical system constituted by the disconnected subsystems of life, consciousness, and communication.

Assuming that its elements and its operations are indistinguishable, Luhmann argues that any system is *autopoietic*. Although a kind of self-reference emerges in our ability to refer to the identity, structure, and constitution of the basic elements of a system,

> there is no ultimate, all-encompassing unity. We have a world only in the sense that some autopoietic systems, certainly conscious systems, can conceive of the identity of the difference

---

[88] Niklaus Luhmann, *Essays on Self-Reference* (New York: Columbia University Press, 1990), p. 107. Acknowledging the growth in developmental complexity in modern societies, Luhmann observes that increasing social differentiation has led to "increasingly generalized symbolic frameworks" that necessitate the redefinition of social roles. He finds any attempt to formulate a theory of the individual in this context problematic.

[89] Like Charles Taylor in *Sources of the Self*, Luhmann sketches a history of theories of the individual. But their conclusions about the history differ. For Luhmann, in the medieval period self-reference provided a stable and safe "refuge" for individuals, given the instability of the social and political conditions. In the more prosperous seventeenth century, widespread practices of individual piety and devotion took root, rendering all forms of self-reference suspect and vain. But sociality again came into vogue in the next century, only to spawn cultures of elitism and privilege. Overcoming the restrictive grip of such social hierarchies, Kant recovered self-reference through his critical distinctions between the general and the particular in aesthetics, and between the transcendent and the empirical in epistemology. This predominance of the individual has prevailed into our own century. See *Essays on Self-Reference*, p. 109.

between themselves and their environments: that the difference is always *one* difference (in distinction to others). Of course, this again does not deny interconnections between systems. As interconnections, however, they have no immanent, natural, or cosmological unity.[90]

To explain action, Luhmann resorts to a decisionism: we are free to choose conscious systems as the system reference most appropriate for what we want to express.[91] But he rejects the possibility that this choice would yield the kind of unified self-determination that Habermas's ethical-existential discourse claims to offer.

While correctly identifying this synthetic reflection in Habermas's understanding of the self, Luhmann argues that reflection can neither improve the observations of the system nor loosen the subject from ideologies. Admitting that *Philosophical Discourse of Modernity* is a "brilliant and keen" exposure of the paradox of self-enlightenment, Luhmann nonetheless insists that Habermas relies too much upon the synthesizing externalization of self-reference: "But since we know that unrestricted self-reference is impossible for purely logical reasons, the idealization of intersubjective communication will only interpret the process of self-referential constitution, and then the question arises: why does self-reference have to operate in this way but not another?"[92] He thus concludes that Habermas employs an historical analysis of the self-enlightening subject without a sufficient analysis of the paradoxical problems of self-referential systems in general.[93]

It should be clear that Luhmann views self-reflection not synthetically as a determination of one's limits relative to another, but only functionally as a kind of self-reproduction. Thus, he paints himself

---

[90] Ibid., p. 116.

[91] Luhmann acknowledges the similarity this bears to what Husserl's transcendental reduction obtains. But actually it is more like Hegel's absolute knowing or Gendlin's notion of the body-centered narcissistic ego. It rejects all possibility of knowledge about consciousness, meaning, language, and, above all, "internal speech." See ibid., p. 118.

[92] Ibid., p. 137.

[93] Luhmann also rejects the unifying form of what he calls Habermas's system/lifeworld "protest" against the functional differentiation of systems. He maintains that Habermas's model requires, but does not provide, a third "higher" transcendent viewpoint to decide whether lifeworld or system more comprehensively describes society. See ibid., p. 125.

into a corner. Like most structuralists he remains enlisted in a quixotic battle against a nineteenth-century view of false totalities that few any longer defend. While attempting to maintain the purity of an analytic understanding of reflection, he ends up implicitly using a synthetic form of reflection *to posit the very totality of the self that he then denies that we can posit.* His denial of the act of self-reflection ends up begging the question.

Concluding Summary

Both discourse ethics and ego-identity theories presuppose the employment of reflexive acts first to posit the illocutionary self/other difference and then to reconcile the difference by a second-person crossover perspective presupposed in discourse. The crossover perspective guarantees the possibility of both action coordination in collective will-formation and intersubjective recognition of one's life projects in individual will-formation. On the level of ego-identity, the recognition of self-determination is cognitive and epistemic, while the recognition of self-actualization—the form that preserves the existential requirements of autonomy and dissent—is performative and existential. The next chapter will examine whether the intersubjectivity that Habermas presupposes in the formation of ego-identity and discourse ethics sufficiently takes into account crucial "existential" and contextual background conditions of a theory of reflective acceptability: the *temporal* limits in which the impartial argumentation between self and the other occurs. Unless participants in discourse can identify themselves and their arguments in a temporal continuum, their use of reflection remains metaphysical and ineffective.

5

The Temporal Background
Conditions of Discourses

We have traversed a considerable distance in formulating the genesis
and mechanics of Habermas's reflective acceptability theory of truth.
We have seen that Habermas replaces the philosophy of reflection
(philosophy of consciousness), in which an isolated subject overcomes its limit or boundedness vis-à-vis an object that opposes it,
with a unique social theory based on reflective acceptability of claims
to truth. In the realm of action, he claims that subjects can overcome
the limits of both the narrowness of their own immediate interests
and the isolation of their lack of intersubjective recognition. They
accomplish this by taking on the impartial illocutionary perspective
of argumentation aimed at unforced agreement. What remains to
be done, as we saw in the Introduction, is to examine the degree
to which Habermas's theory of reflection accounts for the *temporal*
background conditions in which its reflective processes take place.
As Merleau-Ponty argues, "even our acts of reflection take place
within the temporal flow which they seek to capture."[1]

Although Habermas does refer to communicative speech acts that
determine procedures for reflective discourses regarding future
norms, he fails to account for the way these determine *when* we
should engage in these discursive reflections. What rationally motivates us to engage in discourse or clinical reflection at one time and
not at another? An actor must account for these temporal factors to
realize fully the emancipatory force of the reciprocity of perspectives
achieved in argumentation. This chapter will examine the temporality of moral and ethical-existential discourses, since the problem of
temporality is unique with regard to norms of action constituted by
them. I shall defend three theses about the temporal contextualiza-

---

[1] See his *La phénoménologie de la perception* (Paris: Gallimard, 1945), p. ix.

tion of the justification of norms these two types of discourse accomplish.[2]

Thesis 1: Habermas's theory of discourse insufficiently accounts for the *temporal background conditions that condition the very occurrence of discourse*.

Discourse is not an abstract process unrelated to any specific context, but an actual process that takes place in time. Two reflexively determined temporal conditions are fundamental for any discourse. First, reflection posits the limit between the *present* problematization of a norm or way of life and a *future* projected aim in which the problematization will be overcome by validity determination. Second, the participants must determine a given time in which to begin discourse. But Habermas fails to reconstruct adequately the formal skills that provide actors with the competence to know when a norm is properly problematized or when to employ an intersubjective reflection about a norm or life project. Taking up a suggestion of Maeve Cooke's, I shall endorse a broader scope for moral and ethical argumentation, arguing specifically that the competence of knowing when to engage in the practice of discursive reflection ought to be a constitutive element of discourse theory.[3]

It is one thing to maintain *that* temporal background conditions are crucial to the achievement of discursive reflection; it is another to determine *how* such temporal conditions are thematized and utilized in real situations. I shall defend a second thesis about how discourse takes account of temporal context:

Thesis 2: The reconstruction of the temporal conditions of discourse can be determined by an analysis of the actual use of *second-order* discourse involving token reflexive speech acts. A second-order discourse can determine

---

[2] Much of what applies to the temporalization of moral and ethical-existential discourses, which I focus on in this chapter, will also apply to other types of discourse. Moreover, by choosing to analyze only discourses of justification, I am hereby excluding discourses of application, since they have their own unique problems of temporal contextuality that lie beyond the scope of my project here.

[3] Cooke claims that we can "criticize participants and practices" on the basis of their failure to fulfill the normative promise of finding context-transcendent validity claims. See *Language and Reason*, p. 161.

the context of a specific discourse, and specifically *when* the discourse should take place.[4]

One can reconstruct these temporal conditions neither from a phenomenological account of time nor from an analysis of symbolic references to time, but only from a formal pragmatic analysis of the actual speech acts that express the temporal conditions of discourse. (Habermas does refer briefly to *communicative* speech acts that organize speech in everyday conversation. But on my reading they are not explicitly second-order discourse—see TCA 1.326.) An analysis of the token reflexive speech acts that actors raise and redeem *about* the temporal contextualization of a possible discourse—specifically, claims involving when it should or should not occur—provides the very means by which the discourse in question can be properly determined to occur. Thus, although a discourse refers directly to a claim or norm whose validity is questioned, a second-order discourse refers to the conditions of *the raising of the validity claim itself*. I shall reconstruct below the kinds of claims that actors use in second-order discourse which determine when to initiate or terminate moral or ethical-existential discourse. My assumption is that actors do in fact engage in second-order discourse that determines certain times for carrying out discourse that are qualitatively *better* than other times.[5]

Before I go any further, a few distinctions are in order. Three analytically (but not actually) distinct conditions must be fulfilled before discourse about any claim can commence:

(C1) all participants must recognize the claim in question *as binding*, i.e., that its content, once verified, will obligate all participants in all relevant future situations;

(C2) all participants must agree that the claim in question,

---

[4] Habermas uses the term "meta-discourse" for what I will refer to as a "second-order" discourse. As we have already seen, he rejects the possibility of meta-discourse.

[5] I shall not take up the related problems of either the distinction between time and time-consciousness or the distinction between temporal and spatial dimensions of reality. Theorists who look at the spatial dimensions of language and reflection tend to focus on the body as the locus of meaning and expression. For a theory of the bodily aspects of language, see Gendlin's "Philosophical Critique of Narcissism." In giving rise to new symbolic expressions, Gendlin argues that the body "physically restructures" the language already contained in it unconsciously (p. 290).

once recognized as normative, in fact *is problematic* at the present moment, i.e., that it stands in need of a test for validity; and

(C3)   all participants must recognize that the discourse about the problematized claim is *normatively right*, i.e., that it is right to engage in discourse within a specific context of interaction.[6]

Common sense would dictate that a group of scientists, moralists, politicians, or psychologists must first discuss and agree upon several contextual matters regarding a claim—what exactly is the norm at stake? how should it be resolved? who is affected by it? when is a good time to discuss it?—*before* they can begin to determine its validity. Thus, although (C1) is fulfilled when all participants determine that the claim is intended to be generalized to all actors in *all* relevant future situations, (C2) is fulfilled when all affected by a norm determine it to be problematic *here and now*. (C3) entails that there are proper times and settings for discourse, and that participants can and do raise and redeem claims that relate to such situating.

(C1) entails that it is not self-evident that every claim made and defended by a speaker is meant to be valid for all times and in all relevant contexts. For example, though it is generally agreed that normative claims such as "one ought to keep promises" and "we ought to distribute goods justly" when validated by discourse do purport to be binding on all persons indefinitely, evaluative claims such as "that was a good film" and prudential claims such as "you ought to go to bed early" do not.[7] For these latter non-universalistic claims, a second-order discourse is required to determine whether or not they, in fact, intend to be normative indefinitely in the future. No moral discourse is required if they are not understood to be binding indefinitely for all. (C2) entails that there exist cases in which actors fail to engage in discourse about a norm simply because they do not agree that its validity is in question. For example, individuals often

---

[6] I am using here Cooke's analysis of the difference between *normative validity claims* and claims to *normative rightness*. See *Language and Reason*, p. 64. I am applying the latter not only to speech acts, but also to discourse itself.

[7] Ibid. Cooke points out that even some normative validity claims are situation-specific, particularly those raised with acts of warning or advising: for example, "*you* ought to take better care of *your* children."

have difficulties convincing themselves that their life projects are problematic in the first place. Discourse about the present "status" of the norm—whether the consensus that actually determined it in the past is no longer effective or socio-economic conditions have changed, and so on—serve to determine the problematization of a norm as such.[8] Until these claims about the problematic status of the norm are redeemed or rejected, it is not clear *whether* discourse about the norm should actually take place. My primary concern, however, involves (C3) conditions. We must be able to determine when to engage in discourse. This is not a trivial problem, since the aim of the discourse is to generalize the interests of those engaging in it.

By defending these three conditions of reflection, I am setting myself in opposition to prevailing views of discourse theorists.[9] With regard to (C1), most discourse theorists would argue that a moral claim is normative for all participants and an ethical-existential is normative for the individual *simply by definition*. This normativity entails that a validated moral claim demands universal adherence in all relevant situations and that an ethical-existential claim universally prescribes certain behaviors for a subject in a given set of relevant circumstances. This explains the fact that participants assume that the norm is problematic *before* discourse commences; they assume that *once validated* it will be normative. The assumed unconditionality of the outcome guides the deliberation in advance: no discursive procedure is required. With regard to (2), most discourse theorists would argue that the problematization of a norm is determined by non-normative *empirical* factors—our experience of how the norm affects us, whether it can be properly followed, whether it can be properly sanctioned, and so on—not by the formal procedures of discourse itself. For this reason Habermas precludes the very possibility of meta-discourses, arguing that the determination of which claims are to be brought to discourse is accomplished by communicative action alone. On his account, discourse can determine only

---

[8] Schnädelbach speaks of the need to "thematize ways of thematizing." See his "Zum Verhältnis von Diskurswandel und Paradigmenwechsel in der Geschichte der Philosophie," in *Zur Rehabilitierung des animal rationale* (Frankfurt am Main: Suhrkamp, 1992), p. 391.

[9] For another theory of moral discourse besides Habermas's, see Mane Hajdin, *The Boundaries of Moral Discourse* (Chicago: Loyola University Press, 1994).

whether a norm, once determined as normative and problematized, is valid or not; it cannot validate that a claim is normative or problematized. With regard to (C3), most discourse theorists assume that actors either know intuitively or can determine by non-discursive means the proper context of interaction in which discourse should occur. I shall argue instead that specific conditions can be explicated and verified for such determinations.

Discourse theorists thus justify their rejection of second-order determination of conditions of discourse in one of two ways. They claim either that such conditions are *impossible* to determine, due to the sheer gratuitousness of claim problematizations, or that actors simply know these conditions *intuitively*. Some would even claim that positing any second-order level runs the risk of creating the possibility of an infinite regress: a third level to determine the second level, a fourth level to determine the third, and so on. I am claiming, on the other hand, that the conditions for discourse are questions that are neither analytic nor empirical, but discursive.[10] Participants do in fact raise and redeem claims that can be either affirmed or denied regarding these second-order determinations and they do so without running into regress problems. With regard to (C1), I am rejecting the claim that most moral actors assume that a norm, once validated, will be universally applicable in the future *before* they begin deliberation about it. Rather, participants do discursively determine the status of the claim—whether it will be conditioned or unconditioned by temporal factors—in advance of the discourse about it. Regarding (C2), participants in a discourse can and do argue about whether discourse ought to take place. Then, second-

---

[10] I want to avoid the charge often leveled against first- and second-order arguments that they lead to an infinite regress of levels of ordering. I shall simply assert that one can stop with second-order reflections on first-order reflections. Harry Frankfurt argues for the same kind of curtailment of a regress in his claims about first- and second-order desires. He argues that a multiplication of levels of desire can be stopped simply by what he calls "decisive identification" with one desire over another. See his "Identification and Wholeheartedness," in *The Importance of What We Care About* (Cambridge: Cambridge University Press, 1988), pp. 168–169. Making a commitment without reservations means that the person who makes it does so believing that no further accurate inquiry would change her mind; and thus she does not push the inquiry further. He refers to this as the "resonance effect" of the decision. Schnädelbach agrees with Habermas's claim that discourse is a form of reflection that needs to be set within certain limits so as to avoid becoming a procedure that uses an endless progression of superimposed levels of speech.

order claims about the situating of discourse are raised and re-deemed (C3).

My third thesis regards the formulation and use of temporal (C3) conditions in discourse.

> Thesis 3: The temporal conditions of discourse can be expli-
>   cated by means of the same analysis of background
>   conditions as Habermas assumes in his theory of self/
>   world relations.

The temporal contextualization of discourse I propose is consistent with, yet at the same time augments, Habermas's formalization of self/world relations we examined in Chapter 3. Thus, the temporal background conditions that impact the instantiation of agreements conform to the demands of the postmetaphysical world-perspectives he defends. In other words, we can sketch a formal pragmatics of the temporal conditions of rational action that conforms to the overall typology of the formal analysis that he presents.

Habermas and the Contextualization of Truth Claims

My first thesis states that Habermas does not sufficiently account for the formal determination of temporal background conditions of discourse. He excludes these temporal factors from his formal prag-matics on the basis of certain assumptions he makes about the way time functions in a theory of truth.

Truth and Context

Most philosophers hold that the *truth* is predicated of propositions (claims, sentences, statements, beliefs) that are determined to be what is the case. Moreover, once validated, the truth of a proposition transcends the particular times and circumstances in which it is ex-pressed. Habermas adopts both requirements in his truth theory.[11] He argues that truth consists in existing states of affairs (*Sachverhal-*

---

[11] Alessandro Ferrara claims that Habermas's formalistic "warranted assertability" theory of truth is more a "sign" of truth in certain cases than a "fundamental criterion" of truth. See his "A Critique of Habermas's Consensus Theory of Truth," in *Philosophy and Social Criticism*, 13, No. 1 (Fall 1987), 39–67.

ten) that are correlative to verified statements. Though every speech act is a datable and episodic event, a verified state of affairs to which a speech act refers is a non-episodic "invariant claim." Quoting Strawson, Habermas notes: "My saying something is certainly an episode. What I say, is not. It is the latter, not the former, we declare to be true."[12]

Facts are not what true statements "are about," but rather what they actually state.[13] A statement neither mirrors nor discovers a truth; it adequates itself (*passen zu*) to facts (WT 132). Habermas argues that facts are not reducible, as Husserl claims, to objects of experience about which we have evidential certainty, but rather are discursively determined in argumentation about problematized assertions (see WT 150–155).[14] The discursive determination arises either in interpretations of experiential observations or in the course of problematizations, or virtualizations, of facts or states of affairs (see WT 134; JA 164–165).[15] But the facts themselves neither rely on nor are reducible to their discursive determination. The truth that the discourse establishes is based neither on empirical evidence for the claim nor on a logical consistency among claims, but only on the rationally motivating force of the argument that redeems the claim (WT 149).[16]

Habermas then extends the domain of truth, as we have seen, into two other truth-analogous areas: rightness and truthfulness. While a truth claim verifies the existence of a fact or state of affairs, a rightness claim verifies the legitimacy of a norm of behavior, and a truthfulness claim verifies the sincerity of an expression or the authenticity of an aesthetic act. But the way in which a rightness

---

[12] Strawson, "Truth," in *Truth*, ed. G. Pitcher (Englewood Cliffs, N.J.: Prentice-Hall, 1964), p. 33.

[13] Habermas does not clearly distinguish between facts and states of affairs. But, roughly speaking, a fact is an "existing" state of affairs.

[14] Habermas argues that all perceptually based theories are reducible to evidential theories of certainty. But Habermas does allow for various kinds of certainty. We have belief-certainty in the truthfulness of a person, and a meaning-certainty of a perception of a thing or an event (WT 142). Thus, strictly speaking, perceptions cannot be false.

[15] Habermas even uses the term "social facts."

[16] Habermas criticizes both metaphysicians who collapse the theoretical into the practical and positivists who pronounce the two incompatible. He claims that Strauss is an example of the former; Hare, of the latter.

claim is verified has not simply an explicative, but also a constitutive relation to what is verified.

Habermas makes a few qualifications about what constitutes the truth of a claim that separate further the discursive process itself from the validity of what it determines. He argues that neither the comprehensibility of the claim nor the illocutionary offer of the speech act that expresses the claim is itself a matter of truth. Although actors can verbalize the illocutionary component of a claim—with phrases such as "I notify you that" or "I ask you whether"—Habermas maintains that illocutionary expressions cannot refer to anything that is or could be happening in the world. Like Austin, he claims that speech acts are "in order" with respect to typically restricted contexts, but they are "valid" only with respect to the fundamental claim raised (WUP 51–52).[17] Illocutionary acts retain a kind of "supra-valid" status.

Having divorced the illocutionary modality from the truth of a redeemed claim as such, Habermas then argues that all time references belong to illocutionary components of a claim. Though essential to the illocutionary offer, the time in which a claim is raised and redeemed, either in the moment of verification or in the future, has no relevance to the validity of the claim. Habermas does maintain that *eventually* the illocutionary modes are subsumed in the truth claim, stating that the learning processes of the reconstructed structures of communication "should form an arch *in* time bridging all temporal distances, and *in* the world they should realize the conditions whose fulfillment is a necessary presupposition of the unconditionality of context-transcending validity claims" (JA 165). But in the present moment at which the truth of a claim is determined the illocutionary mode is inconsequential.

Since the truth of a claim "p" remains detached from the illocutionary mode "Mp"—whether it is a promise, recommendation, confession, or so on—Habermas excludes *ipso facto* all temporal and spatially specific contexualizing claims from the domain of discourse. Information gathered from ordinary lifeworld communication is decontextualized, "fed into" discourse or self-reflection, and

---

[17] Habermas notes that such illocutionary phrases are reconstructed from actual learning processes.

either redeemed as true or canceled as false.[18] Thus, all communicative actions must satisfy or violate normative expectations or conventions (WUP 35). No assertion can have a private referent or an ungeneralizable meaning. Norms express facts that refer either to possible anticipations of experience or to "controllable outcomes of action."[19] Although facts can be propositionally formulated into different *kinds* of claims—objective (scientific), social (moral), or subjective—they represent neither a thing nor an event that can be dated and localized in the world.[20]

With respect to this context-transcending character of a verified claim, an interesting parallel can be drawn between Habermas's and Quine's theories of truth. Though they differ markedly in *how* truth is grounded, they agree that decontextualizing transformations must be performed on what propositions can be determined *as* true. Quine argues that a sentence is "not an event or utterance, but a universal: a repeatable sound pattern, or repeatable approximable norm."[21] A sentence gains particularization in regard to time and persons by means of its transformation into a proposition. Thus, the sentence "the cat is on the mat" can be transformed into a contextualized proposition such as "I know *that* the cat is on the mat." But Quine claims that even if a proposition includes contextual factors, it is still only an abstract and surrogate vehicle of truth. A proposition with contextualizing elements remains steadfastly true apart from the contextualization factors themselves.[22] The truth of an observation sentence, though an intersubjective matter, does not depend on any particular observer perspective.[23] How does the proposition re-

---

[18] "Nachwort," p. 386. The term Habermas uses is *hineingeben*. Habermas holds that the "adequacy" of a theory of language is a function of the truth of the theorems it can formulate. If we redeem these claims through experience rather than through argumentative reasoning, then theoretical progress would be conceived of only as the product of new experience. Habermas argues instead that progress must result from the shared interpretation and repeatability of the *same* experience: the objectivity of experience guarantees the *identity* of the experience in the various statements interpreting that experience. "Structurally analogous" experiences are data used to legitimate a truth claim. See "Nachwort," pp. 392–393.

[19] Ibid., p. 387.

[20] Ibid., p. 384.

[21] *Word and Object* (Cambridge, Mass.: The MIT Press, 1960), p. 191.

[22] Ibid., p. 192.

[23] See Quine and J. S. Ullian, *The Web of Belief*, 2nd ed. (New York: McGraw-Hill, 1978), p. 28.

main abstracted from the very contextualization it expresses? Quine simply asserts that every proposition can be translated back into a set of decontextualized sentences that stay fixed through time and from speaker to speaker *independent of circumstances*. Habermas holds to this same decontextualized requirements for claims to be tested for validity. He even argues that the thematization of a problematized norm in political discourse, for instance, is decontextualized even from the competencies and responsibilities of those who are affected by the norm. But he also holds that all claims to validity have a "Janus face": although they transcend their context, they must be raised and accepted *here and now* (BFN 21).

Semantics and Contextualization: Habermas's Appropriation of Peirce's Semiotic Theory

Although denying that a valid claim, as justified, can contain an internal relation to its temporal context of verification, Habermas argues that the meaning and expression of a claim does possess a specific temporality.

Habermas makes two preliminary assumptions about time and meaning. First, he assumes that the analysis of our experience of time must be seen in the broader context of modernity. He points out that the reflexive time-consciousness of modernity has resulted in the phenomenon that an increasing number of actions in both system and lifeworld are determined under the conditions of the anticipation of the future (PT 188). An example of such a future anticipation is evident in modern economic systems: most businesses and industries now acquire capital, not on the basis of concrete assets, but from loans made with the expectation that they will be paid back in the future. Second, and more germane to our purposes, Habermas specifies that the structures of linguistic meaning that allow for such a future-directed pragmatic orientation can be derived from Peirce's semiotics.[24] He carefully reconstructs the various points at which Peirce discussed the temporal contextualizing qualities of signs.[25]

---

[24] "On Time and Thought" provides probably Peirce's most comprehensive statement of his temporal characterization of signs. See *Chronological Edition*, 3.68–75.

[25] Expressivist theories of meaning and signification, such as found in Cassirer's *Philosophy of Symbolic Forms*, broaden the role that subjective or inner experience

Peirce developed his sign theory from a semiotic transformation of Kant's critical metaphysics. Peirce bequeathed to signs the same power to establish continuity in the flux of our experience as Kant gave to the "I think" of the transcendental apperception (TK 147). Critical of the atemporality of Kant's view, Peirce took pains to account for the temporal background conditions of sign usage (TK 147).[26] First, he conceived of a sign, not as a form of mediation between an intuition and a concept, but as a threefold mediation between an intuition, object, and interpreter *in time*.[27] A sign refers not only to its intended object, but also both to a spatio-temporal situated interpretant *and* to itself as an episodic event in time. Moreover, Peirce stipulated that signs have a "cinematopographic" nature: each sign has an effect on its temporally succeeding sign.[28] Unlike Hume, Peirce held that this effect is not occasional, but *causal*.[29] The inquiring mind thinks syllogistically in an endless succession of semantically expressed thoughts that constitute the "very essence of representation."[30]

---

plays in meaning. Each assumes that a whole range of non-normative contextual factors can be rationally expressed in language. But Habermas's concern for both the reception of meaning by the other and the justification of meaning in cases of problematization precludes him from adopting an expressivist theory. He excludes any pre-predicative or archetypal symbols, even if universalizable through a kind of *sensus communis*, from the domain of discourse about validity. For Cassier's theory, see *Philosophie der symbolischen Formen*, especially volume I.

[26] Like both Frege and Husserl, Habermas claims that Peirce referred to the operation of signs, not just to the operation of thought. But unlike both of them, Peirce did not fall into "Platonic conclusions about meaning." See PT 93. The early Peirce held to an isomorphism between being and expression. He argued that "whatever is, is a representation" and "as all things are representation alike, they can only be contrasted in their relations." See *Chronological Edition*, 1.324.

[27] Ibid., 3.67. Peirce's theory of signs is extremely complex. He derived an inventory of symbol structures that contained 59,049 types; he later reduced it to a "mere" 66. See his *Collected Papers*, 2.330.

[28] *Chronological Edition*, 3.71; PT 11n3. This is the basis of his principle that all thinking (cognition) is inferred from some other thinking in a linear sequence (1.488). Thus, every statement is the rudimentary form of an argument (2.344). Thought is addressed to one's future self as to a second person (1.xxix).

[29] *Chronological Edition*, 3.74. Peirce argued that this causative linking is "necessarily of the nature of a reproduction." Yet, like Hume, Peirce also claimed that these processes establish an "habitual" connection between thoughts.

[30] See ibid., 3.64, 3.71, 3.108; *Collected Papers*, 5.268, 5.354. But Peirce mitigated the latent psychologism of this conclusion. Although the rationality of the future effect is required in order to ground the possibility that a conclusion can follow from a premise, the finality, "the why," of a conclusion of the process of inquiry

Is there any way of "breaking" this endless future effect of signs so as to subject thought to some kind of fixed verification procedure? Peirce realized that such a break would require a mental process other than mere observation. He argued that the succession of thought produces a second-order effect to which we have subjective access through *memory*. Memory allows us to make judgments about resemblance between two representations because it suspends the otherwise endless translation of sign into sign by retaining two temporally distinct representations in the same moment.[31] Peirce claimed that the mind can conceive of a succession of discrete parts within a conceptual whole constituted by "consciousness running through the time."[32] The mind-imposed whole bestows a coherence on experience. But Peirce realized that the judgments of similarity needed for predication require more than a mere coherence among represented thoughts: "the knowledge that one thought is similar to or in any way truly representative of another, cannot be derived from immediate perception, but must be a hypothesis (unquestionably fully justifiable by facts), and that therefore the formation of such a representing thought must be dependent upon a real effective force behind consciousness."[33] What is this "force behind consciousness" by which a subject effects the simultaneity of two thoughts needed for judgment? Peirce argued that the force is a conceptual whole that can synthesize a series of temporally distinct thoughts. It is an *ideal consensus* that represents the "final opinion" upon which an ideal community of inquirers would agree. Therefore, although the community of inquiry uses signs that are "inside" of time, the ideal consensus that guides their inquiry remains "outside" of time.[34]

A. N. Prior points out that the ambiguity of this dichotomy between a temporal "inside" and an "outside" testifies to Peirce's failure to formulate a coherent semantics of time. Peirce claimed, not

---

cannot be determined in an apriori. We only know that *if* we use these inferential forms, *then* we come nearer to the truth.

[31] See *Chronological Edition*, 3.43, 71–73, 77. As usual, simultaneity is a kind of paradox. Time is always in the present, but from the present we can make inferences about the future (3.317).

[32] Ibid., 3.73.

[33] *Collected Papers*, 5.289.

[34] Peirce in fact admitted that he reached the limits of his temporal analysis of semiotics and inference: "time can only be identified by brute compulsion. . . . we must not go further." See ibid., 5.463.

that a semantics of time was unnecessary, but only that it was inopportune for him to carry out such a project.[35] He realized that "time has usually been considered by logicians to be what is called 'extralogical' matter. I have never shared this opinion. But I have thought that logic had not yet reached the state of development at which the introduction of temporal modifications of its forms would not result in great confusion; and I am much of that way of thinking yet."[36] Peirce never did carry out this task of explicating a temporal logic.

Despite this failure to formulate a coherent account of time, Habermas argues that Peirce's semiotic temporalization suffices for the analysis of the temporal contextualizing required for speech act theory.[37]

> Since the individual experience itself takes up the threefold structure of a sign that simultaneously refers to a past object and a future interpretant, it can extend over timeless distance in a semantic relation to other experiences and thus give origin to a temporal unity in the succession of an otherwise kaleidoscopic fractured diversity. In this way, Peirce explains time relations which are originated through the structure of the sign generally [TK 147–148]).[38]

Thus, Habermas inherits Peirce's refusal to develop a "logical" method for expressing how such a temporal theory of signs can be transformed into a theory of intersubjective inquiry. He does modify Peirce's idea of the ideal community by insisting that it is not a concretely realizable end-state, but an "idealization" that provides a regulative guide for criticizing *current* practices of inquiry (JA 52–

---

[35] *Time and Modality* (Oxford: Oxford University Press, 1957), p. 111.

[36] *Collected Papers*, 4.523.

[37] But Habermas does criticize two aspects of Peirce's theory. First, although Peirce criticizes Hegel for neglecting the "moment of duality" that the externality of an object always expresses, Habermas argues that Peirce himself neglected the same "Secondness" that we confront in communication, as the other's "mind of his own (*Eigensinn*)." See PT 110–111. Second, by focusing on the progress of our representation of reality primarily through inference, Peirce undervalued the full innovative power of the world-disclosing function of language. Habermas argues instead that in cases where we reach the limits of the ability to find agreement, we can step back from the continuity and look at the problematized norm "in the light of a new vocabulary." See PT 106. Here Habermas seems to be mitigating his earlier identitarian assumptions about crossover perspectives in communication by now suggesting that there exists a direct link between world-disclosing language and the overcoming of alterity.

[38] Habermas is referring here to Peirce's *Collected Papers*, 3:68–71, 104.

54).[39] But he maintains that Peirce's model of practical agreement sufficiently explains the relation between the constitutive moment of the formation of a meaning or concept and the transcendent moment of the formation of true judgment that "triumphs over time" (BFN 14).

By relying on Peirce's analysis of the temporal contextualization of sign use, Habermas fails to explain how an idealized and generalizable end of inquiry actually informs the situated contexts in which participants carry out discourse. He defends his use of Peirce's analysis by claiming that the reference to an unlimited communication community serves to replace the moment of eternity (or the time-transcending character) of unconditionality by the idea of an open, but goal-directed process of interpretation that transcends the borders of a social space and historical time from within, from the perspective of an existence in the temporally and spatially finite world (see BFN 15). Two difficulties arise here. First, it remains unclear just how this "inner" transcendence of inquiry is any more coherent as a background condition than an "outer" transcendence of a timeless eternity in truth rests. My contention is that a present/future distinction is more relevant to the issue of transcendence, particularly with regard to moral claims, than an inner/outer distinction. Second, Peirce's analysis fails to provide a salient semantic means of expressing the alterity of the other inquirer's perspective over time. Criticizing Peirce, Habermas suggests that a world-disclosing language is needed to describe the unique situatedness of the other. But Habermas fails to formulate exactly how this grasp of alterity is accomplished only through an exchange of claims that posit normative dispositions. Habermas's reconstruction of Peirce's semiotic theory of temporal contextualization, formulated primarily for constative claims, thus fails to provide the kind of background conditions needed for the discursive determination either of claims as normative (C1) or of norms as problematized (C2) or of the proper contextualization of the practice of moral and ethical-existential discourses (C3). But before suggesting an alternative formulation of temporalization, I need to examine how Habermas views temporalization of discourse within the pragmatics of argumentation.

---

[39] See also William Rehg, "From Logic to Rhetoric in Science: A Formal-Pragmatic Reading of Lonergan," in *Communication and Lonergan*, ed. Thomas J. Farrell and Paul A. Soukup (New York: Sheed & Ward, 1993), pp. 153–172.

Formal Pragmatics and Contextualization

Habermas understands the contextualization of valid claims, not as a correspondence between a subject and a predicate in a spatial and temporal continuum, but as a speaker's adherence to intersubjectively recognized illocutionary rules within a practical lifeworld "action context" (see WUP 7).[40] Like Wittgenstein, he understands contextualization, not as the clarification of the way a statement represents a specific state of affairs, but as the circumstances that determine the way in which a statement makes an offer or claim for actual participants in an interaction. But he admits that his universal pragmatics meets some difficulties when dealing with problems of context.

In *Theory of Communicative Action*, Habermas tries to mitigate some of these contextualization problems by explicating the *empirical* "pragmatic indicators" of speech acts generally. A pragmatic indicator, such as the degree of institutional dependence of a speech act, its temporal status, or its speaker/hearer orientation, helps us to grasp the "illocutionary modification" of validity claims (TCA 1.327). He considers first Marga Kreckel's lexicon of illocutionary functions that serve as pragmatic modal indicators of social space and historical time (TCA 1.321–322).[41] Since few illocutionary acts have grounds that can be identified as universal, Kreckel sets forth pragmatic indicators that indicate speech act contexts such as institutional dependency, the orientation of the speaker to the hearer, and the main topic of communication. On the basis of these pragmatic indicators, Krekel constructs a speech act taxonomy that Habermas claims is "informative, and neither blind nor empty" (TCA 1.327). The pragmatic indicator of time determines whether a speech act is "time neutral" or implies a future, past, or present orientation.

Though acknowledging the need for an empirical determination

---

[40] Habermas chooses speech act theory as the most promising point of departure for universal pragmatics, rejecting analytic theories of action (Danto, Hampshire), intentional action theories (Winch, Taylor), and speaker intention theories (Grice).

[41] See Kreckel's *Communicative Acts and Shared Knowledge in Natural Discourse* (London and New York: Academic Press, 1981), pp. 188ff. Krekel posits a set of general action types correlative to time, such as agreeing or asserting for the present, justifying or accusing for the past, and promising or advising for the future. Habermas does not treat Kreckel's theory at length, however.

of temporal context, Habermas maintains that these classificatory procedures "do not consolidate into intuitive types; they lack the theoretical power to illuminate our intuitions" (TCA 1.323). He stipulates that all such classificatory procedures must be defined by reference to the generalizable dispositions that a speech act contains. Nevertheless, he still admits that this generalizability stipulation renders formal pragmatic analysis "hopelessly distanced" from the context of actual speech use (TCA 1.328). He notes, quite accurately, that this area of the logic of speech acts has not been extensively researched. But he remains convinced that one can address the complexity of natural situations without giving up the idealization of a theory of reflective acceptability altogether. He even proposes eight types of "controlled undoing" of idealization that would in some cases admit into the realm of speech acts elliptically shortened and extraverbally completed phrases that refer a hearer to contingent contextualized conditions of agreement (TCA 1.330). But none of these refers to temporal conditions specifically. Moreover, he stipulates that if a controlled undoing becomes problematized, the participants must proceed to a strategic level of meta-communication, adopting the viewpoint of an intentionalist semantics. The illocutionary success of a speech act still requires the fulfillment of "universal concrete" conditions that remain abstracted from the contextualizing perspectives of the discourse participants.

Habermas also examines Searle's analysis of contextualization. Searle criticizes the claim that literal meaning is independent of context. He uses several empirical examples to invalidate the claim that literal meaning can be determined without reference to a definite set of background assumptions.[42] Although his examples refer to spatial locality, speaker intentions, and the use of imperatives, he also omits any specific reference to *temporal* contextualization. Habermas realizes that he himself is probably among the decontextualizing "literalists" that Searle is criticizing. But Habermas dodges this criticism by arguing that, like Searle himself, he holds for an "art of problematization" by which both speaker and hearer recognize claims as always already contextualized in the lifeworld (TCA 1.336). What remains unclear on both Habermas's and Searle's accounts, however,

---

[42] See his *Expression and Meaning* (Cambridge: Cambridge University Press, 1979), p. 135.

is precisely *how* this background knowledge accounts for the inclusion of context in constative assertions.

In sum, Habermas relies on the basic assumption that all contextualization factors have an illocutionary, and thus intersubjective, component. He argues that subjective conditions (feelings, wishes, and desires) are in fact reflexive and attain content when they are *stabilized*, in a "time-bridging" (*zeitüberbrückend*) way, as intentions capable of giving rise to intersubjectively recognizable future expectations.[43] Thus, all inner episodes and intentions are, in principle, reciprocal. Breaking from *unstable* intentions and motives, actors in discourse resolve to come to an agreement with each other about norms that can restablize these intentions and motives. The illocutionary contextualization is indirectly verified by whether or not it allows for an agreement on the locutionary content. The agreement has to be understood in a very broad sense. Even constative assertions can be problematized and discursively argued. What is the intersubjective expectation involved? The rule is *if* anyone comes into the same set of observable conditions in the future, *then* he or she must make the same determination and everyone can expect action consistent with the determination.

Although Habermas underdetermines the difficulties involved in reaching the symmetry of the crossover perspective and mutual expectations needed for discourse and self-reflection, he is nonetheless aware of the "alterity problem" that Lacan, Ricoeur, Lyotard, Levinas, and others discuss. At several points, as we have seen, Habermas mitigates the idealizing elements of his intersubjective theory by the inclusion of various illocutionary schemes that take into account the alterity of the other: the temporal analysis of intersubjective sign usage, pragmatic indicators, communicative speech acts, intermodal structures, and so on. Yet the reconstructed formal pragmatic structures that inform the attainment of this crossover perspective in discourse and self-reflection construe contextualization only by reference to an "art" of generalizable descriptions of actions, as we have seen. This unduly hinders the applicability of Habermas's formal pragmatic analysis to the determination of specific instances of conflict resolution. Such a non-formalized approach to the conditions of the instantiation of reflection belies his otherwise careful

---

[43] "Nachwort," p. 390.

epistemic analysis of the problems of intersubjectivity and the self. Thus, although Habermas specifies what actors in discourse break *from* (all motives except for the motive to come to an agreement) and what the break *accomplishes* (a symmetry of perspective-taking among participants), he specifies neither the contextual criteria nor the conditions that determine exactly *when this break ought to occur.* There are, in fact, specific temporal background conditions required for this break.

SECOND-ORDER DISCOURSE AND TIME

To review briefly: Habermas's theory of reflective acceptability, carried out in discourse, reconstructs the achievement of a rational agreement about the validity of propositionally formulated problematized claims. He restricts the object domain of what can be agreed upon in discourse to include only "p" propositions that refer to normative characterizations of future dispositions to act (PT 74). "Mp" illocutionary contextualizing factors are thematized only at the level of communicative action.

The temporal contextualization I propose in my second thesis can be achieved neither by a modification of the set of participants allowed into the agreement (which must remain all participants affected by the outcome of the agreement) nor by a modification of the aim of the agreement (which must remain the discursive determination of the validity of a problematized norm), but by allowing time-referential "Mp" claims into discourse.[44] These assertions are reflexive: they refer to specific temporal modalities of either the claims or the participants in the specific agreement itself. On my account, the "Mp" claims that refer to the process of agreement itself—to the thematization of a claim as a norm (C1), or of a norm as problematized (C2), or of the context in which problematization is to be discursively analyzed (C3)—must be included in the domain of claims allowed into discourse.

---

[44] Schnädelbach argues instead for a *pragmatically characterized apriori* that is not an apriori "in itself" but a contextualized apriori for speakers in given situations. This way of understanding aprioricity transforms the methodological "objectivizing" of data into the determination of "observable" data (possible norms) in the descriptive region. This widens the consensus capabilities for the determination of validity. See *Reflexion und Diskurs*, p. 363.

By determining the temporal factors of these conditions, temporal "M*p*" claims can assist us in knowing what Benhabib calls the "right time" to engage in discursive argumentation about a claim or a norm.[45] Schnädelbach also insists that these claims, which he calls "descriptive," form part not only of ordinary communication, but also of discourse as such.[46] He argues that epistemology, ethics, and aesthetics are all disciplines that form modal claims that function to characterize a claim or norm *as* problematized.[47] But how exactly are such temporal conditions expressed and discursively analyzed?

Temporal Contextualization

To justify the inclusion of second-order reconstruction of time reference in discourse, we need to determine how a statement is able to refer to time. But since time is one of the densest and most bewildering of all philosophical topics, I proceed cautiously and without promises of bold insights.[48] I propose here only to sketch in broad outlines how time-referential statements can be verified in order to contextualize discourse.

Time can be thematized only through a cognitive act of reflection. An act of temporal reflection transcends the limits of our immediate attention and determines either a diachronic (linear) or synchronic (simultaneous) temporal ordering of the objects of our attention. This thematization can be characterized in more than one way. *Event-time*, or chronological time, is simply the thematization of a diachronic succession of spatio-temporal events following after each other in an ordered series. This time distinguishes an event at one point in chronological time, $t(1)$, from an event at another point in a continual flow of time, $t(2)$. *Experience-time*, on the other hand, is a subject's capacity to synchronically order the object of its immediate awareness as past, present, or future.[49] Augustine noted that in

---

[45] *Critique, Norm, and Utopia*, p. 321.

[46] See *Reflexion und Diskurs*, pp. 225, 364. Schnädelbach considers Habermas's early use of self-reflection a descriptive discourse because it thematizes intentions as "objects."

[47] See ibid., p. 233.

[48] See Alfred Schutz, "Symbol, Reality, and Society," in *Collected Papers* I, ed. M. Natanso and H. van Breda, 3 vols. (The Hague: Martinus Nijhoff, 1964–1967), p. 290.

[49] For a good description of this event/experience distinction, see Wolfgäng Röd, *Erfahrung und Reflexion: Theorien der Erfahrung in tranzendentalphilosophischer Sicht* (Munich: Beck, 1991), pp. 53–55.

the flow of everyday experience the future and the past are mere abstractions and not "real": we can never escape the immediacy of the present.[50] Despite this synchronic link to the present, most of our life is nevertheless spent in reflection upon either past events or future possibilities. Habermas develops a kind of future-oriented experience-time in which experience develops in a forward direction through cumulative learning processes. Thus, his experience-time is oriented almost exclusively toward problem solving.

In addition to these two forms of time, there exists a third, *inter-subjective-time*, more relevant to discourse about action. Combining synchronic and diachronic forms of time, intersubjective-time coordinates the temporal perspectives of actors aiming to communicate or reach agreement with each other. Alfred Schutz describes two phenomenological characteristics of this intersubjective form of time. The first involves the confrontation with the other person in a "face-to-face" relationship in shared time and space. Schutz claims that many theorists mistakenly assume that this "mutual appresentational comprehension of events in the other's mind leads immediately to communication."[51] But a second determination is needed: an analysis of the *temporal context of the other's perspective.* Synchronization of perspectives requires an account of differences among the actors' biographies. Each speaker must set aside his own specific project at hand in favor of a common project that he shares with the hearer or hearers. Only then can their respective "fluxes" of inner time become synchronous with their event of communication or of agreement.[52] In a similar vein, Mead argued that social actors reconstruct the objective field in which they can cooperate by "ordering" a temporal flow of events: "It is in this field that the continuous flow breaks up in ordered series, in the relation of alternative steps leading up to some event. Time with its distinguishable moments enters, so to speak, with the intervals necessary to shift the scene."[53] Mead concluded that this form of time can account for the reciprocal perspective-taking: the fact that a social actor can at some times "be another and yet himself."[54]

---

[50] See Augustine's *Confessions*, especially Book XI, chapters 14–28.
[51] "Symbol, Reality, and Society," p. 315.
[52] Ibid., p. 317.
[53] *Mind, Self, and Society*, p. 376.
[54] Ibid.

Despite our capacity to reach a symmetry of perspectives with an other, Schutz argues that we still find an "inaccessible zone of the other's private life which transcends my possible experience."[55] Like Habermas, he presumes that we have a kind of lifeworld symmetry with the other's perspective until counter-evidence appears. But, unlike Habermas, he makes it clear that the overcoming of the alterity of perspectives in a synchronicity of intersubjective time requires a special type of second-order determination.

Since participants must make some reference to the chronology of events, to temporal modalities, and to the temporal perspectives of other participants before discourse can occur, how do they express and agree upon these temporal references? I shall sketch a formal pragmatics of temporal reference that can provide for a means of propositional expression of time reference in statements. It can also account for the way these statements are used to determine the temporal conditions of discourse.

Propositional Reference and Time

Aristotle was the first to present a comprehensive analysis of the propositional formulations of meaning generally. The universality of his theory of meaning was based on the mental referents of terms used in utterances: "spoken words are the symbols of mental experience and written words are the symbols of spoken words. Just as all men do not have the same writing, so all men do not have the same speech sounds, but the mental experiences which these directly symbolize are the same for all."[56] Aristotle stipulated that every symbol had to be instantiated in a verbal phrase (*logos*) in order to be affirmed or denied. But he realized that some utterances, such as "the goat-stag is," cannot be affirmed or denied.[57] He thus distinguished propositions that can be affirmed or denied from mere sentential phrases, such as prayers and commands, that cannot.

Prior examines the epistemological and ontological status of vari-

[55] "Symbol, Reality, and Society," p. 326.

[56] See *De interpretatione*, 16a.

[57] A. N. Prior, *The Doctrine of Propositions and Terms* (London: Duckworth, 1976), p. 13. Ricoeur also claims that the problem of strictly logical interpretation for Aristotle involves, not mere utterances, but declarative propositions. See *Freud and Philosophy*, p. 21.

ous post-Aristotelian propositional theories of meaning. He builds his analysis on a critique of the idealism of Bolzano's claim that every proposition is a decontextualized *Satz an sich* that has a truth value independent of whether it is believed by anyone or related to any other propositions.[58] Several alternatives to Bolzano's proposition theory have been proposed. Brentano claimed that propositions derive their meaning from the consciousness of the subject that intends them. Prior rejects this intentionality thesis on the grounds that one can consistently hold that some propositions are true independently of a mind's knowing them. Another version views propositions as the objects of believing and disbelieving, and thus as possible facts. But Prior argues that, since one can understand the meaning of a true statement without knowing what makes it true, this model fails to distinguish between true belief and knowledge.[59] He then considers a third "ascriptive" alternative. According to this theory, a proposition has an ascriber, an ascribed object, and an ascribed *character* of the object. Thus, propositions refer not only to different objects, but also to different modal characteristics of these objects, such as their temporal context.[60]

Since these modal qualifiers refer both to the universal and to the particularizing characteristics of the object, they are reflexive ascriptions of a proposition. Thus, "There is no such thing as *the* object of a belief or judgment (as the 'proposition theory' assumes that there is), not because there can be belief or judgment without any object at all, but because a belief or judgment has not one object but two."[61] Russell in fact claimed that these multiple modes of characterization of objects of judgment led philosophers to speak of thought as discursive in the first place.[62]

Wittgenstein, however, revealed a limitation inherent in the ascriptive model. He argued that the ascriptive model cannot formu-

---

[58] *Doctrine of Propositions and Terms*, p. 13.

[59] Ibid., p. 24. Obviously one could argue that such a distinction does not hold. But, as we have seen, Habermas does hold to the distinction.

[60] Ibid., p. 27. Prior uses a grammatical metaphor: the modal properties are datives, while the asserted predicates are accusatives.

[61] Ibid., p. 29.

[62] A. N. Whitehead and Bertrand Russell, *Principia Mathematica* I, 7th ed. (Cambridge: Cambridge University Press, 1956). Russell later realized certain difficulties in this new mood: it presupposes the existence of a self as one of the terms of the relation.

late the conditions by which two modal ascriptions are able to be compared. Thus, he proposed that the central problem of a theory of meaning is not the ascription of modal properties, but the inter-subjective determination and use of comparable, or identical, propositions. For Wittgenstein the problem of identity determination was in fact closely bound to the idealization of rule-following.[63] Aware of this problem, Habermas argues that two actors arrive at an identity of meaning, not by unifying their outward responses to verbal stimuli, but by following the same rules in coming to an *agreement* about the identity. Following Mead, Habermas argues that actors develop universal "rules of the use of symbols" which can be universally applied in similar situations (TCA 2.15). Mead, however, failed to deal with the problem of how the symbols and gestures actors use to communicate their expectations come to be endowed with identical meaning in the first place. Habermas accounts for this deficiency by stipulating that a rational mode of meaning is based, not upon behavioristic *responses* to the stimulus of a gesture or symbol, but upon yes or no *answers* to validity claims raised in argumentation. Identical meaning thus accrues not only when the actor knows not only how the other *will* react to a certain action, but also how the other *should* react to a valid claim.[64]

Though Prior admits that these *pragmatic* solutions to the problem of identical meaning sustain the plausibility of the ascription theory, he insists that one still needs to analyze how the claims that are "candidates" for an identity refer to the modal contextual conditions of their objects. First, it is necessary to determine whether the identity is, in the terms Peirce used, *token* or *type*.[65] "All x's are y" is a type identity; "x is y" is a token identity. When the reference is context-specific, the identity is token. Second, in cases in which we have determined the identity as token, how do we determine if two

---

[63] For Wittgenstein's theory of rule-following, see *Philosophical Investigations*, trans. G. E. M. Anscombe (Cambridge: Basil Blackwell, 1968), §143–242, especially §225. See also Gordon Hacker's exposition of the problem of rule-following in, "Following Wittgenstein: The Basic Themes for *Philosophical Investigations* §143–242," in *Wittgenstein: To Follow a Rule*, ed. Steven Holtzman and Christopher Leich (London: Routledge & Kegan Paul, 1981), pp. 50–62.

[64] Habermas relies here on Tugendhat's critique of Mead in *Self-Consciousness and Self-Determination*, pp. 230ff. For Mead's arguments, see *Mind, Self, and Society*, pp. 65ff.

[65] *Collected Papers*, 4.537.

sentence tokens are identical? Pragmatic theorists, like Habermas, tend to make this determination by reference, not to constative kinds of sentence tokens, but only to *judgment* tokens. An identity determination by judgment tokens is referred either to a mental act or to a pragmatic disposition to express the assertion "that *x* is *y*," given the *occasion*. Both Wittgenstein and Habermas reject the mentalistic solution and adopt the dispositional one, reducing the identity to the equivalence, not between an object and its particular mode, but between a disposition and an act. But Prior argues that "on this view the distinction between a judgment and a proposition is simply that between a disposition to act in a certain way and the corresponding act, and the difference between 'tokens' and 'type' appears equally in both."[66]

On Prior's account, the type/token identity problem cannot be solved by an appeal only to a dispositional, and thus generalizable, referent for the statement. *The semantic meaning of the type or token cannot be simply "absorbed" into the disposition about which the speaker and hearer formulate a judgment.* Like Prior, Searle argues that token and type are distinguished, not relative to performative utterance, but relative to the inclusion or exclusion of *diachronic context*.[67] Thus, contextual theorists must resolve the problem of how token referents, such as those that refer to the specific temporal context of the assertion itself or the object of the assertion, can be accounted for in generalized dispositions to act. The view that I shall defend holds not only that token claims are redeemable claims, but also that certain temporally referring token claims *must* be redeemed as valid or invalid *before* first-order discourse can commence. They are necessary elements in the process of determining the normativity of a claim and the problematization of a norm.

Semantics and Time Reference

To argue *that* token modal references must form part of discursive acts is one thing, but to specify *how* these semantically formed token

---

[66] *Doctrine of Propositions and Terms*, p. 36. Searle points out that the distinction between token and type does not, as some semanticists hold, parallel the distinction between utterance and sentence. The fact that token sentences are context-dependent and type sentences are not says nothing about the difference between utterance meaning and sentence meaning. Barring diachronic changes, token meanings always are the same as type meanings. See *Expression and Meaning*, p. 119.

[67] *Expression and Meaning*, p. 119.

statements can actually make cogent reference to temporal contexts is another.[68]

The problem of semantic time reference that Prior presents is not new. Aristotle argued that signs refer not only to present, but also to past, future, or even unconscious objects. He pointed out that although nouns refer simply to an object, verbs refer both to an object and to its specific temporal mode (*De interpretatione* 16b). A verb's *tense* determines the temporal mode of the object. There are two forms of temporal attribution: non-reflexive and reflexive. For example, the proposition

(a) "John *plays* baseball"

is a non-reflexive attribution. The "plays" in (a) refers only to the *present fact* of John's proclivity or disposition for playing baseball. It omits specific references to actual temporally locatable *events* (present, past, or future) of John's playing baseball. But

(b) "John *is playing* baseball," or
(c) "John *played* baseball yesterday"

are reflexive attributions, since the "is playing" and "played" refer both to a temporally situated event *and* to the temporally situated attribution itself. Like (a), they can be determined to be true or false: (b) is normally true when John is *actually* playing baseball at the time the utterance is made, but is false at all other times;[69] (c) is true when John played baseball the day before the utterance is made, and is false at all other times. Thus, a token reflexive utterance refers to its object relative to the specific act of its utterance itself.[70] Semantically viewed, all token reflexive utterances—statements that contain the indexical expressions "I," "you," "here," "there," and

---

[68] In his recent *Making It Explicit* (Cambridge, Mass.: Harvard University Press, 1994), Robert Brandom has developed a model of anaphora that accounts for the uptake of temporally specific meaning. To a large extent his account is consistent with the account I offer. But I am interested more in the "categories" of time reference implicit in such an anaphoric context.

[69] In everyday language there are exceptions to this. For example, "I am jogging everyday" does refer to a generalized action. But ordinarily one distinguishes these two types of present tense on these grounds.

[70] Hans Reichenbach, *Elements of Symbolic Logic* (New York: Free Press, 1947), p. 284.

tense inflections of verbs, and so on—share this dual reference both to the object and to the episodic nature of the utterance itself.[71]

Logico-linguistic analysis showed the notion of tense to be self-contradictory.[72] Many modern logicians, such as Quine, transpose token reflexive assertions into equivalent non-reflexive assertions for purposes of truth determination. They claim that (b) and (c) are not propositions able to be determined as true, but phrases that can be *translated into* propositions divested of reference to the episodic context of the utterance. Examples are propositions able to be determined as true or false:

(d)   "John plays baseball on warm afternoons in the summer"
(e)   "It is widely believed that John plays baseball."

Unlike the verbal phrase "is playing," the verb "plays" in both these examples is tenseless and context-neutral.[73] On this reductive account, all propositions have a truth or falsehood that *does not alter with time*. Russell concluded that referential token reflexives such as (b) or (c) can be determined as certain, variable, or impossible, but not as true.

Not all logicians, however, hold to this decontexualizing transposition of the reference of a statement. Rejecting Russell's conclusions, Strawson argues that the question of time reference does arise when we speak of persons and events. He claims that declarative sentences, though ordinarily the sole object of analysis in logic and grammar, are unable to account for temporal reference. He recommends that the study of tenses belongs, not to a theory of entailment, but to a *theory of reference* able to distinguish among tense referents that identify the time of the utterance.[74] Though allowing for temporally neutral sentences, Strawson argues that sentences which contain temporal references have a referential status similar to that of other indexical referents. While admitting that certain temporal determinations, expressed in phrases such as "*When* did Mary and Patricia become sisters?" *can* be decided by declarative sentences, he argues that many others, such as "*When* does the state of affairs of Mary

---

[71] Ibid., p. 336.

[72] McClure, "St. Augustine and the Paradox of Reflection," 317.

[73] I simply assume that the present tense, if not expressed as a gerundive such as "I am playing," is tenseless.

[74] *Introduction to Logical Theory* (London: Methuen, 1952), pp. 150–151, 212.

and Catherine talking to each other obtain?" *cannot*. Strawson calls the function of assertions that can answer the second type of question "situational space-time indication."[75] Such contextualizing assertions do not involve generalizable behaviors, since what one individual tends to do at a particular time cannot be generalized to other individuals (or even to the individual himself) at other times. Yet, by accounting for the actual frequency and duration of the events *when* such temporally specific behaviors or states of affairs have occurred, these assertions serve to contextualize all generalizations that can be drawn from them.

Temporal situatedness thus has an internal relation to the meaning of certain propositions. As Prior argues, expressions such as

(*f*) "it was/is/will be the case at time *x* that *p*"

cannot be "collapsed" to simple "*p*" sentences.[76] Time modalities are intrinsic to the truth of a sentence and integral to the content of the assertion itself. Thus, some propositions include a time-referential token whose interpretation requires a *discursive commitment* on the part of participants to raise and redeem claims about them. Bosanquet argued for a similar distinction between

> the "time of predication" and the "time in predication" (that is, between the time at which a proposition is uttered or a judgment made, and the time which the proposition or judgment is about). It is the time in predication—the time that is part of its "meaning"—that would now be generally taken as fixing the identity of a proposition, rather than the other, the time of its utterance (time "of" predication), though this latter may affect the form of the sentence by which the proposition is expressed.[77]

This "time in predication" provides the contextualization that is constitutive of the truth claim of the predication.

What function would such tensed token reflexives serve in a formal pragmatics of truth? Schutz argued that the "we-relation," which Habermas considers the illocutionary perspective, can be linguistically formulated only through second-order considerations.[78]

---

[75] *Subject and Predicate in Logic and Grammar* (London: Methuen, 1974), p. 95.

[76] *Time and Modality*, p. 121.

[77] As quoted in Prior, *Doctrine of Propositions and Terms*, p. 39.

[78] Schutz defines these expressions as appresentational in which exactly one of its two referents transcends our experience of daily life. See "Symbol, Reality, and Society," p. 331. In many cultures universal symbols emerge to provide transcendent antidotes to the difficulties of the human condition.

Moreover, *the less the social relationships in which we are speaking are stabilized or institutionalized, the more we must clarify them by means of second-order determinations.* Schutz lists four types of claims that serve as pre-conditions for the instantiation of social inquiry:

(1) the determination of an unquestioned problem matrix, or virtualization, with which the inquiry begins;

(2) the determination of the background knowledge that guides the intersubjective interchange;

(3) the determination of specific semantic procedures with respect to signs and symbols that are appropriate for dealing with the problem involved; and

(4) the determination of "typical" conditions under which a problem can be considered as solved and thus the inquiry may be broken off.[79]

My thesis is that the determination of all four types of conditions, but particularly the problematization factor of (1), requires the discursive validation of token reflexive utterances that refer to specific events. Time-referential propositions thus can be the object of the discursive truth determination required to establish the necessary contextualizations needed for the (C1), (C2), and (C3) conditions.[80]

TOWARD A FORMAL PRAGMATICS OF TEMPORAL CONTEXTUALIZATION

Is there any way in which discursive temporal contextualization can be systematized? My third thesis proposes that it is possible to systematize the temporal background conditions of discourse, specifically moral and ethical-existential discourse. I am thereby proposing another level of reflection for formal pragmatics:

event-determining reflection: the act of reflection that grasps temporal limits. This reflection determines events as discrete entities within a temporal background.

---

[79] Ibid., p. 351.

[80] Freud argues that "reference to time is bound with the work of the conscious system." The unconscious is timeless; the act of becoming conscious places us in time. See Freud's "The Unconscious," in *Gesammelte Werke* X (Frankfurt am Main: Fischer, 1968), section V.

For a formal pragmatics, this act of reflection is presupposed not only in the formation of token reflexive speech acts (to determine the distinction between the event of a speech act's utterance and the event of the state of affairs to which it refers), but also in the determination of events of normative determination, norm problematization, and adherence to obligations arising from personal convictions or social norms.

Habermas himself provides some clues for such an reflexive explication of events. In "The Hermeneutic Claim to Universality," he argues that metaphysical concepts, such as cause, space, and time, have a dual meaning: an analytical dimension relative to the identity of objects, and a reflexive dimension relative to speaking and acting subjects.[81] Thus, a postmetaphysical dimension of events demands reference not only to physical events, but also to speaking and acting subjects embedded in a shared lifeworld. On my account, both requirements demand a systematization of events that, although not provided by Habermas, can be coordinated with his own explication of self/world relations. Such a systematization would delimit three kinds of events:

(1) objective or *chronological* events relative to the constative claims of the objective world,[82]

(2) intersubjective or *synchronic* events relative to the moral claims of the social world, and

(3) subjective or *historical* events relative to the expressive claims of the subjective world.

An explication of these three kinds of events would provide a formal pragmatic theory of reflective acceptability with a more comprehensive analysis of the background conditions of the lifeworld context from which the *rational demand* for discursive verification emerges in the first place. Given these three background conditions, we can then formalize the kinds of token reflexives in speech acts that refer to them.

The Pragmatics of Chronological Events

Chronological events occur within a spatio-temporal continuum. For example, when we time a race, the time against which each runner

---

[81] "Hermeneutic Claim to Universality," p. 197.

[82] Roger McClure refers to this as "serial time." See "St. Augustine and the Paradox of Reflection," 320.

is judged is constant and unchanging even though each runner's specific time in the race will vary. Although chronological time is continuous and unbounded, it becomes context-specific when it is bracketed into either the *frequency* of several events or the *duration* of a single event. Empirical and social sciences carry out statistical analyses of the occurrences of a behavior relative to a certain set of initial conditions and a specified chronological time interval. For example, a botanist will observe how often a certain kind of bee pollinates a given flower over a specific period of time, a political scientist will observe how many potential voters actually vote during a given interval of their life spans, and so on. These statistical analyses provide *probabilities* on the basis of which predictions about the future occurrence of the behavior can be made. But statistical assertions are neither explanatory nor normatively binding. They determine neither the causal conditions of a behavior nor whether the behavior will actually occur given the presence of the initial conditions. They assert only the probability of the occurrence of an event relative to a given time interval.

An "objective" statistical analysis of either the frequency of events of agreement about a norm or the frequency of acts of compliance with a norm forms part of the determination of whether a moral norm is problematized in the first place. Examples of such assertions about specific events would be:

(g)   "Over time interval t, actor a . . . complied with norm n a total of x times."

(h)   "Over time interval t, actors a, b, c . . . engaged in discourse about norm n a total of x times."

(i)   "Over time interval t, actor a engaged in actions consistent with concrete ethical way of life z, a total of x times."[83]

Such statistical assertions are token reflexive assertions, since the episodic nature of the claim has a direct relevance to its meaning or truth as such. Actors need to determine the events of norm-following or agreement relative to a set of chronological time intervals in order

---

[83] Klaus Günther, for example, proposes a weaker version of (U) that has "time and knowledge indices" that link a norm's justification to the knowledge that participants have at the point it is made. See *Sense of Appropriateness*, pp. 34–35. See also Vic Peterson's review of Günther's text in *Philosophy and Social Criticism*, 22, No. 1 (1996), 115–124.

to objectively determine whether a new agreement about the claim in question is needed in the present moment.[84] The analysis of the frequency of the events of norm-following, discourse, and consistency in one's chosen way of life fulfills a necessary, though not sufficient, condition for the determination of the validity status, or problematization, of a given norm. Although neither the diminished frequency of the following of a norm nor the increased frequency of reflection about the norm directly entails that the norm is invalid, both constative factors do contribute directly to the determination of the norm's problematization.[85]

The Pragmatics of Synchronic Events

Relativity theory in physics demonstrated that chronological time, although adequate for determining successive diachronic events, is inadequate for determining *simultaneous* events. A non-chronological form of time is needed for either the determination of one event from multiple frames of reference or the determination of several simultaneous events from one frame of reference. Such temporal reference is needed to determine coordinated or synchronized perspective-taking in the social world. Determined by suspensions and resumptions of coordination between the perspectives of social actors, this intersubjective form of time is not continuous or chronological, but simultaneous and synchronized.

Some theorists have attempted to formulate a "science" of such intersubjective-time for various social sciences. Durkheim spoke of a sociological form of time that is not an abstract part of personal existence, but a "category of society" in which all members of the same civilization think.[86] This category of time forms common

---

[84] I want to claim that my reference to rule-following is valid despite Wittgenstein's thorough critique of both the subjective and objective aspects of rule-following in *Philosophical Investigations* §143–252. I am referring here only to the empirical and third-person observable occurrence of "violations" of what are considered to be norms by both actor and others.

[85] I realize that a more rigorist view of obligation would endorse the claim that the following of a norm has little or indeed nothing to do with its problematization. Although intuitively suspicious of this belief, I will not present arguments to defeat it here.

[86] *Die elementaren Formen des religiösen Lebens*, trans. L. Schmidts (Frankfurt am Main: Suhrkamp, 1981), p. 29.

"fixed points" taken from elements in the social world that are crucial for its functioning. He even claimed that we need to have synchronized and regularized "distancings" from life through periodic ceremonies and other social forms of ritual interaction. Such periodic interactions reveal how a normative consensus is "regularly" made actual (TCA 2.52). Arthur Danto developed a kind of intersubjective-time theory for historical interpretation. He claimed that historians must take into account how a single event can be situated in several different temporal wholes, each constituted by a unique relation between the original event and another temporally distinct event.[87] Diachronic analysis alone is inadequate for determining historical meaning and truth.

Lacan formulated a science of time contextualization for psychoanalysis. He argued that natural sciences are defined not so much by the quantity to which they are applied as by the *creative* measure they introduce into the interpretation of the real. Laws of experimental sciences thus function co-extensively with the time measure that makes them possible. Huyghen's clock, for instance, gave experimental science its precision and universal extension by functioning as "the organ embodying Galileo's hypothesis on the equigravity of bodies."[88] In a similar way, the mathematics derived from Boolean logic and set theory provide formulas given in game theory that symbolize the intersubjective-time that structures human action. Human action, as it orders itself according to the action of the other, finds "in the scansion of its hesitations the advent of its certainty; and in the decision that concludes it, the action given to that of the other—which it includes from that point on—together with its consequences deriving from the past, its meaning-to-come."[89] By adopting this mathematically derived periodic analysis, a human science can structurally analyze *times for understanding and moments for concluding*. Psychoanalysis requires such a structure of intersubjective time to ensure its own rigor.

---

[87] *An Analytic Philosophy of History* (Cambridge: Cambridge University Press, 1965), p. 167.

[88] "Function and Field of Speech and Language," in *Écrits: A Selection*, trans. A. Sheridan (New York: Norton, 1977), p. 75.

[89] Ibid. Martin Seel also argues for the crucial importance of time in any game, both for the participant and the spectator. See his "Die Zelebration der Unvermögens: Zur Ästhetik des Sports," in *Merkur*, 47, No. 2 (February 1993), 91–100.

Although forgoing a formal analysis of synchronic events presupposed in intersubjective agreements, Habermas does implicitly take into account several of its conditions. He acknowledges both the lack of stability in everyday intersubjective communication and the fact noted by ethnomethodologists that agreement among actors is achieved only "occasionally" (TCA 2.100). He notes that the intersubjective world exhibits a temporal character and an "intrinsic historicality" much different from the objective world (JA 39). Intersubjective time thus mirrors the fragility and vagaries of those individuals who constitute it. Habermas takes account of such relativity by explicating the self/world relations from which any act oriented toward reaching agreement can be viewed. He assumes that such a decentered model of agreement serves as a necessary background for participants engaged in intersubjective events such as learning processes, seminar discussions, parliamentary hearings, and so on.[90]

Relative to moral and ethical-existential discourse, synchronic events refer to the coordinating of perspectives involved in agreements or clinical advice. The discursive analysis of these events contributes to the determination of the claim's normativity or the norm's problematization. For example, participants make second-order non-reflexive temporal assertions such as:

(j)   "Agreement about the normativity of claim x was determined by actors $a, b, c, \ldots$ at time $t(1)$ and continued until time $t(2)$";

(k)   "Agreement about the authenticity of way of life y was determined by actor $a, \ldots$ at time $t(1)$ and continued until time $t(2)$."

The time reference in these claims is intersubjective; the claims refer primarily to the intersubjective accomplishment of a coordination of temporal perspectives and only secondarily to a chronological event. But even though they are tensed claims, they can and must be discursively validated before actors can engage in a first-order discourse about the specific norm or claim.

An analysis of synchronic events can help to determine the proper frequency of moral and ethical-existential (as well as political) dis-

---

[90] See *Theorie der Gesellschaft oder Sozialtechnologie*, p. 121; JA 31.

course. Certain temporally referential claims must be redeemed before the participants' perspectives can be sufficiently synchronized so as to coordinate their projection of both problematizations of present norms and hypothetizations of new possible claims. These temporally situated claims about intersubjective events of agreement serve to determine when norms are problematized and thus when first-order discourse should commence. If discourse is too frequent, or too infrequent, pathologies can develop: a person can become too introspective about who he or she wants to be; two friends can analyze their friendship too much; a government can schedule too few deliberations about the effectiveness of its present policies and programs; and so on. Determining when to move from ordinary lifeworld interaction to the thematization of normativity and problematization is thus a discursive competence that individuals must acquire. This competence is enhanced by formalizing the kinds of validity claims employed in determining both past agreements about or future re-validizations of the norm in question.

The Pragmatics of Historical Events

While synchronic events refer to actions involving interactions, suspensions of interaction, and incorporation of social memories and anticipations, historical events are actions viewed from the perspective of individual or social experiences.[91] A person or society dwells on past memories and future anticipations for various intervals of time in its experience. We unify these distinct experiences by allowing the different moments of our experience to permeate each other. The historical constitution of an event thus constitutes a uniquely configured social or life history, which I discussed in the last chapter. This development is continuous, even though we experience stages in which we seem to be "going nowhere" or even regressing. This unified duration is nonetheless bounded for the individual, as Heidegger described in Being and Time, by the finite limits of birth and death. If we lose sight of the unique experience of historical constitution of events, we end up in an idealism of timeless theorizing.

---

[91] For a discussion of the concept of duration, see Bergson's discussion of it in Time and Free Will (London: Allen & Unwin, 1910).

How does this historical time function?[92] Through an act of reflection, a subject can cognize his past, evaluate the present, or imagine its future.[93] The past events constitute the background of a life history from which future projections are made. Some of the future projected events are practical: they imagine either conformity to accepted norms or the adoption of new innovative and emancipatory actions. An actor's projection of future actions does, nonetheless, form part of his enduring life history. The *present* is the unique point at which both past and future determinations are made. However, neither of these sets of historical events is normative or generalizable, since they refer only to a temporal experience from the perspective of the subject involved. As McClure argues, reflection not only can arrive at a chronological awareness of one event's being *before* another, but also arrive at a *pre*-reflective awareness of some event *having been* such in the eye of reflection itself. In this mode of time, reflection discloses its event as both inside and outside of time: something the subject knows in the present and does not know as his future. It is knowledge about the event without Cartesian presence.[94]

How does this historical time impact discourse? On my account, it is possible to reconstruct how individual actors interpret both past (remembered) and future (anticipated) events *not only* of their norm-adjudication and norm-following involving moral discourse, but also of their character-formation in ethical-existential discourse. The individual can reflect upon his experience of past events involving a claim's normativity or problematization or about his own determination of a character or way of life. A subject's knowledge about the problematization of a norm or a way of life is derived primarily

---

[92] Reminiscent of Kant, Arnold Gehlen argues that the counter-posing of different words or symbols for the same object can break chronological time and give rise to reflexive awakening. Gehlen also describes how painters, such as Degas, Gauguin, and Toulouse-Lautrec, used visual interference and cross division to give rise to this state of reflexive awakening in the beholder. See Arnold Gehlen, *Zeit Bilder: Zur Soziologie und Ästhetik der modernen Malerei* (Frankfurt am Main: Athenäum, 1960), pp. 63ff.

[93] Alfred Lorenzer, for example, uses Langer's idea that presentative forms of symbols describe the "projective mechanisms" needed for understanding situations in new ways. See his *Spachzerstörung und Rekonstruktion* (Frankfurt am Main: Suhrkamp, 1971), p. 109; Langer, *Philosophy in a New Key*, pp. 61–65. The early Wittgenstein argued that we need rules as "laws of projection" to "read" what are otherwise merely two-dimensional picturings of facts. See *Tractatus*, 4.1041.

[94] McClure, "St. Augustine and the Paradox of Reflection," 320–321.

from the subject's obligation to follow the commitments they entail. The subject forms his will to seek agreement about a norm or way of life on the basis of both memories and anticipations regarding the events of the formation of them. The subject has, not a complete self-present awareness of the past events, but commitments arising from his reflective determination of the events.

When one overcomes the alienation of one's inclinations, one has effectively reached an *agreement* with oneself. Commitments are events, reached in an historical present, regarding either individual or social agreements. These events must be taken into account if the individual's autonomy is to be fully respected in its participation in collective will-formation processes. For example, the token reflexive claims

(l) "I am now committed (or not committed) to the normativity of claim x,"

(m) "I am now committed (or not committed) to the problematization of claim y,"

(n) "I am now committed (or not committed) to my preference for character, or concrete ethical way of life, z" (JA 4)[95]

refer to subjective experiences of norm-adjudication, norm-following, and ethical-existential discourse, respectively. The convictions in all three utterances refer to events that must be understood neither as chronological events nor as synchronized events; rather, they serve as the basis for the determination of a subject's *present dispositional state* regarding the norm. Although the speech act claims used to refer to these convictions refer only to the individual's contextualized and subjective experience of time, intersubjective and normative entailments can be drawn from the redemption of them:

(o) "If I am not committed to the normativity of claim x, I ought to engage in discourse about claim x's normativity";

(p) "If I am not committed to the problematization of norm y, I ought to engage in discourse about norm y's problematization";

(q) "If I am not committed to the value of preference z, I ought to engage in ethical-existential discourse about z."

---

[95] Habermas explicitly adopts Charles Taylor's terminology to describe these characteristics of ethical-existential discourse.

An individual's commitments regarding the normativity of a social norm or way of life serve to determine the proper instantiation of moral and ethical-existential discourse. These token reflexive claims thus play a significant role in determining whether ethical-existential validity determination is needed for the individual, whether an individual is free to dissent from a valid norm, or whether moral norms are normative or problematized for a group of actors.

In sum, the formulation, interpretation, and discursive determination of these three types of events contributes to the development of second-order discourse. This formal pragmatics of time mitigates the context-transcending character of Habermas's idealizations in intersubjective agreement—the "weakness" he attributes to its transcendental claims notwithstanding—by reconstructing the processes by which participants must confront actual norm-adjudication and norm-following and character-forming actions in everyday situations. Although I agree fully with Habermas's rejection of the need for a Rawlsian veil of ignorance or some other neutral construction in order to initiate argumentation regarding these determinations, both the psychologist and the discourse theorist still need to provide not just an empirical, but also a formal pragmatic analysis of how actors determine that reflection ought to be instantiated.

The advantage of formalizing these procedures is that it regularizes and rationalizes discourse competence. Just as formal pragmatics regularizes the argumentation procedures of discourse, so it should also regularize the instantiation conditions for discourse. By broadening its domain from including only "p" assertions to including time-referential "Mp" assertions, Habermas can retain his discourse theory's need for stability over time without losing the context-specificity it needs for emancipation and critique.

Conclusion: Reflection Revisited

We are indebted to Rorty for alerting us to both the puzzles and the pitfalls of reflection. He has exposed a number of dubious "privileged representations" that philosophers of reflection have used to justify their epistemic and ethical claims: Plato's ideal forms, Husserl's essences, Kant's intuitions, and even the "raw feels" of analytic philosophers. Like Sellars and Quine, Rorty sketches a version of pragmatism that discards the need for verification through the mediations of these mental entities altogether.[96] He proposes that the ultimate arbiters of beliefs and actions ought to be simply the *conventions* that give coherence to social practice.

It should be clear that Habermas is, in the final analysis, somewhat ambivalent about Rorty's critique of reflection. On the one hand, he agrees with Rorty's rejection of the mental entities and other hypostatizations to which previous philosophers have appealed. On the other, his theory of reflective acceptability vigorously disputes Rorty's claim that rationality ought to abandon *syllogistic reasoning about facts*.[97] In order to retain a role for rational critique, Habermas espouses the "privilege" of the idealizations that, as a matter of fact, guide all argumentation regarding the truth of claims (JA 164). One and only one well-defined set of reconstructed epistemic assumptions grounds the reflective acceptability of a claim.[98] Thus, justification emerges, not from a de facto consensus, as Rorty holds, but only from an agreement determined by discourse that can reproduce its own validity conditions. Habermas's idea of rationality neither admits of degrees nor appeals to a higher ground: a *tertium non datur*.[99] Reflexive acceptability of validity claims, as we have seen, requires the achievement of a symmetric illocutionary perspective either within a self-reflecting subject or among those engaged in discourse. His reconstruction of this competence is a notable achievement.

In this study I hope that I have occasioned, in addition to a profound respect for Habermas's achievement, a deep appreciation for the problem of reflection itself. Reflection is not merely an interesting philosophical topic; it lies at the very core of the philosophical enterprise. One could even say that those who deny the existence of reflexive acts commit the same "performative contradiction" as those

---

[96] *Philosophy and the Mirror of Nature*, p. 169.

[97] Ibid., p. 190.

[98] Geuss, *Idea of a Critical Theory*, p. 162. This claim that there exists one and only one set of rational procedures leaves Habermas open to the charge that he is a moral realist. For a description of realism in ethics, see David Brink, *Moral Realism and the Foundations of Ethics* (Cambridge: Cambridge University Press, 1989), pp. 17ff.

[99] Geuss, *Idea of a Critical Theory*, p. 31.

who deny the existence of reason, truth, God, or whatever other unassailable grounds to which philosophers have appealed throughout history. One could even claim that modernity itself, turning from the analysis of single entities (persons, semantic terms, social norms) to the *relations between* them (which includes their characterization as events), should have piqued our philosophical interest in reflection. Limit concepts are found throughout all cognitive determinations. We have seen this repeatedly in Habermas's preoccupation with the reflective acceptability of claims.

Every act of reflection crosses over some kind of limit. It relates the two terms in the relation with respect to the limit that separates them. In Habermas's theory of truth and truth-analogous relations, the primary set of terms are a speaker and a hearer; and the limit is the alterity of the hearer as other (or the self understood as other) that is bridged by a synthetic act of reflection in self-reflection or discourse. Thus, discursive reflection yields a harmony or symmetry either between the self and its alienated self, or between the moral actor and the other, or between citizens and their polis. The "temporalized" version of the theory of reflective acceptability I have endorsed simply broadens the domain of assertions, raised by social actors, that are allowed into discourse to include time-referential assertions about the *events* of speech acts, discourse, and rational convictions about the normatization, problematization, and following of normative claims.

There remains, however, a certain necessary tension within any theory of reflection. For Habermas this tension shows up in the way his account of communication in the context of the lifeworld still manifests the basic Husserlian distinction between *Denken* and *Existenz*: the stubborn difference between attaining clearly defined *agreement about problems of social coordination* and the at times harsh and intractable realities of the *actual social world*. Nevertheless, as perhaps the last of the Frankfurt School theorists, Habermas remains steadfastly committed to the conviction that philosophy can provide the rational tools needed to mitigate the human suffering that arises from these alienating aspects of the social world.

BIBLIOGRAPHY

This bibliography is divided into six sections. Since I intend this work to be first and foremost an analysis of Habermas's works, I list them separately. Section 1 lists monographs not already included in Abbreviations; section 2 lists articles. Then I list secondary sources on his work: books in section 3, and articles in section 4. Section 5 includes the works I consulted specifically for the problem of reflection. All other references are placed in section 6.

1. MONOGRAPHS AND COLLECTIONS BY HABERMAS

Das Absolute und die Geschichte: Von der Zweispaltigkeit Schellings Denken. Dissertation, Universität Bonn, 1954.

Eine Art Schadensabwicklung: Kleine politische Schriften VI. Frankfurt am Main: Suhrkamp, 1987. [*The New Conservatism: Cultural Criticism and the Historians' Debate.* Trans. S. W. Nicholsen. Cambridge, Mass.: The MIT Press, 1989.]

Entwicklung des Ichs. Coauthored with Rainer Döbert and Gertrud Nunner-Winkler. Cologne: Kiepenheuer & Witsch, 1977.

Erkenntnis und Interesse. 2nd ed. Frankfurt am Main: Suhrkamp, 1973.

Erläuterungen zur Diskursethik. Frankfurt am Main: Suhrkamp, 1991.

Faktizität und Geltung: Beiträge zur Diskurstheorie des Rechts und des demokratischen Rechtsstaats. Frankfurt am Main: Suhrkamp, 1992.

Kultur und Kritik: Verstreute Aufsätze. Frankfurt am Main: Suhrkamp, 1973.

Legitimationsprobleme im Spätkapitalismus. Frankfurt am Main: Suhrkamp, 1973.

Moralbewußtsein und kommunikatives Handeln. Frankfurt am Main: Suhrkamp, 1983.

Nachmetaphysisches Denken: Philosophische Aufsätze. Frankfurt am Main: Suhrkamp, 1988.

Philosophische Diskurs der Moderne: Zwölf Vorlesungen. Frankfurt am Main: Suhrkamp, 1985.

Philosophische-politische Profile. 2nd ed. Frankfurt am Main: Suhrkamp, 1981.

Technik und Wissenschaft als Ideologie. Frankfurt am Main: Suhrkamp, 1968.

Theorie der Gesellschaft oder Sozialtechnologie: Was leistet die Systemforschung? Coauthored with N. Luhmann. Frankfurt am Main: Suhrkamp, 1971.

Theorie des kommunikativen Handelns. 2 vols. Frankfurt am Main: Suhrkamp, 1981.

Theorie und Praxis. 2nd ed. Frankfurt am Main: Suhrkamp, 1971.

Vorstudien und Ergänzungen zur Theorie des kommunkativen Handelns. Frankfurt am Main: Suhrkamp, 1984.

Vergangenheit als Zukunft. Zurich: Pendo Interview, 1991. [*The Past as Future.* Trans. M. Pensky. Lincoln: University of Nebraska Press, 1994.]

Zur Logik der Sozialwissenschaften. Philosophische Rundschau, Beiheft 5. Tübingen: Mohr, 1967.

Zur Rekonstruktion des historischen Materialismus. Frankfurt am Main: Suhrkamp, 1976.

2. ARTICLES AND INTERVIEWS BY HABERMAS

"Actions, Speech Acts, Linguistically Mediated Interactions, and the Lifeworld." In *Philosophical Problems Today* I. Ed. G. Fløistad. Dordrecht: Kluwer, 1994. Pp. 45–74.

"Arbeit und Interaktion." In *Technik und Wissenschaft als Ideology.* Frankfurt am Main: Suhrkamp, 1968. Pp. 9–47.

"Edmund Husserl über Lebenswelt, Philosophie, und Wissenschaft." In TK. Pp. 34–49.

"Erkenntnis und Interesse." *Technik und Wissenschaft als Ideologie.* Frankfurt am Main: Suhrkamp, 1968.

"Ein Generation von Adorno getrennt." In *Geist gegen den Zeitgeist: Erinnern an Adorno.* Ed. J. Früchtl and M. Calloni. Frankfurt am Main: Suhrkamp, 1991. Pp. 47–53.

"The Hermeneutic Claim to Universality." In *Contemporary Hermeneutics.* Ed. J. Bleicher. Boston: Routledge & Kegan Paul, 1980. Pp. 181–211.

"Historical Consciousness and Post–Traditional Identity: The Western Orientation of the Federal Republic." In *The New Conservatism: Cultural Criticism and the Historians' Debate.* Trans. S. Weber Nicholsen. Cambridge, Mass.: The MIT Press, 1989. Pp. 249–267.

"Interview." *Theory and Society,* 1 (1974), 37–58.

"Law and Morality." In *The Tanner Lectures on Human Values* VIII. Salt Lake City: University of Utah Press; Cambridge: Cambridge University Press, 1988. Pp. 217–299.

"Moralentwicklung und Ich-Identität." In *Zur Rekonstruktion des histori-schen Materialismus*. Frankfurt am Main: Suhrkamp, 1976. Pp. 63–92.

"Morality and Ethical Life: Does Hegel's Critique of Kant Apply to Dis-course Ethics?" In MCCA. Pp. 195–216.

"Nachwort" (1973). In *Erkenntnis und Interesse*. Frankfurt am Main: Suhr-kamp, 1973. Pp. 367–416.

"Psychic Thermidor and the Rebirth of Rebellious Subjectivity." In *Haber-mas and Modernity*. Ed. Richard Bernstein. Cambridge, Mass.: The MIT Press, 1985. Pp. 177–187.

"Questions and Counterquestions." In *Habermas and Modernity*. Ed. Rich-ard Bernstein. Cambridge, Mass.: The MIT Press, 1982. Pp. 192–216.

"Reconciliation Through the Public Use of Reason: Remarks on John Rawls's Political Liberalism." In *The Journal of Philosophy*, 92, No. 3 (March 1995), 109–131.

"A Reply." *Communicative Action: Essays on Jürgen Habermas' Theory of Communicative Action*. Ed. Axel Honneth and Hans Joas. Cambridge, Mass.: The MIT Press, 1991. Pp. 214–264.

"Reply to My Critics." In *Habermas: Critical Debates*. Ed. David Held and John Thompson. Cambridge, Mass.: The MIT Press, 1982. Pp. 219–283.

"Response to the Commentary of Bernstein and Dove." In *Hegel's Social and Political Thought*. Atlantic Highlands, N.J.: Humanities Press, 1980. Pp. 247–250.

"A Review of Gadamer's *Truth and Method*." In *Hermeneutics and Modern Philosophy*. Ed. B. Wachterhauser. Albany: State University of New York Press, 1986. Pp. 243–276.

"Richard Rorty's Pragmatic Turn." In OPC. Pp. 343–382.

"Ruckkehr zur Metaphysik: Eine Tendenz in der deutschen Philosophie?" *Merkur*, 439–440 (October 1985), 898ff.

"Some Difficulties in the Attempt to Link Theory and Practice." In *Theory and Practice*. Trans. J. Viertel. Boston: Beacon, 1973. Pp. 1–40.

"Some Further Qualifications of the Concept of Communicative Rational-ity." In OPC. Pp. 307–342.

"Transzendenz von Innen, Transzendenz ins Diesseits." In TK. Pp. 127–156.

"Wahrheitstheorien." In *Wirklichkeit und Reflexion: Walter Schulz zum 60. Geburtstag*. Ed. H. Fahrenbach. Pfullingen: Neske, 1973. Pp. 127–183.

"Yet Again, German Identity." In *New German Critique*, 52 (Winter 1991), 84–101.

"Zur Einführung." In *Entwicklung des Ichs*. Coauthored with Rainer Dö-bert and Gertrud Nunner-Winkler. Cologne: Kiepenheuer & Witsch, 1977. Pp. 9–28.

3. Monographs on Habermas

Alford, C. Fred. *Science and the Revenge of Nature: Marcuse and Habermas.* Gainesville: Florida University Press, 1985.

Arens, Edmund, ed. *Habermas und die Theologie.* Düsseldorf: Patmos, 1989.

Badillo, Robert Peter. *The Emancipative Theory of Jürgen Habermas.* Washington D.C.: The Council for Research Values and Philosophy, 1991.

Baynes, Kenneth. *From Social Contract Theory to Normative Social Criticism.* Albany: State University of New York Press, 1991.

Baynes, Kenneth, James Bohman, and Thomas McCarthy, eds. *After Philosophy.* Cambridge, Mass.: The MIT Press, 1987.

Bernstein, Richard, ed. *Habermas and Modernity.* Cambridge, Mass.: The MIT Press, 1985.

Calhoun, Craig, ed. *Habermas and the Public Sphere.* Cambridge, Mass.: The MIT Press, 1992.

Cooke, Maeve. *Language and Reason.* Cambridge, Mass.: The MIT Press, 1994.

Dallmayr, Fred, ed. *Materialien zu Habermas' "Erkenntnis und Interesse."* Frankfurt am Main: Suhrkamp, 1974.

Flynn, Bernard. *Political Philosophy at the Closure of Metaphysics.* London: Humanities Press, 1992.

Geuss, Raymond. *The Idea of a Critical Theory: Habermas and the Frankfurt School.* Cambridge: Cambridge University Press, 1981.

Held, David, and John Thompson, eds. *Habermas: Critical Debates.* Cambridge, Mass.: The MIT Press, 1982.

Holub, Robert. *Jürgen Habermas: Critic in the Public Sphere.* New York: Routledge, 1991.

Honneth, Axel. *Kritik der Macht: Reflexionsstufen einer kritischen Gesellschaftstheorie.* Frankfurt am Main: Suhrkamp, 1986.

Honneth, Axel, and Hans Joas, eds. *Communicative Action: Essays on Jürgen Habermas's Theory of Communicative Action.* Trans. J. Gaines and D. Jones. Cambridge, Mass.: The MIT Press, 1991.

Honneth, Axel, et al., eds. *Zwischenbetrachtungen im Prozeß der Aufklärung.* Frankfurt am Main: Suhrkamp, 1989.

Horster, Detlef. *Jürgen Habermas.* Stuttgart: Metzler, 1991.

Ingram, David. *Critical Theory and Philosophy.* New York: Paragon House, 1990.

——. *Habermas and the Dialectic of Reason.* New Haven, Conn.: Yale University Press, 1987.

Keat, Russell. *The Politics of Social Theory: Habermas, Freud, and the Critique of Positivism.* Chicago: The University of Chicago Press, 1981.

Kessler, Alfred. *Identität und Kritik: Zu Habermas' Interpretation des psycho-analytischen Prozesses*. Würzburg: Königshausen & Neumann, 1983.

Lakeland, Paul. *Theology and Critical Theory: The Discourse of the Church*. Nashville: Abingdon Press, 1990.

McCarthy, Thomas. *The Critical Theory of Jürgen Habermas*. Cambridge, Mass.: The MIT Press, 1978.

Rasmussen, David. *Reading Habermas*. Cambridge, Mass.: Basil Blackwell, 1990.

————, ed. *Universalism and Communitarianism*. Cambridge, Mass.: The MIT Press, 1988.

Rehg, William. *Insight and Solidarity*. Berkeley: University of California Press, 1994.

Rockmore, Tom. *Habermas on Historical Materialism*. Bloomington: University of Indiana Press, 1989.

Thompson, John. *Critical Hermeneutics: A Study in the Thought of Paul Ricoeur and Jürgen Habermas*. New York: Cambridge University Press, 1981.

White, Stephen. *The Recent Work of Jürgen Habermas: Reason, Justice, and Modernity*. Cambridge: Cambridge University Press, 1988.

————, ed. *The Cambridge Companion to Habermas*. New York: Cambridge University Press, 1995.

4. ARTICLES ON HABERMAS

Alford, Fred C. "Habermas and the End of the Individual." *Theory, Culture, and Society* (1987), 1–29.

Bernstein, Richard. "The Relationship of Habermas's Views to Hegel." In *Hegel's Social and Political Thought*. Atlantic Heights, N.J.: Humanities Press, 1980. Pp. 233–239.

Bohman, James. "'System and Lifeworld': Habermas and the Problem of Holism." *Philosophy and Social Criticism*, 15 (1989), 381–401.

Bubner, Rüdiger. "Summation." *Cultural Hermeneutics*, 2, No. 4 (February 1975), 360–361.

Cooke, Maeve. "Habermas, Autonomy, and the Identity of the Self." *Philosophy and Social Criticism*, 18, Nos. 3–4 (1993), 269–292.

Doody, John. "MacIntyre and Habermas on Practical Reason." *American Catholic Philosophical Quarterly*, 65, No. 2 (Spring 1991), 143–158.

Eder, Klaus. "Critique of Habermas's Contribution to the Sociology of Law." *Law and Society Review*, 22, No. 5 (1988), 931–944.

Ferrara, Alessandro. "A Critique of Habermas's Consensus Theory of Truth." *Philosophy and Social Criticism*, 13, No. 1 (1987), 39–67.

Fraser, Nancy. "What's Critical About Critical Theory: The Case of Habermas and Gender." In *Unruly Practices: Power, Discourse and Gender in Contemporary Social Theory*. Minneapolis: University of Minnesota Press, 1989. Pp. 113–143.

Gadamer, Hans-Georg. "Hermeneutics and Social Science." *Cultural Hermeneutics*, 2 (1975), 313–317.

Gasché, Rodolphe. "Postmodernism and Rationality." *The Journal of Philosophy*, 85 (1988), 528–538.

Geiman, Kevin-Paul. "Habermas's Early Lifeworld Appropriation: A Critical Assessment." *Man and World*, 23 (1990), 63–81.

Griffioen, Sander. "The Metaphor of the Covenant in Habermas." *Faith and Philosophy*, 8, No. 4 (October 1991), 524–540.

Heath, Joseph. "The Problem of Foundationalism in Habermas's Discourse Ethics." *Philosophy and Social Criticism*, 21, No. 1 (January 1995), 77–100.

Henrich, Dieter. "Was ist Metaphysik—was Moderne?: Zwölf Thesen gegen Jürgen Habermas." In *Konzepte: Essays zur Philosophie der Zeit*. Frankfurt am Main: Suhrkamp, 1987. Pp. 11–43.

Hesse, Mary. "Science and Objectivity." In *Habermas: Critical Debates*. Ed. David Held and John Thompson. Cambridge, Mass.: The MIT Press, 1982. Pp. 98–115.

Ingram, David. "Dworkin, Habermas and the CLS Movement on Moral Criticism in Law." *Philosophy and Social Criticism*, 16, No. 4 (1990), 237–268.

Jay, Martin. "The Debate over Performative Contradiction: Habermas versus the Poststructuralists." In *Zwischenbetrachtungen im Prozeß der Aufklärung*. Ed. Alex Honneth et al. Frankfurt am Main: Suhrkamp, 1989. Pp. 171–189.

Kelly, Michael. "MacIntyre, Habermas, and Philosophical Ethics." *Philosophical Forum*, 21 (1989–90), 70–93.

Loiacono, James. "Liberation as Autonomy and Responsibility: Habermas and Psychoanalytic Method in the Analysis and Critique of Values." In *The Social Context and Values*. Ed. G. McLean and O. Pegoraro. New York: University Press of America, 1989. Pp. 75–121.

Matustik, Martin. "Jürgen Habermas at 60." *Philosophy and Social Criticism*, 16, No. 1 (1990), 61–80.

———. "Habermas's Readings of Kierkegaard: Notes from a Conversation." *Philosophy and Social Criticism*, 17, No. 4 (1992), 313–324.

McCarthy, Thomas. "Translator's Introduction." In LC. Pp. vii–xxiv.

———. "Rationality and Relativism. In *Habermas: Critical Debates*. Ed. David Held and John Thompson. Cambridge, Mass.: The MIT Press, 1982. Pp. 57–78.

Mette, Norbert. "Identität ohne Religion." In *Habermas und die Theologie*. Ed. E. Arens. Düsseldorf: Patmos, 1989. Pp. 160–198.

Meynell, Hugo. "Habermas: An Unstable Compromise." *American Catholic Philosophical Quarterly*, 65, No. 2 (Spring 1991), 189–201.

Moss, Lenny. "Ethical Expertise and Moral Maturity: Conflict or Complement?" *Philosophy and Social Criticism*, 16, No. 3 (1990), 227–235.

Nichols, Christopher. "Science or Reflection: Habermas on Freud." *Philosophy of the Social Sciences*, 2 (1972), 261–270.

Olafson, Frederick. "Habermas as a Philosopher." *Ethics*, 100 (April 1990), 641–657.

Pippin, Robert. "Hegel, Modernity, and Habermas." *The Monist*, 74, No. 3 (July 1991), 329–357.

Postone, Moishe. "Habermas's Critique of Marx." In *Time, Labor, and Social Domination*. Cambridge: Cambridge University Press, 1993. Pp. 226–260.

Rajchman, John. "Habermas's Complaint." *New German Critique*, 45 (Fall 1988), 163–191.

Rasmussen, David. "Advanced Capitalism and Social Theory: Habermas on the Problem of Legitimation." *Cultural Hermeneutics*, 3, No. 4 (1976), 349–366.

———."Communicative Action and Philosophy." *Philosophy and Social Criticism*, 9 (1982), 1–18.

Rasmussen, Douglas. "Political Legitimacy and Discourse Ethics." *International Philosophical Quarterly*, 32, No. 1 (March 1992), 17–34.

———. "Reply to Habermas." *The Journal of Philosophy*, 92, No. 3 (March 1995), 132–180.

Rehg, William. "Discourse Ethics and the Communitarian Critique of Neo-Kantianism." *Philosophical Forum*, 22, No. 2 (Winter 1990), 120–138.

———. "Discourse and the Moral Point of View: Deriving a Dialogical Principle of Universalization." *Inquiry*, 34 (1991), 27–48.

Rorty, Richard. "Epistemological Behaviorism and Analytic Philosophy." In *Hermeneutics and Praxis*. Ed. R. Hollinger. Notre Dame: University of Notre Dame Press, 1985. Pp. 89–121.

———. "Two Meanings of 'Logocentrism.' " In *Philosophical Papers* II. New York: Cambridge University Press, 1991. Pp. 107–118.

Scharff, Robert. "Habermas on Heidegger's *Being and Time*." *International Philosophical Quarterly*, 31, No. 2 (June 1991), 189–201.

Steele, Meili. "The Ontological Turn and Its Ethical Consequences: Habermas and the Poststructuralists." *Praxis International*, 11, No. 4 (January 1992), 428–446.

Thiebaut, Carlos. "The Complexity of the Subject, Narrative Identity, and the Modernity of the South." *Philosophy and Social Criticism*, 18, Nos. 3–4 (1993), 313–332.

Trey, George. "Communicative Ethics in the Face of Alterity: Habermas, Levinas, and the Problem of Post-Conventional Universalism." *Praxis International*, 11, No. 4 (January 1992), 412–427.

Wagner, Gerhard, and Heinz Zipprian. "Intersubjectivity and Critical Consciousness: Remarks on Habermas's Theory of Communicative Action." *Inquiry*, 34, No. 1 (March 1991), 49–62.

Warnke, Georgia. "Communicative Rationality and Cultural Values." In *The Cambridge Companion to Habermas*. Ed. S. White. Cambridge: Cambridge University Press, 1994. Pp. 120–142.

———. Review of David Rasmussen. *Reading Habermas. The Philosophical Quarterly*, 42 (January 1992), 129–131.

Wolin, Richard. "On Misunderstanding Habermas: A Response to Rajchman." *New German Critique*, 49 (Winter 1990), 139–154.

5. The Problem of Reflection

Apel, Karl-Otto. *Transformation der Philosophie*. 2 vols. Frankfurt am Main: Suhrkamp, 1973.

———."The Transcendental Conception of Language-Communication and the Idea of a First Philosophy." In *The History of Linguistic Thought and Contemporary Linguistics*. Ed. H. Parret. New York: de Gruyter, 1976. Pp. 32–61.

Breazeale, Daniel. "Editor's Introduction." In Johann Gottlieb Fichte. *Foundations of Transcendental Wissenschaftslehre nova methodo (1796/ 99)*. Trans. and ed. Daniel Breazeale. Ithaca, N.Y.: Cornell University Press, 1992. Pp. 1–49.

Bubner, Rüdiger. "Selbstbezüglichkeit als Struktur transzendentalen Argumente." In *Kommunikation und Reflexion*. Ed. W. Kuhlmann and D. Böhler. Frankfurt am Main: Suhrkamp, 1982. Pp. 304–333.

Cassirer, Ernst. *Philosophie der symbolischen Formen*. 2nd ed. 3 vols. Oxford: Bruno Cassirer, 1954.

Fichte, Johann Gottlieb. "Grundlage der gesamten Wissenschaftslehre (1794)." *Ausgewählte Werke* I. Ed. F. Medicus. Darmstadt: Wissenschaftliche Buchgesellschaft, 1962. Pp. 275–520.

———. *Johann Gottlieb Fichtes sämmtliche Werke*. 17 vols. Ed. I.. Fichte. Berlin: Veit, 1845–1846.

———.*Science of Knowledge*. Trans. P. Heath and J. Lachs. Cambridge: Cambridge University Press, 1970.

Flach, Werner. *Negation und Andersheit: Ein Beitrag zur Problematik der Letztimplikation.* Würzburg: Ernst Reinhardt, 1959.

Gasché, Rodolphe. *The Tain of the Mirror: Derrida and the Philosophy of Reflection.* Cambridge, Mass.: Harvard University Press, 1986.

Hadjin, Mane. *The Boundaries of Moral Discourse.* Chicago: Loyola University Press, 1994.

Hegel, G. W. F. "Differenz des Fichteschen und Schellingschen Systems der Philosophie." In *Jenaer Kritische Schriften* I. Hamburg: Felix Meiner, 1979. Pp. 1–116.

———. *Early Theological Writings.* Ed. T. M. Knox. Philadelphia: University of Pennsylvania Press, 1981.

———. *Enzyklopädie der philosophischen Wissenschaften.* Ed. F. Nicolin and O. Pöggler. Hamburg: Felix Meiner, 1959.

———. *Faith and Knowledge.* Trans. W. Cerf and H. Harris. Albany: State University of New York Press, 1977.

———. *Phänomenologie des Geistes.* Frankfurt am Main: Suhrkamp, 1970. [*Phenomenology of Spirit.* Trans. A. V. Miller. Oxford: Oxford University Press, 1977.]

———. *The Philosophy of Right.* Trans. T. M. Knox. New York: Oxford University Press, 1967.

———. *System of Ethical Life (1802/1803) and First Philosophy of Spirit.* Trans. H. S. Harris and T. M. Knox. Albany: State University of New York Press, 1977.

———. *Wissenschaft der Logik.* 2 vols. Frankfurt am Main: Suhrkamp, 1969. [*Science of Logic.* Trans. A. V. Miller. Atlantic Highlands, N.J.: Humanities Press, 1969.]

Henrich, Dieter. "Dunkelheit und Vergewisserung." *All-Einheit: Wege eines Gedankens in Ost und West.* Stuttgart: Klett-Cotta, 1985. Pp. 33–52.

———. "Fichte's Original Insight." In *Contemporary German Philosophy* I. Trans. D. Lachterman. University Park: Pennsylvania State University Press, 1982. Pp. 17–55.

———. *Fluchtlinien.* Frankfurt am Main: Suhrkamp, 1982.

———. "Hegels Logik der Reflexion: Neue Fassung." In *Hegel-Studien* 18. Bonn: Bouvier, 1978. Pp. 204–324.

———. "Identität: Begriffe, Probleme, Grenzen." In *Identität.* Ed. O. Marquand and K. Stierle. Munich: Wilhelm Fink, 1979. Pp. 113–187.

———. "Selbstbewußtsein: Kritische Einleitung in eine Theorie." In *Hermeneutik und Dialektik* I. Ed. R. Bübner. Tübingen: Mohr, 1970. Pp. 257–284.

———. *Die Wissenschaft der Logik and die Logik der Reflexion.* Bonn: Bouvier Verlag Herbert Grundmann, 1978.

Husserl, Edmund. *Cartesianische Meditationen und Pariser Vorträge.* Ed.

S. Strasser. The Hague: Martinus Nijhoff, 1950. [*Cartesian Meditations*. Trans. D. Cairns. The Hague: Martinus Nijhoff, 1960.]

―――. *The Crisis of European Sciences and Transcendental Phenomenology*. Trans. D. Carr. Evanston, Ill.: Northwestern University Press, 1970.

―――. "Die intersubjektive Gültigkeit phänomenologischer Wahrheit." In *Husserliana* XIV. Ed. I. Kern. The Hague: Martinus Nijhoff, 1973. Pp. 305–308.

―――. *Experience and Judgment*. Trans. J. Churchill and K. Ameriks. Ed. L. Landgrebe. Evanston, Ill.: Northwestern University Press, 1973.

―――. *Husserliana*. 23 vols. Ed. M. Biemel et al. The Hague: Martinus Nijhoff, 1954―.

―――. *Ideen zu einer reinen Phänomenologie und phänomenologischen Philosophie*. Ed. M. Biemel. 2 vols. The Hague: Martinus Nijhoff, 1950, 1952.

―――. *Logical Investigations*. Trans. J. Findlay. New York: Humanities Press, 1970.

―――. *Phenomenology and the Crisis of Philosophy*. Trans. Q. Lauer. New York: Harper & Row, 1965.

―――. "Philosophy as Mankind's Self–Reflection." In *The Crisis of European Sciences and Transcendental Phenomenology*. Trans. D. Carr. Evanston, Ill.: Northwestern University Press, 1970. Pp. 335–342.

Kant, Immanuel. *Kritik der praktischen Vernunft*. Frankfurt am Main: Suhrkamp, 1974. [*Critique of Practical Reason*. Trans. L. Beck. New York: Bobbs–Merrill, 1956.]

―――. *Kritik der reinen Vernunft*. 2 vols. Frankfurt am Main: Suhrkamp, 1956. [*Critique of Pure Reason*. Trans. Norman Kemp Smith. New York: St. Martin's, 1956.]

―――. *Kritik der Urteilskraft*. Frankfurt am Main: Suhrkamp, 1957. [*Critique of Judgment*. Trans. J. Meredith. Oxford: The Clarendon Press, 1973].

―――. *Schriften zur Metaphysik und Logik*. Frankfurt am Main: Suhrkamp, 1977.

Kern, Iso. "Einleitung des Herausgebers." In *Husserliana* XIII. Ed. Iso Kern. The Hague: Martinus Nijhoff, 1973. Pp. i–xlviii.

Marx, Werner. *Absolute Reflexion und Sprache*. Frankfurt am Main: Klostermann, 1967.

Marx, Wolfgang. *Reflexionstopologie*. Tübingen: Mohr, 1984.

McClure, Roger. "St. Augustine and the Paradox of Reflection." *Philosophy*, 69 (1994), 317–326.

McCumber, John. Review of Rodolphe Gasché. *The Tain of the Mirror*. *Philosophical Review*, 100, No. 2 (April 1991), 302.

Mead, George Herbert. *Mind, Self, and Society*. Ed. C. Morris. Chicago: The University of Chicago Press, 1934.

———. *Selected Writings: George Herbert Mead*. Ed. A. Reck. Chicago: The University of Chicago Press, 1964.

Peirce, Charles Sanders. *Collected Papers of Charles Sanders Peirce* I–VI. Ed. Charles Hartshorne and Paul Weiss. Cambridge, Mass.: The Belknap Press of Harvard University Press, 1931–1935. VII–VIII. Ed. Arthur Burks. Cambridge, Mass.: The Belknap Press of Harvard University Press, 1958.

———. *Writings of Charles S. Peirce: A Chronological Edition*. Ed. Nathan Hauser et al. 5 vols. to date. Bloomington: University of Indiana Press, 1982–.

Roberts, Julian. *The Logic of Reflection: German Philosophy in the Twentieth Century*. New Haven, Conn.: Yale University Press, 1992.

Röd, Wolfgang. *Erfahrung und Reflexion: Theorien der Erfahrung in transzendentalphilosophischer Sicht*. Munich: Beck, 1991.

Rorty, Richard. *Contingency, Irony, and Solidarity*. Cambridge: Cambridge University Press, 1989.

———. "Is Derrida a Transcendental Philosopher?" In *Philosophical Papers* II. New York: Cambridge University Press, 1991. Pp. 119–128.

———. *Philosophical Papers*. 2 vols. New York: Cambridge University Press, 1991.

———. *Philosophy and the Mirror of Nature*. Princeton, N.J.: Princeton University Press, 1979.

———. "Philosophy as Science, Metaphor, Politics." In *Philosophical Papers* II. New York: Cambridge University Press, 1991. Pp. 9–26.

———. "Wittgenstein, Heidegger, and the Reification of Language." In *Philosophical Papers* II. New York: Cambridge University Press, 1991. Pp. 50–65.

Rotenstreich, Nathan. "Can Expression Replace Reflection?" *Review of Metaphysics*, 43 (March 1990), 607–618.

Schelling, F. W. J. *Sämmtliche Werke*. 14 vols. Stuttgart, 1859.

———. *System des transzendentalen Idealismus*. Hamburg: Felix Meiner, 1957.

Schnädelbach, Herbert. "Bermerkungen über Rationalität und Sprache." In *Kommunikation und Reflexion*. Ed. W. Kulhmann and D. Böhler. Frankfurt am Main: Suhrkamp. Pp. 347–368.

———. *Reflexion und Diskurs: Fragen einer Logik der Philosophie*. Frankfurt am Main: Suhrkamp, 1977.

———. "Zum Verhältnis von Diskurswandel und Paradigmenwechsel in der Geschichte der Philosophie." In *Zur Rehabilitierung des animal rationale*. Frankfurt am Main: Suhrkamp, 1992. Pp. 391–399.

Schütz, Alfred. *Collected Papers*. Ed. M. Natanso and H. van Breda. 3 vols. The Hague: Martinus Nijhoff, 1964–67.

———. *The Phenomenology of the Social World*. Trans. G. Walsh and F. Lehnert. Evanston, Ill.: Northwestern University Press, 1967.

————. "Das Problem der transcendentalen intersubjecktivität bei Husserl." *Philosophische Rundschau* (1957).

Schütz, Alfred, and Thomas Luckmann. *Strukturen der Lebenswelt*. Darmstadt, Luchterhand, 1975.

Seidel, George. *Fichte's Wissenschaftslehre of 1794: A Commentary on Part One*. West Lafayette, Ind.: Purdue University Press, 1992.

Spaemann, Robert. "Der Streit der Philosophen." In *Wozu Philosophie?* Ed. H. Lübbe. Berlin: de Gruyter, 1978.

————. "Unschuld und Reflexion." In *Fénelon: Reflexion und Spontaneität*. Stuttgart: Klett-Cotta, 1990.

Spaemann, Robert, and Reinhard Löw. *Die Frage Wozu: Geschichte und Wiederentdeckung des teleologischen Denkens*. Munich: Piper, 1981.

Surber, Jere Paul. "Introduction." In G. W. F. Hegel, *The Difference Between the Fichtean and Schellingian System of Philosophy*. Trans. Jere Paul Surber. Resada, Calif.: Ridgeview Publishing, 1978.

Taylor, Charles. *Hegel*. Cambridge: Cambridge University Press, 1975.

Taylor, Mark C. "Foiling Reflection." In *Tears*. Albany: State University of New York Press, 1990. Pp. 87–104.

Valiati, Ezio. "Leibniz on Reflection and Its Natural Veridicality." *Journal of the History of Philosophy*, 25, No. 2 (April 1987), 247–262.

Wagner, Hans. *Philosophie und Reflexion*. Würzburg: Ernst Reinhardt, 1959.

Williams, Robert. *Recognition: Fichte and Hegel on the Other*. Albany: State University of New York Press, 1992.

6. Background Material

Adorno, Theodor. *Negative Dialektik*. Frankfurt am Main: Suhrkamp, 1966. [*Negative Dialectics*. Trans. E. B. Ashton. New York: Seabury, 1973.]

Adorno, Theodor, and Max Horkheimer. *Dialectic of Enlightenment*. Trans. J. Cumming. New York: Herder and Herder, 1972.

Apel, Karl-Otto. "Normative Begründung der kritischen Theorie durch Rekurs auf lebensweltische Sittlichkeit?" In *Zwischenbetrachtungen Prozeß der Aufklärung*. Ed. Alex Honneth et al. Frankfurt am Main: Suhrkamp, 1989. Pp. 15–65.

————. "Szientismus oder transzendentale Hermeneutik?" In *Hermeneutic and Dialektik* II. Tübingen: Mohr, 1970.

————. "Wissenschaft als Emanzipation? Eine kritische Würdigung der Wissenschaftskonzeption der kritische Theorie." In *Materialien zu Habermas' "Erkenntnis und Interesse."* Ed. Fred Dallmayr. Frankfurt am Main: Suhrkamp, 1974. Pp. 314–348.

———. "Zurück zur Normalität." In *Diskurs und Verantwortung*. Frankfurt am Main: Suhrkamp, 1990. Pp. 370–474.

Austin, J. L. *How to Do Things With Words*. Cambridge, Mass.: Harvard University Press, 1962.

Benhabib, Seyla. *Critique, Norm, and Utopia: A Study of the Foundations of Critical Theory*. New York: Columbia University Press, 1986.

———. *Situating the Self*. New York: Routledge, 1992.

Bergson, Henri. *Time and Free Will*. New York: Macmillan, 1910.

Bernstein, Richard. "Introduction." In *Habermas and Modernity*. Cambridge, Mass.: The MIT Press, 1985. Pp. 1–32.

———. *The Restructuring of Social and Political Theory*. Cambridge, Mass.: Blackwell, 1976.

Blanchette, Oliva. "Language, the Primordial Labor of History." *Cultural Hermeneutics*, 1 (1974), 325–382.

Brandom, Robert. *Making It Explicit*. Cambridge, Mass.: Harvard University Press, 1994.

Brink, David. *Moral Realism and the Foundations of Ethics*. Cambridge: Cambridge University Press, 1989.

Brower, Bruce. "Dispositional Ethical Realism." *Ethics*, 103 (1993), 221–249.

Brown, Kathryn. "Language, Modernity, and Fascism: Heidegger's Doubling of Myth." In *The Attractions of Fascism: Social Psychology and Aesthetics of the "Triumph of the Right."* Ed. J. Milfull. New York: Berg, 1990. Pp. 137–154.

Caputo, John D. *Radical Hermeneutics: Repetition, Deconstruction, and the Hermeneutic Project*. Bloomington: University of Indiana Press, 1987.

Carr, David. *Phenomenology and the Problem of History*. Evanston, Ill.: Northwestern University Press, 1974.

Cerf, Walter. "Speculative Philosophy and Intellectual Intuition: An Introduction to Hegel's *Essays*." In *Faith and Knowledge*. Trans. W. Cerf and H. Harris. Albany: State University of New York Press, 1977. Pp. i–xxvi.

Chomsky, Noam. *Aspects of the Theory of Syntax*. Cambridge, Mass.: The MIT Press, 1965.

Cobb-Stevens, Richard. "Transcendental Philosophy and Emancipatory Communication." Unpublished.

Colletti, Lucio. *Marxism and Hegel*. Trans. L. Garner. London: NLB, 1973.

Dallmayr, Fred. *Polis and Praxis*. Cambridge, Mass.: The MIT Press, 1984.

Danto, Arthur. *An Analytic Philosophy of History*. Cambridge: Cambridge University Press, 1965.

Delueze, Gilles, and Felix Guattari. *Anti-Oedipus: Capitalism and Schizophrenia*. Trans. R. Jurly, M. Seem, and H. Lane. Minneapolis: University of Minnesota Press, 1983.

Dilthey, Wilhelm. *Gesammelte Schriften.* 12 vols. Leipzig and Berlin: Teubner, 1927.

———. "Introduction to the Human Sciences." In *Selected Works* I. Ed. R. Makkreel and F. Rodi. Princeton, N.J.: Princeton University Press, 1989. Pp. 245ff.

Döbert, Rainer, and Gertrud Nunner-Winkler. *Adoleszenzkrise und Identitätsbildung.* Frankfurt am Main: Suhrkamp, 1975.

Dreyfus, Hubert, and Stuart Dreyfus. "What Is Morality? A Phenomenological Account of the Development of Ethical Expertise." In *Universalism vs. Communitarianism.* Ed. D. Rasmussen. Cambridge, Mass.: The MIT Press, 1990. Pp. 237–264.

Duhem, Pierre. *The Aim and Structure of Physical Theory.* Trans. P. P. Wiener. Princeton, N.J.: Princeton University Press, 1954.

Durkheim, Émile. *Die elementaren Formen des religiösen Lebens.* Trans. L. Schmidts. Frankfurt am Main: Suhrkamp, 1981.

Feuerbach, Ludwig. *Gesammelte Werke* I. Ed. W. Schaffenhauer. Berlin: Akademie Verlag, 1981.

Forst, Rainer. "How (Not) to Speak About Identity." *Philosophy and Social Criticism,* 18, Nos. 3–4 (1993), 293–312.

Frankfurt, Harry. "Identification and Wholeheartedness." In *The Importance of What We Care About.* Cambridge: Cambridge University Press, 1988. Pp. 159–176.

Freud, Sigmund. *Beyond the Pleasure Principle.* Trans. J. Strachey. New York: Norton, 1961.

———. "The Interpretation of Dreams." In *The Complete Psychological Works of Sigmund Freud* IV–V. Trans. J. Strachey. London: Hogarth Press, 1953. Pp. 1–630.

———. "Konstruktion der Analyse." In *Gesammelte Werke* XVI. 3rd ed. Frankfurt am Main: Fischer, 1968. Pp. 43–56.

———."Das Unbewußte." *Gesammelte Werke* X. 3rd ed. Frankfurt am Main: Fischer, 1968. Pp. 264–303.

Frye, Northrup. "Ethical Criticism: A Theory of Symbol." In *Anatomy of Criticism.* Princeton, N.J.: Princeton University Press, 1957. Pp. 71–128.

Fukuyama, Francis. *The End of History and the Last Man.* New York: Free Press, 1992.

Gadamer, Hans-Georg. *Philosophical Hermeneutics.* Trans. D. Linge. Berkeley: University of California Press, 1976.

———. "Rhetorik, Hermeneutik, und Ideologiekritik. *Kleine Schriften* I. Tübingen: Mohr, 1967. Pp. 113–130.

———. "Die Universalität des hermeneutischen Problems." In *Kleine Schriften.* Tübingen: Mohr, 1967.

———.*Wahrheit und Methode.* Tübingen: Mohr, 1975. [*Truth and Method.* Trans. G. Barden and J. Cumming. New York: Seabury, 1975.]

Gadamer, Hans-Georg, and Jürgen Habermas. *Zwei Reden aus Anlass der Verleihung des Hegel–Preises 1979.* Frankfurt am Main: Suhrkamp, 1979.

Geach, Peter. "Ontological Relativity and Relative Identity." In *Logic and Ontology.* Ed. M. Munitz. New York: New York University Press, 1973. Pp. 287–302.

Gehlen, Arnold. *Die Seele im technischen Zeitalter.* Hamburg: Rowohlt, 1957.

———. *Zeit Bilder: Zur Soziologie und Ästhetik der modernen Zeit.* Frankfurt am Main: Athenäum, 1960.

Gendlin, Eugene. "A Philosophical Critique of Narcissism." In *Pathologies of the Modern Self: Postmodern Studies on Narcissism, Schizophrenia, and Depression.* Ed. D. Levin. New York: New York University Press, 1987. Pp. 251–304.

Gilligan, Carol. *In a Different Voice.* Cambridge, Mass.: Harvard University Press, 1982.

Grünbaum, Adolf. *The Foundations of Psychoanalysis: A Philosophical Critique.* Berkeley: University of California Press, 1984.

Günther, Klaus. *The Sense of Appropriateness: Application Discourses in Morality and Law.* Albany: State University of New York Press, 1993.

Hacker, Gordon. "Following Wittgenstein: The Basic Themes for Philosophical Investigations §143–242." In *Wittgenstein: To Follow a Rule.* Ed. Steven Holtzman and Christopher Leich. London: Routledge & Kegan Paul, 1981. Pp. 50–62.

Harris, H. S. *Hegel's Development: Night Thoughts.* Oxford: Clarendon Press, 1985.

Harris, William. *Hegel's Logic.* New York: Garland, 1984.

Heidegger, Martin. *Basic Problems of Phenomenology.* Trans. A. Hofstadter. Bloomington: Indiana University Press, 1982.

———. "Foreword." In William Richardson. *Heidegger: Through Phenomenology to Thought.* The Hague: Martinus Nijhoff, 1963. Pp. 1–24.

———. *Identity and Difference.* Trans. J. Stambaugh. New York: Harper & Row, 1969.

———. *Introduction to Metaphysics.* New Haven, Conn.: Yale University Press, 1958.

———. "Letter on Humanism." In *Basic Writings.* Trans. D. Krell. New York: Harper & Row, 1977. Pp. 213–266.

———. "Nietzsche's Word: God Is Dead." In *The Question Concerning Technology.* Trans. J. W. Lovitt. New York: Harper & Row, 1977. Pp. 53–114.

———. *Sein und Zeit.* Tübingen: Max Niemeyer, 1957. [*Being and Time.* Trans. J. Macquarrie and E. Robinson. New York: Harper & Row, 1962.]

Heidtmann, Bernhard. "Systemwissenschaftliche Reflexion und gesell-

schaftliches Sein: Zur dialektischen Bestimmung der Kategorie des objektiven Scheins." In *Marxistische Gesellschaftsdialektik oder
"Systemtheorie der Gesellschaft?"* Berlin: Marxistische Blätter, 1977. Pp.
69–87.

Horkheimer, Max. "Materialism and Metaphysics." In *Critical Theory: Selected Essays*. Trans. M. O'Connell. New York: Herder and Herder, 1972.
Pp. 10–46.

———. "Traditional and Critical Theory." In *Critical Theory: Selected Essays*. Trans. M. O'Connell. New York: Herder and Herder, 1972. Pp. 188–
243.

———. "Zum Problem der Wahrheit." In *Kritische Theorie*. Ed. A.
Schmidt. Frankfurt am Main: Suhrkamp, 1968.

Humboldt, Wilhelm von. *Werke* III. Darmstadt: Wissenschaftliche Buchgesellschaft, 1963.

Hume, David. *An Inquiry Concerning Human Understanding*. Ed. C. Handel. New York: Macmillan, 1955.

Jackall, Robert. *Moral Mazes: The World of Corporate Managers*. Oxford:
Oxford University Press, 1988.

Jay, Martin. *The Dialectical Imagination*. Boston: Little, Brown, 1973.

Jeanrond, Warner. *Text and Interpretation as Categories of Theological
Thinking*. New York: Crossroads, 1988.

Klein, Wolfgang. "Argumentation und Argument." *Zeitschrift für Literaturwissenschaft und Linguistik*, 38/39 (1980), 9ff.

Kojève, Alexandre. *Introduction to the Reading of Hegel: Lectures on the
Phenomenology of Spirit*. Trans. J. Nichols. Ed. A. Bloom. Ithaca, N.Y.:
Cornell University Press, 1969.

Korthals, Michiel. "On the Justification of Societal Development Claims."
Philosophy and Social Criticism, 18, No. 1 (1992), 1–17.

Kreckel. M. *Communicative Acts and Shared Knowledge in Natural Discourse*. London and New York: Academic Press, 1981.

Kroner, Richard. "Introduction." In G. W. F. Hegel. *Early Theological Writings*. Trans. T. M. Knox. Philadelphia: University of Pennsylvania Press,
1981. Pp. 1–66.

Lacan, Jacques. *Écrits: A Selection*. Trans. A. Sheridan. New York: Norton,
1977

———. "Function and Field of Speech and Language." In *Écrits: A Selection*. Trans. A. Sheridan. New York: Norton, 1977. Pp. 30–113.

Langer, Susanne. *Philosophy in a New Key*. 3rd ed. Cambridge, Mass.: Harvard University Press, 1957.

Lauer, Quentin. *A Reading of Hegel's Phenomenology of Spirit*. New York:
Fordham University Press, 1976.

Lorenzer, Alfred. *Konstructive Wissenschaftstheorie*. Frankfurt am Main:
Suhrkamp, 1974.

————. *Sprachzerstörung und Rekonstruktion*. Frankfurt am Main: Suhrkamp, 1970.

Luhmann, Niklaus. *Essays on Self–Reference*. New York: Columbia University Press, 1990.

Lukes, Steven. "Making Sense of Moral Conflict." In *Liberalism and the Moral Life*. Ed. N. Rosenblum. Cambridge, Mass.: Harvard University Press, 1991. Pp. 127–141.

————."Of Gods and Demons: Habermas and Practical Reason." In *Habermas: Critical Debates*. Ed. David Held and John Thompson. Cambridge, Mass.: The MIT Press, 1982. Pp. 134–148.

MacIntyre, Alasdair. *After Virtue: A Study in Moral Theory*. 2nd ed. Notre Dame, Ind.: Notre Dame University Press, 1984.

————. *Three Rival Versions of Moral Enquiry*. Notre Dame, Ind.: Notre Dame University Press, 1990.

————. *Whose Justice? Which Rationality?* Notre Dame, Ind.: Notre Dame University Press, 1988.

Makkreel, Rudolf. *Imagination and Interpretation in Kant*. Chicago: The University of Chicago Press, 1990.

Marx, Karl. "The German Ideology." In *Karl Marx, Friedrich Engels: Collected Works* V. New York: International Publishers, 1976. Pp. 19–539.

Marx, Werner. *Das Selbstbewußtsein in Hegels Phänomenologie des Geistes*. Frankfurt am Main: Klostermann, 1986.

McCarthy, Thomas. "Philosophy and Social practice: Avoiding the Ethnocentric Predicament." In *Zwischenbetrachtungen in Prozeß der Aufklarung*. Frankfurt am Main: Suhrkamp, 1989.

McCarthy, Thomas, and David Couzens Hoy. *Critical Theory*. Cambridge, Mass.: Blackwell, 1994.

Merleau-Ponty, Maurice. *La phénoménologie de la perception*. Paris: Gallimard, 1945.

Monk, Ray. *Ludwig Wittgenstein: The Duty of Genius*. New York: The Free Press, 1990.

Parfit, Derek. *Reasons and Persons*. Oxford: Clarendon, 1984.

Parsons, Talcott. *The Social System*. Glencoe, Ill.: The Free Press, 1951.

Peterson, Vic. Review of Klaus Günther. *The Sense of Appropriateness: Application Discourses on Morality and Law*. *Philosophy and Social Criticism*, 22, No. 1 (1996), 115–124.

Pippin, Robert. *Hegel's Idealism: The Satisfactions of Self-Consciousness*. Cambridge: Cambridge University Press, 1989.

Postone, Moishe. *Time, Labor, and Social Domination*. Cambridge: Cambridge University Press, 1993.

Prior, A. N. *The Doctrine of Propositions and Terms*. London: Duckworth, 1976.

————. *Time and Modality*. Oxford: Oxford University Press, 1957.

Putnam, Hilary. "Why Reason Can't Be Naturalized." In *After Philosophy*. Ed. Kenneth Baynes, James Bohman, and Thomas McCarthy. Cambridge, Mass.: The MIT Press, 1987. Pp. 222–244.

Quine, W. V. *Word and Object*. Cambridge, Mass.: The MIT Press, 1960.

Quine, W. V., and J. S. Ullian. *The Web of Belief*. 2nd ed. New York: McGraw Hill, 1978.

Rasmussen, David. "Critical Theory: Horkheimer, Adorno, Habermas." In *Routledge History of Philosophy* VIII. London: Routledge, 1993. Pp. 254–289.

————. "Marx: On Labor, Praxis, and Instrumental Reason." *Creativity and Social Life*, 3 (1979), 37–52.

————. "Reflections on the 'End of History': Politics, Identity and Civil Society." *Philosophy and Social Criticism*, 18, Nos. 3–4 (1993), 235–250.

————. *Symbol and Interpretation*. The Hague: Martinus Nijhoff, 1974.

Rawls, John. *Political Liberalism*. New York: Columbia University Press, 1993.

Rehg, William. "From Logic to Rhetoric in Science: A Formal-Pragmatic Reading of Lonergan." In *Communication and Lonergan*. Ed. Thomas J. Farrell and Paul A. Soukup. New York: Sheed and Ward, 1993. Pp. 153–172.

Reichenbach, Hans. *Elements of Symbolic Logic*. New York: The Free Press, 1947.

Ricoeur, Paul. *The Conflict of Interpretations*. Trans. D. Idhe. Evanston: Northwestern University Press, 1974.

————. *Freud and Philosophy*. Trans. D. Savage. New Haven, Conn.: Yale University Press, 1970.

————. "Hermeneutics and the Critique of Ideology." In *Hermeneutics and the Human Sciences*. Trans. J. Thompson. New York: Cambridge University Press, 1981. Pp. 63–100.

————. *The Rule of Metaphor*. Trans. R. Czerny. Toronto: University of Toronto Press, 1977.

————. *The Symbolism of Evil*. Trans. E. Buchanan. Boston: Beacon, 1967.

————. *Time and Narrative*. 3 vols. Trans. K. Blamey and D. Pellauer. Chicago: The University of Chicago Press, 1988.

Sachs, Jeffrey. "Father of Radical Reform." *Time*, July 22, 1991, pp. 54–55.

Sartre, Jean Paul. *Being and Nothingness*. Trans. H. Barnes. New York: Citadel, 1964.

Schwalbe, Michael. "Meadian Ethical Theory and the Moral Contradictions of Capitalism." *Philosophy and Social Criticism*, 14, No. 1 (1988), 25–50.

Searle, John. *Expression and Meaning*. Cambridge: Cambridge University Press, 1979.

Seel, Martin. "Die Zelebration der Unvermögens: Zur Ästhetik der Sports." *Merkur*, 47, No. 2 (February 1993), 91–100.

Selman, Robert. *The Growth of Interpersonal Understanding*. New York: Academic Press, 1980.

Singer, Alan. "The Adequacy of the Aesthetic." *Philosophy and Social Criticism*, 20, Nos. 1–2 (1994), 39–72.

Sokolowski, Robert. *Husserlian Meditations: How Words Present Things*. Evanston, Ill.: Northwestern University Press, 1974.

Solomon, Robert. *In the Spirit of Hegel: A Study of G. W. F. Hegel's Phenomenology of Spirit*. Oxford: Oxford University Press, 1983.

Strawson, P. F. *Individuals: An Essay in Descriptive Metaphysics*. London: Methuen, 1979.

———. *Introduction to Logical Theory*. London: Methuen. 1952.

———. *Subject and Predicate in Logic and Grammar*. London: Methuen, 1974.

———. "Truth." In *Logico-Linguistic Papers*. London: Methuen, 1971. Pp. 190–213.

———. "Truth." In Truth. Ed. G. Pitcher. Englewood Cliffs, N.J.: Prentice-Hall, 1964.

Taylor, Charles. *Sources of the Self: The Making of Modern Identity*. Cambridge, Mass.: Harvard University Press, 1989.

Taylor, Mark C. *Tears*. Albany: State University of New York Press, 1990.

Teubner, Gunther. "Substantive and Reflexive Elements in Modern Law." *Law and Society Review*, 17 (1983), 239ff.

Theunissen, Michael. *Der Andere*. 2nd ed. Berlin: de Gruyter, 1977.

———. *Selbstverwirklichung und Allgemeinheit*. Berlin: de Gruyter, 1982.

Toulmin, Steven. *The Uses of Argument*. London: Cambridge University Press, 1958.

Tracy, David. *The Analogical Imagination*. New York: Crossroads, 1981.

Tugendhat, Ernst. *Self-Consciousness and Self–Determination*. Trans. Paul Stern. Cambridge, Mass.: The MIT Press, 1986.

———. *Vorlesungen zur Einführung in die sprachanalytische Philosophie*. Frankfurt am Main: Suhrkamp, 1976.

Wagner, Hans. *Kritische Philosophie: Systematische und historische Abhandlungen*. Ed. K. Bärthlein and W. Flach. Wurzburg: Königshausen & Neumann, 1980.

Weber, Max. *The Protestant Ethic and the Spirit of Capitalism*. Trans. T. Parsons. New York: Charles Scribner's Sons, 1958.

Westphal, Merold. *History and Truth in Hegel's Phenomenology*. Atlantic Heights, N.J.: Humanities Press, 1979.

White, Alan. *Schelling: An Introduction to the System of Freedom*. New Haven, Conn.: Yale University Press, 1983.

Whitebook, Joel. "Reason and Happiness: Some Psychoanalytic Themes in Critical Theory." *Praxis International*, 4, No. 1 (1984), 15–31.

Whitehead, Alfred North, and Bertrand Russell. *Principia Mathematica* I. 7th ed. Cambridge: Cambridge University Press, 1956.

Wingert, Lutz. *Gemeinsinn und Moral*. Frankfurt am Main: Suhrkamp, 1993.

Wittgenstein, Ludwig. *Philosophical Investigations*. Trans. G. E. M. Anscombe. Cambridge: Basil Blackwell, 1968.

———. *Tractatus logico-philosophicus*. London: Routledge & Kegan Paul, 1922.

INDEX